THE WRITINGS OF RABASH

ESSAYS

Volume Five

LAITMAN
KABBALAH
PUBLISHERS

Rav Baruch Shalom Halevi Ashlag

The Writings of RABASH
Volume Five—Essays

Copyright © 2023 by Michael Laitman All rights reserved
Published by Laitman Kabbalah Publishers

Contact Information
E-mail: info@kabbalah.info
Web site: www.kabbalah.info
Toll free in USA and Canada: 1-866-LAITMAN

1057 Steeles Avenue West, Suite 532, Toronto, ON, M2R 3X1, Canada

No part of this book may be used or reproduced in any manner without written permission of the publisher, except in the case of brief quotations embodied in critical articles or reviews.

ISBN: 978-1-77228-142-2

Translation: Rinah Shalom, Chaim Ratz
Translation Assistance: Mickey Cohen, Moshe Eisenberg
Content Editing: Noga Bar Noye
Editing and Proofreading: Mary Pennock, Mary Miesem
Internal Design: Gill Zahavi
Cover Design: Baruch Khovov/Inna Smirnova
Executive Editor: Chaim Ratz
Printing and Post Production: Uri Laitman

SECOND EDITION: SEPTEMBER 2023

Table of Contents

Tav-Shin-Nun-Aleph (1990 - 1991)

What Is, "We Have No Other King But You," in the Work? 9
What Is, "Return, O Israel, Unto the Lord Your God," in the Work?... 20
What Is, "The Wicked Will Prepare and the Righteous Will
  Wear," in the Work? 30
What Is, "The Saboteur Was in the Flood, and Was Putting
  to Death," in the Work? 41
What Is, "The Good Deeds of the Righteous Are
  the Generations," in the Work? 51
What Is, "The Herdsmen of Abram's Cattle and the Herdsmen
  of Lot's Cattle," in the Work? 61
What Is "Man" and What Is "Beast" in the Work?............................ 72
What Is, "And Abraham Was Old, of Many Days," in the Work?......... 82
What Is, "The Smell of His Garments," in the Work? 92
What Does "The King Stands on His Field When the Crop
  Is Ripe" Mean in the Work?.. 102
What It Means that the Good Inclination and the Evil Inclination
  Guard a Person in the Work 112
These Candles Are Sacred 122
What "You Have Given the Strong to the Hands of
  the Weak" Means in the Work 130
What Does It Mean that Man's Blessing Is the Blessing of
  the Sons, in the Work? 141
What Is the Blessing, "Who Made a Miracle for Me in
  This Place," in the Work? 150

Why We Need "Reply unto Your Heart," to Know that the Lord, He Is God, in the Work 160
What Is, "For I Have Hardened His Heart," in the work? 170
What It Means that We Should Raise the Right Hand over the Left Hand, in the Work 177
What Is, "Rise Up, O Lord, and Let Your Enemies Be Scattered," in the Work? 187
What Is, "There Is Nothing that Has No Place," in the Work? 197
What Does It Mean that We Read the Portion, *Zachor* [Remember], Before Purim, in the Work? 206
What Is "A Lily Among the Thorns," in the Work? 216
What Is the Meaning of the Purification of a Cow's Ashes, in the Work? 226
What Does It Mean that One Should Bear a Son and a Daughter, in the Work? 236
What Does It Mean that One Who Repents Should Be in Happiness? ... 246
What Is Revealing a Portion and Covering Two Portions in the Work? ... 256
What Is, "If a Woman Inseminates First, She Delivers a Male Child," in the Work? 266
What Are Holiness and Purity, in the Work? 276
What Does It Mean that a High Priest Should Take a Virgin Wife, in the Work? 286
What Does It Mean that One Who Was On a Far Off Way Is Postponed to a Second Passover, in the Work? 296
What Does It Mean that Charity to the Poor Makes the Holy Name, in the Work? 306
What Are Banners in the Work? 317
What Does It Mean that the Creator Favors Someone, in the Work? ... 327
What Is Eating Their Fruits in This World and Keeping the Principal for the Next World, in the Work? 337
What Is the Meaning of "Spies," in the Work? 347
What Is, "Peace, Peace, to the Far and to the Near," in the Work? 357
What Is the "Torah" and What Is "The Statute of the Torah," in the Work? 367
What Is the "Right Line," in the Work? 377
What Does It Mean that the Right Must Be Greater than the Left, in the Work? 387
What Are Truth and Falsehood in the Work? 397
What Should One Do If He Was Born With Bad Qualities? 407
What Is, "An Ox Knows Its Owner, etc., Israel Does Not Know," in the Work? 417
What Is, "You Will See My Back, But My Face Shall Not Be Seen," in the Work? 427

What Is the Reason for which Israel Were Rewarded
    with Inheritance of the Land, in the Work? 437
What Does It Mean that a Judge Must Judge Absolutely
    Truthfully, in the Work? 448
What Is the Son of the Beloved
    and the Son of the Hated in the Work? 459
What Does It Mean that the Right and the Left Are
    in Contrast, in the Work? 469

Tav-Shin-Nun-Aleph

(1990 - 1991)

What Is, "We Have No Other King But You," in the Work?

Article No. 1, Tav-Shin-Nun-Aleph, 1990/91

We should understand what it means when we say, "We have no other king but You." It implies that when we praise the Creator that "We have no other king but You," then we are not like the nations of the world, who have many gods, while we have only You as our king.

It follows as though the Creator is greater than them. Why is this so important if the Creator is more important than they are, and we chose the Creator? We can say this in the manner that is written in *The Zohar* ("Introduction of The Book of Zohar," Item 161), "Rabbi Aba said, 'It is written, 'Who would not fear You, King of the nations, for it is Your due?" What kind of a praise is this? Rabbi Shimon said to him, 'This verse does not give Him much respect, for it is written, 'For among all the sages of the nations and in all their kingdoms, there is none like You.' Why this comparison to people, who have no existence?'"

While there are many interpretations to this, we will explain it in the work. It is known that the order of the work begins first of all on the basis of faith. Right at the beginning of the work, we take upon ourselves the burden of the kingdom of heaven, which is to believe that the Creator is the leader of the world. That is, He watches over the world with private Providence, as said in the article, "The Order of the Work, from Baal HaSulam."

Afterward, we must know that the faith we take upon ourselves is of inferior importance, meaning that if everything were known and we would not have to believe, this knowledge would be more important to a person. Now a person must believe that although faith is of little importance to a person, he still chooses to go specifically in this path of faith above reason, since he believes in the sages, in what they attained and said.

But one who has no faith in the sages says that if knowledge were more successful for man's work than faith, as one thinks and says that if serving the Creator were in a state of knowing and we would not have to believe, there would probably be many more servants of the Creator, and many people would dedicate themselves to the work. But when a person must believe in both the Creator and the sages, the faith that people must believe pushes them away from being workers.

However, a person who wants to approach the Creator must believe in the sages, who told us that if the way of knowledge were truly better for guiding the world, the Creator would give us the work in a manner of knowing.

Instead, the Creator knows that the most successful way for a person to achieve the goal, which is His desire to do good to His creations—for man to be able to receive the delight and pleasure without the bread of shame—is specifically through faith.

However, since man is born with a nature of self-love, the body enjoys that which is closer to self-love. For this reason, when a person is told that he must observe Torah and *Mitzvot* [commandments/good deeds] on the basis of faith, it is difficult for him. He would be happier if everything were known.

However, there are many discernments concerning faith, meaning what a person should believe. The matter is simple: A

What Is, "We Have No Other King But You," in the Work?

person should believe only in reward and punishment. That is, if he observes Torah and *Mitzvot* he will be rewarded, and if he does not observe he will be punished.

There is reward and punishment on all levels. The only difference lies in what is the reward and what is the punishment. In this there are differences between the degrees. This also applies to corporeal matters. For example, a child is told that if he does not want to eat he will be punished, such as when all the children who eat go on a trip, the child who does not want to eat will stay home.

Sometimes the reward and punishment are expressed in the eating itself, in that someone who does not do what the parents command will not get food today and will stay hungry. It follows that it is the same for all people: The reward and punishment give man the push to advance.

For this reason, sometimes a person believes that by observing Torah and *Mitzvot* he will be rewarded in this world, as it is written in *The Zohar*, "There are people whose fear is in reward and punishment of this world, meaning long life, health, etc., and there are those whose reward and punishment are in the next world, meaning they have the Garden of Eden. Also, there are people whose fear is *Lishma* [for Her sake], meaning "because He is great and ruling," who are privileged that they are serving the King, and this is their reward, and they do not need any other reward.

In other words, they cancel their own authority, have no concern for themselves, and their only worry is to bring contentment to the Maker. Since the body, called "will to receive," does not accept this, it resists this work. Therefore, precisely here, in work where one wants to work in order to bestow, there are ascents and descents.

In this work, "reward and punishment" are completely different from those applied in the work to receive reward. When a person has some flavor in the work and he feels he has some nearing to the Creator, this is his reward. If he feels that he has been thrown out from the work of the Creator, meaning he does not feel any flavor in the work, a person considers this "the biggest punishment."

In other words, he has no feeling of work. Yet, one should say that this pushing away that he is feeling is because he is far from the Creator, since a person understands that if he were closer to the Creator, he would have to feel differently than he is feeling now, as it is written, "Strength and joy are in His place."

This means that when a person feels that he is in a place of *Kedusha* [holiness], and it is written about *Kedusha*, "Strength and joy," but now he feels that he has no vitality and sees everything as black, and he cannot overcome the state that he is in, to a person who wants to come to work for the sake of the Creator, this is considered the biggest punishment.

When a person wants to overcome the state that he is in, he sees that it is impossible to approach the Creator. Sometimes he falls into despair, meaning he wants to escape the campaign and decides that he will never be able to achieve a degree where he has no concern for his own benefit but only for the benefit of the Creator.

So, the question is, which is the truth? That is, is he wrong, and it is actually possible to come to a state where all his actions are for the sake of the Creator, or is it not? That is, does overcoming help, and a person does have the strength to do by himself everything for the sake of the Creator?

The answer is as it is written, "We have no other king but You," for we are powerless to overcome and take upon ourselves Your being our king and that we will serve You only because of the importance of the King, and we will not do anything for ourselves except that which is beneficial to You. Only You can give us this power, the second nature, which is the desire to bestow.

Therefore, first we say, "Our Father, our King, we have sinned before You." That is, a person cannot say, "We have no other king but You," meaning that only the Creator can give this power. And how does one know that it is not within his power? Therefore, first he must do all that he can, as it is written, "Everything that you can do with your hand and strength, do."

What Is, "We Have No Other King But You," in the Work?

At that time, a person comes to a state where he feels how remote he is from the Creator, meaning that he cannot do anything for the sake of the Creator. Then, the person feels that although he is observing Torah and *Mitzvot*, he is still regarded as a sinner because he sees that he is not working for the sake of the Creator. Therefore, first, a person must say, "Our Father, our King, we have sinned before You." Even though he is observing Torah and *Mitzvot*, he feels that he has sinned by not doing anything for the sake of the Creator.

Afterward, he says wholeheartedly, "Our Father, our King, we have no other king but You." In other words, only the Creator can help make Him our king, so we can work because we are serving the King, and this is our reward, that we have the privilege of serving the King. This means that only then can we do everything for the sake of the Creator.

In other words, if the Creator does not give him this power, to feel that "we have a great King," he has no strength to work for the sake of the Creator, for the body claims, "What will you get from bestowing upon the Creator?" In other words, as long as the will to receive dominates, a person is powerless. Sometimes he doubts the beginning, meaning says that now he sees that he has worked in vain and did not gain anything by his labor. Now he really sees that all his work was to no avail.

Therefore, when the Creator helps him and gives him the desire to bestow, and he feels that he has a great King, only the Creator can give this. This is the meaning of what is written, "Our Father, our King, we have no other king but You." Namely, "Only You can make us feel that we have a great King and it is worthwhile to work for Him, to bring Him contentment."

According to the above, we should interpret what is written in *The Zohar* (*Haazinu*, Item 210), "Happy is he who calls on the King and knows how to call on Him properly. If he calls but does not know Whom he has called, the Creator moves away from him, as it is written, 'The Lord is near to all who call upon Him.' To whom is He close? He reiterated and said, 'To all who call upon Him in truth.' But does anyone call upon Him falsely? Rabbi Aba said, 'Yes, it is he who calls but does not know whom he calls.' It is written, 'to all who call on Him in truth.' What is 'in truth'? It is with the King's signet ring."

We should understand what he says about "in truth" and "falsely," that only those who call "in truth" are heard. He asks, "What is 'in truth'?" Also, we should know what is "falsely," meaning what it means that a person calls on the Creator falsely in the work.

The *Sulam* [Ladder commentary on *The Zohar*] ("Introduction of The Book of Zohar," Item 175) brings the words of our sages as follows: "Upon the creation of the world, when He said to the angels, 'Let us make man in our image,' *Hesed* [mercy] said, 'Let him be created, for he does mercies.' *Emet* [truth] said, 'Let him not be created, for 'he is all lies.'" What did the Creator do? He took Truth and cast it to the earth, as it is written, 'cast truth to the earth.'" Interpretation: It is known that our sages said, "One should always engage in Torah and *Mitzvot* even if *Lo Lishma* [not for Her sake], since from *Lo Lishma* he comes to *Lishma* [for Her sake]." Because of his lowliness, man cannot engage in His *Mitzvot* right away in order to bring contentment to his Maker. For this reason, he must first engage in *Mitzvot Lo Lishma*, meaning for his own benefit. And yet, he still draws abundant *Kedusha* while performing the *Mitzvot*. Through the abundance he extends, he will eventually come to engage in *Mitzvot Lishma*. This is what the truth complained about man's creation, who said that he is all lies.

According to the above, we see that "truth" means *Lishma*, meaning for the sake of the Creator, and "falsely" means *Lo Lishma*, meaning for his own sake. By this we can interpret what *The Zohar* says, "near to all who call upon Him in truth." It is known that "far and near" in spirituality mean that equivalence of form is called "near," and disparity of form is called "far."

It follows that a person who comes to a state of "truth," where he feels that unless the Creator helps him come to work for the sake of the Creator, he has no hope of ever achieving the degree of *Lishma* by himself, meaning to do everything only for the sake of the Creator. Therefore, he calls on the Creator to help him and give him the quality of truth, called "for the sake of the Creator."

In other words, he asks the Creator to give him the quality of truth, called "equivalence of form." To that man, the Creator is near. In other words, he wants to be in equivalence of form with the Creator, who is called "as He is merciful, so you are merciful." This is called, "The Lord is near to those who want to be near," which is called "equivalence of form."

Conversely, to those people who call on the Creator falsely, meaning who want the Creator to help them with *Lo Lishma*, which is called "disparity of form," the Creator is far from them, since they do not want to draw near to the Creator, which is called *Dvekut*, "equivalence of form." This is the meaning of what he says, "Truth is called 'the King's ring,'" which is truth, meaning that the kingdom of heaven that they take upon themselves is regarded as "truth," meaning for the sake of the Creator.

However, man must first prepare a *Kli* for this light, called "desire to bestow." A *Kli* is called "a need," meaning that a person does not call on the Creator to help him before he has begun the work of bestowal and sees that he is utterly incapable of attaining this by himself. At that time, a person asks to be given help from above.

For this reason, once a person has done all that he could and saw that he is utterly incapable of obtaining this desire, he comes to realize that no one can help him but the Creator. Then, a person says, "Our Father, our King, We have no King, meaning that there is no way that we will have faith in a king whom we will be able to serve 'because He is great and ruling,' but You," meaning that only the Creator can help him.

There, in *The Zohar*, he interprets that the King's ring is called the "middle line," and the middle line is called "truth." In other words, each line in itself is incomplete. We can understand this with an allegory: Two people prepared a meal for guests. One prepared meat and fish, and other things, and the other prepared only spices, salt, and vinegar, and so forth. But then, a dispute broke out between them, and each one said that he will call the guests over to him and will give them the meal. When the one who promised to provide only spices let them eat the spices, meaning to drink the vinegar and eat the salt, etc., who could eat? And the other one, who gave meat, fish, and other things to eat, who could eat meat and fish without salt, etc.? Since people could not eat at either place, they had to make peace between them and mix the food with the spices, and out of the two, a good meal emerged.

Likewise, when a person begins to walk in *Lo Lishma*, he is in a state of wholeness. This is called "one line." But when he shifts to the left line and begins to criticize the order of his work, meaning with what intention he is working, namely what reward he wants for his work, he feels a bitter taste.

In other words, he sees that he is not all right. Put differently, he sees that he cannot do anything for the sake of the Creator. In that state, each line in itself is incomplete, since the completion of the "right" is only because he is content with his lot, meaning says that he is very privileged that he has a small grip on spirituality, even if it is *Lo Lishma*, for in terms of actions, he has something, in that he observes the *Mitzvot* of the Creator. Although the faith in the Creator is only partial faith (as it is written in the "Introduction to The Study of the Ten Sefirot," Item 14), that part is still important to him.

This is not so with the left line, where he sees that he is full of faults and feels a bitter taste in his life. It is like a spice given in order to sweeten the food. But a spice without food is not a dish. It follows that each line in itself is incomplete, but when using both lines, right and left, from this we come to the middle line.

In other words, the Creator gives the soul, as our sages said, "There are three partners in a person: his father, his mother, and the Creator." The father is called "right." He gives the white. "White" means that there is no lack there. Mother is called the "left line." She gives the red, which is called "lacks." From the two of them together there can emerge the middle line, which is called "The Creator gives the soul." At that time, the quality of "man" emerges.

What Is, "We Have No Other King But You," in the Work?

We should know that when a person shifts to the left line and begins to see how far he is from the desire to bestow, and that he is immersed in self-love, and sees his faults to an extent that he had never imagined—that he would be so removed from working for the sake of the Creator—he begins to think that foreign thoughts must have come to him from the *Sitra Achra* [other side], who gives him these thoughts and desires that are inappropriate for someone who wishes to be a servant of the Creator. Even for an ordinary person, who is not working, it is inappropriate to have such thoughts and desires. At that time, a person must overcome through faith in the sages, and believe that all those thoughts come from above, as it is written in the essay, "Other Gods." In other words, the Creator sends them to a person, but he should not think that these are new thoughts and desires that did not previously exist in the person but came now. This is not so.

Rather, they were previously within man's body but were not revealed because nothing is done without a reason. Now that he wants to walk on the path of truth and wants to correct himself, he is shown from above what he has in his body, and which is not apparent outwards. Now that a person wants to correct himself, these thoughts are shown to him so he will know what to correct.

To understand this, we should look in the book *A Sage's Fruit* (Part 1, p 55), where it is written, "I admit that you are right about that; I do not feel those pains that you feel whatsoever. On the contrary, I rejoice in those revealed corruptions and the ones that are being revealed. I do, however, regret and complain about the corruptions that have not been revealed. If they appeared now, there is no doubt that they were here to begin with, but were hidden. This is why I am happy when they come out of their holes. I remember discussing similarly with you on the first day of *Rosh Hashanah* [the first day of the Jewish year], *Tav-Reish-Peh-Aleph* [September 13, 1920], upon our return from the house of A.M. You shared with me very sad things that you saw that morning during the morning service [prayer] (he was the prayer-leader of the morning service). I was filled with joy before you and you asked me, 'Why the joy?' I replied to you the same then, that when buried wicked appear, although they have not been fully conquered, their very appearance is regarded as a great salvation and causes the sanctity of the day."

Therefore, we should not be alarmed if a person feels that he has suffered a descent, as though he were thrown from above. On the contrary, at that time a person should believe that the Creator is tending to him and guides him so he will be able to achieve *Dvekut* [adhesion] with Him, as it is written, "And to cleave unto Him."

At that time, a person comes to a state where he feels that he has sinned. That is, before he began the work of bestowal, he thought that he was incomplete, but that in general, he was fine, since he saw the lowliness of other people, whereas he, thank God, was not as bad. But now he sees that he is the worst. That is, no one has such thoughts and desires.

The answer is that in order for a person to be able to receive a complete thing, he must have a complete lack. Hence, from above, he is shown his deficiencies each time, which were concealed within his body. It therefore follows that a person must say that the Creator was merciful with him in that He revealed to him his faults, just as He is giving him the filling, for "There is no filling without a lack."

By this we can interpret what is written (Psalms 89), "I will sing of the mercies of the Lord forever, generation after generation I will make known Your faith with my mouth." We should understand the meaning of "sing forever." How can one sing to the Creator when he sees that he is full of faults and his heart is not whole with the Creator, and he feels far from the Creator? And sometimes, he even wants to escape the campaign. How can he say that this is the Lord's mercies and he is singing about this to the Creator?

According to the above, a person should say that the fact that he in a lowly state is not because now he has become worse. Rather, now, since he wants to correct himself so that all his actions will be for the sake of the Creator, from above he is shown his true state—what is in his body, which until now was concealed and was not apparent. Now the Creator has revealed them, as it is written in the book *A Sage's Fruit*.

What Is, "We Have No Other King But You," in the Work?

A person says about this that it is mercy that the Creator has revealed to him the bad in him so he would know the truth and would be able to ask of the Creator for a real prayer. It follows that on one hand, now he sees that he is far from the Creator. On the other hand, a person should say that the Creator is close to him and tends to him, and shows him the faults. Hence, he should say that they are mercies.

This is the meaning of the words, "I will sing of the mercies of the Lord forever." That is, on one hand, he is happy and is singing about this. On the other hand, he sees that he must repent. In other words, he must ask of the Creator to bring him closer and give him the desire to bestow, which is a second nature.

This is the meaning of the words, "generation after generation I will make known Your faith." "Generation after generation" means that there is cessation in the middle, which is the meaning of ascents and descents. A generation is positive, and the cessation is negative. However, specifically by this, the light of faith appears.

What Is, "Return, O Israel, Unto the Lord Your God," in the Work?

Article No. 2, Tav-Shin-Nun-Aleph, 1990/91

The writing says, "Return, O Israel, unto the Lord your God, for you have failed in your iniquity. Take with you words and return to the Lord. Say unto Him: 'Remove all iniquity and take good, and we will pay with the fruit of our lips.'" We should understand the connection, for it is implied that since "you have failed in your iniquity," therefore, "return to the Lord your God." Also, what is, "Say unto Him: 'Remove all iniquity'"? And we should also understand what our sages said, "Great is repentance, for it reaches unto the throne, as it was said, 'unto the Lord your God'" (*Yoma* 86).

It is known that in the work, we should make two discernments: 1) that which pertains to the general public. Their work is in practice and they do not work on the intention, meaning to aim that it will be in order to bestow. For this reason, in terms of practice, everyone thinks that they are fine. Each one believes that it is impossible to be a perfect human being, so in general, he thinks that he is complete, and when he looks at his friends he sees their faults, that they are not all right.

He, on the other hand, is fine. Although he is lacking something, he excuses himself with the verse, "There is not a righteous man on earth who will do good and will not sin." Therefore, he has faults, as well, and he is careful with the quality of lowliness, as our sages said, "Be very, very humble." Although he sees that he is higher than the rest of the people, he has faith in the sages and believes above reason that he, too, is probably lowly, meaning that he is worse than the rest of the people. However, to him, this is faith above reason.

It follows that when those who belong to the general public engage in Torah, they cannot feel that they have iniquities or that they are worse than other people. Rather, in general, they are happy with their work. Therefore, come month of *Elul* [last month in Hebrew calendar] and the Ten Penitentiary Days, which is the time to make repentance, they have a lot of work to find iniquities within them on which they must repent.

Otherwise, they might be judged in the courthouse of above and could be punished for their actions. They understand that it is possible that the reward that they think they deserve might not happen, meaning that they will be rewarded less. But punishments? This is out of the question, since they know about themselves that they have much Torah and many *Mitzvot* [commandments/good deeds].

Conversely, those who work in the individual manner, who want to be rewarded with *Dvekut* [adhesion] with the Creator, and who understand that the Torah and *Mitzvot* they are observing are merely in the form of 613 counsels by which to adhere to the Creator, meaning so they will have only one concern—how to bring contentment to the Maker and to have no concern for themselves.

The body certainly resists this and presents just arguments why what it says is correct. It begins to present him with evidence from the whole world that no one is walking on such a path of annulling the will to receive for oneself and working only for the sake of the Creator. That person wants to overcome the iniquities that the will to receive brings him thoughts that contradict faith, which is Pharaoh's argument, who said, "Who is the Lord that I should obey His voice?"

It follows that the person failed in the iniquity of heresy. The more a person strengthens, the more it comes and prevails over the person. That is, as much as one wants to believe that the Creator watches over the world in a manner of good and doing good, the body shows him the opposite. Naturally, he is always failing and sees that this is endless and he is in ascents and descents, and he does not know what to do against it.

The writing says about this, "Return, O Israel, unto the Lord your God." And why must it be "unto the Lord your God"? It is because "You have failed in your iniquity." That is, since you have failed in your iniquity, meaning the iniquity of faith, and now you feel that you are the lowliest person in the world, since the thoughts and desires that you have are the lowest in the world, and you feel that you are utterly removed from spirituality.

In other words, the secular do not say that they are far from spirituality because they do not even believe that there is spirituality in the world. The same goes for the religious, who believe in Torah and *Mitzvot*—they do not feel that they are removed, since each one feels that he is more or less fine. And if they see some faults in themselves, they are certain to have an excuse for it. And especially, a person sees that the whole world leads a tranquil life, while he is in a state where he is full of failures and iniquities, and he sees no way out of that state.

Therefore, he has no other counsel besides "Return, O Israel." A person must return to the Creator and not retreat from Him until he is rewarded with the Creator being "your God." That is, until he is rewarded with complete faith. Otherwise, he will remain in the failures. For this reason, a person must try to do all that he can until there is mercy on him from above and he is given the power called "desire to bestow."

What Is, "Return, O Israel, Unto the Lord Your God," in the Work?

According to the above, we can understand what is written, "Take with you words." That is, these words that the body speaks to you and claims that it is not worthwhile to work for the sake of the Creator, take these words when you return to the Creator. Say to Him: "Remove all iniquity," since these words that the body tells us, we cannot overcome. Take these words when you return to the Creator. It says "all" because only You are all mighty; You can give us a second nature, called "desire to bestow." You will remove the iniquity, meaning that You can accept our iniquity and correct it, for only You are the carrier of our iniquity, while we are completely powerless.

However, we believe that all those words that the body speaks to us, You gave it these words, and You must have sent them to us, and it is certainly for our best. Therefore, "Say unto Him: 'Remove all iniquity and take good.'" That is, take this good that You sent us. In other words, those words that the body argued against the Creator, You must give another nature, called "desire to bestow," for otherwise we are lost, since we are full of failures.

This is the meaning of the words, "And we will pay with the fruit of our lips." We want that where we are, instead of our lips, where lips is considered the end of the matter, meaning outside of *Kedusha* [holiness], therefore since we are outside of *Kedusha* because of our desires, we ask You to "pay with the fruit of our lips." That is, where we are in the lips, at the end, we want to be whole with fruits, where "fruits" means fertilization and multiplication with good deeds.

According to the above, we can understand what our sages said, "Great is repentance, for it reaches unto the throne." That is, those people who belong to the general public do not feel that they have failures in the iniquity, called "the first iniquity," since they feel that they have faith and they are fine. Although they have only partial faith, as is explained ("Introduction to The Study of the Ten Sefirot," Item 14), they do not feel it. For this reason, they think that they are complete.

Conversely, those who belong to the individuals, who want there to be only one authority, the singular authority, who want to annul their self-authority called "will to receive," and to have only the authority of the Creator revealed in the world, they feel how the body objects to this. They want to repent, to return to the Creator, and this repentance reaches unto the throne.

However, we should understand the meaning of the throne in the work. It is known that *Malchut* is called "the throne," as it is written in the "Introduction of The Book of Zohar" (Item 31), "There are two discernments in the throne: 1) Covering the King, as it is written, 'He made darkness His hiding place,' for which it is called *Kisse*, from the word *Kissui* [covering/hiding]. 2) She reveals the glory of *Malchut* in the worlds, as it is written, 'And on the *Kisse* [throne] was a figure with the appearance of a man.'"

The thing is that we must believe that the *Tzimtzum* [restriction] and concealment that took place are a correction for the creatures. In other words, specifically by the concealment and covering that were made, the creatures will achieve their completion. We must believe above reason that the guidance by which the Creator leads the world is one of good and doing good. The reason we do not see that the guidance of good and doing good is concealed from us, we must believe that in truth, the guidance truly is of good and doing good, but there is a cover on this, which covers it.

Although the body objects to this, and to believing above reason, for it claims, "The judge has only what his eyes see," the person wants to overcome the arguments of the body. This is hard work and comprises ascents and descents.

When a person cries out to the Creator to help him be able to take upon himself this covering, meaning to be able to believe that Providence really is in the manner of good and doing good, except he has still not been rewarded with seeing it, through this work he becomes a chariot to the throne. In other words, he takes upon himself this throne although it is truly a concealment. At that time, that chair [*Kisse*] becomes the throne, meaning he is rewarded with the *Shechina* sitting on the throne.

It follows that to the extent that previously he was in the form of a *Kisse*, which is concealment, when he was as "*Shechina* in the dust," now it has become the throne. This is the meaning of the saying that the throne covers the King, as in, "He made darkness His hiding place." In other words, the throne does not shine and is in a state of darkness. We must overcome the darkness and say, "They have eyes but they will not see."

It follows that in the period of *Kisse*, that state is called "for you have failed in your iniquity." In the state of *Kisse*, a person has ascents and descents, and he does not see that this work will ever end. Rather, it is a perpetual to and fro, since during the concealment, it is difficult for a person to overcome and say that the Creator behaves in a manner of good and doing good.

Therefore, that person must repent, meaning that from the *Kisse*, which is "He made darkness His hiding place," the second state of the *Kisse* will appear, when it reveals the glory of *Malchut* in the world, as it is written, "And on the *Kisse* [throne], high up, was a figure with the appearance of a man."

This is the meaning of the words, "Great is repentance, for it reaches unto the throne." That is, repentance must be that a person must be rewarded with the second discernment in the meaning of *Kisse*, which is the throne. This is the meaning of "Return, O Israel, unto the Lord your God."

We should interpret that the meaning of "For you have failed in your iniquity" is that when a person wants to repent, meaning he is separated from the Creator because of the will to receive, which is opposite in form from the Creator, and he wants to connect with the Creator, to have equivalence of form, he sees that "The concealed things belong to the Lord our God."

In other words, when he wants to do something for the Creator, for the sake of the Creator, it is a "hidden" taste. In other words, the flavor of the work is hidden from him. Conversely, when he works for his own benefit, called "for us and for our children," the flavor is revealed to us. In other words, "concealed" and "revealed" pertain to the taste.

This means that when a person works for the sake of the Creator, called "to the Lord our God," the taste in the work is concealed. But when it is for one's own sake, called "for us and for our children," the taste is called "revealed," meaning the taste of the work is revealed. It follows that this causes our failures, as it is written, "For you have failed in your iniquity." Hence, there is no other way but to return to the Creator, as was said about it, "Remove all iniquity and take good."

According to the above, we should interpret what is written in the blessing for the food: "May we find grace and good understanding in the eyes of God and man." We should understand why we must ask the Creator to be liked by people. What does it mean that people should respect us and honor us? What does this have to do with the work? Rather, we ask the Creator to be liked by the Creator, and what do we want from Him? To give us the quality of "man," since by nature, man was created with a desire to receive, called *Malchut*, which is the name *BON*, which is "beast" in *Gematria*.

For this reason, we ask to be liked by God, so He will give us the quality of "man," as our sages said, "You are called 'man,' and not the nations of the world." Man is MA in *Gematria*, which is a giver. In other words, we ask to be liked by the Creator so He will give us the quality of "man." This is the meaning of the words "May we find grace in the eyes of God and man," so He will give us the quality of man.

It follows that man should pray for only one thing—for the Creator to bring him closer. "Closeness" in spirituality is called "equivalence of form." That is, he wants the Creator to give him the desire to bestow, called "second nature."

By this we should interpret what is written (Psalms 147), "who heals the brokenhearted." We should understand what it means that the Creator heals the brokenhearted. The thing is that it is known that the essence of man is the heart, as our sages said, "The Merciful one wants the heart." The heart is the *Kli* [vessel] that receives the *Kedusha* from above. It is as we learn about the breaking of the vessels, that if the *Kli* is broken, everything you put in it will spill out.

Likewise, if the heart is broken, meaning the will to receive controls the heart, abundance cannot enter there because everything that the will to receive receives will go to the *Klipot* [shells/peels]. This is called "the breaking of the heart." Hence, a person prays to the Creator and says, "You must help me because I am worse than everyone, since I feel that the will to receive controls my heart, and this is why nothing of *Kedusha* can enter my heart. I want no luxuries, only to be able to do something for the sake of the Creator, and I am utterly incapable of this, so only You can save me."

By this we should interpret what is written (Psalms 34), "The Lord is near to the brokenhearted." That is, those who ask the Creator to help them so their heart will not be broken and will be whole, this can happen only if a person has been rewarded with the desire to bestow. For this reason, he asks the Creator to give him the desire to bestow, since he sees that he lacks nothing in the world but the ability to work for the sake of the Creator. It follows that he is asking only the nearness of the Creator, and there is a rule, "measure for measure." Hence, the Creator brings him closer. This is the meaning of the words, "The Lord is near to the brokenhearted."

According to the above, we can understand what is written there: "Keeps all his bones, not one of them broken." Man's bone [in Hebrew, *Etzem* means both "bone" and "essence"] is the heart, the desire in the heart. The desires in man's heart constantly change through the ascents and descents, and the Creator guards their desires so that the will to receive will not mingle into the desires of *Kedusha*.

This is the meaning of the words, "not one of them broken." In other words, since the will to receive causes the breaking of the vessels, when the Creator keeps him, meaning brings a person closer, called "equivalence of form," by giving him a second nature called "desire to bestow," this is regarded as the Creator keeping, as in the verse, "The Lord keeps the fools." In other words, one who feels that he is a fool, that he is mindless, should keep himself from falling until the control of the *Sitra Achra* [other side], called "will to receive for oneself." He asks the Creator to keep him. It follows that the person gives the awakening from below, which is called "a desire" and a *Kli*, and then the Creator gives him the light.

But when a person is in an ascent, he thinks that he no longer needs the Creator's help, since now he has a basis of feeling, which he called "knowledge." In other words, now he knows for what purpose he is working. His work is no longer above reason because he has a basis to rely on, meaning this feeling that he feels that this state is good for him. On this basis he determines the work.

At that time, he is immediately thrown from above and it is as though he is asked, "Where is your wisdom? You said that you already know on what the work relies." Thus, as long as one thinks of himself as a fool, meaning that the basis of the work is above reason, and that he needs the help of the Creator, the person says, "Unless the Lord builds the house, they who labored in it worked in vain." Specifically in this way, the Creator is called "The Lord is the keeper of Israel."

By this we understand what it means that the person is in trouble in the work. The answer is that it is known that "narrow" means lack of *Hassadim* [mercies/plural of *Hesed*]. Hence, when a person sees that he cannot do anything in order to bestow, this is considered being unable to act in *Hesed*, unless for his own benefit. He sees that in the state he is in, he will never be rewarded with *Dvekut* with the Creator, and he regrets it. What can one do? One cannot do anything but cry out to the Creator, and the Creator hears. "From all their troubles [also "narrowness"]," meaning from every state, when he is in a state of "narrowness," which is lack of *Hassadim*, when he cannot overcome his actions, the Creator saves him, as it is written, "From all their troubles, He saves them." When it is written, "He has no troubles," it means that he does not regret that he cannot do something in order to bestow. Therefore, he has no *Kli* for the Creator to save him because he feels that he is fine where he is.

Accordingly, we should interpret what our sages said (*Hulin* 133), "Anyone who teaches an unworthy disciple falls to Hell." We should understand this, since it is written, "The Creator said, 'I have created the evil inclination; I have created the Torah as a spice.' Thus, one who has evil inclination and cannot overcome it, He said, I have created the Torah as a spice." So we see that we should learn Torah even when we are unworthy.

We should interpret this as Baal HaSulam said about what is written, "will give wisdom to the wise." It should have said "to the fools." The answer is that one who searches wisdom, although he still does not have it, he is already called "wise," since he desires to be wise. We should also interpret here that one who wants to be worthy is already called "a worthy disciple."

That is, one who wants to learn Torah because he wants to be worthy is already called "worthy," for because he feels that he is far from serving the Creator, since he can work only for his own sake, which is being unworthy, and he wants to be worthy but is unsuccessful, it was said to them: "The Creator said, 'I have created the evil inclination; I have created the Torah as a spice.'"

For this reason, we should interpret "It is forbidden to teach the Torah to an unworthy disciple" that one who wants to be a worthy disciple may learn.

What Is, "The Wicked Will Prepare and the Righteous Will Wear," in the Work?

Article No. 3, Tav-Shin-Nun-Aleph, 1990/91

The *Zohar* says (*Emor*, Item 232), "From good deeds that a person does in this world, a high, stately garment is made for him in that world, to clothe in. When a person has established good deeds but bad deeds overcame him, then he is wicked, since the faults are greater than the merits, and he ponders and regrets the good deeds he did before. At that time, he is completely doomed. He asks, 'What does the Creator do with those good deeds that that sinner did before?' And he replies, 'Even though that wicked one, that sinner, was lost, those good deeds and the merits he had done are not lost, since there is a righteous who walks in the ways of the upper King and fashions garments from his good deeds, but before he completes his garments, he departs from the world. The Creator completes his garments for him out of those good deeds that that

What Is, "The Wicked Will Prepare and the Righteous Will Wear"?

wicked sinner did. This is the meaning of the words, 'The wicked will prepare and the righteous will wear.' That sinner corrected and the righteous is covered with what he had corrected.'"

We should understand what it means when it says that we are speaking of a person who did good deeds, and why the bad deeds overcome him. After all, there is a rule, "A *Mitzva* [commandment/good deed] induces a *Mitzva*," so why did the bad deeds overcome him to such an extent that he came to a state where he pondered the beginning, at which time he is completely lost, since he doubts the beginning? We should also understand why if the a righteous is deficient of garments made of good deeds, he should receive the deeds of a wicked. He says that this is the meaning of "The wicked will prepare and the righteous will wear." From the literal meaning of "the wicked will prepare," it seems as though the wicked can only do bad deeds, but here he says that the righteous will wear the good deeds of the wicked. This means that the righteous takes good deeds and not bad ones.

It is known that the order of the work divides into two kinds:

1) Actions: That is, one who engages in Torah and *Mitzvot* [plural of *Mitzva*] and observes the commandments of the King, will be rewarded in return both in this world and in the next world. These people are usually fine in terms of their qualities, as much as possible. Each of them tries to observe Torah and *Mitzvot* and each works according to the measure of faith that he has. This is called "partial faith," as explained in the "Introduction to The Study of the Ten Sefirot" (Item 14), "And each one feels that he is called 'a servant of the Creator.'" Normally, each one always sees that the other one is wrong, where concerning himself, he always has excuses why he is fine. He feels that he has many merits, so naturally, that person can never come to such bad thoughts that he will doubt the beginning.

2) These are people who want to achieve *Dvekut* [adhesion] with the Creator, namely equivalence of form. They want to work only because of the greatness of the King, where to the extent that they believe in the greatness of the King, to that extent they have the

strength to work for the sake of the King. And if they cannot depict to themselves the greatness and importance of the King, then they have no fuel to be able to work for the sake of the Creator.

At that time he sees that he is called "a sinner," meaning that to the extent that he does good deeds, to the extent that he does things in order for it to cause him an "awakening from below," although the body does not agree to work in order to bestow and resists with all its might, he hopes that through coercion, when he forces this work of bestowal on himself, he will be able to do everything for the sake of the Creator.

But in the meantime, he sees that according to the good deeds that he has done, he should have been adhered to the Creator, but in fact, he sees that the bad deeds have increased, meaning that he regressed and has come to a state of despair and he doubts the beginning. *The Zohar* says about this that he loses everything, and this is why he now feels that he is wicked. Thus, the question is, What good deeds does he have if he doubts the beginning, since he loses everything?! According to this, it is perplexing when he says, "There is a righteous who walks in the ways of the upper King and fashions garments from his good deeds, but before he completes his garments, he departs from the world. The Creator completes his garments for him from those good deeds that that wicked sinner had done."

In the work, we should interpret this in one person, meaning when he begins to walk on the path toward achieving *Dvekut*, which is equivalence of form, meaning to bestow, and he did good deeds in the manner of 613 *Eitin* [Aramaic: counsels], by which to be rewarded with the desire to bestow. However, it is known that to the extent of one's work, so it is revealed to him from above how he is immersed in self-love. At that time, he sees the truth—there is no way that he can emerge from the governance of the will to receive and that all his concerns will be only about bringing contentment to his Maker, and that in all that he does, he will want that through his actions, he will cause His great name to grow and be sanctified.

He sees that all this is far from him. Finally, he decides that there is no way that he will achieve this level. As a result, he says, "I worked in vain," and he doubts the beginning. At that time, he is called "a sinner," "wicked."

At that time begins a procession of ascents, since each time, he is given an awakening from above and he begins to do good deeds once more. And then, once more, a descent. Such is the order until all the bad within the person surfaces. At that time, he prays to the Creator to help him because then, too, he must believe above reason that in the end, he will receive help from above, meaning the Creator will give him the desire to bestow, which is called "a second nature," meaning he will emerge from the governance of the will to receive for himself and will want only to bestow contentment upon his Maker.

It follows that there are three stages here:

1) In the beginning of the work, when he begins to do good deeds, the bad deeds overcome him and then he is a "wicked."

2) When he is rewarded with help from above, meaning the desire to bestow, and begins to do good deeds in order to bestow. At that time, he is called "righteous, who walks in the ways of the upper King." But before he completes his garments, he departs from the world. He completes his garments for him out of the good deeds that that wicked sinner did. We should interpret that "Before he completes his garments, he departs from the world" means before he fashioned the garments from the time when he was wicked. "Departs from the world" means that he has departed from the world called "will to receive," and ascended to the level of the "desire to bestow."

It follows that although now when he does good deeds in order to bestow, those deeds are fine, he lacks the completion in order to correct the *Kelim* [vessels] that were in the form of "pondering the beginning." He calls them "good deeds" because only those deeds that he did caused to make all the efforts so the Creator would bring him closer, meaning give him the desire to bestow.

It follows that the deeds on which there was the state of "pondering the beginning" were now corrected in that through them, the desire to bestow has now been revealed. This is why now the deeds—when he said he doubted the beginning—are now good deeds, since now their benefit is apparent, namely that they caused him to make efforts to ask the Creator to bring him closer; otherwise, he sees that he is lost. Through them, he ascended to *Kedusha* [holiness].

This is as it is written in the "Introduction of The Book of Zohar" (Item 140), "Yet, sometimes the thoughts prevail over a person until he wonders about all the good deeds he has done and says, 'What profit is it that we have kept His charge, and that we have walked in mourning before the Lord of hosts?' At that time, he becomes a complete wicked and loses all the good deeds he had done by this bad thought, for they will complete the correction of all the vessels of reception, so they will be only in order to bestow contentment upon the Creator. At that time, we will evidently see that all those punishments from the time of descents, which brought us into pondering the beginning, were purifying us since now they have been turned into merits. This is why those who speak those words are regarded as 'Those who fear the Lord and esteem His name.'"

According to the above, we can see how the deeds when they were in a state where the bad deeds overcame them, when they said, "We served the Lord in vain," and "we have walked in mourning before the Lord of hosts," meaning in low spirit because of the Creator, and all those things that they experienced during the descent, all join the good deeds and become garments for the righteous who walks in the ways of the upper King. Once he has departed from this world, meaning from a state of reception, into the next world, called *Bina*, which is bestowal, now he has good deeds only from vessels of bestowal. Yet, he lacks the wholeness, meaning the deeds he did before he was rewarded with the next world. Those deeds should also come into *Kedusha* and should not remain without correction. This is the meaning of the deeds becoming garments.

3) It follows that the third state is when the good deeds that he regretted have already joined. That is, he came to a state of pondering the beginning. After he has departed from this world, meaning from the will to receive, and has received the next world, meaning *Bina*, which is the desire to bestow, and once he has the desire to bestow comes the third state, namely that the deeds that were lost for him because he doubted the beginning now join as good deeds.

According to the above, we can understand what is written, "The wicked will prepare and the righteous will wear." This refers to the good deeds that the person did, and for which he was rewarded with a revelation from above that showed him the bad in him, but which was concealed because "He who is greater than his friend, his desire is greater than him." In other words, a person is not shown more evil than he is able to correct. This means that the good and the bad should be balanced. Otherwise, if a person sees all the bad in him before he has good, that person will escape the campaign and will say that this work is not for him.

It follows that only according to his work and labor in doing good deeds, which he wants to do, called "all his works will be for the sake of the Creator," this is called "good deeds." But if a person works for his own benefit, this is called "bad deeds," since self-benefit is called "receiving for oneself," and is in disparity of form from the Creator.

It turns out that these deeds remove him from the Creator. The good deeds that a person does, wanting to achieve *Dvekut* with the Creator, cause him to see the truth each time, that in truth, he is far from the Creator in terms of disparity of form, to the point that sometimes he comes to a state where he says that it is impossible that he will have the strength to defeat the distance, that he is so far from the Creator, to the point that he doubts the beginning.

Our sages said about this in *The Zohar*, "When a person has established good deeds but bad deeds overcame him, then he is wicked." This means that by doing good deeds, he was shown from above that there is evil in him and he is wicked. This is the meaning of the words "but bad deeds overcame him," meaning that from above he was given additional bad deeds.

This is the meaning of the words, "The wicked will prepare and the righteous will wear." In other words, the fact that the bad deeds grew, for which he is called "wicked," this was a preparation so that he would know that no one can help him but the Creator Himself. It follows that those bad deeds became garments that the righteous wears once he has become righteous, meaning after he has corrected his deeds, meaning after he has been rewarded with *Dvekut* with the Creator. At that time, the causes, meaning those revelations of evil that he had, for which he is called "wicked," now receive correction, too.

There are two things to discern here:

1) The good deeds that a person does, meaning the exertion to reach a state where all his works are for the sake of the Creator.

2) The bad deeds. He saw that because he did good deeds before, he was later notified from above that there are bad deeds within him, meaning that within him there is not a spark of desire to do everything for the sake of the Creator and not for his own sake. This is regarded as "the good deeds that he did caused him bad deeds," as was said, "When a person has established good deeds but bad deeds overcame him." And since he has come to a state where the bad deeds caused him to come to a state of pondering the beginning, now both have become bad deeds, since he lost all the deeds and they were included in the bad deeds. Now that he has been rewarded with entering the *Kedusha*, meaning with the desire to bestow, they were all corrected and everything was made into garments of *Kedusha*.

This is the meaning of what he says, "The wicked will prepare." That is, the state where everything becomes bad by coming to a state of pondering the beginning, but without the previous states, he would not be able to come into *Kedusha*. It follows that "The wicked will prepare," meaning without the preparation of the two above-mentioned discernments, where everything became bad, which is called "wicked," from this "the righteous will wear" is made.

What Is, "The Wicked Will Prepare and the Righteous Will Wear"?

By this we will understand what is written (in the concluding prayer), "And You desire the repentance of the wicked, and You have no wish for their death. 'I do not want the death of the wicked, but rather that the wicked turn back from his way and live.'" This means that when a person does good deeds, meaning wants to achieve *Dvekut* with the Creator, he is shown from above the evil within him, and he reaches the degree of wicked. At that time, a person wants to escape the campaign and says that this work is not for him, since he sees the truth each time, that by nature, the will to receive cannot agree that the person will cast it out and take instead the desire to bestow.

And who revealed to him this state, that he is wicked? It was the Creator who revealed it to him. The question is, Why did the Creator reveal it to him? Is it in order for him to die wicked? But the Creator does not want the death of the wicked. Thus, why did He reveal to him that he is wicked? It is only in order for him to repent, as it is written, "that the wicked turn back from his way and live."

For this reason, a person should not be alarmed when foreign thoughts come to him, which are not in the spirit of *Kedusha*. A person should believe that the Creator has sent him the awareness that he is wicked so that he may repent, meaning return to the will of the Creator, called "desire to bestow." In other words, the person, too, will ask the Creator to give him the desire to bestow, as we explained, "Annul your will before His will," meaning that the person will annul his will to receive before the will of the Creator, which is the desire to bestow. In other words, a person should throw and revoke the will to receive before the will to bestow, meaning take the desire to bestow in its stead.

It therefore follows that during the descents, when a person often comes to a state of despair where he doubts the beginning, he should take upon himself faith and believe in the Creator, that the Creator sends him these thoughts so that through them he will repent. In other words, a person should try to take upon himself the kingdom of heaven whether at a time of ascent or at a time of descent.

This is as it is written in "Introduction of The Book of Zohar" (Item 202), "Rabbi Elazar replied, 'Certainly, this fear must not be forgotten in all the *Mitzvot*, much less in the *Mitzva* of love—fear should be attached to it, since love is good on one side, when He gives him wealth and bounty, long life, sons, and nourishments.' At that time, fear should be awakened, to fear lest he will cause the sin. It is written about this, 'Happy is he who is always fearful.' Thus one should evoke the fear on the other side, of harsh judgment. It follows that fear clings to both sides, the side of good and love, and the side of harsh judgment."

Here, too, we should interpret similarly, meaning that one should assume the kingdom of heaven whether he feels good about engaging in Torah and *Mitzvot*, meaning whether he is in a state of ascent, at which time it is called "The side of the good" (meaning a state where he is happy), or from the side of harsh judgment (meaning when he feels bad). A person should believe in the Creator, that He watches in a manner of good and doing good. That is, the state in which a person feels bad is also for his best. Hence, during the descents he should still take upon himself the matter of fear.

For this reason, a person should be careful during the descent, and think about who is giving him the descents. If he believes that the Creator has given him the descent, then he is already close to the Creator, according to the famous rule, "In the place where a person thinks, there he is." Hence, when he thinks that the Creator has given him the descent, he already has contact with the Creator.

If he believes in this, this faith, when he thinks about the Creator, that connection can lift him from the state of descent. But if a person thinks about himself, that he is in a descent, then he is in a descent together with his body, since he is attached to the descending person and does not think of the Creator, and no longer has any connection with the Creator.

However, we must understand why the Creator gave him the descents. We can understand this through an allegory. Two students came to learn a trade from a craftsman. To one student, the teacher did not pay attention whether he was working well. To the other one, he kept commenting on his mistakes all day. That student went and said to his father, "Why does the teacher yell at me all day that I do not know how to work, and to the other one, who works worse than me, he says nothing? It must be that his father pays him more, and this is why he never criticizes him. Therefore, I am asking my father to also pay him more than other students pay, and then the teacher will not tell me my faults, just as he does not criticize other students."

His father went to the teacher and said, "Why have you no mercy on my son? Is it because I am not paying as much as other people, so you are taking revenge on my son?" So the teacher said to him, "Know that of all the students, I enjoy only your son, since I see that he is gifted and can be a star in the world. This is why I make such efforts with him, since it is worth my while, since my work will not go to waste. As for other students, I teach them more generally, since they are not as gifted as your son. This is why I criticize him on every detail.

"Therefore, you are wrong when you think that I want to fail your son because I am angry with you because you pay me little money. Know that if I did not want to embarrass you by teaching your son for free, believe me, I would teach him for nothing, since I enjoy him and it is worth my while to make all the effort that I exert in him."

The lesson is that all the descents that the Creator gives to those who want to walk on the path of bestowal for the sake of the Creator, specifically with them the Creator pays attention to how they work. Each time a person tries to do good deeds, the Creator shows him the faults—how immersed he is in self-love and cannot work for the sake of the Creator. It follows that the criticism that the Creator is showing him, that his actions are improper, is because the Creator sees that he is trying to work for the sake of the Creator, called "good deeds," so the Creator shows him that they are not all right, as in the allegory.

Conversely, those who work in the manner of the general public, the Creator does not show them criticism, that their deeds are not in order, since they are still unfit for individual work. It follows that when the general public work and their faults are not revealed, it is because it is pointless.

Hence, a person should not complain when the Creator always gives him descents, which show him that he is wicked. It is not because he is worse than other people. On the contrary, he is given a personal treatment, called "special treatment," since only he is fit to come into the holy work. Therefore, a person should not say that now he sees that he is not being looked after although he prays to the Creator to help him. On the contrary, he must believe that he is given a special treatment since he is worthy of this work of bestowal.

It therefore follows that he cannot receive the good from the Creator, called "desire to bestow," before he has a real need for it. That is, when he sees that he is wicked, he cries out to the Creator, "Save my soul from the netherworld, for I see that I am totally and utterly lost."

By this we can interpret what is written, "There is not a righteous man on earth who will do good and will not sin." We should explain that "There is not a righteous man on earth" means that it is impossible to be righteous, and for the Creator to help him, unless he sins first. In other words, first he must come to a state of sin, meaning see, as it is written in *The Zohar*, that once he has done good deeds, the bad deeds overcome him. Then he cries out to the Creator to help him, he receives the help of the Creator, and the Creator delivers him from the hand of the wicked, and he becomes righteous. In other words, the Creator gives him the second nature, called "desire to bestow."

What Is, "The Saboteur Was in the Flood, and Was Putting to Death," in the Work?

Article No. 4, Tav-Shin-Nun-Aleph, 1990/91

It is written in *The Zohar*, Noah: "There was a flood and the saboteur was sitting inside." Baal HaSulam asked what is the difference between the saboteur putting to death or the flood putting to death. He said that the flood caused corporeal suffering, and the saboteur causes spiritual suffering. In other words, within the corporeal suffering there is a saboteur who kills a person's spirituality, meaning that the torments of the body bring him foreign thoughts until these thoughts sabotage and kill the spirituality.

We should interpret his words. The flood and the rain are called "revealed," meaning that which is visible to our eyes, that the saboteur was killing the people. That is, what a person thinks, that if the will to receive had what it demands, meaning knowledge and not faith, if it could understand everything about His guidance, as the will to receive requires, he would serve the Creator properly. However, this is not so, and as a result, because it is difficult for a person to suffer, he moves away from the Life of Lives and wants the Creator to impart upon him only pleasures. This is why he moves away.

However, within the corporeal suffering, meaning a person's inability to understand His guidance, why the Creator does not give him what the will to receive understands that He should give, and he suffers, from this extends death in spirituality, meaning spiritual suffering that causes death in spirituality. In other words, he falls into heresy.

That is, the fact that he suffered the corporeal suffering because the Creator did not give him what he thought, and it pained him, these sufferings cause death in corporeality, as it is written, "The dead is as important as the dead, and one who has no sons is as important as the dead." However, afterward, he comes to spiritual suffering, meaning that he cannot overcome the faith and believe in the Creator, that He leads the world with a guidance of good and doing good. At that time, he comes to heresy.

This is called "spiritual death," when a person falls into the vacant space of the *Sitra Achra* [other side]. Later, when a person reenters the work, it is considered "the revival of the dead." At that time a person must believe that the fact that now he has begun the work once more is not by his own strength, but he rather received from above the "dew of resurrection." This is considered "the revival of the dead," with which he has been rewarded because he received an awakening from above. For this reason, a person must say each day, "Blessed are You, Lord, who returns souls to dead corpses." Also, one should say (in the Eighteen Prayer), "You are certain to revive the dead."

Thus, there are two things here concerning suffering: 1) Corporeal suffering, when a person suffers in corporeal matters because of what he needs, and he suffers death because of it, as in "The dead is as important as the dead, and one who has no sons is as important as the dead," etc. It follows that this death is not related to spirituality. However, afterward, it causes him spiritual death

What Is, "The Saboteur Was in the Flood, and Was Putting to Death"?

because he cannot believe that the Creator leads the world in a manner of good and doing good.

It follows that this is spiritual death and not corporeal death. This is the meaning of saying that within the flood of rain, which is corporal suffering, he later comes to spiritual suffering, when he cannot justify Providence, and therefore falls into spiritual death.

This is as it is written in the "Introduction of The Book of Zohar" (Item 138), "Prior to the end of correction, *Malchut* is called 'the tree of knowledge of good and evil,' since *Malchut* is the guidance of the Creator in this world. As long as the receivers have not been completed so they can receive His whole benevolence, the guidance must be in the form of good and bad, reward and punishment. It is so because our vessels of reception are still tainted with self-reception. Thus, we necessarily sense evil in the operations of Providence in relation to us. It is a law that the creature cannot receive disclosed evil from the Creator, for it is a flaw in the glory of the Creator for the creature to perceive Him as an evildoer, for this is unbecoming of the complete Operator. Hence, when one feels bad, denial of the Creator's guidance lies upon him and the superior Operator is concealed from him to that same extent. This is the worst punishment in the world."

It therefore follows that when a person receives bad from Him, it makes the operator become concealed from Him. This is called "death" in spirituality. And who caused him to receive bad from Him? Why did he receive bad? It is because those *Kelim* [vessels] were still dirty with self-reception. Hence, there must be guidance in a manner of concealment and hiding. For this reason, suffering causes death in spirituality.

Because of this, a person must go above reason and not be impressed by the reason he sees and on which he builds his work in holiness, so he may be rewarded with entering the *Kedusha* [holiness], since this reason came because he received ills, and according to reason, if the Creator is good and does good, why does He not give a person what the person thinks he needs, and instead, the Creator does what He wants? It follows that reason is built on the basis of a guidance of good and evil. Hence, a person's only choice is to say that what reason tells him is incorrect, as was said about this, "For My thoughts are not your thoughts, nor are your ways My ways." Instead, he should not be alarmed by the reason and say that he is going above reason.

However, concerning the feeling of nearing the Creator, there are two manners to discern: 1) Sometimes he is worried that he should obtain something he needs. Normally, when a person needs something, he prays to the Creator to satisfy his need. If he needs this thing and does not see a natural way to obtain it, and a miracle happens and he receives what he asked for, the person fills with love of the Creator for helping him obtain the matter, and he attributes obtaining the matter to the Creator. It follows that nearing the Creator came to him by reception of delight and pleasure; this was the cause for nearing the Creator.

The same applies for a sick person who has been healed. He was already despaired, and suddenly a change for the better occurred and he was cured. He, too, sometimes draws near to the Creator, for the reason that receiving the good from the Creator brought him closer to the Creator.

At times it is to the contrary. A person suffers torments, and the torments push him to draw near the Creator. That is, it occurs to him that if he takes upon himself the burden of Torah and *Mitzvot* [commandments/good deeds], the Creator will save him from his troubles. It follows that the suffering caused the nearing to the Creator. It should be said about this that since at a time of trouble, a person is in a state of lowliness, since it is written, "The Lord is high and the low will see," it follows that the fact that he is in lowliness because of the troubles and torments that have afflicted him, he is ready to receive help from above, as it is written, "The Lord is high and the low will see." However, usually, we see that suffering pushes a person away from the Creator since he cannot attribute the suffering to the one who is good and does good. Hence, this causes him death in spirituality.

However, concerning lowliness, there are many interpretations. In other words, when a person lowers himself, the question is, What is lowliness? How is it expressed that a person is in lowliness? The literal meaning is that lowliness is when one subdues oneself and works above reason. This is called "lowliness," when he lowers his reason and says that his reason is worthless.

In other words, man's reason dictates that if the Creator gives him all his needs, which the will to receive understands that it deserves, then he can love the Creator. That is, he loves Him because he satisfies all his needs. If He did not, he would not be able to lower himself and say that his reason is worthless. Rather, at that time he would depart from the Creator and say that it is not worthwhile to serve the Creator if He does not grant him his wishes. It follows that this is called "proud," since he wants to understand the ways of the Creator, in what is He regarded as good and doing good, if the body does not get what it demands. About such a proud person the Creator says, "He and I cannot dwell in the same abode."

But if he lowers himself and says, "I cannot understand the ways of the Creator," and he says that what his reason dictates is worthless, but he is going above reason, this is called "lowliness," and it was about him that the verse, "The Lord is high and the low will see" was said. He is rewarded with the Creator bringing him near Him.

Accordingly, we can interpret what our sages said, "Anyone who chases greatness, greatness runs from him" (*Iruvin* 13). That is, a person says, "I can serve the Creator on condition that He sends me greatness. That is, if I feel His greatness, I will be able to work for the sake of the Creator. Otherwise, I cannot work for the sake of the Creator." He is told, "greatness runs from him."

But when a person says, "Now I want to be a servant of the Creator unconditionally, and I do not need greatness," but he rather wants to serve the Creator in utter lowliness, meaning although he has no feeling of the greatness of the Creator, but above reason, which is called "lowliness," then he is rewarded with greatness because he lowers himself since he wants to work only for the sake of the Creator and not for his own sake.

Hence, when he says that he cannot work unless he feels the greatness of the Creator, it follows that the will to receive says that if he does not understand the greatness of the Creator within reason, he will not be able to work for the sake of the Creator. It follows that only the will to receive is the operator, but on the will to receive there were *Tzimtzum* [restriction] and concealment. Hence, it is utterly impossible to be rewarded with greatness. Instead, a person must always run from greatness. At that time, it can be said as it is said, "He who runs from honor, honor chases him."

It therefore follows that there are several stages here in the order of the work: 1) A person must first chase greatness and honor, since otherwise, he has no *Kelim* [vessels] at all for honor and greatness, since the thought acts on what a person demands. If he has no *Kelim* for reason, how can he go above reason? For this reason, when a person begins the work, he must think how to receive greatness of the Creator, so that when he has a feeling of the greatness of the Creator, the body will not resist because it is natural for the small to annul before the great. There is no work on this, since there is a rule that the body does not resist anything that comes by nature.

But if he has no yearning for reason, meaning to want to serve a great King, then his work is only in the action, and he has no need for the Creator to help him, since then he works only to receive reward. To the extent that he believes in reward and punishment, to that extent he can work and he has no need for the greatness of the Creator. In other words, even though the King is not so great, he does not mind since he looks at the reward, and not at the giver of the reward.

But if he begins to work for the sake of the Creator then he needs the greatness of the King. It follows that if he does not yearn for the greatness of the King, it is a sign that he is not working for the sake of the Creator. Thus, specifically when he chases greatness, it is a sign that he wants to achieve a state where he can say that all his actions are for the sake of the Creator. Afterward, when he feels that he must know that he has a great and important King, and he sees that this is to him the main disruptor, what he needs in order to be able to overcome the will to receive, he comes to the second stage, when he has to run away from greatness and wants to work for the sake of the Creator unconditionally, which is called above reason.

In other words, although his reason tells him, "You see that you believe in only a small king," a person should still say, "To me you are a great King, as though I felt it. I believe above reason that You are a great King as though I felt it." Hence, at that stage, he runs from greatness and from honor and then the greatness and the honor chase him and catch up with him although he does not want to receive the greatness because only then is there equivalence with the Creator.

This is the same as we learn about *Zivug de Hakaa* [coupling by striking]: To the extent that the *Masach* [screen] rejects the light, although it has *Aviut* [thickness], meaning a desire and yearning for the light, it still does not receive it because it wants to be a giver and not a receiver. Hence, by the rejection in the *Masach*, the *Ohr Hozer* [Reflected Light] is born in him, and in this *Ohr Hozer* he receives a new *Kli* [vessel] for reception of the light.

It is likewise here. First, a person needs to acquire a desire and yearning to obtain the greatness of the Creator, and then a person must acquire strength to reject the greatness and not want to receive it because he wants equivalence of form. At that time he obtains the *Ohr Hozer*, and in this *Ohr Hozer* he receives the greatness and the might.

It follows that there are three stages here:

1) To want specifically the greatness of the Creator.

2) To reject the idea of yearning, meaning that although he understands that if he has a true feeling of the greatness of the Creator, the body will surrender to do the holy work. Still, he runs from the honor and the greatness and says that he wants to work for the sake of the Creator. Although he has no feeling, he asks the Creator to give him the strength to be able to defeat the will to receive, even though it disagrees with it.

3) When he does not need the feeling of the greatness of the Creator and works for the sake of the Creator unconditionally. At that time, he is rewarded with the greatness of the Creator and the glory of the Creator. Then, the words, "He who runs from honor and from greatness, honor chases him and wants to cling to him," come true because he already has equivalence of form, meaning that he wants to work in order to bestow.

Accordingly, once a person understands that it is worthwhile to receive the feeling of the greatness of the Creator because then the body will agree to serve the King, and once he has a demand for this, since he wants to work for the sake of the Creator but the body resists it because as long as long he does not feel the greatness of the Creator, he does not want to believe above reason, then comes a state where a person must run away from this because this is only an argument of the will to receive.

But when he does not feel the greatness of the Creator, the body does not agree to this work, and then a person must say, "But our sages said, 'Anyone who chases greatness, greatness runs from him,'" since a person must work for the sake of the Creator even when the body does not enjoy the work, since for the sake of the Creator means not considering one's own benefit whatsoever.

This is as it is written in the "Introduction of The Book of Zohar" (Item 199), "Whole love is whole on both sides, whether in judgment or in mercy. And even if He takes your soul, your love in the Creator is in complete wholeness, as when He gives you abundance. There is one who loves Him so as to have wealth, long life, sons around him, rule over his enemies, and success on his way. Thus, he loves Him. If it were to the contrary, and the Creator would reverse the fortune upon him with harsh judgment, he would hate Him and not love Him whatsoever. For this reason, this love is not love that has a foundation. Complete love is love on both sides, in judgment or in mercy and successful ways. He will love the Creator as we learned, even if He takes His soul away from Him. This love is complete."

What Is, "The Saboteur Was in the Flood, and Was Putting to Death"?

We should interpret that a person having to love the Creator in ascent—when he feels that the Creator leads the world as The Good Who Does Good, since during the ascent, a person wants to annul before Him unconditionally—but this is like a candle before a torch, where he annuls without any mind or reason. This is regarded as a person serving the Creator when he has a soul.

An ascent means that the person is alive and has the breath of life. At that time a person has love for the Creator, and this is called "the side of goodness" in the work.

But a person must also love the Creator when He takes his soul away, meaning when the Creator takes from him the breath of life. This is called "the time of descent," when he has no feeling of vitality, when his soul is taken from him and he has no vitality. If he has love for the Creator in such a state, as well, this is called "complete love."

Such a thing can be only above reason, since within reason he has no vitality so as to have the strength to overcome. Hence, a person must work during the preparation on escaping from the greatness and honor before he obtains any nearness on the part of the Creator. That is, he should not say that only if the Creator gives him the breath of life he will be able to work in order to bestow, but without vitality, meaning without the spirit of life, he cannot work for the sake of the Creator. This is not the view of Torah.

Rather, a person must ask the Creator to give him the strength to love the Creator even when He takes his soul away, and he is left lifeless, to be able to overcome and love the Creator under any circumstances.

According to the above, we should interpret the meaning of "He made darkness His hiding place." It means that when the Creator wants to hide Himself from a person, which is certainly for man's best because he is still not ready for revelation, He gives a person darkness. That is, He takes from him the breath of life, and then he falls into a place of darkness, where the light of *Kedusha* does not shine.

A person should believe that this is concealment. Concealment means that he believes that there is a great Creator who leads the world in a manner of good and doing good, but this is concealed from him. He should believe that this is only a concealment, and if he succeeds in believing that this is only a concealment but it is not really as he sees it, then he is rewarded with the light shining on this *Kisse* [cover], meaning that light will shine within this darkness.

Accordingly, a person should learn from the state of descent and from the state of ascent. That is, the state of descent comes to a person when he wants to make great efforts to achieve *Dvekut* [adhesion] with the Creator. Yet, he sees otherwise, as though he did nothing, but he is in the same state as before he began the work on the aim to bestow. At that time, a person should have faith in the sages and what they say, and not in what a person thinks and says, since these descents give him room to ascend and draw near to the Creator.

What Is, "The Good Deeds of the Righteous Are the Generations," in the Work?

Article No. 5, Tav-Shin-Nun-Aleph, 1990/91

RASHI brings the words our sages about "These are the generations [offspring] of Noah; Noah was a righteous man." Why does it not mention the names of the sons, Shem, Ham, and Yaphet, but rather "These are the generations [offspring] of Noah; Noah was a righteous man"? It is to teach you that the offspring of the righteous are primarily good deeds.

We should understand if saying that the offspring of the righteous are good deeds, is this information for other people to know or is it something that the righteous themselves should know? It is known that in the work, we learn everything within one person. It follows that the rest of the people having to know that the offspring of the righteous are good deeds is also in the same body. That is, the righteous himself should know that his offspring should be good deeds. We should know this with relation to the righteous himself, what this information adds to him in the work.

To understand this, we first need to know what are good deeds or bad deeds in the work. Good deeds means that it is known that in observing Torah and *Mitzvot* [commandments/good deeds], we should discern the practice, when a person observes Torah and *Mitzvot* in practice, meaning that he believes in the Creator, observes His *Mitzvot*, and allocates times for the Torah. However, he does not pay attention to the intention, meaning for whose sake he is working, whether it is for himself, so that he will be rewarded for observing Torah and *Mitzvot*, which is called "self-benefit," or is he working for the sake of the Creator, which is not in order to receive reward.

The difference between them is that when a person still works for his own benefit and is still immersed in self-reception, on this reception there were *Tzimtzum* [restriction] and concealment. That is, concerning the purpose of creation, which is to do good to His creations, he cannot receive the delight and pleasure. It follows that the deeds where the aim is for one's own benefit are called "bad deeds," since these actions move him away from receiving the delight and pleasure. It follows that when a person does deeds, he should gain, but here he is losing because he is separated from the Creator.

But if a person does everything for the sake of the Creator, so the Creator will enjoy it, then he is walking on a line and a path leading to *Dvekut* [adhesion] with the Creator, which is called "equivalence of form." When there is equivalence of form, the *Tzimtzum* and concealment are removed from him, and a person is rewarded with the delight and pleasure that were in the thought of creation, which is to do good to His creations. For this reason, what a person does for the sake of the Creator is called "good deeds," since these actions lead him to be rewarded with the good.

According to the above, we should interpret that the righteous should know that the offspring of the righteous are good deeds. Offspring are called "fruits," which are the results of the previous

What Is, "The Good Deeds of the Righteous Are the Generations"?

state. This is called "cause and consequence," or "father and offspring." It follows that when a person observes Torah and *Mitzvot* and wants to be righteous, how can he know whether or not he is righteous, as our sages said (*Berachot* 61), "Rabba said, 'One should know in one's heart whether he is righteous or wicked'"? Yet, how can one know this?

For this reason, they said, "the generations [offspring] of righteous are good deeds." If a person sees that his engagement in Torah and *Mitzvot* yields for him good deeds, meaning that the Torah and *Mitzvot* he does causes him to do everything in order to bestow, which is for the sake of the Creator, it is a sign that he is righteous.

However, if the Torah and *Mitzvot* he performs do not yield for him the offspring of good deeds, but rather bad deeds, meaning that he works only for his own benefit and does not bring him the ability to do good deeds, which is for the sake of the Creator, then he does not fall into the category of "righteous," even if he observes Torah and *Mitzvot* in all their details and precisions. However, this is so only in the work. For the general public, one who observes Torah and *Mitzvot* with all the precisions is considered righteous.

This is why concerning the verse, "Noah was a righteous man, complete in his generations," RASHI brings the words of our sages, "Some praise him and some condemn him." We should interpret why they praise and why they condemn, meaning which is the truth.

In the work, when relating everything to one person, the offspring, too, do not pertain to several bodies but to one body at several times. Therefore, what is the meaning of praising and condemning? It is written in the "Introduction of The Book of Zohar" (Item 140), "'Day to day pours forth speech, and night to night reveals knowledge.' Often, the guidance of good and evil causes us ascents and descents. You should know that for this reason, each ascent is regarded as a separate day because due to the great descent that he had, pondering the beginning, during the ascent he is as a newly born child. This is why each ascent is considered a specific day, and similarly, each descent is considered a specific night. At the end of correction they will be rewarded with repentance from love, for they will complete the correction of the vessels of reception, so they will work only in order to bestow contentment upon the Creator, and all of the great delight and pleasure of the thought of creation will appear to us. At that time, we will evidently see that all those punishments from the time of descents, these sins will be inverted into actual merits. And this is 'Day to day pours forth speech.'"

According to the above, we should interpret "Noah was a righteous man, complete in his generations," that there should be praise here, as well as condemnation, and both are true. In other words, if it is written, "in his generations," in plural form, it means that the generation divided into several intervals. Hence, there are many generations. This is possible when during the work he had ups and downs; hence, they divided into several generations.

It follows that the time of descent is considered a condemnation, as he says in the *Sulam* [Ladder commentary on *The Zohar*], that sometimes we come to a state of "pondering the beginning." There is no worse condemnation than this. It follows that condemnations pertain to the descents. Also, there are praises, meaning the time of ascents. It is praise because then he has connection with the *Kedusha* [holiness].

"Complete" means that all the generations have become wholeness, which is called "complete." In other words, he has been rewarded with the end of correction, meaning that they have completed the correction of the vessels of reception to receive in order to bestow. It follows that the proliferation of generations, where there were intervals in between, meaning descents, have been corrected and he became complete in his generation. This is the meaning of condemning and praising, and both are true, and both become one matter, called "complete in his generations."

However, for the most part, those who engage in Torah and *Mitzvot* in practice have no ascents or descents to the point that they can come to a state of pondering the beginning, since as long as they do not want to blemish the will to receive, the body does not

What Is, "The Good Deeds of the Righteous Are the Generations"?

object to the work so much. Hence, these people regard themselves as complete. When they look in the Torah, they see themselves as not so bad, more or less fine.

This is called "*Ayin* [eye/seventy] faces to the Torah," meaning that there are two discernments to make here:

1) Narrow-eyed turns his face to the Torah. That is, he interprets the Torah in the manner of a narrow-eyed, called "narrow in *Hassadim* [mercies]." In other words, he does not understand how there can anything more than self-benefit. For this reason, he interprets the Torah in a manner that no harm will come to his self-benefit. This is as our sages said (*Avoda Zara* 19), "One learns only where one's heart desires." That is, if he is narrow-eyed, the *Ayin* faces of the Torah are in a manner that will yield self-love.

2) There is the blessed *Ayin*, as it is written, "The good-eyed, he will be blessed." This means that one who has a good eye, who likes to bestow, which is the opposite of the narrow-eyed, since he wants to work in order to bestow, when he looks in the Torah, he sees that in all the places in the Torah, a person must work in order to bestow. This is regarded as learning from the place where he is. In other words, he sees that we must work only in order to bestow. It follows that the good-eyed is rewarded with the blessings called *Hesed* [mercy/grace], namely with *Dvekut* [adhesion]. By this, he is later rewarded with the delight and pleasure that were in the thought of creation.

It follows that a person must work in order to obtain the need that the Creator will help him and give him the second nature, called "desire to bestow." However, each person wants the reward first, and to work next. That is, each one wants to first be given the desire to bestow, although he still does not understand that he needs the desire, but he heard that the reward one receives for the work is that from above he is given the desire to bestow. Hence, he wants to be given that desire, but his intention is only that he will not have to work in order to obtain it.

However, there is no light without a *Kli* [vessel]. That is, a person must first toil in order to have a desire and a need for it, since there is no filling without a lack. Therefore, a person must accept descents each time, since through the descents he acquires a need that the Creator will help him and give him the strength to be able to defeat the will to receive in him so he is rewarded with the desire to bestow.

Therefore, we ask the Creator to give us the desire to bestow in order to have *Dvekut* with the Creator, while for our part, we are unable to overcome our will to receive and subdue it so it will cancel itself and give its place so that the desire to bestow will govern the body.

The order of the prayer is as it is written, "Our Father, our King, do for Your sake if not for our sake." This phrasing is perplexing. Normally, when we ask a person for a favor, we tell him, "Do me a favor for you, meaning for your sake. If you do not want to do me a favor because it will be to your benefit, do it only for my benefit."

But it is certain that if he does not want to help him although it will be for his own benefit, too, and he still does not want to, then if he does not derive any benefit from this, he will not do him the favor. So what does it mean "Do for Your sake," and if not, meaning if not for Your sake, then "Do for our sake," meaning only for our benefit? Can this be?

We should interpret this: We say, "Our Father, our King, do for Your sake." We ask the Creator to give us the strength so we can perform all our actions for You, meaning for the sake of the Creator. Otherwise, meaning if You do not help us, all our actions will be only for our own benefit. That is, "If not," meaning "If You do not help us, all our actions will be only for ourselves, for our own benefit, for we are powerless to overcome our will to receive. Therefore, help us be able to work for You. Hence, You must help us." This is called "Do for Your sake," meaning do this, give us the power of the desire to bestow. Otherwise, we are doomed; we will remain in the will to receive for our own sake.

However, a person must know that there is no light without a *Kli*, no filling without a lack. For this reason, he must first feel that he lacks the desire to bestow. In other words, he does not regard wanting the desire to bestow as an accessory, that he is actually fine but he would like to be more complete. We should know that this is not regarded as a lack with respect to spirituality. In spirituality, everything must be complete, meaning a complete light, complete lack. Accessories are not regarded as complete lacks, and therefore the complete light cannot enter.

Hence, the light, regarded as the Creator giving a person the desire to bestow, is called "light of repentance," since before a person receives the desire to bestow, he is placed under the governance of the will to receive, which is the opposite of *Kedusha* [holiness], called desire to bestow, as the will to receive belongs to the *Klipot* [shells/peels]. This is why our sages said, "The wicked in their lives are called 'dead.'"

This is the meaning of what is written in *The Study of the Ten Sefirot* (Part 1, *Histaklut Pnimit*, Item 17), "For that reason, the *Klipot* are called 'dead,' since their oppositeness of form from the Life of Lives cuts them off from Him and they have nothing of His Abundance. Hence, the body, too, which feeds on the leavings of the *Klipot*, is also severed from the Life of Lives. All this is because of the will only to receive. Thus, 'The wicked in their lives are called 'dead.'"

Accordingly, a person cannot acquire the desire to bestow, which the Creator will bestow upon him, before he has a complete lack, meaning that he feels that he is wicked because he is under the governance of the will to receive and is separated from the Creator, and he wants to repent, to adhere once more to the Creator so as not to be separated, since separation causes death, as was said, "The wicked in their lives are called 'dead.'"

It follows that unless a person feels himself as wicked, he does not have a complete lack for the Creator to give him the help, the power of the desire to bestow, which Baal HaSulam calls "a second nature." Hence, in terms of the work, it is not considered that he has repented before he first feels that he is wicked.

Afterward, he asks the Creator to help him because he wants to repent. Yet, he sees that he is powerless to repent without the

Creator's help. In such a state he has a complete lack, called "a complete *Kli*," and then he is fit to receive the complete help from the Creator, namely the desire to bestow.

However, our sages said, "A person does not regard himself as wicked" (*Ketubot* 18). The reason is that in the work, "transgressing and repeating," our sages said "becomes to him as permitted." Thus, a person does not view himself as wicked and can say that he has a complete *Kli*, that he is so truly remote from the Creator that he feels himself as dead. That is, we should interpret that "The wicked in their lives are called 'dead'" is when a person can say that he feels that he is wicked before the Creator. That is, when he feels himself as dead—that has no vitality of *Kedusha*—he feels himself as wicked.

But from where does one take such a feeling? The answer is as we said in previous articles: Such awareness and feeling come from above, as it is written in *The Zohar* about the verse, "Or, make it known to him that he has sinned." He asks, "Who made it known?" And he replies, "The Creator made it known to him." It follows that the awareness and feeling that he has sinned also comes from above. In other words, both lack and filling, both light and *Kli*, come from above.

However, it is known that everything requires an awakening from below. The answer is that first a person must do good deeds. That is, the work begins when a person wants to do good deeds, which is considered that he wants to work for the benefit of the Creator, regarded as working for the sake of the Creator. Then, by wanting to come closer to the Creator and thinking that he needs only a little bit of wholeness, but in fact, he is fine, since it is seen above that he wants to approach the Creator, he is given each time the deficiency that is in him—that he is actually completely removed from the Creator.

It is not as he thought before, that he lacked a little bit of wholeness. Rather, he is shown from above that he is remote from the Creator to the point of oppositeness of form, to the point that the person feels that he is wicked toward the Creator and cannot do anything in order to bring contentment to his Maker.

At that time, he achieves the degree of "wicked" and sees that he has no vitality of *Kedusha*, and that he is truly "dead." Then, he has a complete lack, called a "complete *Kli*," and then the Creator can give him a complete light, meaning complete help, which is the desire to bestow. This is considered that he has repented.

However, we should know that in the work, we should discern that there is faith, which is above reason, called "law," and there is the Torah, called "sentence" [verdict]. Baal HaSulam said that "Law means faith above reason, and sentence means the Torah," where it is specifically within reason. He said that "One who does not know the commandment of the upper one, how will he serve Him?" Hence, a person must try to understand the words of Torah, called "sentence."

By this we should interpret what is written (Genesis 4:19), "Lemech took to himself two wives: the name of the one was Adah, and the name of the other, Tzillah." We should understand what it teaches us in the work, how many wives he had, as well as their names. The thing is that Lemech has the letters of *Melech* [king], which implies that a person should make good conjunctions, meaning to be rewarded with feeling that there is a King to the world, and it is a great privilege for a person if he is rewarded with serving the King of the world.

"Wives" means assistants, as it is written, "It is not good for the man to be alone; I will make for him a help made against him," so a woman means an assistant. That is, how does she help? She is called "wife" in her assistance to him, meaning she completes his work by his using her quality. This is why it is considered that she helps him achieve his completion.

We should know that the completion of the work is in two discernments: 1) *Mitzva* [singular of *Mitzvot*], 2) Torah. It is known that *Mitzva* is called "faith above reason," and "reason" is considered "sun," as it is written, "If the matter is as clear to you as day." It follows that "above reason" is the opposite of the sun. This is called "a shadow."

By this we should interpret that if a person wants to feel that there is a king, he must take a shadow, meaning faith above reason. This is the meaning of the words, "and the name of the other, Tzillah [Hebrew: shade]." In other words, he receives help to be rewarded with serving the King through faith. However, this is still not considered wholeness because the shade on the sun, meaning the above reason, which should be on the faith, is still not regarded as complete work.

The Torah is also required, which is called "sentence" and knowing, since what we do not understand does not fall into the category of Torah but into the category of faith. Torah, on the other hand, is called "testimony." It is known that there is no testimony by hearing, but by seeing, since seeing is considered knowing.

This is the meaning of the words "The name of the one was Adah," from the word *Edut* [testimony], where a person should receive help from the assistant, called "wife," who helps him in a manner of Torah, which is light and not shadow. Precisely when he has Torah and *Mitzva*, he is considered a complete human being.

Adah = *Ed* [witness] of the Creator about the Creator is the Torah, called *Edut*.

Tzillah = *Tzel* [shade] of the Creator is a shadow on the Creator, meaning faith.

What Is, "The Herdsmen of Abram's Cattle and the Herdsmen of Lot's Cattle," in the Work?

Article No. 6, Tav-Shin-Nun-Aleph, 1990/91

It is written (Genesis 13:7), "And there was a quarrel between the herdsmen of Abram's cattle and the herdsmen of Lot's cattle." Baal HaSulam said about this, that "cattle" means "possessions," that the quarrel was among the herdsmen of Abraham's cattle, who said, "How can we be rewarded with spiritual possessions, which are regarded as *Av-Ram* [High-Father], meaning specifically the quality of *Ram* [high] which is above reason, for the quality of Abraham is *Av* [father] of the faith.

Av-Ram means that he would want—*Av* comes from the word *Ava* [wanted], as in "He did not *Ava* [did not want] to send them away."

Ram means above. That is, Abram went above the desire that exists within man, called "will to receive," and above the desire that exists within man, and which is called "desire to know and understand what he is doing, and does not want to believe." Abram went above those two, meaning the mind and the heart. This is called "herdsmen," for only in this way would he like to guide himself.

This is not so with the "herdsmen of Lot's cattle." Lot means *Alma DeEtlatia* [Aramaic: cursed world], from the word "curse," referring to the will to receive, which is the serpent, meaning the will to receive for oneself. Lot was a chariot for the quality of the serpent. They would say that we must go and delight ourselves because this is how the Creator created the creatures—with a will to receive for ourselves. Otherwise, He would not have created the will to receive, since who does something in the world in order not to use it? Hence, since He created in us the will to receive, we must work for it, so the will to receive will take its satisfaction. Otherwise, it is considered that the Creator created it in vain.

Therefore, when considering the work, Abram and Lot are qualities within the same body. There is a dispute in the body: Some think like Abram, and some think the opposite and side with Lot. Hence, there is a quarrel between them as to how a person should behave in the work. That is, should man's work be for the sake of the Creator, and to achieve this, one must go above reason, which is the quality, *Av-Ram*, or should it be within reason, which is the will to receive for one's own sake, and since there was a *Tzimtzum* [restriction] and concealment on it, this quality is called Lot, a curse, where there is no delight and pleasure—as was in the thought of creation, which can enter there—and it remains a vacant space devoid of light.

In the work, "herdsmen" means a guide how to behave, as in Moses being called "the faithful shepherd," who guided the people of Israel with the quality of faith. Lot and Abram mean the good inclination in the person and the evil inclination in the person.

According to the above, we should interpret what *The Zohar* says (*Lech Lecha*, Item 162), "'Abram was very heavy with cattle, and silver, and with gold.' 'Very heavy' means from the east, which is *Tifferet*. 'With cattle' means from the west, which is *Malchut*. 'And silver is from the south, *Hochma*, and 'with gold' means from the north, *Bina*."

We should understand this in the work. It is known that east and west are two opposites. East means that which shines, such as the sunrise, and west is the opposite, meaning that which does not shine. Where the sun sets and does not shine, this is the west. The middle line, which is *Tifferet*, includes everything. For this reason, it is called "east," since it illuminates because it contains the whole work that emerged from all the lines.

This is not so with the west, which is called "the kingdom of heaven." We must accept the kingdom of heaven "with all your heart and with all your soul," even if He takes your soul away. Also, we must take upon ourselves the kingdom of heaven, called "faith," with love, as it is written (Article No. 4, *Tav-Shin-Nun-Aleph*), that even if he has no vitality, which is called "even if he takes his soul away," meaning that he has no vitality. This is called "west," meaning it does not illuminate. Still, a person should be in a state of faith above reason.

This is called "cattle," by which we buy spiritual possessions, called "the herdsmen of Abram's cattle." In other words, specifically through faith above reason, meaning even if he feels darkness on this path, and even though he understands that if *Malchut* had illuminated openly and not in concealment, and the body would feel the greatness of the Creator, it would be easier for him to move further and be rewarded with always being in a state of work and he would have no descents, he nonetheless chooses to go above reason. This is called "the herdsmen of Abram's cattle." This is called "west," meaning that even though it does not shine for him, he is still with all his might, as though everything illuminated for him openly.

This is the meaning of what is written, "Abram was very heavy," meaning east, *Tifferet*, which is the middle line. It is called "east" because the middle line includes all the work he had, and it was sweetened by him, since he already went through all the work that needs to be done, and the light shines there anyhow. This is why the east is called "very heavy," since the glory of the Lord, meaning the greatness and importance of the Creator is already very much revealed, meaning that at that time the light of the Creator shines.

For this reason, it is regarded as we explained (in Article No. 4, *Tav-Shin-Nun-Aleph*), "Anyone who runs from honor, honor chases him." In other words, once he passed the dispute between the two lines, called "two writings that deny one another," he is rewarded with the middle line, where the glory of the Creator is revealed and shines. This is called *Tifferet*, "east."

However, the main work is in the west. This is the place of the work because when a person is still in a state of darkness, where there are ascents and descents, since all the concealments are on this place, called "west." "West" indicates the kingdom of heaven, and in general, *Malchut* is called "faith," and the matter of good and evil applies there, as it is written in *The Zohar*, that *Malchut* is called "the tree of good and evil." If he is rewarded, she is good and the evil is concealed. If he is not rewarded, the good is concealed and the evil becomes revealed outward, and anything that is outside rules.

For this reason, "west" is called "cattle," since this is the main possession that one should acquire, which is the kingdom of heaven. If he does not have it, meaning *Malchut*, called "faith," then he has nothing. For this reason *Malchut* is called "cattle," as it is written, "Abram was very heavy with cattle." Because of it, cattle is called *Malchut* and west, since from here begins all the possessions of *Kedusha* [holiness], as it is written, "The beginning of wisdom, the fear of the Lord."

This is the meaning of the words "Silver is from the south, *Hochma*," as our sages said, "He who wants to grow wise should go south," meaning to be rewarded with a garment of *Hassadim* [mercies], where *Hesed* [singular of *Hassadim*] is called "love," when he wants to give and to bestow. He wants to annul before Him, and this is called "silver," from the word *Kisufin* [longing], as it is written, "My soul longed and also yearned." "South" means right, wholeness, when he needs nothing and his only passion is to be passionate about the Creator. He has no thought of himself, and only after the stage of the right can we be rewarded with the left, called *Bina*.

This is the meaning of "with gold means from the north, *Bina*." "Gold" means as it is written, "Gold means from the north." Gold is regarded as *Bina* that returns to being *Hochma*. Also, it is written, "Wisdom is for the humble," meaning that *Hochma* [wisdom] should be clothed in a garment of *Hassadim*, which is called "humbleness," by clothing in *Bina* and not being seen without a garment of *Hassadim*.

The thing is that it is known that *Hochma* dresses in vessels of reception. For this reason, she needs keeping so that the vessels of reception will always work in order to bestow. Hence, since he is using vessels of reception, guarding is required. For this reason, *Hassadim* must be extended, as this is the light that shines in vessels of bestowal. By this, the light of *Hochma* that can shine in vessels with the aim to bestow can shine.

This is why they said that south is *Hochma*, meaning that one who wants to grow wise should go south. He who wants the wisdom to remain in him and not depart needs the south, meaning *Hesed*, called "yearning," from the words "My soul longed and also yearned." Those two, south and north, which are *Hochma* and *Bina*, illuminate in the middle line, called "east," *Tifferet*, where everything is included. However, the essence of the work begins in the west, which is the quality of *Malchut*, called "cattle," which is regarded as *Malchut*, and "west."

Concerning *Malchut*, called "west," and "cattle," we should know that the order of the work begins with the kingdom of heaven. Before every *Mitzva* [commandment/good deed], a person must take upon himself the burden of the kingdom of heaven, called "faith," where he believes that the Creator leads the world in a manner of good and doing good. For this reason, he blesses Him.

This is as our sages said, "One should always establish the praise of the Creator and then pray." We should ask, What is the praise of the Creator that a person should establish? The answer is that since a person says to the Creator that he believes that He leads the world in a manner of good and doing good, this is called "the praise of the Creator." Afterward, he should pray.

Baal HaSulam said about this that when a person asks something of his friend, the order is that 1) he knows that his friend has what he asks of him, and 2) his friend has a kind heart and likes to do favors. In that state, it is relevant to ask from his friend.

Hence, when a person asks the Creator to give him what he is asking, he should believe that the Creator can give him what he wants, and that He is good and does good. Because of it, the beginning of man's work is to establish the praise of the Creator, meaning to believe that He is good and does good, although the body disagrees with what he says, and he sees that it is only lip service. At that time, he should say that he wants to believe above reason and he is happy that at least he knows the truth about what one must believe.

Although these words that he says are compulsory, meaning that the body will not agree to what he says, he is happy about that, too, that he can say with his mouth words of truth.

"And then pray" means that once he has established the praise of the Creator, that the Creator leads the world in a manner of good and doing good, if this were within reason, of course he would be happy. But since this is only above reason, although it is compulsory, still, sometimes he has the strength to pray to the Creator to give him the power to believe that this is really so and he will be able to say all day the praise of the Creator by the Creator only doing good to him.

In this work there are ascents and descents. A person must believe that he has a point in the heart, which is a spark that shines. But sometimes, it is only a black dot and does not shine. We must always awaken that spark because at times that spark awakens by

What Is, "The Herdsmen of Abram's Cattle and the Herdsmen of Lot's Cattle"?

itself and reveals a lack in a person, where he feels that he needs spirituality, that he is too materialistic and he sees no purpose that enables him to emerge from these states.

That spark gives him no rest. That is, as a corporeal spark cannot illuminate, but using the spark, a person can light up things, so that through the things that the spark touches, a great fire can ignite. Likewise, the spark within man's heart cannot shine, but that spark can light up his actions so they will illuminate because the spark pushes him to work.

However, sometimes the spark quenches and does not shine. This can be in the middle of the work, and this is regarded as a person having a road accident. In other words, in the middle of the work, something happened to him and he descended from his state and was left unconscious. Now he does not know that there is spirituality in reality, he has forgotten everything, and he has entered the corporeal world with all of his senses.

Only after some time does he recover and sees that he is in the corporeal world and he begins to climb up once again, meaning to feel the spiritual lack. Then, once again, he receives a drive to approach the Creator.

Afterward, he descends from his degree once more, but he must believe that each time he raises his spark to *Kedusha* [holiness]. Although he sees that he has descended from his state and fell back to the place where he was at the beginning of his work, each time he nonetheless raises new sparks. That is, each time, he raises a new spark.

In the "Introduction to The Book of Zohar" (Item 43), he says, "When man is born, he immediately has a *Nefesh* [soul] of *Kedusha*. But not an actual *Nefesh*, but the *Achoraim* [posterior] of it, its last discernment, which, during its *Katnut* [smallness/infancy], is called a 'point,' and it dresses in man's heart."

We should interpret that this "point," which is still in the dark, reveals and shines each time according to one's work on purifying his heart. At that time, the point begins to shine. This means that each time a person begins to ascend once more after the descent, he should believe that this is a new discernment from what he had during the previous ascent, for he has already elevated it to *Kedusha*. Thus, each time he begins a new discernment.

Since in every beginning a person must start over the acceptance of the kingdom of heaven, it is not enough that yesterday he had faith in the Creator. For this reason, every acceptance of the kingdom of heaven is considered a new discernment. That is, now he receives a part of the vacant space that was devoid of the kingdom of heaven, and admits that empty place and fills it with the kingdom of heaven. It follows that now he sorted out a new thing, which did not exist before he took that empty place and filled it with the kingdom of heaven. This is regarded as elevating a new spark into the *Kedusha*. Finally, from all the ascents, he always raises sparks from the vacant space into the *Kedusha*.

It follows that from each descent he arrives at a new beginning and raises new sparks. Hence, when a person sees that he has descents, he should be careful not to escape from the campaign, even though he sees that he is not progressing. Rather, he must try to start anew each time. That is, the fact that he begins to ascend does not mean that he returned to his previous degree. This would mean that he did nothing by his work, since he thinks that he is now ascending to his previous level. Rather, he must believe that this is a new discernment, that each time, he raises different sparks, until he raises the sparks that pertain to his essence.

According to the above, we should interpret what our sages said (*Bava Metzia*, Chapter 7), "Elazar said, 'Thus, the righteous speak little and do much, and the wicked speak much and do not even do little.'"

Concerning "wicked" and "righteous" in the work, we should interpret that all those who want to observe Torah and *Mitzvot* for the sake of the Creator are called "righteous" in the work, meaning they want to be righteous. Conversely, those who engage in Torah and *Mitzvot* not for the sake of the Creator are called "wicked,"

What Is, "The Herdsmen of Abram's Cattle and the Herdsmen of Lot's Cattle"?

in the work, since they are in disparity of form from the Creator. Hence, they are regarded as wicked (though among the general public they, too, are considered righteous).

Among those who work in the manner of the general public, we can say, for example, when a person is forty, he knows that since the time of his Bar Mitzva [age 13], meaning since he was thirteen until he turned forty, he has acquired a possession of 27 years of Torah and *Mitzvot*. It follows that they say that they have a lot. This is the meaning of "speak much." In other words, they have much Torah and *Mitzvot*. However, they do not work even in the least for the sake of the Creator.

But the righteous "speak little." That is, they say that they have been engaging in Torah and *Mitzvot* for 27 years but have not been rewarded with doing anything for the sake of the Creator. However, they must believe that they are doing much, meaning that from each doing that they see that they are incapable of doing it for the sake of the Creator, and it pains them, this is called "a prayer."

In other words, they make a lot of prayers, by seeing how far they are from the Creator, from having a desire and yearning to bring contentment to the Maker. In other words, they are far because they haven't the ability to appreciate the greatness of the King. Hence, they do not have the power to do anything for the sake of the Creator, but only for themselves. It follows that they do a lot in order for the Creator to bring them closer to Him.

It follows that one need not be impressed when he wants to work for the sake of the Creator and sees each time that he is regressing. He must believe that he is doing much in order to approach the Creator and be rewarded with the Creator giving him the desire to bestow. That is, specifically through the descents and ascents, a person can pray to Him to really bring him closer, for each time, he elevates new sparks into the structure of *Kedusha* until he elevates all the sparks that belong to him. Then he will be rewarded with the Creator giving him the second nature called "desire to bestow." Then, he will be rewarded with permanent faith.

But before he is rewarded with all his works being for the sake of the Creator, there is no room for faith. This is as it is written ("Introduction of The Book of Zohar," Item 138), "It is a law that the creature cannot receive disclosed evil from the Creator, for it is a flaw in the glory of the Creator for the creature to perceive Him as an evildoer. Hence, when one feels bad, denial of the Creator's guidance lies upon him and the superior Operator is concealed from him to that same extent."

In other words, as long as a person does not have the desire to bestow, he is unfit to receive delight and pleasure. Therefore, when a person suffers, he loses the faith. But once he has been rewarded with the desire to bestow, he receives delight and pleasure from the Creator and is rewarded with permanent faith. It follows that all those ascents and descents bring him to a state where the Creator helps him achieve the desire to bestow, and then all his works are for the sake of the Creator.

However, a person must know that when he comes to a state where he does not see how he will ever be able to emerge from self-love and he wants to escape the campaign, he must know that there are two matters here, which are opposite from one another, as our sages said (*Avot*, Chapter 2:21), "It is not for you to finish the work, nor are you free to idle away from it."

Thus, on one hand, a person must work and never idle away from it. That is, it is within man's power to attain, since he says, "nor are you free to idle away from it." This means that one should work because he is guaranteed to get what he wants, meaning to be able to work for the sake of the Creator in order to bring contentment to his Maker.

On the other hand, he says, "It is not for you to finish the work." This implies that it is not within man's hands, but rather, as it is written, "The Lord will finish for me." This means that it is not within man's ability to obtain the desire to bestow.

However, there are two matters here: 1) A person must say, "If I am not for me, who is for me?" Hence, he should not be alarmed by the fact that he has not been rewarded with obtaining the desire to bestow, although in his opinion, he has made great efforts. Nonetheless, he should believe that the Creator waits until he reveals what he must do. 2) Afterward, the Creator will finish for him, meaning that at that time, he will receive what he wants at once, as it is written, "The salvation of the Lord is as the blink of an eye."

What Is "Man" and What Is "Beast" in the Work?

Article No. 7, Tav-Shin-Nun-Aleph, 1990/91

It is written in *The Zohar* (*VaYera*, Items 1-2), "'The buds appear on the earth.' This means that when the Creator created the world, He placed in the earth all the power it deserves. Everything was in the earth, but it did not bear fruit until man was created. When man was created, everything appeared in the world and the land revealed its fruits. Similarly, the heaven did not endow the earth with force until man came, and the heavens halted and did not rain upon the earth since man was absent. When man appeared, the buds immediately appeared in the land."

We should understand what this comes to teach us. We should know that the purpose of creation was because of His desire to do good to His creations. However, in order to bring to light the perfection of His deeds, there were *Tzimtzum* [restriction] and concealment, where the good is not revealed to the created beings before they are rewarded with working for the sake of the Creator. Otherwise, there is the matter of shame because of the disparity of form in the vessels of reception of the created beings. Hence, a person cannot receive the purpose of creation, which is the delight and pleasure, due to shame. This is called "separation and remoteness from the Creator." That is, we understand the matter of the bread of shame as separation from the Creator to such an extent that this disparity of form makes it as "The wicked in their lives are called 'dead.'"

Therefore, man's work emerges from the beastly state and acquires the quality of "man." It is as our sages said (*Yevamot* 61), "Rabbi Shimon Bar Yochai says, 'You are My sheep, the sheep of My pasture, you are 'man.' You are called 'man,' and the idol-worshippers are not called 'man.'" We already explained the importance of "man," that the nations of the world are not called "man." It is as our sages said (*Berachot* 6), "'In the end, all is heard, fear God and observe His commandments, for this is the whole of man.' What is 'for this is the whole of man'? Rabbi Elazar said, 'The whole world was created only for this.'" In other words, one who has fear of God is called "man," and one who does not have fear of God, it means he is a "beast" and not "man."

It therefore follows that before a person is rewarded with having fear of God, with doing everything for the sake of the Creator, he is still not regarded as a human being but as a beast. In other words, everything they do is only for their own sake, like beasts. And since there were *Tzimtzum* and concealment on the will to receive for one's own sake, although for His part, the delight and pleasure are already revealed in *Kedusha* [holiness], since there is equivalence of form there between the light and the *Kli* [vessel], the lower ones—which were created—still do not have the quality of man, as it is written, "Man is born a wild ass." It follows that he is placed under the *Tzimtzum* and the concealment, where there is no disclosure of light.

Thus, although all the delight and pleasure in the purpose of creation has emerged and been revealed by Him, it is all concealed from the lower ones. They see no delight and pleasure, but only a tiny light from the *Kedusha*, which fell into the *Klipot* [shells/peels], and on this the whole of the corporal world is sustained.

By this we can interpret what we asked concerning the interpretation of *The Zohar* about the verse, "'The buds appear on the earth.' When the Creator created the world, He placed in the earth all the power it deserves. Everything was in the earth, but it did not bear fruit until man was created." We should interpret that although from the perspective of the Creator, everything has emerged, but they were all under the *Tzimtzum* and the concealment, meaning that there was no one who could enjoy it, since the concealment blocks everything and they did not see that there are delight and pleasure in the world.

"When man was created, everything appeared in the world and the land revealed its fruits." This means that once a person acquires the quality of "man," when he has fear of God, meaning that everything he does is for the sake of the Creator, the concealment is removed from him and he sees all the fruits that there are in the world, which he did not see before he acquired the quality of "man."

When it says, "Similarly, the heaven did not endow the earth with force until man came," it means that before one is rewarded with the quality of "man," a person cannot have permanent faith that powers are given to the earth. That is, from above they give powers below, to the created beings, so they can ascend on the rungs of holiness. But afterward, when he is rewarded with the quality of "man," he sees that all that exists on earth, in the lower ones, comes from above, and then he does not need to believe this, since then he attains it.

This is regarded as when the quality of man comes, everything is revealed in the world. This means that all that has been renewed now, existed also before, except he did not see this. This is the meaning of the words, "and the heavens halted and did not rain upon the earth since man was absent." That is, before the quality of man is revealed, he would say that he is praying to the Creator every time but he is not being answered from above. This is called, "and the heavens halted and did not rain," meaning he received nothing for his prayers.

The reason he could not see if he is answered is that he still did not have the quality of man. Hence, everything was concealed from him, and he could only believe that the Creator does hear the prayer of every mouth. But afterward, when man appeared, promptly, "the buds appeared in the land." In other words, all the things that were thus far concealed became visible. When the quality of man came, everything appeared. That is, then we see the delight and pleasure that were in the purpose of creation has already been revealed in the world.

For this reason, one should be careful not to escape the campaign and say that the Creator does not want to help him, since he sees that he has asked him many times to help him, and he thinks as though he is not being looked at from above. However, whether or not he is praying, it is all the same, unchanging. Therefore, he does not see anything that will help him. Instead, he sees that he is as an empty *Kli* [vessel] that has nothing, and whatever the Creator wants to do, He will do. But for man's part, he is powerless to do anything.

There is a rule: Where one sees no progress, one cannot make any effort. At that time, the only way is to have faith in the sages, who tell us that we must believe that such is the order of the work, that a person must not see what he is doing. He should believe that this concealment is for his best, that it will lead him to be rewarded with *Dvekut* [adhesion] with the Creator. If he overcomes and believes that it is all for his best and the Creator does hear the prayer of every mouth, but there should be an awakening from below, "and the salvation of the Lord is as the blink of an eye," meaning when all the sparks gather, one should scrutinize and ask that they will enter the *Kedusha*, and then he receives the help at once.

However, when one feels that he is empty, meaning that he feels that he has neither Torah nor *Mitzvot* [commandments/good deeds] or any good deeds, what can he do? At that time, he should ask the Creator to shine for him so he can obtain the greatness and exaltedness of the Creator above reason. In other words, although he is still unworthy of feeling the greatness and exaltedness of the Creator, since he has still not been rewarded with the quality of "man," and the *Tzimtzum* and concealment of the Creator are still on him, as it is written, "Do not hide Your face from me," he still asks the Creator to give him the strength to receive greatness and importance of the Creator above reason.

It is as Baal HaSulam says about what our sages said (*Iruvin* 19), Even the empty ones among you are filled with *Mitzvot* like a pomegranate." He said that *Rimon* [pomegranate] comes from the word *Romemut* [exaltedness], which is above reason. Hence, the meaning of "Even the empty ones among you are filled with *Mitzvot* like a pomegranate" is that the measure of the filling is according to his ability to go above reason, which is called "exaltedness."

In other words, emptiness can be precisely where there is no presence and he feels that he is devoid of Torah, *Mitzvot*, and good deeds. When this continues over time when a person wants to work for the sake of the Creator and not for himself, then he sees that everything he does is not for the sake of the Creator but only for his own benefit. In that state, he feels that he has nothing and he is completely empty, and he can fill this place only with a pomegranate, meaning if he goes above reason, which is called "exaltedness of the Creator." In other words, he should ask the Creator to give him the power to believe above reason in the greatness of the Creator. That is, the fact that he wants the exaltedness of the Creator does not mean that he says, "If You let me attain the exaltedness and greatness of the Creator, I will agree to work." Rather, he wants the Creator to give him the power to believe in the greatness of the Creator, and with this he fills the emptiness in which he is in right now.

It follows that were it not for the emptiness, that is, if he did not work on the path toward achieving *Dvekut*, meaning in equivalence of form, called "in order to bestow," but rather like the general public, who suffice for the practices they observe, these people do not feel themselves as empty, but as full of *Mitzvot*.

However, specifically those who want to achieve bestowal feel the emptiness within them and need the greatness of the Creator. They can fill this emptiness specifically with exaltedness, called "full of *Mitzvot*," to the extent that they ask the Creator to give them the power to be able to go above reason, which is called "exaltedness." In other words, they ask the Creator to give them power in exaltedness that is above reason in greatness and importance of the Creator. They do not want the Creator to let them attain this, since they want to subjugate themselves with unconditional surrender, but they ask for help from the Creator, and to that extent they can fill the empty place with *Mitzvot*. This is the meaning of "filled with *Mitzvot* like a pomegranate."

According to the above, we should interpret the words of *The Zohar* (*VaYera*, Item 167), "When the Creator loves a person, He sends him a gift. What is the gift? A poor, so as to be rewarded by Him. And when he is rewarded by Him, the Creator draws upon him a string of grace that extends from the right side, spreads over his head, and registers him so that when the *Din* [judgment] comes to the world, that saboteur will be careful not to harm him. For this reason, the Creator first gives him something with which to be rewarded."

We should understand what is poor in the work, and what is "a string of grace," and what is the judgment that comes to the world. It is known that "poor" means poor in knowledge. What is poor in knowledge? There are two categories in the work:

1) The general public, who are primarily about practicing. Concerning the intention, to make everything for the sake of the Creator, they pay no attention to this. They engage in Torah and *Mitzvot* and are generally whole, feeling no deficiencies about themselves. But because our sages said that one should be humble, they search for deficiencies in themselves in order to observe, "Be very, very humble" (*Avot* 4:4).

2) Those who want to work in order to bestow and engage in Torah and *Mitzvot* so it will bring them to be able to do everything in order to bestow and not for their own sake. This is as our sages said, "I have created the evil inclination; I have created the Torah as a spice." Thus, these workers understand that each day they should advance, be rich in knowledge, meaning to understand each time

that it is worthwhile to work only in order to bestow. Yet, in fact, they see that each day when they want to walk on the path where everything is only for the sake of the Creator, the body understands differently each time. It begins to understand that it is better to work for one's own sake than to work for the sake of the Creator. At that time, they are baffled over why it turns out the opposite of what they thought. They pray to the Creator to send them the understanding and the knowledge so the body will understand that it is worthwhile to work for the sake of the Creator. Yet, they see otherwise, and many times they despair because the Creator, does not hear the prayer, and sometimes they want to escape the campaign.

The answer, says *The Zohar*, is that "When the Creator loves a person, He sends him a gift. And what is the gift? A poor." In other words, the fact that one sees that he is poor in knowledge, that the body does not understand why it needs to work for the sake of the Creator and not for its own sake, the Creator sends him the gift of the thought and the feeling that he is poor, since He loves him. But why does the Creator love him? It is because he wants to work for the sake of the Creator. For this reason, the Creator loves him.

However, he cannot, even though he wants to, since it is against nature. Man was born with a will to receive for his own benefit. Since there is a correction that as long as one is not ready to walk on the path of truth, he will not be able to see the truth because it will harm him, those people who do not intend to walk on the path of bestowal are not shown the truth, that they are incapable of going against the nature of the will to receive. They think that all they lack is some desire, meaning that if they agree to walk on the path of for the sake of the Creator, they can do everything for the sake of the Creator. For this reason, anything that a person thinks that he can do by himself, he does not suffer from not doing it, since it is easy. Therefore, it does not pain him that he is not working for the sake of the Creator although he knows that we should do everything for the sake of the Creator.

This stems from the rule that our sages said, "Anything that is about to be collected is deemed collected" (any debt that a person is going to receive back from the borrower, it is as though he already took his debt because it is certain, he knows he will receive). Hence, because he knows that whenever he wants, he will be able to do everything for the sake of the Creator, he does not feel a lack although he is still not doing it. This is the correction for those who work in the manner of the general public.

However, those who truly want to walk on the path of doing everything in order to bestow, the Creator loves those people, as it is written in *The Zohar*, the Creator sends them a gift. What is the gift? A poor, meaning poor in knowledge. In other words, the body does not understand how there can be such a thing that we will be able to work for the sake of the Creator, as it is against nature. At that time, he sees that he is poor even in actions. That is, he is not only poor in knowledge, but in practice, too. Put differently, he sees that he does not have even one deed that is for the sake of the Creator. Rather, everything is for his own benefit.

Then, a person becomes needy of the Creator to help him because he is the poorest of all, in mind as well as in heart. He sees then that he is truly wicked, meaning that he cannot justify how the Creator behaves with him, and he sees that even the prayers he prays to the Creator are as if the Creator does not hear his prayers, and many times he falls into despair. However, a person must believe that all those feelings that he feels come to him from above, that the Creator sends them to him, and that they are a gift from above.

This is the meaning of saying "And what is the gift? A poor, so as to be rewarded by him." The question is, How can we say that poverty is a gift? He answers this, "so as to be rewarded by him." In other words, by seeing that he is poor, that he has nothing, a person has a complete lack, meaning a complete desire for the Creator's help, for in order to receive the filling from the Creator, one needs a complete desire—when one sees that no one can help but the Creator. Thus, through poverty, he acquires a need to make his vessels of reception worthy of the Creator giving him the desire to bestow instead of the will to receive.

This is the meaning of the words "And when he is rewarded by him," meaning that through the poor he acquired a complete need and lack, then "the Creator draws upon him a string of grace that extends from the right side." Put differently, the Creator gives him the desire to bestow, called *Hesed*, meaning a giver, which is called "right," meaning he receives the second nature called "desire to bestow."

This is the meaning of the words, "spreads over his head." "Head" means knowledge. The *Hesed* that a person receives is on his head, meaning above his head, meaning above reason. Through the string of *Hesed*, he can walk above reason.

He says, "When the *Din* [judgment] comes to the world, that saboteur will be careful not to harm him." This means that since the string of *Hesed* is on his head, meaning that he is in faith above reason, when the judgment comes—meaning the will to receive, on which there was a judgment that no light shines in it—and he wants to harm a person with its questions, since the string of *Hesed*, called "faith above reason," is stretched over that person's head, it can no longer harm him. The saboteur comes with the arguments of the will to receive, called "the quality of judgment," meaning that he argues with his reason. Hence, once he has been rewarded with a string of *Hesed* in both mind and heart, and goes above reason in regard to everything, thanks to the string of *Hesed*, it cannot harm him any longer.

However, when a person feels that he is poor, meaning that he has no awe when he wants to work for the sake of the Creator, but to the contrary, at that time he sees that to him, the *Shechina* [Divinity] is in the dust. That is, to him, she has the form of dust. "Dust" is as it is written about the serpent, that the Creator said to the serpent, "You shall eat dust all your life." Our sages explained that whatever the serpent eats, it tastes the taste of dust. In the work it means that as long as one has not corrected the sin of the tree of knowledge, he tastes the taste of dust. When one wants to do his deeds in order to bestow, which is called "*Shechina* in the dust," he must not tell his body, called "will to receive."

In other words, he must not tell the will to receive for oneself that he does not feel any awe with regard to spirituality. He should not even discuss work matters with his will to receive, since he must know that no arguments with the will to receive will help him. Therefore, when a person comes to a state of being poor, he must only ask the Creator to help him and give him the strength to overcome it.

This is as our sages said (*Avot de Rabbi Natan*, end of Chapter 7), "If a man comes to the seminary and is treated disrespectfully, he should not go and tell his wife." We must understand what this teaches us in the work. Also, is one permitted to demand respect? After all, our sages said, "Be very, very humble."

We should interpret that a person coming to the seminary to learn Torah, the Torah is as in "for they are our lives and the length of our days." In other words, the Torah is respected because all the good things are in it. He came to the seminary but the Torah did not respect him. That is, the Torah was concealed from him and he was not shown any of the glory and importance that there are in the Torah. Instead, he tastes the taste of dust. For this reason, he wants to consult with his will to receive if he should continue. They say, "He should not go and tell his wife," meaning the will to receive. Instead, he should tell everything to the Creator, meaning that the Creator will open his eyes and he will be rewarded with the glory of the Torah.

What Is, "And Abraham Was Old, of Many Days," in the Work?

Article No. 8, Tav-Shin-Nun-Aleph, 1990/91

It is written in *The Zohar* (*VaYeshev*, Item 3), "'A poor and wise child is better than an old and foolish king.' 'A wise child is better' is the good inclination, which is a child from few days with man, since he is with man from thirteen years of age onward. 'An old and foolish king' is the evil inclination, called 'King and man's ruler in the world over people.' He is certainly 'old and foolish,' since he has been with man from the day he is born into the world. Therefore, he is 'an old and foolish king.' But 'a wise child is better' is as it is written, 'I was a youth and I grew old.' This is a youth who is a poor child with nothing of his own. Why is he called 'a youth'? It is because he has the resumption [renewal] of the moon, which is always resumed, and he is always a child."

It appears from the words of *The Zohar* that "old" indicates the evil inclination, whereas the good inclination is called "a child." If this is so, what is the meaning of "And Abraham was old, of many

What Is, "And Abraham Was Old, of Many Days," in the Work?

days"? What does it come to tell us when it says, "Abraham was old"? What merit is there to Abraham being old and of many days, for it seems as though the text is praising Abraham.

It is written in the "Introduction of The Book of Zohar" (Item 140) about the verse, "Day to day pours forth speech, and night to night reveals knowledge." It says there, "Prior to the end of correction, before we qualified our vessels of reception to receive only in order to give contentment to our Maker and not to our own benefit, *Malchut* is called 'the tree of good and evil,'" since *Malchut* is the guidance of the world by people's actions.

"Hence, we must receive the guidance of good and evil from the *Malchut*, as this guidance qualifies us to ultimately correct our vessels of reception. Often, the guidance of good and evil causes us ascents and descents, and each ascent is regarded as a separate day because due to the great descent that he had, while he doubted the beginning, during the ascent he is as a newly born child. Thus, in each ascent, it is as though he begins to serve the Creator anew. This is why each ascent is considered a specific day, and similarly, each descent is considered a specific night."

Now we can interpret what we asked, Why does it say, "And Abraham was old, of many days"? What is the merit in Abraham being old? The answer is "many days." That is, there is one who is old, which is one state that extends over a long period of time, and the prolonging turns this state into an old one. It is written about it in *The Zohar*, "Why is the evil inclination called 'old'?" It says that it is because of the prolonged time, "since he is with man from the day one is born into the world." In other words, there is no change in his situation and he has been the same since he was born. This is called "An old and foolish king."

We should ask, But he is an angel, as it is written, "For He will command His angels over you, to keep you in all your ways." *The Zohar* interprets that this pertains to the good inclination and the evil inclination. So how can we say that it is a fool?

The answer is that every angel is named after its task. Hence, since the evil inclination installs a spirit of folly in a person, as our sages said, "One does not sin unless a spirit of folly has entered him," for this reason the evil inclination is named "fool," accordingly. However, he always plays the same role—installing the spirit of folly in people. This is why he is called "An old and foolish king."

However, in *Kedusha* [holiness], when a person begins to work on the path toward achieving *Dvekut* [adhesion] with the Creator, meaning that all his actions will be for the sake of the Creator, the person should first come to the recognition of evil, meaning to know the measure of the evil within him. It is as our sages said, "To the wicked, the evil seems like hairsbreadth, but to the righteous, it seems like a high mountain." This is so because one is not shown more evil that exists within him than he has good, since the good and the bad must be balanced, for only then can we speak of choice, as our sages said, "One should always see oneself as half guilty, half innocent." Hence, those who want to achieve the work of bestowal undergo ascents and descents, as said in *The Zohar*, which interprets "Day to day pours forth speech, and night to night reveals knowledge."

It follows that the quality of "old" in one who works in order to bestow is not in the sense that one state has taken a long time. Rather, he is "old" because he has had many days and many nights. This is why it says, "Abraham was old, of many days." To interpret "many days," "And the Lord blessed Abraham with all," what is "with all"? Since he had many days, he must have had many nights in between, for if there are no nights in between, there cannot be many days. "The Lord blessed Abraham with all" means that the nights were also blessed with him. This is the meaning of "And the Lord blessed Abraham with all."

According to the above, we should interpret the words "A wise child is better," as it is written, "I was a youth and I grew old." In other words, although "I" grew old, "I" remain a youth. This is so because the order of the work is that when a person should take upon himself faith above reason, since the body objects to this, this work is daily. In other words, each day a person must take upon himself faith, and it is not enough that yesterday he took it upon himself, as it is written (Deuteronomy 26:16), "This day the Lord your God commands you to do." RASHI interprets, "Each day, they will be as new in your eyes, as if on that day you were commanded them."

It follows that each day is its own discernment, since each day he is a youth and must begin anew the acceptance of the kingdom of heaven. This is as the ARI says (*Shaar HaKavanot*, p 61), "In each and every prayer, the *Mochin* enter, and after the prayer they depart. You should know that the matter is not as it seems, meaning that the *Mochin* that come are the ones that depart, and they are the ones that return with each prayer. The thing is that with each prayer new *Mochin* come."

This means that although a person begins anew each day, it does not mean that he begins from the same place he began. Rather, "of many days" means that he has many new days. It follows that "I was a youth and I grew old." That is, the old age is not from one state, because that state was prolonged. Rather, "old" in *Kedusha* means that he has had a long time of many resumptions, meaning that growing old came from being many days in a state of "youth," meaning a child. Thus, the meaning of "I was a youth and I grew old" pertains only to the times of "youth"; from this he became old.

This is the meaning of the words, "This is a youth who is a poor child with nothing of his own." In other words, all the work, which is only to bestow upon the Creator and not for his own sake, this work is against the body, where he wants to work specifically for his own sake and not for the sake of the Creator. At that time, a person sees that after each ascent, he immediately has a descent, and from this he gets the matter of "nights and days."

This continues until a person decides that he is powerless to do anything, since he sees that everything he does in order to advance, he sees the opposite, that each time, he has more evil. At that time, he decides and says, "Unless the Lord builds a house, they who built it labored in vain." For this reason, when a person is rewarded with the Creator giving him the desire to bestow, meaning that he has been rewarded with being able to do all his actions for the sake of the Creator, he sees that he is a "child." That is, he has no more power than that of a child, meaning he has nothing of his own. In other words, he has achieved nothing by himself, but rather the Creator gave him everything.

At that time, he sees that the Creator gave him the descents, as well, and for himself, he has nothing. This is the meaning of "Why is he called 'a youth'? It is because he has the resumption [renewal] of the moon." In other words, as the moon has no light of itself except what it receives from the sun, likewise, when man is rewarded with *Dvekut* with the Creator, he sees that he has gained nothing by his own strength, but the Creator gave him everything, while he is always a "child." In other words, in every situation, he is as a child, doing nothing, and having only what a child is given, while he himself cannot do anything. This is why one should always ask the Creator to give him the power to prevail in the work, and the person himself is completely powerless.

According to the above, we should interpret what is written (Genesis 15:6), "And he believed in the Lord and He regarded it to him as righteousness." This seems perplexing. What is Abraham's praise in that he believed in the Creator? After all, any person who had the revelation of Godliness and the Creator would speak to him would believe in the Creator. We should interpret that once Abraham saw that he had no power of his own to be rewarded with anything in *Kedusha*, since the will to receive is the ruler, as it is written, "an old and foolish king," and he was powerless to emerge from its governance and be rewarded with *Dvekut* with the Creator, this is why it is written in general, "And he believed in the Lord and He regarded it to him as righteousness."

In other words, the fact that Abraham could be rewarded with faith is only charity from the Creator; the Creator gave him charity and delivered him from the governance of the old and foolish king, who objects to faith above reason. *Av-Ram* [high father] means that he wanted to go specifically above reason, which is regarded as "the herdsmen of Abraham's cattle" (as written in Article No. 1, *Tav-Shin-Nun-Aleph*).

But the whole body resists it. Hence, when the Creator gave him the power of faith above reason, Abraham regarded it as having been rewarded with faith, as it is written, "And he believed in the Lord," meaning what he could believe in the Lord, to Him, to the Creator. "As charity," that the Creator gave him charity by giving Abraham the power of faith.

However, in the order of the work, we see that there are ascents and descents. During an ascent, when one feels the importance, when he feels that he is close to the Creator and has some feeling of the importance and greatness of the Creator, and wants to annul before Him because he feels a little bit of love of the Creator and wants to annul before Him as a candle before a torch, in that state he does not remember that he ever suffered a state of descent. Moreover, he does not want to remember that there is such a thing called "a state of descent," and he yearns for his state of ascent to be permanent.

But in the end, he suffers a descent. Sometimes, he falls into such a lowly state that he says that there is no way he will ever be able to do something for the sake of the Creator. When it occurs to him that we must work and observe Torah and *Mitzvot* [commandments/good deeds] for the sake of the Creator, so why do I not want to do this, he gives himself a true answer, in his opinion, that there is nothing to reply to this, since man, meaning the will to receive within man, is the ruler during the descent, and it says that it is willing to do everything for the sake of the Creator, but on condition that I will know what my will to receive will gain from this.

In other words, he is willing to work for the sake of the Creator but on condition that his self-benefit will profit from this. It follows that during the ascent, if he looks at the descents that he receives each time, he is impressed with how such a thing can be—that there will be such a difference between ascents and descents, as the gap between heaven and earth. In other words, during the ascent, he thinks that he is already in heaven, that he no longer has any connection to corporeality, and that from this day forth, his only engagement in the world will be that which concerns spirituality. He even becomes upset with the Creator for giving him corporeality, to engage in worldly matters and that he must dedicate time and effort to these things, to obtaining corporeality.

At that time, a person does not understand for what purpose the Creator created this. The whole corporeal world seems to him redundant. But along with all the good calculations, he suddenly suffers a descent and falls to the ground. Sometimes, during the descent, he loses consciousness altogether and completely forgets about spirituality. Sometimes, he does remember that there is such a thing as spirituality in the world, but sees that this is not for him.

However, we should understand why the Creator gives us these descents. That is, first, one must believe that the Creator gives us these descents, and then a person asks for what purpose the Creator gave me these descents. In other words, when one believes that the Creator is sending this to him, the descents come to a person after he had a state of ascent and he asked the Creator to bring him closer to Him, and he believes that the Creator hears a prayer.

But what did he receive in return for his prayer? He thought that after the prayer he would receive an ascent to a higher degree than the state he was in during the prayer. But in the end, he sees that the Creator has given him a worse state than he was in before he prayed to the Creator. The answer is as Baal HaSulam said, that there is the matter of "as the advantage of the light from within the darkness." He said that a person cannot appreciate the importance of the light, and to know how to keep it, unless from within the darkness. At that time, a person can discern the distance between the light and the darkness.

We should interpret his words with an allegory. When one gives a present to a friend, which is worth 100 shekels in the eyes of the receiver, the receiver is happy with the fact that his friend appreciates him and sends him a gift, and he accepts it with great joy. However, if the recipient finds out afterward that the gift is worth 10,000 shekels, we can understand how the recipient would be happy now, and how his love for the giver of the gift would be established in his heart, and how he would keep the gift from being stolen

The lesson is that when a person receives an awakening from above, when the Creator brings him closer to Him, the person feels some importance in feeling that he is speaking with the Creator, but a person cannot accept the real joy from this nearing, since he still cannot appreciate the greatness and importance of the Creator so as to receive the delight and pleasure from the Creator speaking to him.

The reason is as said above, "as the advantage of the light from within the darkness." Since a person does not suffer because he is far from the Creator, he cannot appreciate the greatness and importance of a situation where he is close to the Creator, and he also cannot appreciate the suffering of being away from the Creator, if he never felt what it means to be close to the Creator. For this reason, the order of the work walks on two legs—right and left, as our sages said (*Sotah* 47), "The left should always reject, and the right pull nearer."

"Right" means wholeness. During the ascent, when a person feels that now he is close to the Creator, he has vitality and joy, and he lives in a world that is all good. Afterward, it is desired above that he will feel the importance of the Creator bringing him closer to Him, so he can enjoy and be happy, not as one appreciates it as in the allegory, as worth 100 shekels. Therefore, when he suffers a descent and feels suffering from being in a descent, although during the descent he does not always feel that he is in a descent, meaning if he has descended from his level and does not suffer because he fell, it is not considered a descent, for who knows that he has fallen if the person does not feel it?

Rather, this is like a person who was injured in a road accident and does not feel that he has fallen under the car, since he is unconscious. Who does know that he has fallen under the truck? only people on the outside. But what does he feel from other people seeing that he is unconscious?

It is the same in spirituality when he suffers a descent. It is known above, but once a person recovers, he realizes that he is in a state of descent, and then begins a new procession and he is given from above another ascent, and then another descent. From this, a person acquires the distinction between light and darkness. Also, from this, a person acquires letters by which to appreciate it when the Creator brings him closer, and by this he will know how to keep himself from dropping anything into the *Klipot* [shells/peels], meaning into his vessels of reception, since he knows what he is losing because "as the advantage of the light from within the darkness." This is the meaning of descents and ascents that a person has to go through these state.

One who is clever and wants to save time does not wait until he suffers a descent from above. Rather, while he is in an ascent and wants to acquire the importance of the state of closeness to the Creator, he begins to depict to himself what is a state of descent, meaning how he suffered from being far from the Creator compared to how he feels now that he is close to the Creator. It follows that even during the ascent he learns from the discernments as though he were in a state of descent. At that time, he can calculate and discern between an ascent and a descent.

At that time he will get a picture of the advantage of light over darkness, since he can create a depiction of how he was back in the state of descent, and thought that the whole matter of the work of bestowal does not pertain to him, and how he suffered from these states when he wanted to escape the campaign, and only from one place he could get some relief, meaning only from one hope, that he thought, "When will I be able to go to sleep?" for then he would escape from all the states of impatience, when he felt that the world has grown dark on him.

Now, during the ascent, he sees everything differently. At that time, he wants to work only for the sake of the Creator, and he has no concern for his own benefit. From all those calculations that he will do during the ascent, it follows that now he has a place where he can discern between light and darkness, and he does not need to wait until he is given from above a state of descent.

According to the above, we should interpret what our sages said (*Shabbat* 152), "I search for what I did not lose." RASHI interprets, "I search for what I did not lose out of old age, I walk bent, swaying, and I seem as though I seek something that I lost." We should understand this in the work, what it comes to teach us. An old man is considered wise, meaning he wants to be a wise disciple.

As Baal HaSulam said, the Creator is called "wise," and His manner is bestowal. When a person wants to learn from His ways, meaning to also be a bestower, that person is called "a student of the Wise." That person does not wait until he suffers a descent and then comes to ask to be elevated again, meaning that he lost his state of ascent and he asks to be lifted up once more. Instead, before he loses the state of ascent, he searches as though he has already lost it. By this he saves time. It follows that as far as descents are concerned, there is room for man to rise and receive a place to discern the advantage between light and darkness.

What Is, "The Smell of His Garments," in the Work?

Article No. 9, Tav-Shin-Nun-Aleph, 1990/91

"Rabbi Zira said about the verse, 'And he smelled the smell of his garments and blessed him. And he said, 'The smell of my son is as the smell of a field that the Lord has blessed' (Genesis 27:27). 'The smell of his garments,' do not call it Begadav [his garments], but Bogdav [his traitors], for even the traitors among them have a smell to them'" (Sanhedrin, 37a).

We should understand the words of Rabbi Zira. What is the connection between "garments" and "traitors"? "Garments" are clothes that a person wears, meaning there is a connection between the clothes and the person. It is a good thing that the person has clothes. But "traitors" are the complete opposite, since when one person betrays another, it is a bad thing for that person. In other words, a person feels so bad in his situation that he wants to come out of that state, and he has no other choice but to betray the person who put him in the bad state he is in. Therefore, how come Rabbi Zira explains about the verse that "garments" means "traitors"?

What Is, "The Smell of His Garments," in the Work?

It is known that the order of the work is that person should correct himself and enter *Kedusha* [holiness], since man was born with the evil inclination, which comes to a person and as soon as he is born, it is with him. *The Zohar* says about it (*VaYeshev*, Item 1), "And when one comes into the world, the evil inclination immediately appears to partake with him, as it is written, 'Sin crouches at the door,' for then the evil inclination partakes with him." It says there (Item 7), "'An old and foolish king' is the evil inclination. From the day he was born, he never parted from his *Tuma'a* [impurity]. And he is a fool because all his ways are toward the evil way, and he walks and incites and lures people."

It is known that the order of the work divides into the work of the general public, meaning what the general public can do, and the work of the individual, what the general public cannot do. This is expressed by the words *Lishma* [for Her sake] and *Lo Lishma* [not for Her sake]. In other words, the work of bestowal pertains specifically to individuals. But work that is in order to receive reward is work that the general public can do, as well. Maimonides says about it, "Therefore, when teaching little ones, women, and uneducated people, they are taught to work only out of fear and in order to receive reward. Until they gain much knowledge and acquire much wisdom, they are taught that secret little-by-little" (*Hilchot Teshuva*, Chapter 4).

Therefore, when a person wants to walk on the path of individuals, to do everything in order to bestow, the evil inclination, called will to receive, which is concerned with its own benefit, can work only in order to receive reward. When a person wants to work for the sake of the Creator, the evil inclination objects to this work, since it conflicts with the nature with which he was born. Hence, here begins man's work with a hard battle, since the person tells his body when the body asks him why he observes Torah and *Mitzvot* [commandments/good deeds], "What will you get out of it?" The person tells him that our sages said, "The Creator said, 'I have created the evil inclination; I have created the Torah as a spice.'"

"Therefore, since I haven't the power to annul you, by engaging in Torah I will have the strength to annul you and remove you from your kingship over me, as it is written, "You are an old and foolish king." Therefore, I want to remove you from your governance that you govern me, and take upon myself the governance of the King of all kings, the Creator."

What should the evil inclination, called "will to receive for oneself," do? It has no other choice but to interrupt with all its might. However, normally, a person does not make efforts to obtain something if he can obtain it easily. Therefore, when a person begins to work and makes little efforts to emerge from its dominance, the body does not need to resist a person with all its might. Rather, the evil in a person emerges gradually, with greater force each time, depending on man's work.

In other words, the order of the work is balanced, so that one will have a choice to elect the good and reject the bad. This is as our sages said, "One should always see oneself as half guilty, half innocent. If he performs one *Mitzva* [singular of *Mitzvot*], happy is he, for he has sentenced himself to the side of merit" (*Kidushin* p 40b). The reason one should see oneself as "half guilty, half innocent" is so as to have a choice. Conversely, if one thing is more than the other, he can no longer make the decision.

Therefore, if a person performs one *Mitzva*, he has already sentenced to the side of merit, so how can he make a choice once more, since the side of merit has already prevailed? The answer is that if the bad in a person sees that the person has overcome it, the evil uses greater force, meaning brings him just arguments why it is not worthwhile to work for the sake of the Creator. It makes one taste the taste of dust when he wants to do something to bestow, and gives him a greater flavor in work for self-benefit.

In other words, each time, he gives him a greater pleasure is self-benefit. In other words, he never thought that there is so much pleasure in self-benefit, since when he makes more efforts, he sentences to the side of merit. Hence, he must give him more evil in order to be able to choose. That is, it does not mean that he gives him more bad deeds. Rather, it means that he gives him greater pleasure in self-benefit, to the point that it is difficult for him to retire from self-benefit and work in order to bestow.

This is regarded as a person suffering great descents. That is, when the evil appears to him with greater force and it is difficult to overcome it, the person sometimes comes to a state of "pondering the beginning," meaning that he sees that he has labored and toiled in vain, since in fact, it is impossible to emerge from the governance of evil. Thus, it is a shame that I exerted for nothing. It follows that during the descent, he betrays the work of the Creator. Afterward, when the Creator sends him an awakening from above, he ascends to spirituality once more and thinks that now he will be in a state of *Kedusha*.

However, afterward the evil appears within him once again, and with greater force, and he suffers another descent, just as before. Each time he thinks the same, meaning that each time, he falls into betrayal in the work. It follows that "He who is greater than his friend, his inclination is greater than him," since otherwise, there would not be choice. It follows that one who is greater has more betrayals in the work, where as one who does not have the strength to overcome, the evil does not need to show its full strength.

Hence, the question is, If he has committed a transgression, woe unto him, for he has sentenced himself to the side of fault, since he has already decided, so how can he later make a choice? The answer is as our sages said, "Transgressed and repeated? It becomes as though permitted to him." In other words, he does not feel the power of the evil that there is in the transgression, and naturally, he does not need excessive overcoming. Rather, with a small overcoming, he can choose the good and loathe the little bit of evil that is in him.

Conversely, one who is great, that person has many ups and downs. That is, often, he betrays the work of bestowal, as the complaint of the spies who slandered the land of Israel, which is the kingdom of heaven. In other words, his taking upon himself the kingdom would not be for his own sake, called *Eretz* [land] but because of the *Shamayim* [heaven]. Put differently, the person wants to take upon himself the burden of Torah and *Mitzvot* in order to bring contentment to his Maker, so the spies slandered it, as it is written in *The Zohar* (*Shlach*, Item 63): "'And they returned from touring the land.' 'They returned' means that they returned to the bad side, returned from the path of truth, saying, 'What did we get out of it? To this day we have not seen good in the world. We have toiled in Torah and the house is empty. Who will be awarded that world? Who will come and be in it? It would have been better had we not toiled so. We learned in order to know the part of that world. That upper world is good, as we know in the Torah, but who can be rewarded with it?'"

We should understand the argument of the spies. After all, they said what they felt. When a person is in descent, he does not lie; he says what he feels. Hence, during the ascent, he wants to annul before Him as a candle before a torch, since he feels that he will be happy from this. Conversely, during a descent, he sees that all that the will to receive argues is correct. Thus, why does the verse say as it is written, "And they slandered the land"?

According to what Baal HaSulam says, the answer is that they had to believe that since the Creator promised to the people of Israel that He would give them the land of Israel, which is a land "flowing with milk and honey," the Creator will certainly give them. But the situation that they saw was that they had to believe that this revelation of the bad came to them from above, meaning the revelation of the evil that exists in man by nature, and that one is unable to emerge from the governance of evil and be rewarded with *Dvekut* [adhesion] with the Creator. Rather, it is only the Creator Himself. They had to believe that the Creator would give them a second nature, which is the desire to bestow, and by this they will receive all the delight and pleasure called "a land flowing with milk and honey." Then, when they have the vessels of bestowal, the *Tzimtzum* [restriction] and concealment are lifted from them and they are rewarded with the delight and pleasure that were in the purpose of creation. At that time, it is a "land flowing with milk and honey."

It follows that these descents are required in order to reveal the evil, so that afterward they will know that only the Creator can

What Is, "The Smell of His Garments," in the Work?

help. His help comes specifically on a complete lack, for then the complete help can come. This means that if the evil were not completely exposed, there would not be a complete lack. Hence, first we must see that the evil is revealed.

Subsequently, the filling called "help from the Creator" comes and fills his lack. This follows the rule, "There is no light without a *Kli*." We could ask, Why must we wait so long? That is, there are many accents and many descents, but the bad could have appeared at once. The answer is that if the bad were revealed in full, no one would be able to begin the work, since the bad would prevail and there would not be room for choice. Hence, the bad appears according to the level of the good that a person increases in the work.

According to the above, we should interpret what we asked, What does it mean that Rabbi Zira interprets the verse, "And he smelled the smell of his garments and blessed him." He says, "Do not call it *Begadav* [his garments], but *Bogdav* [his traitors], for even the traitors among them have a smell to them."

We should interpret that since Jacob was rewarded with wholeness, meaning that from all the descents he achieved wholeness, so that the help from above could come, since all the bad has been revealed in him. It follows that the descents, which are the betrayals, are called "sins." When the light appears through them, we now see that the sins have become as merits, that were it not for the descents, we would not be able to achieve wholeness. This is why Rabbi Zira interprets that the smell of his garments was because he achieved his completion, meaning that the betrayals were also corrected. It follows that the betrayals were as fragrant as the merits, since everything was corrected in him. This is why he says, "the smell of his traitors."

Therefore, when a person is in a state of ascent, he must learn from his state during the descent in order to know the difference between light and darkness, as it is written, "as the advantage of the light from within the darkness." However, for the most part, a person does not want to remember the time of darkness because it pains him, and people do not want to suffer for no reason. Rather, a person wants to enjoy the state of ascent that he is in.

However, one must know that if he considers the descents while he is in an ascent, he will learn two things from this, which will benefit him and he will therefore not suffer from descents for no reason: 1) He must know how to keep himself as much as he can from falling into a descent. 2) "As the advantage of the light from within the darkness." At that time, he will have more vitality and joy from the state of ascent, and he will be able to thank the Creator for bringing him closer to Him. That is, now a person has a good feeling from being in a state where he understands that it is worthwhile to be a servant of the Creator, since now he feels the greatness and importance of the King.

But during the descent, it is the complete opposite. The body asks him, "What will you get out of wanting to annul before Him and cancel yourself from this entire world, and care only about how to bring contentment to the Creator?" When a person considers both extremes, he sees the differences between them. At that time he has the values of a different importance than he thought about the ascent. It follows that by looking at the descent, the ascent rises in him to a higher level than he feels without looking at the descent.

It follows that when he thinks about the time of betrayals that he had during the descents, all the descents are sweetened and filled with the blessing of the Creator, since they are causing an ascent. Hence, when a person completes the work, everything is corrected into merits. This is the meaning of what he says, "And he said, 'The smell of my son is as the smell of a field that the Lord has blessed.'" This means that then the smell of my son's betrayals is as the smell of *Malchut*, who is called "a field that the Lord has blessed." That is, he already received all the bestowals of delight and pleasure from the Creator.

Accordingly, we should interpret the words, "And the Lord said to her, 'Two nations are in your womb, and two peoples will be separated from your abdomen, and one nation shall be stronger than the other.'" RASHI interprets "'Two nations' as 'There is no nation but *Malchut*.' 'Will be separated,' one to his wickedness and one to his wholeness. 'One nation shall be stronger than the other,' they will not be the same in greatness; when one rises, the other falls."

We should understand what the RASHI interpretation adds to us. Here the writing brings the order of the work when we want to achieve *Dvekut* with the Creator. He says "nation" as "There is no nation but *Malchut*." That is, a person must know that there are two discernments in *Malchut*: 1) an old and foolish king, 2) the King of all kings.

The evil inclination belongs to the old and foolish king, but there is also the good inclination in him, which pertains to the King of all kings. Therefore, he says, "'Will be separated,' one to his wickedness and one to his wholeness. 'One nation shall be stronger than the other,' They will not be the same in greatness; when one rises, the other falls." This pertains to ascents and descents, where each wants to overcome the other, meaning that specifically by quarreling, each one grows, as was said, "All who is greater than his friend, his inclination is greater than him."

This is called "One nation shall be stronger than the other," meaning that both grow, and each one grows through the other. In other words, the descents, which is the old and foolish king, his power grows through the ascents of the good inclinations. It is as our sages said, "To the righteous, the evil inclination seems like a high mountain," since he has many ascents, which in plural form is called "righteous." That is, in the work, when speaking of one person, that he is a small world, there are many righteous in a person, meaning many ascents. They come by overcoming the wicked. Concerning "many wicked in one person," this is called "many descents," since in each descent he becomes wicked. It follows that each one grows through the other. This is the meaning of "One nation shall be stronger than the other."

Conversely, those who do not walk on the path toward achieving *Dvekut* with the Creator, which is to obtain the desire to bestow, are called "wicked" in that they are not walking on a path where they will be able to do everything for the sake of the Creator, but rather for their own sake.

Yet, here, "wicked" is a different discernment, a completely different interpretation. That is, there are no righteous there in the middle, but all their actions are as wicked, meaning not for the sake of the Creator, but for their own sake.

In the work, they are called "wicked," but to the general public, who observe Torah and *Mitzvot*, they are called "righteous." They are called "wicked" only in terms of the intention, in terms of the work, to work only for the sake of the Creator and not for their own sake. And since they do not have a quality of "righteous" in between, their evil does not receive an addition, for only if there is a righteous in between, meaning an ascent, when he wants to work only in order to bestow, then the bad must receive more bad so as to be able to lower him from his degree.

Hence, "To the wicked, the evil seems like hairsbreadth," and the bad does not grow in them. Instead, "Transgressed and repeated? It becomes as though permitted to him." In other words, he has no sensation of the evil. This is as our sages said, "And one nation shall be stronger than the other." As RASHI interpreted, "They will not be the same in greatness; when one rises, the other falls."

But how come when he rises he then falls? Each time, someone else receives an addition. Once the good receives an ascent from above and the bad falls, and when the bad receives bad from above, the good falls. This is the order of descents and descents, until all the evil within man is revealed specifically by a person receiving good each time, which is called "ascents." This is the meaning of "And one nation shall be stronger than the other." Hence, a person should not be alarmed by the descents. Instead, he should ask the Creator each time to bring him closer to Him.

According to the above, we should interpret, "Thus far, Your kindness has assisted us and Your mercies have not left us, the Lord our God." We should ask, In which state is he in now, and what was his state before, of which he comes to say something new, as though now he is in a state of delight and pleasure? It seems as though he was not in a good state, but was in a state where he was

What Is, "The Smell of His Garments," in the Work?

not happy, and now he has come to realize that thus, what we felt have been help from above, from the side of mercy. Although he did not feel them as mercy, now he sees that that then, too, his feelings, which we felt as bad, were also from the side of kindness. "And Your mercies have not left us" means that then, too, Providence was from the side of mercy and not from the side of judgment.

We should understand how this is so, meaning to say that the bad state was also mercy. The thing is that there is no light without a *Kli*, since a person cannot be given something if he has no need for it. It is like a person who cannot eat if he is not hungry. Therefore, when a person begins to walk on the path of the Creator to achieve *Dvekut* with the Creator, he cannot receive help from the Creator because normally, a person does not ask for help from someone unless he cannot obtain that thing by himself.

Therefore, when one thinks that he can come to work in order to bestow alone, he does not ask the Creator to help him. Thus, when one begins to work for the sake of the Creator, and sees each time that he is incapable of achieving the degree of work in order to bestow, he becomes needy of the Creator's help. It follows that all the descents he had, to the point that sometimes he despaired and came to "pondering the beginning," and wanted to escape the campaign, and certainly, these state are called "bad states," and he was in a state of "wicked." But afterward, when he has satiated the lack of the *Kli*, when he saw that his *Kli* was full of lacks, the Creator gives him help, which is the desire to bestow, a second nature. At that time, he sees that thus far, the many descents he felt, and thought that the reason was that he was unsuitable for it, and this is why he suffered the descents, now he sees that thus far it was also help from the Creator.

This is the meaning of "Thus far, Your kindness has assisted us," and it was all mercy, as it is written, "and Your mercies did not leave us."

What Does "The King Stands on His Field When the Crop Is Ripe" Mean in the Work?

Article No. 10, Tav-Shin-Nun-Aleph, 1990/91

Our sages said about the verse, "The Lord stood over him" (presented in *The View of Elders*, from the authors of the Tosfot, *VaYetze*), "We did not find this in the rest of the patriarchs. Rabbi Simon said, 'The king does not stand on his field, neither when it is plowed, nor when it is sowed, but when the crop is ripe.' This is how Abraham plowed it, as it is said, 'Arise, walk through the land.' Isaac sowed it, as it is said, 'And Isaac sowed.' Jacob came and he is the ripening of the crop, as it is said, 'The holiness of Israel is for the Lord, its first fruits,' he stood over it."

We should understand what this comes to teach us in the work: What is "a field," what is "When the crop is ripe," and what is the allegory of the King who stands over his field? It is known that our work is essentially only on the kingdom of heaven, which is called

What Does "The King Stands on His Field When the Crop Is Ripe" Mean?

"faith." Our sages said about it, "Habakkuk came and founded them on one: 'A righteous lives by his faith.'" Faith means the necessity to believe in the Creator, that He leads the world in guidance of good and doing good.

And even though one still does not have this feeling, he should still believe and say that the fact that he is not seeing how the good is revealed in the world, he should still believe above reason that he does not see the good revealed before his eyes, since as long as he is not out of the dominion of self-love, he cannot see. This is because there was a *Tzimtzum* [restriction] on the *vessels of reception* so that the light cannot shine there due to disparity of form, as it is written in the *Sulam* [Ladder commentary on *The Zohar*] ("Introduction of the Book of Zohar," Item 138).

For this reason, one cannot see the truth. Instead, he must believe that this is so. And in the work of the general public, the states of guidance of reward and punishment are not so apparent. But in individual work, when a person wishes to try to achieve the degree where all his actions are for the sake of the Creator, when he begins to strain to reach the degree of a giver, his entire basis should be built on the greatness of the Creator. It is said about it in *The Zohar*, "One should fear Him because He is great and ruling," and then begins the work primarily on this faith—that the Creator leads the world as The Good Who Does Good.

And then states of ascents and descents come to him. In other words, at times, he has reward and he can believe in the Creator, that He is good and does good, and one can love the Creator because of His greatness. This comes to a person through great efforts in faith in reward and punishment. This means that if one works with faith above reason, he is rewarded, and his reward is that he comes to feel the Creator's love for him. And the punishment is that if he wants to go specifically within reason, he thus becomes remote from the love of the Creator.

Worse yet, sometimes he becomes the opposite, a hater of the Creator, since he has many complaints against the Creator because he has already prayed to the Creator many times and he sees that the Creator does not hear the prayer. And from that, a person comes to a state of ascents and descents. However, if one overcomes, goes above reason, and says "They have eyes but they will not see," he is temporarily rewarded and feels close to the Creator.

It is written about it in the "Introduction to The Study of the Ten Sefirot" (Item 132), "We must know that the above attribute of 'medium' applies even when one is under Providence of concealment of the face. By great exertion in faith in reward and punishment, a light of great confidence in the Creator appears to them. For a time, they are granted a degree of disclosure of His face in the measure of the medium. But the drawback is that they cannot permanently remain in their degrees, since standing permanently in a degree is possible only through repentance from fear."

It follows that the order of our work comprises three periods before we reach the exit from the work, which is the discernment of Adam [human being]. Our sages said about it (*Nidah* 31), "There are three partners in a person—the Creator, his father, and his mother. His father gives the white; his mother gives the red; and the Creator places a spirit and a soul [*Ruach* and *Neshama*, respectively] within him." This is explained in the work, as we learn that there are three lines—*Hesed* [mercy/grace], *Din* [judgment], and *Rachamim* [pity/mercy].

It is as we said in previous essays, that for a person to be able to walk, one needs two legs, right and left. These are like the two verses that refute one another until the third verse comes and sentences between them. Thus, the two lines have given birth to the decisive line.

With that, we can interpret the meaning of "plowing," "sowing," and the "ripened crop" in the work. The right line is the plowing. This is the order of man's work of wanting to be admitted into the work of bestowal. Man is created to care only for himself. And since there was a correction over the will to receive for himself, to avoid the matter of shame due to the disparity of form from the

Creator—since what we see of Him is only how He bestows upon the creatures and there is no self-reception in Him whatsoever—hence, a *Tzimtzum* [restriction] and concealment were made over the will to receive for oneself so the creatures cannot receive the delight and pleasure that He wishes to impart upon the creatures.

This was in order to enable man to correct the *vessels of reception* to work only in order to bestow. In other words, man must invert the will to receive in him and receive a desire to bestow, instead. That is, what was previously of highest importance to him—the will to receive—will now be of inferior importance. He will not wish to use it, but on the contrary, the will to bestow, which was of inferior importance for him and which he did not want to use, will now be of high regard. This means that now this will to bestow is important for him and he wants to use only the desire to bestow.

This is called "plowing," when the soil is overturned so that what was above becomes below, and what was below becomes above. This is called "right line," Abraham, *Hesed*. In other words, now he wishes to engage only in *Hesed*, called "the desire to bestow," and the right line is called "wholeness." Thus, although one sees that he still cannot perform *Hesed*, he should imagine that he has already been rewarded with bestowal, called *Hesed*, and thank the Creator for rewarding him with doing things in order to bestow.

All this is only above reason. And although if he considers the situation he is in, he will see otherwise, it is a matter of above reason. This means that he must imagine that he has already been rewarded with a desire to bestow, as though he has already been rewarded with plowing.

Also, one should lower himself and say, "I am content and thankful for whatever thought and desire to do something in spirituality the Creator gives me, for rewarding me with doing a little service to the Creator, meaning that I can do something for the Creator." And he is happy with that because he sees that the Creator did not give the rest of the people the chance to serve Him. This is why he is happy with that. This is regarded as "wholeness," since now he believes above reason that the Creator leads the world in a manner of good and doing good, and thus he can now show love for the Creator and always be happy.

However, at the same time one needs to walk with the other leg, the left, meaning to criticize his actions. He should have a desire to see the truth, how much effort he can give in order to bestow, and how much is the importance of spirituality. Does he really understand that it is better to work only for the Creator and not for himself?

In that state, he sees very differently: All his actions while he was walking on the right line, when he thought that he was truly a whole man, now that he has shifted to the left line he sees that he has nothing that is truly for the sake of the Creator.

This is called "sowing." For example, when taking good wheat seeds and sowing them in the field, if there is a person who does not know about field work, he would look at the person who took the seeds and sowed them in the ground as though he were insane. Similarly, here, when one takes good states that contain wholeness, for which he has already thanked the Creator, now he cancels them. It is like that man who took good wheat seeds and sowed them in the field.

But in truth, one cannot walk on one leg. Those two legs are considered two verses that refute one another. This is why Isaac is regarded as sowing his field, which is left. Our sages said about it, "One should always repel with the left and attract with the right" (*Sotah* 47). We should interpret that when one feels that he is close to the Creator, it is called, "attracting with the right." "Repelling with the left" means that when he criticizes, he sees that he is being repelled from the work of bestowal. That is, our sages come to tell us that man needs two things, right and left, since we cannot walk on a single leg. This is considered "Isaac," which is called "sowing."

Abraham, who is called "right," meaning *Hesed*, wholeness, is called "whiteness," as was said above that there the three partners are his father, his mother, and the Creator. His father is the first discernment—the first line, which is *Hesed*—showing wholeness. Wholeness is called "white," as it is written, "Though your sins be as scarlet, they shall be as white as snow." This is called "The right attracts," when he feels that he is being brought closer to the Creator.

"And his mother sows the red." Red points to a deficiency, *Nukva* [Aramaic: female], where he sees that he is being completely repelled from the work of bestowal. Thus, he is in a state of ascents and descents. This is regarded as having only partial faith, as he says ("Introduction to The Study of the Ten Sefirot," Item 14) that it is because he has many descents, and during the descent he is without faith.

However, one must not spend much time on the left line, called "the second line," since at that time one is in a state of separation. Thus, for the most part, one's work should be in a state of wholeness. This is called "the renewal of the moon." It means that one must constantly renew the white in him, the right line, which is whiteness.

But during the descent, faith departs from him and he sometimes remains unconscious, like a person who falls under a truck and is hurt, though he does not know that he has fallen. The lesson is that the person lies under his load, as it is written, "If you see the donkey of your enemy lying under its burden" because he cannot go above reason, as the work of going above reason is an intolerable load and burden to him. Hence, if he gets distracted from it, he immediately falls under the truck. This is called "being injured in a road accident." Hence, one must always be careful and keep to the right.

It follows that the correction of a person walking on the left line is because he does not wait to get a decline and fall, and then he will wait until an awakening from above comes to him. Instead, he draws upon him the left, and then he sees that he is in a state of descent, meaning that he does not have a single spark of desire to work in order to bestow and not for his own benefit. And then he can pray.

It is as Baal HaSulam said about what our sages said of David, who said, "I awaken the dawn, and the dawn does not awaken me." That is, King David did not wait for the dawn, which is called "black," which is darkness, meaning that the darkness awakens him. Instead, he awakens the darkness. He prays to the Creator to illuminate His face for him and thus he gains time from having the preparation for the darkness, and then it is easier to correct it.

And the two above-mentioned lines—right and left—beget a third line, the middle line. It is as our sages said, "And the Creator places the spirit and soul within him." Thus, after a person has completed the work in two lines, all the evil is revealed in him. This came to him because those two lines are as two verses that refute one another. And one sees that there is no end to the ups and downs, and then he makes an honest prayer for the Creator to help him receive the desire to bestow.

When the Creator helps him, he is rewarded with complete, permanent faith, since he already has the vessels of bestowal. Before one obtains the vessels of bestowal, it is impossible for him to have permanent faith, since during the descent he loses his faith and cannot permanently believe in the Creator.

It is explained ("Introduction of The Book of Zohar," Item 138), "Since we use the *vessels of reception* contrary to how they were created, we necessarily feel the acts of Providence as evil, against us. Hence, when a person feels bad, he is accordingly heretical against His Providence, and the Operator is hidden from him."

Thus, we see that before one is rewarded with vessels of bestowal, he cannot have permanent faith. However, by being rewarded with the desire to bestow—which extends from the work in the two lines, by which all the evil appears completely—one comes to a resolution that only the Creator can help him. Then he toils in this work and does not escape the campaign, and he is rewarded with the middle line, called "the Creator gives the spirit and the soul." This is called "disclosure of the face." It is regarded as what is written, "How is there repentance, when He who knows the mysteries will testify that he will not turn back to folly."

With this we can interpret what we asked, "What does it mean in the work that it is written, 'Jacob came and he is the ripening of the crop,' as it was said, 'The holiness of Israel is for the Lord, its first fruits,' he stood over it." Our sages gave an allegory about that, "The King does not stand on his field, unless when the crop is ripe."

We should interpret that the king standing on his field refers to a man. Man extends from *Malchut*, and *Malchut* is called "a field." And man should come to a state of "A field which the Lord has blessed." This is done by labor in the above-mentioned two lines—the plowing of Abraham and the sowing of Isaac.

Afterward comes the discernment of "When the crop is ripe," when you can already see the reward from the work—the crop—which is Jacob. It is as we said above—after he has been rewarded with help from the Creator, when the Creator has given him the soul, called "disclosure of the face," it is considered that the Creator stands over him permanently, meaning that then he is rewarded with permanent faith. This is the meaning of what is written, "And the Lord stood over him." In other words, once a person has reached the degree of the middle line, which is considered Jacob, the Creator is over him, as mentioned in the allegory above, where the King stands on his field when the crop is ripe.

It is written ("Introduction to The Study of the Ten Sefirot," Item 54), "When the Creator sees that one has completed one's measure of exertion and finished everything he had to do in strengthening his choice in faith in the Creator, the Creator helps him. Then, one attains open Providence, meaning the revelation of the face. Then, he is rewarded with complete repentance."

He says ("Introduction to The Study of the Ten Sefirot," Item 56), "In truth, one is not absolutely certain that he will not sin again before he is rewarded with the above attainment of reward and punishment, meaning the revelation of the face. And this revelation of the face, from the perspective of the Creator's salvation, is called 'testimony,' …it guarantees that he will not sin again." This means that at that time he is rewarded with permanent faith.

Now we can interpret what is written, "The Lord lives, and blessed be my Rock." "My soul shall be glorified in the Lord." We should understand the meaning of "The Lord lives," in regard to the Creator. What kind of praise of the Creator is it? In the work, we should interpret "Lives." Who is He who is called "The Lord lives"? It is one who believes in the Creator, that He watches over the world benevolently. This person is called "Lives."

"Blessed by my Rock" is one who receives from the Creator the shape of this faith, where the Creator is His desire to do good to His creations. That man blesses the Creator for giving him the faith, since alone he would not be able to take upon himself faith above reason, for this is the gift of God.

We should also interpret, "My soul shall be glorified in the Lord." "In the Lord" means in the Creator bringing him close to Him. For this, his soul is glorified, meaning that man's soul is deeply thankful to the Creator for bringing him closer. This is called "The Creator gives the spirit and the soul." With his own strength, a person would not be able to achieve this. For this, he praises the Creator—that now that he has faith. He blesses the Creator only for what the Creator gave him. Also, the Creator is called "the middle line," as was said above, that only by working in the two previous lines, one is later rewarded with the Creator giving the spirit and the soul.

Thus, only the Creator can help one exit the dominion of the *vessels of reception*. Therefore, during the descent one must not argue with his will to receive and plead that it is better for him if the will to receive left the premises and made room for the desire to bestow, and he wants to make it understand so it will surrender before him. One should know that the body will never agree to this; it is a waste of words.

Instead, he should ask the Creator, for only He has the strength to annul it, and none other. In other words, the body will never agree to this; hence, it is pointless to argue with the body. But when

What Does "The King Stands on His Field When the Crop Is Ripe" Mean?

he wishes to do something for the sake of the Creator, he should ask the Creator to give him the strength to overcome the will to receive for himself.

With the above said, we should interpret what they said (*Avot*, Chapter 1:5), "Do not extend in conversation with the woman." This was said about his woman. It is all the more so about his friend's woman. Although the literal meaning is the main one, in the work, we can interpret that the woman and the man are in one body. Man's woman is called "the will to receive," which is called "a female," and which always wants only to receive.

Hence, sometimes, when one wishes to do something in order to bestow, which is called "male," a man, and the will to receive resists, and a man wishes to extend in discussion with his will to receive to make it understand that it is better for it to let him work in order to bestow, our sages said that it is a waste of words. They said, "This is said about his own woman," meaning the will to receive in himself. "It is all the more so in his friend's woman," meaning to argue with the friends' will to receive—that he will argue with them and make them see that it is better to do everything in order to bestow—since only the Creator can help them emerge from the domination of the will to receive for oneself.

Hence, such people—who wish to walk on the path of reaching a state where all their actions are for the sake of the Creator—must not reproach their friends about why they do not engage in the work of bestowal. This is because if he wants to correct a friend's will to receive, it is as though that man has power. But in truth, what a person does in order to bestow is only by the power of the Creator. This is why it is forbidden to rebuke one's friend.

What It Means that the Good Inclination and the Evil Inclination Guard a Person in the Work

Article No. 11, Tav-Shin-Nun-Aleph, 1990/91

The Zohar says (VaYishlach, Items 1-4), "Rabbi Yehuda started, 'For He will give His angels charge over you, to keep you in all your ways.' When a person comes to the world, the evil inclination immediately comes with him. It is written, 'My sin is ever before me,' for it makes man sin before his Master. The good inclination comes to a person from the time he comes to be purified. And when does one come to be purified? When he is thirteen years of age. At that time, a man connects in both, one on the right, and one on the left, the good inclination on the right, and the evil inclination on the left. And these are really two appointed angels. When a man comes to be purified, the evil inclination surrenders before him and the right governs the left. And both the good inclination and the evil inclination join to keep man in all the roads he travels."

We should understand that when we are speaking in terms of the work, we understand that the good inclination guards a person when he walks on the path of the Creator and wants to achieve *Dvekut* [adhesion] with the Creator, so he receives the guarding of the good inclination. Yet, what guarding does one receive from the evil inclination, for which he will achieve *Dvekut* with the Creator? This implies that if he is not guarded by the evil inclination, he will not be able to achieve *Dvekut* with the Creator.

The verse says (Genesis 25:23), "And the Lord said to her, 'Two nations are in your womb, and one nation shall be stronger than the other, and the older shall serve the younger.'" RASHI interprets, "'One nation shall be stronger than the other,' they will not be the same in greatness; when one rises, the other falls." That is, they will not be in greatness at the same time.

It is known that the order of the work is to come to a state where all your work is for the sake of the Creator. This is out of one's hands. Rather, this force is something he should receive from above, as our sages said, "He who comes to purify is aided." However, achieving a degree of bestowing contentment upon one's Maker permanently comes to a person after he has revealed all the bad in him. At that time, a person receives this power called "second nature," which is the desire to bestow.

In other words, a person must first reveal all the bad in him, which is called that he already has a complete *Kli* [vessel], meaning a complete lack. At that time he receives the complete light, as our sages said, "The light in it reforms him." However, before he has the revelation of this *Kli*, meaning a need for the help of the Creator—since the help must be complete help, as our sages said, "From above, there is no giving of half a thing, but rather a complete thing"—the lower one's deficiency must also be complete.

And since it is impossible to reveal to a person all the evil because while he still does not have good, he will not be able to subdue the bad, since the bad will be more than the good, therefore, when a person begins to engage in Torah and *Mitzvot* [commandments/ good deeds], he increases the good each time, and to that extent he is shown the evil. At that time, man's work is balanced, as our sages said (*Kidushin*, p 40), "One should always see oneself as half guilty, half innocent."

For this reason, he is shown the evil gradually, according to his effort to acquire the good through his efforts in Torah and *Mitzvot*.

According to the above, when a person wants to walk on the path of achieving *Dvekut* with the Creator and do all his work for the sake of the Creator, meaning to bestow contentment upon his Maker and not for his own sake, as it is against human nature, who was created with the will to receive for his own sake, and all of man's work is that he is told that he will not obtain this by his own strength, but only the Creator can give him this power called desire to bestow, and a person should only prepare the *Kli* to receive this power called "second nature," it follows that specifically through the evil inclination, which grows within him to its completion, a person sees his real deficiency—that he is unable to obtain the desire to bestow by himself. This brings him to a state where the Creator gives him the desire to bestow.

Thus, both the good inclination and the evil inclination lead a person to achieve the goal of equivalence of form, called "*Dvekut* with the Creator."

By this we can interpret what we asked, Why does *The Zohar* say, "For He will give His angels charge over you, to keep you in all your ways," which pertains to the evil inclination, too, which guards a person so he will achieve *Dvekut* with the Creator? But if it guards a person so he will achieve *Dvekut* with the Creator, why is it called "evil inclination"? "Evil inclination" implies that it brings a person thoughts and desires that object to *Kedusha* [holiness]. That is, it makes a person think that it is not worthwhile to exert in Torah and *Mitzvot*, so how does it guard a person so he will achieve *Dvekut* with the Creator, so he will do everything for the sake of the Creator and not for his own sake?

The Good Inclination and the Evil Inclination Guard a Person

The answer is that if the evil is not revealed to a person to its true extent, he cannot receive help from the Creator because he still does not have a real need. It follows that he still does not have a real *Kli*. The evil inclination gives him thoughts and desires against the *Kedusha*, and this is called "the evil inclination," as Baal HaSulam said, that the evil inclination means "a depiction of evil," meaning that the evil inclination depicts to a person that if he works for the sake of the Creator and not for his own sake, it will be bad for him. When the evil inclination draws such depictions to a person, it makes him leave the work of bestowing upon the Creator.

For this reason, when a person comes to feel the depictions of the evil inclination, he wants to escape from this work that is only for the sake of the Creator. At that time, he sees that it is impossible to overcome the depictions that the evil inclination draws for him. Yet, only then can he overcome and say that the Creator will help him emerge from the control of the evil inclination, since then he sees that this is above nature for a person to be able to do something against the black state where a person sees the depiction of the evil inclination.

From these depictions, a person sees what is bad, meaning what measure of evil exists in man's heart, who cannot do anything for the sake of the Creator unless he sees there something for his own benefit, too. Through these depictions, a person acquires an image of the bad each time. One cannot see these images all at once, for he will not be able to endure them. Rather, one is shown a little bit, and that depiction soon leaves. Then, it is as though the person forgets the depiction of working for the sake of the Creator and not for himself. Hence, he has the strength to start the work of bestowal once again. When he thinks that he is already at a stage where he can work only for the sake of the Creator, the evil inclination promptly comes to him and gives him another depiction of work for the sake of the Creator. This depiction moves him once again from working for the sake of the Creator.

It follows that specifically through the evil inclination, a person can achieve the state of truth, meaning that one cannot deceive oneself and say that he is serving the Creator and all his work is for the sake of the Creator, since when the evil inclination gives him the depictions of what for the sake of the Creator means, he sees that he is far from this work. It follows that a person cannot fool himself that he is walking on the path of truth, since he sees how the body objects to this, to such an extent that he must believe above reason that the Creator can help him emerge from the governance of self-love.

It follows that without the keeping of the evil inclination he would never be able to see the truth. Thus, just as everyone understands that the good inclination guards a person on the way to achieving his completion of being adhered to the Creator, meaning to work entirely to bestow, likewise, without the evil inclination, a person would think that he is doing everything for the sake of the Creator.

But when the evil inclination comes to him with bad depictions and tells him that it is not worthwhile to work for the sake of the Creator, it becomes utterly clear to a person that everything he did in Torah and *Mitzvot* before was all for his own benefit, since now he sees that when the evil inclination shows him the state of working only for the sake of the Creator, he agrees that the evil inclination is correct and the person really does not see what he will gain by working for the sake of the Creator.

This causes a person a state of descent. That is, before the evil inclination came to him with these depictions, he knew that everything he did was for the sake of the Creator, meaning that he was observing what the Creator commanded man to do. Otherwise, why would he observe Torah and *Mitzvot*? But not for the sake of the Creator? Everyone knows that someone who works not for the sake of the Creator, his work is worthless, so when a person engages in Torah and *Mitzvot*, he is certain that he is working for the sake of the Creator.

But now that the evil inclination came to him with the bad depictions of work in order to bestow, he sees that he is far from working for the sake of the Creator, and working not for the sake of the Creator is unworthy work, so he wants to leave the work of observing Torah and *Mitzvot* altogether, since by nature, a person cannot work for no reason. When a person works, he must see that he is doing something. Hence, if he sees that he cannot work for the sake of the Creator—as the evil inclination made him see about what it means to work entirely for the sake of the Creator and not at all for his own sake, and not for the sake of the Creator is worthless—he comes to a state where he wants to escape the campaign altogether.

Now we understand how *The Zohar* interprets the verse, "For He will give His angels charge over thee, to keep thee in all thy ways." Without the evil inclination, a person would never be able to achieve the work of bestowal, since only the Creator can give this power of being able to do everything in order to bestow, and without a lack, a person cannot receive anything. But he does not have this lack for the Creator to give him the other nature, meaning the desire to bestow, since he thinks that he is doing everything for the sake of the Creator, since as long as one does not want to work for the sake of the Creator, the body does not object to the point where a person needs the help of the Creator.

But when a person wants to work in order to bestow, the work of the evil inclination comes to him and begins to make him think that it is not worthwhile to work for the sake of the Creator. At that time, the evil engenders in him a need for the help of the Creator. It follows that specifically by the bad, he comes closer to the Creator. That is, the evil inclination keeps him from fooling himself that he is working for the sake of the Creator.

It follows that when a person prays to the Creator to help him, the prayer must be clear. That is, he must know what he is missing, meaning that the lack will be revealed in him without any doubt, for if the deficiency is not revealed to him for certain, but he is unclear about the lack he feels, this is not a prayer. Hence, when the evil inclination comes to him with bad depictions, the person knows for certain what he needs, and this is called "a complete deficiency."

This is similar to what is written about Jacob, who said "Deliver me, I pray Thee, from the hand of my brother, from the hand of Esau; for I fear him, that he will come and strike me and the mothers with the children" (Genesis 32:11 and *VaYishlach*, Item 70). It says, "This implies that one who prays his prayer, his words should be properly interpreted. When he said, 'Deliver me, I pray Thee,' it seems as though it should have sufficed, since he does not need more than deliverance. Yet, he told the Creator, 'And should You say that You have already saved me from Laban?' This is why he explained, 'from the hand of my brother.' And if you say that other kin are called brothers, too, as Laban said to Jacob, 'Because you are my brother, should you therefore serve me for nothing?' He therefore explained, 'from the hand of Esau.' What is the reason? It is because we need to interpret the matter properly."

We should ask about this: We can understand that when we speak of a flesh and blood king, the one who seeks help should have a clear request, so that the king will understand what he is asking. However, when someone asks for something of the Creator, why should the request be so clear? Does the Creator not know what is in one's heart? He certainly knows man's thoughts, since the Creator is called "He who knows the thoughts," as we say, "He who knows the thoughts, please save." Therefore, why must we clarify the prayer and request that we pray that we will "interpret the matter properly"?

The answer is that a person must clarify the prayer so it is clear and interpreted to the person. That is, a person must know what he missing, since sometimes he thinks that he needs luxuries and prays for them with all his might, while about things that concern his life, without which he cannot receive a life of *Kedusha* [holiness], this he relinquishes. He thinks that he needs things by which he will come to be a respectable and perfect man, and this is what he asks, when in fact, he is lacking things that pertain to his life, meaning that without them he will remain as though dead, as our sages said, "The wicked in their lives are called 'dead.'"

Therefore, when the evil inclination pictures for him bad depictions about the work of bestowal contentment upon his Maker, through this evil he sometimes comes to a state of "pondering the beginning," like the spies who slandered the land of Israel, as *The Zohar* interprets. At that time he sees that he is truly evil and has no faith in the Creator.

It is as Baal HaSulam said, that one should see to it that on the path he is walking, he will make every effort he can make, as an awakening from below, to obtain faith in the Creator. This is called "I am the Lord your God and you will have no other gods." These are regarded as *Kaneh* [trachea] and *Veshet* [gullet], which are two signs that the life of animals depend on. That is, in corporeality, if these signs stop, life ceases from an animal. Likewise, in the work, if the "I am ... and you will have now..." stops, the spiritual life departs from him.

For this reason, sometimes a person cries and prays to the Creator to help him with what he thinks. But even though he cries bitterly, his request is not answered, since he is in mortal danger yet asks to be given nonsense. That is, a person thinks that he is fine, that all he needs, in his view, is some complementary thing, when in truth, he is lifeless. Therefore, the angel called "evil inclination" comes and through its depictions, shows him that it is not worth it to annul before Him because the will to receive will gain nothing from it. At that time a person can see the truth—he is truly wicked.

It is follows that specifically the revelation of this evil keeps him, so he will ask the Creator to give him life, called "faith in the Creator," so he can adhere to the Creator, as it is written, "And you who cleave unto the Lord your God are alive every one of you this day." It is as *The Zohar* says, "For He will give His angels charge over thee, to keep thee in all thy ways." That is, both the good inclination and the evil inclination keep the person, so he will achieve *Dvekut* with the Creator. Without the evil inclination, he would not know the truth, what help to ask of the Creator.

According to the above, we should interpret what our sages said, "To the righteous, the evil inclination seems like a high mountain." We should explain and say that when a person sees that the evil inclination is so big, like a high mountain, this is a sign that he is righteous, meaning that he is walking on the path of truth, by which to come to be righteous. Otherwise, the evil inclination would not appear to him as a high mountain. This is so because a person is shown the evil in him only to the extent of the good that he has, since the good and the bad must always be balanced. Then, it can be said that a person should decide and choose the good.

By this we can interpret what is written (Genesis 28:12), "And behold, the angels of God were ascending and descending on it." The famous question is, Why did the angels of God ascend first? It should have said "descending" first, and then "ascending." In the work, we should interpret that "angels of God" are those people who want to be messengers of the Creator, to do the holy work, as our sages said (*Sukkah* 10), "We are messengers of *Mitzva* [singular of *Mitzvot*]."

Therefore, those who want to be as angels, to do everything for the sake of the Creator, are called "messengers of the Creator." They must first rise in degree, meaning do good deeds, which is called "an ascent in degree," and then, when they are in an ascent, when they are in a state where they are walking on the path of wholeness, they might think that they are in utter wholeness. But since they desire to achieve *Dvekut* with the Creator, they are shown from above the truth, that they are still far from doing everything for the sake of the Creator. Through the recognition of evil, a person descends from his degree and begins to see the truth, to see what he is missing.

This is the order of the work. First, a person receives an ascent from above, and then he receives a descent from above. It is all for the above-mentioned reason that through the ascents and descents, the person obtains a complete lack. And the lack is so great that no one in the world can fill the lack but the Creator Himself. This is called "a complete *Kli*," ready to receive His help.

It is as Baal HaSulam said about what our sages said (*Avot*, Chapter 2:21), "It is not for you to finish the work, nor are you free to idle away from it." He said that "It is not for you to finish the work" refers to the work of achieving a state where all his actions are for the sake of the Creator. A person cannot finish this work. Therefore, why should one begin this work, which he cannot finish anyway? Normally, a person does not begin a work that he knows he cannot finish. Thus, why did they say, "nor are you free to idle away from it"? This implies that a person should begin this work. So, the question is for what purpose should he start?

The answer is that in everything, there must be desire and yearning to obtain the required matter. Otherwise, when, if we receive something without a prior need for it, it is impossible to enjoy, as it is known that there is no light without a *Kli*. For this reason, a person must begin the work of bestowal, and then he sees that after he has made many efforts to obtain that force, yet he cannot have it, later, when the Creator gives him this power of bestowal, he can enjoy it.

Baal HaSulam said about this, that this is the meaning of "We will do and we will hear," which Israel said when the nations of the world did not want to receive it, since they saw that it was impossible to go against nature. But the people of Israel said, "We will do by force, even though our heart does not want this, and by this we will be rewarded with hearing. In other words, the Creator will let us hear that this work is acceptable to the heart. This is called "Reply unto your heart."

These Candles Are Sacred

Article No. 12, Tav-Shin-Nun-Aleph, 1990/91

Baal HaSulam said about what is written, "These candles are sacred and we have no permission to use them, but only to see them," that we must know the difference between the miracle of Hanukkah and the miracle of Purim. On Hanukkah, the decree pertained only to spirituality, that the people of Israel were prevented from observing the *Mitzvot* [commandments/good deeds]. The miracle was that when they prevailed over the Hasmoneans, they could observe the *Mitzvot*. Since spirituality has no *Kelim* [vessels], since *Kelim* are called specifically "vessels of reception," which is called "creation existence from absence," which is the will to receive, this is why the intimation comes, "These candles are sacred and we have no permission to use them."

This is not so with the miracle of Purim. Then the decree was over the bodies, too, as it is written, "To destroy, to kill, and to annihilate" (Esther 3:13). It follows that the miracle was on the bodies. "Bodies" are called "vessels of reception." Hence, on Purim, it is written, "Joy, feast, and a good day," where a feast pertains to the body. On Hanukkah, we were given the miracle, "no permission to use them, but only to see them."

This is the meaning of what our sages said, that Hanukkah means *Hanu-Koh* [parked here]. He asked, What is the meaning of "parked"? He said that "parked" meaning parking, and he gave an allegory about it. Many times, in the middle of a war, soldiers are given a vacation and they go home so that afterward they will have the courage to be brave soldiers. After the parking they return to the battlefield. But some fools think that the soldiers were given a vacation because the war must be over so they are not needed anymore.

But the smarter ones among them understand that they were given a vacation in order to rest, so they would be re-energized to fight against the enemy. Therefore, they understand that the rest is in order to acquire strength to fight.

It is likewise here. On Hanukkah, the redemption was only on spirituality, since the decree was only on spirituality, as it is written ("About the Miracles"), "When the wicked kingdom of Greece arose over Your people, Israel, to make them forget Your law and remove them from the rules of Your will, You with Your great mercies stood by them in their time of trouble."

It follows that the redemption was only about spirituality, and in the work, "spirituality" is called "vessels of bestowal," called "light of *Hassadim* that dresses in vessels of bestowal." But here, when we are rewarded with vessels of bestowal, it is only half the work, half a war. That is, a person must be rewarded with the vessels of reception also entering the *Kedusha* [holiness], meaning to use them with the aim to bestow.

Once the vessels of reception have also entered the *Kedusha*, this is considered that he has *Kelim* to receive, as well. At that time, this degree is called "sweetening of the *Gevurot*." In other words, before he obtained the vessels of reception that work in order to bestow, he could not use the light that was revealed over vessels of bestowal, for vessels of bestowal means that a person gives something, and in return for the giving, he does not want anything, since he believes that he is serving a great King. Therefore, he is happy that he has been rewarded with serving a great King.

But when he uses the vessels of reception, meaning takes pleasures from the Creator, since through reception he becomes separated from the Creator because of the disparity of form, these vessels of reception are called "bitter *Gevurot*," because it is bitter for him that he is far from the Creator. *Gevurot* means that a person has two kinds of *Kelim*: One is called *Hesed*, meaning he gives, and one is called *Gevura*, which is that he receives. It is called *Gevura* since there is the matter of *Hitgabrut* [to overcome] here, not to receive. If he does receive, he will be far from the Creator, and that state is bitter for him. Hence, when he can place the aim to bestow on the will to receive, then the previous *Gevurot*, where he used the vessels of reception, are bitter for him because of the disparity of form.

But now they have been sweetened, meaning that now that he is using the vessels of reception, he feels some sweetness because his intention is in order to bestow, and this is already regarded as equivalence of form. Hence, now he can enjoy them, since in reception in this manner, in order to bestow, there is no bitterness and all is good.

We say (in the song *Mighty Rock of My Salvation*), "Greeks have gathered over me, then in the days of the Hasmoneans, and broke the walls of my towers." "Greeks" are those people who go within reason, who cannot do anything if it is against reason. At that time, there was the governance of the Greeks, meaning this dominion governed over the people of Israel.

This authority is called "the wicked kingship of Greece," whose role was to make them "forget Your Torah and move them from the laws of Your will." That is, the governance is to go specifically within reason. This is what causes the breaching of the wall that guards the tower. A "tower" means that within man, there is a certain measure of greatness of the Creator. This "wall" is called "faith above reason," and specifically by faith above reason one can come to feel the greatness of the Creator, as well as depict to himself the greatness of the Creator.

When a person feels the greatness of the Creator, he is "like a candle before a torch," annulled before Him. But the Greeks, meaning dominion of within reason, which did not let them go above reason, is regarded as "breaking the walls of my towers." In other words, the faith above reason, which is a wall. Within this wall we can build towers, meaning obtain the greatness of the Creator, which is called "a tower." That is, specifically through faith above reason we are rewarded with the "reason of *Kedusha*."

It follows that man's greatness, who is rewarded with feeling the greatness of the Creator, comes specifically by lowering himself, meaning lowering his reason. At that time he can be rewarded with the greatness of the Creator called "reason of *Kedusha*."

By this we can interpret what is written ("And [the Lord] Will Give You," for After Shabbat), "Rabbi Yochanan said, 'Wherever you find the greatness of the Creator, there you find His humbleness.'" There is certainly a simpler explanation, but when we speak in terms of the work, we should understand what is written, that we find the Creator's humbleness, that He is humble. We should understand how is there the quality of humbleness in the Creator, for it means lowliness, and how can we speak of this quality in the Creator. Normally, it is written, "The Lord is King, He wears pride."

We should interpret that this refers to the person. That is, wherever a person is rewarded with His greatness, to attain something of the greatness of the Creator, "there you find the humbleness of a person." According to the greatness of the Creator with which a person is rewarded, to that extent the person sees his lowliness.

In other words, precisely when a person goes above reason, the reason comes to him and wants to obstruct him, and begins to argue with him. At that time, the person sees that he has nothing to reply. Then a person sees the evil within him, that he needs more strengthening so he can be saved from the reason of the evil inclination, which is called "Greeks." At that time, he sees according to the evil that is revealed in him, that no one is as low as he, since the evil in him is revealed more than in the rest of the people. As said above, this is according to the good that a person does, if he walks on the path of truth and wants to do everything in order to bestow.

It follows that when one is rewarded with even a little bit of the greatness of the Creator, he does not know why the Creator helped him more than other people, since he feels that he is worse than all the people in the world. He tells himself that if the rest of the people knew the path of truth the way he understands it, they would certainly be virtuous people, not like him. It follows that when one feels a little bit of the greatness of the Creator, he comes to a state of lowliness at the Creator helping someone as base as he. This is the meaning of the words "Wherever you find the greatness of the Creator, there you find His humbleness."

Therefore, when one says to the Creator, "You lend a hand to criminals and Your right is stretched out to welcome the returning" (Conclusion prayer), this means that when one asks the Creator to bring him closer, it is regarded as stretching out the hand for reconciliation, "and Your right is stretched out to welcome the returning." In other words, a person says to the Creator, "I feel my situation, that I am more wicked and more criminal than the rest of the world." This comes to him because from above, he was shown the evil. As said above, a person is not shown more evil than what is in him.

As we interpreted what our sages said, "To the wicked, the evil inclination seems like a hairsbreadth, and to the righteous, like a high mountain." It seems as though it should have been the opposite. The wicked, who cannot overcome the evil inclination, should say that the evil inclination is like a high mountain, and the righteous, who did have the power to overcome, the evil inclination should have been in their eyes like a hairsbreadth.

The answer is that a person is not shown the evil in him but only according to the good within him, so that the good and the bad will be balanced. Therefore, the righteous, who have many ups and downs, all the descents are from the evil inclination. As a result of the many descents, a "high mountain" is built. The word *Har* [mountain] means *Hirhurim* [reflections/thoughts]. This means that any reflection, where one doubts the quality of the Creator, when he does not believe in His Providence, that He is good and does good, this is called "a bad thought."

Therefore, to the righteous, the evil inclination becomes a high mountain, whereas to the wicked, who have no ascents and descents, since it is impossible to descend before you ascend, as we explained concerning Jacob's dream, where it is written, "Behold, angels of God were ascending and descending on it," where it should have written first "descending" and then "ascending."

But in the work, all the people came into this world to carry out the mission of the Creator, and an "angel" is called a "messenger." Therefore, first one must ascend in the degree of the work, when feeling some nearness to the Creator, and afterward, there can be descents. For this reason, the wicked, who have no ascents, naturally have no descents. Indeed, why do they not ascend? It is because the evil inclination disrupts them from ascending. For this reason, they remain in the evil inclination that is only as a hairsbreadth.

Hence, the righteous, who have the real form of the evil, when the Creator helps them, they feel their lowliness, that the Creator brought them closer, and this is called as it is written, "He lifts the poor up from the trash." That is, the person says, "I was in the trash, enjoying everything that animals take as their nourishments, meaning trash." This is the meaning of "In the place where you find the greatness of the Creator, you find His humbleness."

However, we should interpret this as said above, that one should not say, "Now that I have been rewarded with the greatness of the Creator, I no longer need faith above reason because I have what to build my work on—the basis that I have now been rewarded with the greatness of the Creator."

Rather, as Baal HaSulam said, a person should be careful when he is rewarded with some nearness on the part of the Creator. He should not say that now he knows that it is worthwhile to do the holy work because now he feels a good taste in the work. Rather, he should say, "Now I see that it is worthwhile to work above reason because specifically by wanting to go above reason, the Creator is giving me some nearness to Him."

Hence, he takes this nearing as a sign that he is walking on the path of truth. Therefore, he resolves that henceforth, he will not want to accept any work within reason. Rather, everything will be above reason. It follows that he does not take the nearing to the Creator as a basis on which he says that it is worthwhile to be a servant of the Creator, "since I already have a basis." On the contrary, from now on he will work only above reason.

This is the meaning of what is written, "In the place of the greatness of the Creator, there you find His humbleness." That is, "In the place of His greatness," meaning in the place where one attains some greatness of the Creator, there you must find His humbleness. In other words, there, in the place where a person finds the greatness of the Creator, a person should find man's humbleness, which is faith above reason, called "lowliness," "humility."

Since faith is regarded as being of inferior importance, faith is called "below." That is, when one finds the greatness of the Creator, he should search and find a place to work in faith, and not in the sense that he has found a place of the greatness of the Creator.

Since one should say that the fact that he has been rewarded with finding some greatness of the Creator, it is because first he went with faith, which is called "low," "lowly." Hence, he continues on the path of faith above reason since he sees that this is the path of truth, and the proof of this is that specifically through this preparation, the Creator brings him closer to Him.

This is the meaning of what is written, "Greeks have gathered over me ... and broke the walls of my towers." This means that a person should guard this wall, called "faith in the Creator above reason." In other words, a person must not wait until he understands that it is worthwhile to learn and to pray, etc. Rather, he should not consider what the reason advises him. Instead, he should follow the way that the Torah obligates a person. This is how one must behave. Only in this way, called "unconditional surrender," can one be rewarded with the reason of *Kedusha*.

And the most important is the prayer. That is, one must pray to the Creator to help him go above reason, meaning that the work should be with gladness, as though he has already been rewarded with the reason of *Kedusha*, and what joy he would feel then. Likewise, he should ask the Creator to give him this power, so he can go above the reason of the body.

In other words, although the body does not agree to this work in order to bestow, he asks the Creator to be able to work with gladness, as is suitable for one who serves a great King. He does not ask the Creator to show the greatness of the Creator, and then he will work gladly. Rather, he wants the Creator to give him joy in the work of above reason, that it will be as important to a person as if he already has reason.

What "You Have Given the Strong to the Hands of the Weak" Means in the Work

Article No. 13, Tav-Shin-Nun-Aleph, 1990/91

Here is the order of the work: When a person wishes to do everything for sake of the Creator, that his actions will be in order to bestow and not to receive reward, it is against nature because man was created with a desire to receive for his own benefit. This is why we were given the work of exiting self-love and working only in order to bestow for the sake of the Creator.

To be able to perform this work of exiting the domination of self-love, we were given the *Mitzva* [commandment/good deed], "love your neighbor as yourself," which, as Rabbi Akiva says, "Is a great rule in the Torah." As it explains in the book *The Giving of the Torah*, through it we will exit the domination of the will to receive for ourselves and will be able to work for the sake of the Creator.

What "You Have Given the Strong to the Hands of the Weak" Means

And concerning "love your neighbor as yourself," we should make two interpretations:

1) Literally, between a man and his friend.

2) Between man and the Creator, as our sages said, (*Midrash Rabbah, Yitro,* 27:1), "Do not leave your friend and the friend of your father." "Your friend" is the Creator, as it is written, "For the sake of my brothers and my friends," which is interpreted as the Creator, who called them "brothers" and "friends." It follows that "love your neighbor as yourself" refers to achieving love for the Creator as for yourself.

Thus, there are two discernments in "love your neighbor as yourself":

1) We should say, as a cure. In other words, the reason why one must love his friend is only because through it, he will be able to come to love the Creator, too, as presented in the book *The Giving of the Torah*. Hence, as with love of friends, when a person wishes to cling to friends, he chooses with whom to bond. In other words, when a person chooses for himself friends, he searches for those who will have good qualities.

Likewise, when one wishes to love the Creator, he should try to see the greatness and importance of the Creator. This evokes the love of the Creator in a person. If he cannot see the greatness and importance of the Creator because the evil in man slanders the Creator, one must pray for the Creator's help to have the strength to overcome and say above reason, "I want to believe in the greatness and importance of the Creator so that I can love Him," as it is written, "And you shall love the Lord your God with all your heart and with all your soul." In other words, love of friends is a means by which to attain the goal, which is the love of the Creator.

By this we can interpret what our sages said, "It is good to have Torah with the right conduct, since toil in both mitigates iniquity." This means that toiling in the right conduct, which is the work between a man and his friend, is a cure by which one can come to love the Creator, who is called "Torah." The essence of the Torah is that through the Torah, one connects to the giver of the Torah. Our sages said about this, "The Creator said, 'I have created the evil inclination; I have created the spice of Torah.'" That is, through the Torah, which is the spice, one is rewarded with *Dvekut* [adhesion] with the Creator, and this is regarded as "reforming him."

This is the meaning of, "Toil in both mitigates iniquity." In other words, through labor between a man and his friend and between man and the Creator, meaning by exerting in the Torah, it mitigates iniquity. That is, the iniquity of the tree of knowledge, from which the iniquities extend, is corrected by both.

The writing says (Psalms 33, *Rejoice ... You Righteous*), "Behold, the eye of the Lord is toward those who fear Him, toward those who await His mercy; to deliver their souls from death, and to keep them alive in famine." We must understand what is meant by "The eye of the Lord is [specifically] toward those who fear Him." After all, the eyes of the Creator roam everywhere. We must believe that the Creator watches over the whole world in private Providence, as The Good Who Does Good, and not necessarily those who fear Him.

We should interpret that we speak of the Creator only from the perspective of "By your actions, we know You." This means that it is specifically those who fear Him who feel that the eye of the Creator watches over the whole world. In other words, only those who fear the Creator attain that the Creator watches over the world in private Providence, as The Good Who Does Good. But as for the rest of the world, for them there is concealment of the face on Providence, since they cannot attain His Providence as being The Good Who Does Good.

It is written in the "Introduction of The Book of Zohar" (Item 138), "As long as the receivers have not been completed so they can receive His whole benevolence, which He had contemplated in our favor in the thought of creation, the guidance must be in the form of good and bad."

In other words, as long as our vessels of reception are littered with self-reception, it is impossible to see Providence as good and doing good. Rather, those who can see the eye of the Creator, that His guidance is good and doing good, are only those who "Await His mercy." This is because "His mercy" means that they yearn to receive the quality of *Hesed* [mercy] from the Creator—the quality of bestowal—which is called "equivalence of form," known as "*Dvekut* [adhesion] with the Creator."

Therefore, when they are rewarded with the quality of bestowal, their *vessels of reception* are no longer littered. At that time, they are rewarded with "The eye of the Lord," to feel that His Providence is one good and doing good. But those who do not wish to obtain the quality of *Hesed*, meaning vessels of bestowal, are under the influence of good and bad.

But to whom does the Creator give the *Hesed*, called "vessels of bestowal," which is the second nature? Not to everyone. There are many people who await His mercy—for the Creator to give them the quality of *Hesed*. However, the Creator does not give the *Hesed*, called "vessels of bestowal," to those people who think that the matter of *Hesed* is only an addition, meaning those who consider themselves whole and need the Creator to give them the quality of *Hesed* as a good supplement.

This is so because only those with *Kelim* [vessels] for the filling are given from above. In other words, if there is no real deficiency, it is impossible to fill it. So precisely when is it possible to satiate a need? When a person does not ask for luxuries but for necessity. Then a person receives because luxuries are not considered a deficiency.

When it is written, "The eye of the Lord is toward those who fear Him, toward those who await His mercy," who are these above-mentioned people who await His mercy? That is, for what purpose are they yearning for the Creator to give them the quality of *Hesed*? It is specifically such people who feel that they need the quality of *Hesed*, "to deliver their souls from death."

In other words, it is precisely in those people who wish to achieve *Dvekut* with the Creator, to adhere to the Life of Lives. Otherwise, if they have no *Dvekut*, they feel that they are tantamount to the dead, as our sages said, "The wicked, in their lives, are called 'dead.'" For this reason, they ask of the Creator to deliver them from death because disparity of form separates them from the Life of Lives.

Dvekut with the Creator is considered life, as it is written, "But you who cleave unto the Lord your God are alive every one of you this day." It follows that the reason they are asking for the quality of *Hesed* is because they do not wish to be as "The wicked, in their lives, are called 'dead,'" and it is to them that the Creator gives the quality of *Hesed*, meaning vessels of bestowal.

When it is written, "To deliver their souls from death," meaning his request of the Creator to give him the quality of *Hesed* is in order to "Deliver their souls from death," this is called "a deficiency," which is a *Kli* [vessel] that can receive the filling. But those people who need the help of the Creator as a luxury have no real *Kelim* [plural of *Kli*], no real need for the Creator to give them the *Kelim* "to deliver their souls from death," but as a luxury.

Hence, they remain with the *vessels of reception*, caring only for their own benefit. They do not feel that they have soiled *Kelim*, that it is impossible to insert *Kedusha* [holiness] into these *Kelim*, since *Kedusha* and self-benefit are opposites.

It therefore follows that only those who understand that if they cannot perform acts of bestowal they will become separate from the Life of Lives will ask the Creator to give them the power to bestow. This is a second nature, as Baal HaSulam said that as the Creator gave the first nature, the desire to receive, it is impossible to change the first nature into a second one. Rather, only the Creator can do this.

As in the exodus from Egypt, the Creator Himself delivered them from the dominion of Pharaoh, King of Egypt, as our sages said in the Passover Haggadah [Passover narrative], "The Lord brought us forth from Egypt, not by an angel, not by a seraph, and not by a messenger, but the Creator Himself."

However, when does one receive the help that the Creator will deliver him from the rule of Egypt, which is the will to receive for himself? It is precisely when a person has a real need and not a luxury. Hence, if one wishes to achieve *Dvekut* with the Creator, one receives help for the need. In other words, he should feel that he is lacking, meaning not lacking completeness, but lacking life, since the evil in him is so extensive. Hence, he is informed from above that he is a sinner, as it is written in *The Zohar* about what is said, "Or make his sin known to him." It asks, "Who made it known to him?" And it replies, "The Creator made it known to him that he has sinned."

This means that the Creator shows him the truth of how remote he is from the Creator and that he is in real need of a life of *Kedusha*. Thus, then one asks of the Creator to help him and give him the desire to bestow because he is deficient of life. And then, since he already has a real need, the Creator gives him the desire to bestow, which is the second nature.

According to the above, we should interpret what is written (in "And of the Miracles"), "And You, in Your great mercy, have placed the strong in the hands of the weak, the many in the hands of the few, and the impure in the hands of the pure." This comes to tell us that before a person comes to a state where he sees how weak he is, how the evil in him is in such profusion that he cannot overcome, and how impure he is, it is impossible to receive the filling from above. This is because he still does not have a complete *Kli* that can receive the filling, which relates to the deficiency of the *Kli*.

This is why it is written, "For you were the fewest of all peoples." In other words, "The Lord did not set His love upon you, nor choose you because you were more in number than any people, for you were the least of all peoples." Thus, when a person sees that he is worse than the whole world, specifically in the state of lowliness does the Creator choose you and deliver you from the domination of Egypt, as it is written, "I am the Lord your God, who brought you forth from the land of Egypt, ...to be your God."

It is written (in the psalm, *Hanukkah Song*), "I will extol You, O Lord, for You have lifted me up, and have not let my enemies rejoice over me." We must understand who are David's enemies, of which

David said, "And have not let my enemies rejoice over me." We should interpret that it is known that David is considered *Malchut*, meaning the kingdom of heaven. That is, the creatures should take upon themselves the burden of the kingdom of heaven with the aim not to receive reward, but because "He is great and ruling," and not for self-benefit.

But the whole world resists this and hates doing everything for the Creator and not for self-benefit. Therefore, *Kedusha* is entirely to bestow, meaning to benefit the Creator, as it is written, "You shall be holy for I the Lord am holy." Thus, as the Creator only bestows upon the creatures, the creatures should bestow upon the Creator, for this is called "equivalence of form," which is considered *Dvekut* with the Creator.

It turns out that all those who wish to work only for themselves and not for the Creator are called "the Creator's enemies," meaning the enemies of the kingdom of heaven. By this they are called "David's enemies," and this is the meaning of David's words, "And have not let my enemies rejoice over me."

Generally speaking, there are only two discernments to speak of: 1) the Creator, 2) the creatures. In other words, the Creator created the creatures to impart them with delight and pleasure, as it is written, "His desire to do good to His creations." Prior to the sin, *Adam HaRishon* had wholeness of his *Neshama*, for at that time, he had *NRN* from *BYA* and *NRN* from *Atzilut*. Only after the sin was there departure of his *NRN* and he remained only with *Nefesh*.

Then he had to repent, to raise all of his *Kelim*, which fell to the *Klipot*, and reunite them with the *Kedusha*, meaning to adhere unto Him once more in order to bestow. This is called "repentance" [Hebrew—"to return"], as it is written in *The Zohar*, "The *Hey* shall return to the *Vav*."

Hey means *Malchut*, which receives in order to receive and all the souls extend from her. This is why *Malchut* is called "the assembly of Israel," which contains all the souls. A correction was placed over this *Malchut*, to correct her into working in order to bestow. This work was given to the creatures, where by engaging in Torah and *Mitzvot* [commandments] in order to bestow, they cause each one to work in order to bestow at the root of his soul in *Malchut* of *Atzilut*. In so doing, they cause unification above, called "the unification of the Creator and His *Shechina* [Divinity]," meaning *Malchut*, who is called *Shechina*, with ZA, who is called "*Vav* of *HaVaYaH*." This is the meaning of "repentance" when *The Zohar* says, "The *Hey* shall return to the *Vav*."

In general, we should make three distinctions: "one," "unique," and "unified." It is written in *The Study of the Ten Sefirot* (Part 1, Item 1), "One indicates that He is in uniform equivalence. Unique indicates what extends from Him, that in Him, all those multiplicities are uniform, like His essence. And Unified indicates that although He affects the many actions, a single force operates all of them and they all return and unite in the form of unique."

The meaning of One is that He is in uniform equivalence, meaning that He created creation with a single desire—to do good to His creations. Unique means that although we see that there are many actions, meaning good and bad, that is, He appears as doing good and bad, He is called "Unique" because His various actions all have a single result—doing good. It follows that He is unique in every single action and does not change through all His various actions. Over each act, there rides a single form—doing good.

One must believe that. In other words, even though a person feels that this action comes from the Creator and it is not a favorable action, one should still believe that this action will enable him to attain the good. This is man's work, to believe that this is so, even though he does not understand it, and to give thanks to the Creator for it.

Our sages said, "One should bless for the bad as one blesses for the good." In other words, a person must believe that it is for his own good, or the Creator would not let him feel those states, since His desire is to do good to the creatures, for this was the thought of creation.

"Unified" means that a person has already been rewarded with seeing how all the many singular ones have adopted the shape of the Unique, meaning he was rewarded with seeing how for each bad, he already received the good that belongs to it. One is rewarded with being unified only after he has corrected his *Kelim* to work in order to bestow. At that time, a person is rewarded with the purpose of creation, which is all good.

This is the meaning of what is written in the psalm, *The Opening of the House for David*. The "opening of the house" refers to the Temple. In the work, a man's heart should be a Temple for the Creator, as it is written, "And let them make Me a sanctuary, that I may dwell among them." One should be rewarded with the presence of the *Shechina*, as our sages said, "The Merciful one needs the heart," meaning that all the Creator needs is man's heart, so as to give him what He wishes to give him.

And when a person is rewarded with being Unified, he sees that he has been rewarded with the construction of the Temple. David said about that, "I will extol You, O Lord, for You have lifted me up, and have not let my enemies rejoice over me." This means that all the enemies—which are desires for self-reception—who were obstructing the *Kedusha*, the Creator saved him from all the enemies and he was rewarded with admittance into *Kedusha*. This is the meaning of the words, "O Lord, You have brought up my soul from the nether-world; You have kept me alive, that I would not go down to the pit."

We say (in "Help of Our Fathers"), "You are the first; You are the last; and besides You, we have no King who redeems and delivers." We also say, "You are before the world was created; You are after the world was created; You are in this world; and You are for the next world." We understand it literally as relating to the greatness of the Creator. However, what does this come to tell us in the work?

It is known that the order of the work is that one must correct his vessels of reception so as to have the strength to do everything in order to bestow. And one should exert and do all that he can.

What "You Have Given the Strong to the Hands of the Weak" Means

At that time, he comes to a resolution that without the help of the Creator, there is no way that he will exit the control of the will to receive for himself. This is called "redemption," when he emerges from the exile in Egypt, that is, the control of the will to receive.

Everyone understands that redemption is a matter for the Creator, since a person sees that it is utterly impossible to emerge from exile by himself. And yet, we should ask, "How does one know that emerging from the exile of the will to receive depends solely on the Creator and is beyond man's capabilities?"

The answer is that in his view, he has already done what he could do but did not move an inch from his will to receive. On the contrary, he sees that since he started the work, in order to reach the degree where all his actions will be for the Creator, now he sees completely differently—that he is regressing!

In other words, he sees that now he is more immersed in self-love than ever. For this reason, when a person is rewarded with redemption, with emerging from this exile, he says that only the Creator can deliver the people of Israel from Egypt, meaning that redemption belongs to the Creator.

However, entering the exile, meaning surrendering to the dominion of the will to receive, this certainly belongs to man. In other words, it is man's fault that he cannot overcome the will to receive for himself. Thus, a person goes into exile by himself.

To that, the writings tell us that this is not as we understand it. And although one should say, "If I am not for me, who is for me?" meaning that everything depends on man's decision, one should still believe that everything is under Providence, meaning that everything depends on the Creator. It is said about that, "You are before the world was created." It is known that *Olam* [world] comes from the word *He'elem* [disappearance] and concealment. And we should know that concerning the exile, there are two discernments to make: 1) when a person does not feel that there are disappearance and concealment, and 2) when a person feels that he is in a state of disappearance and concealment.

This is the meaning of the words, "You are before the world was created." In other words, the fact that a person does not feel that he is in a state of concealment is the Creator's doing. This is for man's benefit, since before a person can correct the evil in him, there is a correction of not seeing the bad. Thus, the Creator created the situation that precedes man's entrance into the disappearance and concealment.

This is the meaning of "You are before the world was created," meaning before the concealment was created. Afterward, a person comes to a state of disappearance and concealment. One comes into that state precisely according to his effort in Torah and *Mitzvot* to achieve a degree where all his actions are in order to bestow.

This is the meaning of the words, "You are after the world was created." Thus, the fact that one came into disappearance and concealment was from You. This is the meaning of "You are after the world was created." And after he is already in exile, then comes redemption, and this is, "You are the first, and You are the last."

What Does It Mean that Man's Blessing Is the Blessing of the Sons, in the Work?

Article No. 14, Tav-Shin-Nun-Aleph, 1990/91

It is written in *The Zohar* (*VaYechi*, Items 371-372), "He asks about the verse, 'And he blessed Joseph and said, 'will bless the lads.'' We should look in this verse, for it says, 'He blessed Joseph,' but we find no blessing for Joseph here, that he blessed Joseph, but his sons. He replies, 'Rabbi Yosi said, '*Et* [of]' is precisely it, since *Et* implies *Malchut*.' It is written, 'blessed Joseph,' which is the blessing of his sons, since his sons—Menashe and Ephraim—are regarded as *Malchut*, which is called *Et*. And when his sons are blessed, he is blessed first. This is why it writes Joseph, too, since a man's sons are his blessing."

We should understand what it means that if the sons are blessed, Joseph is also blessed, in the work. What does this tell us?

It is known that all our work is that we must achieve *Dvekut* [adhesion] with the Creator, which is equivalence of form, meaning to bestow, just as the Creator bestows upon the lower ones. Because of it, we were given the work in Torah and *Mitzvot* [commandments/good deeds], to do them in order to bestow. By this, one becomes corrected at the root of his soul, which is *Malchut de Atzilut*, which is regarded as the whole of Israel. This is why *Malchut* is called "the assembly of Israel," since all the souls come from her.

Hence, to the extent that they work in order to bestow, they cause *Malchut*, who is called *Shechina* [Divinity], to unite with the Creator, called *ZA*, or *Yesod de ZA*, for *Yesod* is called "righteous," who bestows upon *Malchut*. However, when *Malchut* is receiving for herself, she has no equivalence with the Giver, called "the Creator," and this is regarded as the *Shechina* being far from the Creator due to disparity of form. This is considered that the Creator cannot bestow upon *Malchut*, and thus the souls have no abundance.

When the Creator cannot bestow upon the lower ones, due to the disparity of form between them, this is called "the sorrow of the *Shechina*." That is, from the perspective of the receiver, she cannot receive abundance because if she receives abundance for the lower ones, it will all go to the *Klipot* [shells/peels], called "receiving in order to receive." It is also called "sorrow" from the perspective of the Giver because the thought of creation is to do good to His creations, but now He cannot give them the delight and pleasure because everything that the creatures will have will go to the *Klipot*.

Hence, the Giver is sorry that He cannot give, like a mother who wants to feed her baby but the baby is sick and cannot eat. At that time, there is sorrow on the part of the Giver. In the words of *The Zohar*, this is considered that there is sorrow above that there cannot be unification, meaning for the Giver to give abundance to the receiver. The Giver of abundance to the lower ones is called *Malchut*, who receives abundance from *ZA*. In the words of our sages, this is called "Israel nourish their Father in heaven." What is the nourishment? It is that Israel qualify themselves to become fit to receive abundance. This is His nourishment, since this was the purpose of creation, which is to do good to His creations.

Therefore, when the lower ones engage in Torah and *Mitzvot* with the aim to bestow, they cause unification above, meaning that *Malchut*, too, who receives the abundance for the lower ones, to become a giver. This is called the "unification of the Creator and the *Shechina*." That is, there is contentment above because the lower ones cause abundance to flow downward.

But if the lower ones do not work with the aim to bestow, it causes the sorrow of the *Shechina*. That is, there is sorrow above that *Malchut*, who is called *Shechina*, cannot bestow delight and pleasure to the creatures.

However, we should make two discernments concerning the sorrow of the *Shechina*. We should discern that there is sorrow from the perspective of the Giver, called "Creator," and there is the sorrow of the *Shechina*, who is called "the mother of the sons," meaning the "assembly of Israel," who engendered the souls of Israel.

Also, we attribute to *Malchut* the giving of vitality to the *Klipot* [shells/peels], as it is written, "And her legs go down to death." The meaning of "her legs" is *Malchut* at her end, which is called "legs." She descends in order to bestow vitality to the *Klipot*, who are called "death," so as to sustain them. Otherwise, the *Klipot* would not exist. Since the *Klipot* are needed, as it is written, "and God made it so they would fear Him," *Malchut* sustains them just so they persist, meaning the amount that enables them to exist.

This is also called "very thin light," so they can exist. That is, we see that there is pleasure in the corporeal world, and that the whole world chases this pleasure in order to obtain it. In general, this pleasure is clothed in three things, called "envy," "lust," and "honor." Were it not for the thin light there, which places the pleasure within these corporeal things, who could exist in the world? since without pleasure, it is impossible to live because the purpose of creation was with the aim to do good to His creations. Hence, without good, it is impossible to live.

However, we should understand why it is called "the sorrow of the *Shechina*," since the Creator created the world in order to do good to His creations. Thus, it should have been called "the sorrow of the Creator." That is, the fact that the creatures do not engage in Torah and *Mitzvot* in order to bestow causes that the Creator will be unable to bestow, so the sorrow should be attributed to the Creator, not to the *Shechina*, who is called *Malchut*.

Baal HaSulam said, What is the difference between the Creator and the *Shechina*? He said that it is one thing. It is as *The Zohar* says, "He is *Shochen* [dweller] and she is *Shechina*." This means that both names are one thing, but are light and *Kli* [vessel]. That is, the place where the *Shochen* is revealed is called *Shechina*. Hence, they are the same thing, but where the light cannot be revealed because of the disparity of form between the light and the *Kli*, it is considered that the *Shechina*, where the *Shochen* should be revealed, is deficient.

For this reason, we relate to the *Shechina*, since the *Shochen* cannot be revealed to the lower ones due to the disparity of form. And since we are speaking only from the perspective of the *Kelim* [vessels], we call the exile "*Shechina* in the dust," "*Shechina* in exile," since we are speaking from the perspective of the *Kelim* and not from that of the lights. This is why it is called "the sorrow of the *Shechina*," as though she suffers from her inability to bestow upon the lower ones. But if we elaborate on the details, we should say that there is also sorrow here on the part of the Giver, who is called "the Giver to the lower ones." But when we speak from the perspective of the *Kelim*, we call it "the sorrow of the *Shechina*."

According to the above, in order to have contentment above because "He spoke and His will was done." This means that in order for His desire to do good to His creations to be carried out, so the creatures will receive from Him delight and pleasure, which is the joy that the created beings cause above—as our sages said, "There has never been such joy before Him as on the day when heaven and earth were created"—when the creatures walk on the straight path, when all their actions are in order to bestow contentment upon their Maker, they make *Malchut*, which is the root of the souls, work in order to bestow what she receives for the souls, meaning for the souls, so they become able to receive in order to bestow. This is considered that the creatures cause the unification of the Creator and His *Shechina*.

By this, abundance is bestowed upon the lower ones because the abundance that is extended is for the purpose of correction. That is, through this reception, in a manner that is in equivalence of form, there is pleasure above, since during the reception of the abundance there is no shame there because of the correction that they receive in order to bestow.

According to the above, we will understand what we asked, What is "A man's blessing is the blessing of the sons"? When the sons, meaning the created beings, who are called "the sons of the Creator," receive the abundance in a correction of a blessing, meaning that they want to receive only because they want to bestow contentment upon the Maker, for "blessing" means bestowal, which is *Hesed* [mercy], meaning to bestow, as it is written in *The Zohar* ("Introduction of The Book of Zohar," Item 37), that the letter *Bet* is *Hesed*, which indicates blessing, which is *Hassadim*, which is the hall of *Hochma*, who is included in the *Bet*.

It follows that by the sons engaging in blessing, meaning working in order to bestow, they cause *Malchut* above to connect with ZA. This is called "the unification of the Creator with His *Shechina*." From this unification, they can bestow above, as well, since the sons engage in bestowal. This causes the blessing at the root above to be drawn down to the sons, and this is considered that the people of Israel receive the abundance from their father in heaven.

It is written in *The Zohar* (*Beresheet*, Item 131), "The reason why the great *Mochin* of Shabbat [Sabbath] are called 'inheritance' is that all the *Mochin* that the children of Israel receive from their father in heaven is by an awakening from below, as they said, 'I labored and found, believe.' It is as people purchase possessions in this world. The greater the possession, the greater should be the exertion that they give for it. But the lights of Shabbat do not require any labor."

The reason that the lights of Shabbat do not require labor is that Shabbat is the completion of heaven and earth, a semblance of the end of correction, when everything is corrected. Hence, before Shabbat, there are the six weekdays, which imply the six thousand years of work until we achieve the end of correction. Likewise, there are the six workdays, which is the time of work, and Shabbat is the rest.

This is why our sages said (*Avoda Zarah* 3), "He who did not toil on the eve of Shabbat, what will he eat on Shabbat?"

It follows that by exerting to emerge from the control of self-love and be rewarded with vessels of bestowal, which is a blessing, by this there is contentment above, in that they can bestow upon the sons.

Now we can understand what *The Zohar* answers about what is written, "He blessed Joseph," and we did not find a blessing here that he blessed Joseph, but rather his sons. He explains that when his sons are blessed, he is blessed. This is why it is written, "Joseph," too, since "man's sons are his blessing." That is, Joseph is called "the giver," and his "sons," explains *The Zohar*, "his sons—Menashe and Ephraim—are regarded as *Malchut*, which is called *Et*."

This means that *Malchut*, who is called *Et* [of], is because she contains all the letters from *Aleph* [first letter in the Hebrew alphabet] to *Tav* [last letter], since the letters are called *Kelim* and the receivers of the abundance, which is called "his sons," since she receives for the created beings. It follows that by his sons being blessed, he becomes blessed, too. That is, the giver, who is Joseph, called *Yesod*, gives to *Malchut*, when *Malchut* can receive for the sons. At that time, *Malchut* is called "The mother of the sons is glad, Hallelujah."

When the lower ones engage in Torah and *Mitzvot* in order to bestow, they cause at the root of their soul, which is *Malchut*, to equalize in form with the Giver. This is called "unification." At that time, the abundance is poured to the lower ones. Thus, they cause *Malchut* to be able to receive abundance for them. Hence, *Malchut* is called "the mother of the sons is glad."

What Does It Mean that Man's Blessing Is the Blessing of the Sons?

Hallelu-KoH [Hallelujah] means *Hellolu* [praise] *Yod-Hey* [the Creator] are called *Hochma* and *Bina*, who give the abundance to the quality of Joseph, and from Joseph, who is *Yesod*, to *Malchut*, who is called *Et*. This is the meaning of what is written, "He blessed Joseph," and this is the meaning of "man's blessing are his sons." If the sons are blessed, it is considered a blessing for man, when he can bestow delight and pleasure.

However, this work, for all his actions to be in order to bestow, is hard work, since all the organs of the body object to it. This is against man's nature, who was created with a desire to receive for his own benefit. This is the meaning of what is written (Psalms 22), "And I am a worm and not a man, a disgrace of man and despised by the people."

We should interpret that "I" refers to "I am the Lord your God," that this quality in him is as a worm, meaning as weak as a worm. "And not a man" means that when I want to cling to "I am the Lord your God," they say that it is unbecoming of an intelligent and reasonable person to go above reason. This is more like an insane person.

"A disgrace of man" is the work of faith above reason. This is a disgrace for a person who thinks that man's main purpose is to cling to "I am the Lord your God." In other words, wanting to be rewarded with "I" being as "the Lord your God," means that he will be rewarded personally, and this is called "your God." At that time, they curse and swear, meaning they say that this work belongs to angels, not to people, that it is a disgrace for a person to want to do this, even though he tells them, "But you see that there many people are walking on the path toward being rewarded with the Lord being their God."

At that time, they say about these people that they are simply "despised by the people," meaning that the nations of the world in one's body tell him that this work, for a person to be rewarded with the quality, "I am the Lord your God," belongs to the despised, meaning to lowly people, that it is a disgrace to even speak to them, since they are walking on the path of the Creator like mindless fools.

In any case, when one wants to overcome their complaints, it is hard work and there are ascents and descents here. A person needs extra efforts because the arguments of the nations of the world in a person stand ready to find some weakness in the work so as to show man that he is wasting his efforts, since this work is not for him, and they advise him to escape the campaign. A person is powerless to stand against them, but only to increase his prayer that the Creator will help him defeat the enemies within him.

This is the meaning of the verse (Psalms 32), "Many are the afflictions of the wicked, and he who trusts in the Lord, *Hesed* [mercy] will surround him." We should understand what is "Many are the afflictions of the wicked." It seems as though because of it, "He who trusts in the Lord, *Hesed* will surround him." But in the work, we speak of one person who comprises the entire world.

The meaning is that as long as one is under the control of the will to receive, he is called "wicked," since he cannot say that His guidance is good and does good. Hence, he suffers torments when he wants to work in order to bestow. A person asks, "Why did I not suffer afflictions when I engaged in Torah and *Mitzvot* before I began to do the holy work, that it will be in order to bestow? I had joy in the work and I was always happy, since I believed in reward and punishment, and this is why I observed Torah and *Mitzvot*."

But now that he has begun the work of bestowal, he feels pain when he wants to engage in Torah and *Mitzvot*, and it is hard for him to do anything for the sake of the Creator. Each time, he sees how far he is from *Kedusha* [holiness], for *Kedusha* means equivalence of form, and now he sees that he is far from it.

The answer is that he should believe that the fact that now he has become farther from the Creator and he is asking, this feeling that he feels, that now he is worse than when he worked in order to receive reward, is not because he is really worse than before. It is not that now more evil has been added to him and because of it he is worse. Rather, it is because now that he has done many good deeds, the truth was revealed to him, that the evil in him governs him.

Conversely, before he had the good, he could not be shown the truth, since the bad and the good must always be balanced. It follows that he is not in such a descent that he thinks that this work is not for him and he wants to escape the campaign. Rather, this feeling comes to him precisely when he has good.

Yet, he believes in the Creator that he was given from above to feel these states of pain. While one is still in a degree of "wicked," when he cannot believe in a guidance of delight and pleasure, when that person overcomes, it is called "He who trusts in the Lord." At that time he is rewarded with "*Hesed* will surround him." We should interpret that *Yesovevnu* [will surround him] comes from the word *Mesovav* [consequence]. In other words, the pains that the wicked suffered was the reason for the *Hesed*, with his meriting the quality of *Hesed*. It follows that "Many are the afflictions of the wicked" caused him to be rewarded with *Hesed*.

What Is the Blessing, "Who Made a Miracle for Me in This Place," in the Work?

Article No. 15, Tav-Shin-Nun-Aleph, 1990/91

Our sages said (*Berachot* 54), "A person had a miracle and was saved from a lion. Raba told him, 'Whenever you come there, bless, 'Blessed is He, who made a miracle for me in this place.''" We should understand what this comes to teach us in the work.

It is known that the purpose of creation was because his desire is to do good to His creations. For this purpose, He created in the creatures a desire and yearning to receive delight and pleasure. Otherwise, if there is no desire for the pleasure, a person cannot enjoy, as we see in nature that if a person has no desire for something, he cannot enjoy. For example, if a person is not hungry, he cannot enjoy eating, etc. Therefore, we see and say that the Creator created within our nature a desire to receive delight and pleasure.

What Is the Blessing, "Who Made a Miracle for Me in This Place"?

We should not ask, Why did the Creator create such a nature? Since our sages said (*Hagigah* 11), "If one asks about before the world was created, the writing tells us, 'since the day when God created man on the earth.'" This means that we cannot ask anything about why when He created the world, He created it specifically with this nature that we see. After all, He could have created with a different nature. We cannot ask about this, but we learn everything by way of "By Your actions, we know You." That is, we begin to learn from the actions we see and not before.

Also, we see another nature, that the branch wants to resemble its root. That is, as the quality of the root of the creatures, which is the Creator, is to bestow and not receive, likewise, when one must eat the bread of shame, he is ashamed. In the words of *The Zohar*, this is called "the bread of shame." According to this nature, it follows that when a person receives from the Creator into one's vessels of reception, which contradict the quality of the Creator, who is the Giver, he feels unpleasantness. Because of this, there was a correction called "*Tzimtzum* [restriction] and concealment," where as long as the lower one has no equivalence of form, called "desire to bestow," a person is placed under concealment and hiding of the *Kedusha* [holiness]. We also should not ask about this, Why did the Creator create a nature of shame? And why did He make the branch want to resemble its root? It is all for the above reason, that we cannot ask about prior to creation.

The *Kli* of the created beings is the desire to receive pleasure. Before the will to receive was created, we have nothing to speak of. We attribute this *Kli* [vessel] to the Creator, meaning that we need not work with this *Kli*, but every person who is created, if he did not corrupt the *Kli*, that *Kli* is perfect. That is wherever the will to receive sees that there is a place from which it is possible to derive pleasure, it immediately runs there.

This is not so with the *Kli* called "desire to bestow," since a person wants equivalence of form. Since we attribute this *Kli* to the created being, meaning a person has to make this *Kli*, since the creature wants equivalence of form, for this reason, it is up to a person to do this.

This is as Baal HaSulam said about the verse, "which God has created to do." "Has created" refers to the *Kli*, called "will to receive," and "to do" pertains to the creatures, who must make the *Kli* called "desire to bestow." This is not from the nature that the Creator created. Rather, He began creation from the will to receive, and you, the created beings, must make the desire to bestow. Therefore, when a person must begin to work in order to bestow, it is a different nature than the one with which man was created.

For this reason, all that one should do in the work of the Creator is to make the *Kli*, which is the opposite action to the *Kli* with which man was created. When one begins to come into the work of bestowal, he still does not feel how much his will to receive interrupts his work of bestowal. This is a correction so that man will not see the truth about the measure of evil within him, since when he sees the evil within him he will certainly run from the work and will not even want to begin this work. This is why Maimonides says that we must first accustom a person in *Lo Lishma* [not for Her sake], "until they gain knowledge and acquire much wisdom," and then they are shown the matter of *Lishma* [for Her sake], called "in order to bestow."

We should know that a person being governed by the will to receive for oneself is called "exile in Egypt," since when we begin this work, we are gradually shown from above the measure of governance of evil on us, as it is written, "And the children of Israel sighed from the work." That is, they saw that they could not perform the work of bestowal that they started to do, since the Egyptians controlled them. At that time, they saw that they could not emerge from the exile in Egypt, but the Creator can deliver them. This is called "a miracle," for anything that one cannot do by himself, but by help from above, is called "a miracle." This is the miracle of the exodus from Egypt

We should know that when a person wants to achieve *Dvekut* [adhesion] with the Creator, he has ascents and descents. The order is that during the descent, when a person comes into a state of despair, he sometimes comes to a state of wondering about all the labor he has done in vain. This is called "pondering the beginning," when he wants to escape from the work of the Creator altogether. But suddenly, he receives an awakening from above and receives vitality and passion for the work, and completely forgets that he ever had a descent. Rather, he is content with the ascent. At that time, a person cannot enjoy the ascent more than when he was placed under the governance of evil during the descent.

We should know that the exile he feels, that he is in exile, is measured not by the exile, but by the sensation of bad and suffering that he suffers because he is in exile. Then, when he is tormented because he is under the rule of oppressors and he must do all that they demand of him, and he has no right to do what he wants, but he must serve and carry out all that the nations of the world in his body demand, and he is powerless to betray them, to the extent of the pain he feels and his desire to escape them, to that extent he can enjoy the redemption.

As we see, it is written about a Hebrew slave (Exodus 21:2), "If you buy a Hebrew slave, he shall serve for six years, and on the seventh he shall go free for free." Certainly, the slave should be happy that he has been liberated and is in his own right, and that he has no master over him. Yet, we see what the Torah says, "And if the slave says, 'I love my master, my wife and my children, I will not go free.'" We see that it is possible that a person will want to remain a slave. And yet, it is written (Deuteronomy 16:12), "Remember that you were a slave in Egypt."

This means that being a slave is a bad thing, yet sometimes a person wants to remain a slave. Thus, what does it mean that it is written, "Remember that you were a slave in Egypt"? And who says that being a slave is so bad? After all, there are people who want to be slaves, as was said, that the slave said, "I love my master." The thing is that exile is according to the level of suffering and pain that one feels in the exile. To that extent, it is possible to be happy about the redemption. This is like light and *Kli* [vessel], meaning that the suffering we suffer from something is the *Kli* that can receive light if it liberates itself from the suffering.

For this reason, in the exile in Egypt, where it is written, "Remember that you were a slave in Egypt," it means that being a slave is so bad because there, in Egypt, the people of Israel suffered. This is why the writing says "Remember," meaning that we must remember the suffering we suffered there, and then it is possible to be happy about the redemption from Egypt.

There, in Egypt, the writing says, "I also heard the groaning of the children of Israel because the Egyptians are enslaving them, and I remembered My covenant." It follows that in Egypt, when they were slaves, it is written, "We were slaves to Pharaoh in Egypt," because they suffered. He also says, "And the children of Israel sighed from the work." Therefore, we were given the commandment to remember Egypt, as it is written, "so that you remember the day when you came out of the land of Egypt all the days of your life."

It follows that according to the rule, "There is no light without a *Kli*, no filling without a lack," although we have already come out of Egypt, we should rejoice at the redemption from Egypt. For this reason, we must remember the exile in Egypt, meaning remember and imagine how the people of Israel suffered in the exile in Egypt. Then we can enjoy the redemption from Egypt even today.

Otherwise, we cannot rejoice over the redemption from Egypt because the suffering are called "the *Kelim* [vessels] to receive the joy." This is why we see about the Hebrew slave that he did not want to go free. We could ask, How can someone not want to go free? The answer is that because he did not suffer while being a slave, he does not want to go free, as is explained when he says, "I love my master, my wife and my children, I will not go free." But concerning the exile in Egypt, it is written, "so that you remember the day when you came out of the land of Egypt," since there they suffered, as it is written, "And the children of Israel sighed from the work."

Accordingly, we can understand what we asked, What does it mean in the work when a person should bless in the place where a miracle was done to him. The thing is that when a person begins the work of bestowal, he comes to states of ascents and descents. An ascent is that after a person has been under the governance of the will to receive, enslaved to fulfill all its wishes, and he wanted to overcome it and not obey it, but the will to receive was stronger than him, that person suffered from being removed from the Creator.

Afterward, he received an awakening from above and began once more to feel some elation of *Kedusha*. At that time, the person wants to annul before Him "like a candle before a torch," and then a person enjoys the state of ascent. However, one cannot elicit from the ascent, progress in the work because he does not appreciate the nearing he has now received from the Creator, since he does not have the *Kelim* [vessels]. In other words, during the ascent, he forgets that he once had a descent. Thus, although he feels that now he is close to the Creator and he appreciates it, he soon forgets. Naturally, he no longer has a *Kli*, meaning a lack, so he can appreciate, as it is written, "as the advantage of the light from within the darkness." For this reason, he makes no progress as he should be making through the ascent.

Hence, during an ascent, he must remember and say, "In this place, where I now have an ascent, I had a descent and the Creator saved me and raised me from the netherworld, and I emerged from death, called 'removal from the Creator,' and I have been rewarded with some measure of nearing to the Creator, which is called 'some measure of *Dvekut* with the Life of Lives.'"

For this, a person should be thankful, for by this he has now come to a state where there he suffered, and now he is in a mood of delight and pleasure because the Creator bringing him closer has given him new *Kelim* of a lack that he can fill with the state of ascent that he is in now.

It follows that he extends a light of joy in new *Kelim* that he has obtained now by looking at the miracle that he has had, where the Creator saved him. Therefore, when he considers the suffering, it is as though now he is the recipient of the suffering, and now he fills them up with pleasure.

It follows that depicting to himself the state of descent causes him that the ascent he has received now will spread in new *Kelim* according to the rule "There is no light without a *Kli*." Hence, during the ascent, when he begins to contemplate the state of descent that he had, the suffering of the descent are regarded as *Kelim* in which the light of the ascent may spread.

This is similar to what was said above concerning exile and redemption, that according to the suffering he feels during the exile, so he can enjoy the redemption. That is, the exile is the *Kelim* of the redemption. This means that the redemption cannot fill more than the *Kelim* it has from the exile. This is why in the work, when a person depicts to himself the state of descent, this is considered what our sages said, that a person should make a blessing, "Blessed is He who made a miracle for me in this place."

There are many ways to depict the suffering. Let us take as an example, a person who wants to rise before dawn, and he set the alarm clock. But when the alarm goes off, the body does not want to get up. The body feels suffering if he should rise out of bed now. Nevertheless, he sluggishly overcomes and comes to the seminary. When he sees that there are many people sitting and learning, he receives a desire and yearning to participate in the lessons, and he becomes happy and high-spirited, and forgets in what way he got out of bed and came to the seminary. And if a person wants to receive new *Kelim* in which there will be joy, he must depict to himself in what way he got out of bed, meaning what level of desire he had then, and what mood he is in now. Then he can also say, "Blessed is He who made a miracle for me in this place," meaning how the Creator now gave him nearness to Him. From this he acquires new *Kelim* where the joy over the Creator bringing him closer to Him can spread.

Likewise, a person should accustom himself with anything to compare between the time of suffering and the time of pleasure, and to bless for the miracle of delivering him from suffering to a state of pleasure. By this, he will be able to thank the Creator and enjoy in the new *Kelim* that have been added to him now when he compares the two times to one another. From this, a person can advance in the work.

This is as Baal HaSulam said, that it does not matter whether a person receives from the Creator something great or small. What matters is how much a person thanks the Creator. To the extent of his gratitude, so grows the giving that the Creator gives. Therefore, we must take note to be grateful, to appreciate His gift, so we can approach the Creator. Hence, when a person always looks during the ascent at the state he was in while in descent, meaning how he felt during the descent, he can make a distinction as in, "as the advantage of the light from within the darkness," and he already has new *Kelim* in which to receive joy and be thankful to the Creator. This is the meaning of what is written, that a person should bless, "Blessed is He who made a miracle for me in this place," meaning in the place where he is now, during the ascent, since there cannot be an ascent if there was no prior state of descent.

However, how can there be a descent if a person was not previously in an ascent and descended from it? The answer is that usually, every person thinks that he is fine the way he is. That is, a person does not see that he is worse than other people in his surroundings. Therefore, he goes with the flow of the rest of the world—a little bit of learning, a little bit of praying, a little bit of charity and good deeds and so forth. But his main concern is to earn well and have a nice apartment and furniture, etc.

This is so because he feels that if he has made an arrangement for himself with the Creator concerning how much he should work for Him, once he has done all his spiritual chores, he feels complete and is free to worry about improving his material state. That person always sees that as much as he may try to make his corporeality complete, he always sees that he is in deficit compared to others. This is regarded as a person being in a state of wholeness.

However, when he begins the work of bestowal, he comes to a state of descent, since he sees how far he is from the intention to bestow. It follows that now that he has descended from the previous period, when he understood that all he needed was to observe Torah and *Mitzvot* [commandments/good deeds], and did not pay attention to the intention to bestow, but then he received an awakening from above and began to annul before Him like a candle before a torch, and forgot the state of descent that he had. Then, when he is now in a state of ascent, he can say, "Blessed is He who made a miracle for me in this place." In other words, previously he was in a state where he had a road accident and he became unconscious about spiritual life. That is, he completely forgot about the need to work in order to bestow. Afterward, the Creator helped him and he came to, meaning regained contact with the Creator. By this depiction, he can receive new *Kelim* so he can receive abundance of joy at the Creator helping him.

However, we must know that when a person asks the Creator to bring him closer to His work, meaning to do the holy work for the sake of the Creator, and a person thinks that the Creator does not hear his prayer, and he has already prayed many times, but it is as though the Creator does not hear his prayer, Baal HaSulam said about that that one should believe that the fact that now he is praying to the Creator, he should not say that this was by his own awakening, to pray to the Creator to bring him closer. Rather, even before he came to pray, the Creator already answered his prayer. That is, a person should appreciate the fact that now he can pray to the Creator; this is regarded as having contact with the Creator. This is a very important thing, and he must be delighted at the fact that the Creator has given him a desire and yearning to pray to Him.

Accordingly, we should interpret what our sages said (*Megillah* 29), "Rabbi Shimon Bar Yochai says, 'Come and see how fond is the Creator of Israel, for wherever they exile, the *Shechina* [Divinity] is with them.'" We should interpret that "the exile of Israel" means that the quality of Israel in a person has drifted from the Creator, meaning that a person suffers because the quality of Israel in him, meaning the desire *Yashar-El* [straight to the Creator], where one should do everything for the sake of the Creator, that desire is in exile under the rule of desires of the nations of the world, and he regrets it.

We should ask, Why specifically now is he feeling removed from the Creator, while prior to this state, he felt that he was far from buying a bigger flat or nicer furniture? All of a sudden, he received suffering from a different remoteness—that he is far from the Creator! The answer is that "the *Shechina* is with them," meaning that the *Shechina* gave him this feeling that he is far from the Creator. This is the meaning of, "Before one prays to the Creator, the Creator gives him a desire and yearning to pray."

Why We Need "Reply unto Your Heart," to Know that the Lord, He Is God, in the Work

Article No. 16, Tav-Shin-Nun-Aleph, 1990/91

The *Zohar* asks (*VaEra*, Items 89-90), "'Know this day and reply unto your heart that the Lord, He is God.' He asks, 'This verse should have said, 'Know this day that the Lord, He is God,' and in the end, 'And reply unto your heart,' since knowing that the Lord is God qualifies him to reply so to the heart. And if he already replied to his heart, it is especially so if he already has knowledge. Also, it should have said, 'reply unto your heart' [with one *Bet*] instead of 'heart' [with a double *Bet*].' He replies, 'Moses said that if you want to insist on this and to know that the Lord, He is God, then 'reply unto your heart.' Know that heart [with a double *Bet*] means that the good inclination and the evil inclination, which reside in the heart, have mingled in one another and are one, so the bad qualities of the evil inclination will become good, meaning he will serve the Lord with them and will not sin through them. Then you will find that the Lord [*HaVaYaH*] is God, that the quality of judgment, called 'God,' is included in *HaVaYaH*, which is the quality of mercy."

We should understand what it comes to teach us when *The Zohar* says that it is impossible to know that "The Lord, He is God," before a person achieves the degree of "Reply unto your heart." We should know what is the quality of "God" in the work, and what is the quality of mercy in the work, which is called *HaVaYaH*. We should also understand what is the evil inclination in the work, and what is the good inclination in the work. That is, in the work, when a person wants to achieve *Dvekut* [adhesion] with the Creator, what is the evil inclination and what is the good inclination?

For the general public, this is simple: Those who observe Torah and *Mitzvot* [commandments/good deeds] are regarded as following the way of the good inclination. If they transgress the Torah and *Mitzvot*, this is regarded as following the advice of the evil inclination. But what is it in the work, when walking on the path toward achieving *Dvekut* with the Creator?

It is known that the creatures were born with a nature called will to receive for one's own sake. For this reason, man cannot do anything that does not yield some benefit for oneself. Hence, the Torah tells us, "If you observe Torah and *Mitzvot*, I will reward you, as it is written, 'If you indeed obey My commandments, I will give the rain for your land in its season, and you will eat and be satiated.'"

Maimonides says (*Hilchot Teshuva*, Chapter 5), "They are taught to work only out of fear and in order to receive reward. Until they gain much knowledge and acquire much wisdom, they are taught that secret little-by-little." It follows that for the general public, the evil inclination and the good inclination pertain only to the observance of Torah and *Mitzvot*, but they do not speak at all about the prohibition to work in order to receive reward.

However, when speaking about the work of bestowal, the evil inclination and the good inclination have completely different meanings. The good inclination means that it leads a person to obtain the delight and pleasure that He wished to impart upon His creations, as it is written, that the purpose of creation is because of His desire to do good to His creations. But in order to avoid the shame, there were *Tzimtzum* [restriction] and concealment where the creatures cannot receive the good before they have equivalence of form, called *Dvekut*. This is obtained by doing everything for the sake of the Creator. At that time, the *Tzimtzum* is lifted and there is room for the good to spread within it. This is called the "good inclination."

The evil inclination is when the inclination advises a person to work only for self-benefit, meaning only to receive. Since this is disparity of form from the Creator, whose desire is only to bestow, and that disparity of form causes man never to be able to receive the delight and pleasure, therefore, this inclination is called "bad" because it harms a person by not letting him work in order to bestow, which causes him not to be able to receive delight and pleasure.

According to the above, we can interpret what it means that a person should work with himself to love the Creator with both inclinations. The thing is that as long as one has two inclinations, they are disputed. Sometimes the good prevails, and sometimes the bad prevails. It follows that two forces work within man in a mixture. This is called "light and darkness working together." As long as the bad has not surrendered, the *Tzimtzum* and concealment that were on the *Kelim* [vessels] of the evil inclination—called "will to receive for oneself"—control it, and he cannot receive the delight and pleasure.

It follows that then a person does not obtain the good. For this reason, he is in a state of "judgment," meaning he says that he does not see the Creator's mercy, so he will be able to say that the Creator leads the world with the quality of mercy, but rather with the quality of judgment, since the person cannot see His guidance as delight and pleasure.

Thus, as long as one has no vessels of bestowal, a person does not have *Kelim* in which to be able to receive delight and pleasure. Naturally, he remains devoid of delight and pleasure.

The person says, "Who is to blame for this? Only the Creator, for not giving the creatures what He should give." That is, since creation was in order to delight His creatures, because of the correction so that there would not be the bread of shame, the creatures are unfit to see it because of the inherent evil in man, which is called in the work, "evil inclination."

Accordingly, we can understand what we asked, "What is judgment and what is mercy in the work? Also what is the good inclination and what is the evil inclination in the work?" "Judgment" means that a judgment was passed over the vessels of reception, called "will to receive for oneself," that the light does not shine within it. It follows that when we say that there is judgment in the world, it means that there are no vessels of bestowal that can receive delight and pleasure in the world. For this reason, suffering and lack reign in the world.

But when there are vessels of bestowal in the world called "mercy," as our sages said about the verse, "And to cleave unto Him, as He is merciful, so you are merciful," meaning that as the Creator is the giver, so man should see that he has vessels of bestowal. When man has vessels of bestowal, the Creator's quality of mercy becomes apparent, meaning that the Creator bestows delight and pleasure to the creatures in the *Kelim* of mercy that the creatures have.

Thus, once a person obtains the vessels of bestowal, meaning that the evil inclination has surrendered to the good, it means that the evil inclination already wants to work in order to bestow. This is called "Reply unto your heart," meaning both hearts. Then he realizes that "the Lord [*HaVaYaH*], He is God." In other words, until now, it was only mercy and not judgment. That is, what he saw, that His guidance was judgment, now he sees that this was a reason to come to the quality of mercy. Therefore, now they see that "the Lord, He is God," that the quality of judgment is included in the *HaVaYaH*, which is all mercy. But before he achieved the state of "Reply unto your heart," His guidance seemed to him as good and bad.

By this we can interpret the meaning of the verse, "And God made it that He would be feared." That is, the Creator deliberately made it so there would be governance to the *Klipot* [shells/peels], so "He would be feared," meaning to create a need to obtain the greatness of the Creator. Otherwise, everyone would remain still, without knowledge of *Kedusha* [holiness], and would settle for the work of observing Torah and *Mitzvot* without any need to work to be rewarded with the greatness of the Creator. They would remain with the same mind they had when they were little children and would have no need for the Creator's help.

We must know and understand what our sages said, "I have created the evil inclination; I have created the Torah as a spice." This means that only when a person has evil inclination, he needs the spice that is found in the Torah. Otherwise, he does not need the Torah, since he can observe *Mitzvot* without the Torah. But when he has the evil inclination and he comes and asks "What is this work for you?" or when he asks Pharaoh's question, "Who is the Lord that I should obey His voice?" and he must overcome him, then he needs His help.

The Zohar says that the help of the Creator is the light of Torah. That is, it is considered that he is given a soul from above, by which he can overcome the bad within him. It follows that if there were no *Klipot*, man would have no need to receive the help of Torah from above. This is called "And God made it that He would be feared."

There are many issues concerning the help that comes from above:

1) The help is simple: The Creator gives him the kingdom of heaven called "permanent faith." Since before a person is rewarded with vessels of bestowal, it is impossible to have faith because there is disparity of form between the creature and the Creator, a person is still unfit to receive the good. Therefore, when he receives bad, he must lose the measure of faith that he had, since this is a correction so he would not slander the Creator. For this reason, before one is rewarded with faith, he must have vessels of bestowal, since when he has equivalence of form, the *Tzimtzum* that was on the vessels of reception is lifted from him and he receives delight and pleasure. Only then can he be at the degree of permanent faith. It follows

that the Creator must give the first assistance, giving him vessels of bestowal, which are called "second nature."

2) By having constant disturbances from the *Klipot*, he always needs the help of the Creator. By this, a person needs the Creator's help, and through the help that he receives from above each time, it is possible that the NRNHY that he has in his soul will be revealed to him. It is known that there is no filling without a need. Hence, the *Klipot* are the cause of the revelation of the *Kedusha*, as it is written, "And God made it that He would be feared."

According to the above, it follows that the thoughts that the *Klipot* send to a person cause deficiencies in a person, and deficiencies are called "*Kelim* to receive fillings to fill the lack in the *Kelim*." In other words, the questions that the *Klipot* ask, which are the wicked's questions and Pharaoh's questions, called "Who" and "What," cause a deficiency in a person, which pushes him to ask the Creator to help him overcome those questions. It follows that these *Klipot* keep a person walking on the right path that leads to *Dvekut* with the Creator. At that time, we see that the *Klipot* were not enemies of the *Kedusha*, as it seemed during the work. Rather, now we see that they are the ones that caused being rewarded with the *Kedusha*.

The like of this is presented in *The Zohar* (*Beresheet*, Item 175), "'And there is no God with Me' refers to other gods, which are SAM and the serpent, for then it will be revealed that SAM and the serpent never separated between the Creator and His *Shechina* [Divinity], and was but a servant to hurry the redemption of our souls. The Creator's guidance from the beginning will appear throughout the world, and then, 'Sinners will cease from the earth, and the wicked shall be no more.' That is, unlike what it seems to us during the 6,000 years, that there is a governance that objects to *Kedusha*, which are SAM and the serpent."

We see from this that the matter of *Klipot* that the *Kedusha* must sustain as in "God has made one opposite the other," is that we need the *Klipot* to be a servant helping the *Kedusha*. This becomes revealed only at the end of correction in the general public, and to individuals, at the end of the work. At that time, the matter becomes revealed in retrospect, as it says, "and was but a servant to hurry the redemption of our souls."

It is said in *The Zohar* (*Tazria*, Item 6), "'Her price is far above pearls.' He asks, 'It should have said 'worth,' meaning that it is harder to buy her than pearls; why does it say 'her price"? He replies, 'She sells and turns over to other nations all those who do not fully cling to her and are not whole with her. And then they are all far from those high and holy pearls, which are the secrets and the internality of the Torah, for they will have no part in them. This is the meaning of 'Her price is far above pearls.'"

It therefore follows that the *Klipot*, which are other nations, she sells them. That is, since there is the quality of "other nations," when person begins to walk on the path toward achieving *Dvekut*, and in the middle of the work he becomes negligent in the work, meaning falls into the governance of the nations, who control him, he cannot emerge from their control and achieve *Dvekut* with the Creator, called "equivalence of form." At that time, he thinks that it is because he is incapable of this work, and this is why he is under their governance.

At that time, the writing tells us that the fact that he has fallen under the control of other nations is for his own good, so he will not fool himself and think that he is walking on the right path and can continue in this state without feeling that he is marching on the wrong way. For this reason, there are *Klipot* called "other nations," outside of *Kedusha*, and then a person sees that he is in a state of descent, and he has no connection to the *Kedusha*. At that time, he should seek advice how to be saved from them and march on the right path that leads to *Dvekut* with the Creator. It follows that the *Klipa* [singular of *Klipot*] keeps the *Kedusha*.

This means that if there were no *Klipa* that the *Shechina* could sell him there to be under their governance, man would remain in his lowliness and he would think that he is advancing on the path toward *Dvekut*. But when he is shown from above the deficiencies that he is in, he can feel that he must correct his way. This is the meaning of the words "Her price is far above pearls," meaning that the *Shechina* gives the man to the authority of the *Klipa*.

In other words, at that time he sees how immersed he is in self-love and that he has no desire to be a giver. That is, he is so immersed in self-love that he never thought that he was such a sordid person, the worst. It follows that we should interpret that the words "And God made it that He would be feared," mean that specifically through this *Klipa*, when he sees that it governs him, this pushes him to do all that he can to achieve *Dvekut* with the Creator.

However, when a person sees that he is under the governance of the *Klipot*, since he sees that they are the ones who sent him the known questions of "Who" and "What," and he cannot provide them with the right answers that will settle in the heart, he thinks that he must be so ignoble that he cannot answer them these simple questions. At that time, one should know that this is not as he thinks, that these questions really are tough.

This is so because the Creator gave power to the *Klipot* to ask tough questions, so that a person will know his real situation, that he was created in disparity of form from the Creator, and that he should achieve equivalence of form. It was done on purpose that man would not be able to answer these questions, so he would need the Creator, meaning that only the Creator can answer him because man's entire intellect is built on a basis of doing everything within reason, and man's reason understands only that which concerns one's own benefit. Therefore, they are correct.

However, one must know that we were given the path of observing Torah and *Mitzvot* above our reason, since our entire reason understands nothing but that which concerns self-benefit. This is called "faith above reason." Before a person can go above reason, anyone who comes to him and asks questions that are built on the reason of the body, it is impossible to answer them in a manner that the reason will understand.

Therefore, why did the *Klipa* come and ask these questions, which a person certainly cannot answer? The *Klipot* know that they are correct and that they will not get answers for them. But the question is according to the rule that is known in the work, that the fact that the *Klipa* comes and asks those questions comes from the side of *Kedusha*, as was said, "And God made it that He would be feared."

Thus, why do these questions come to him? The answer is that he is sent these questions from above, for specifically through these questions, he can observe the *Mitzva* of faith above reason. This is the meaning of "God made it that He would be feared." This means that the questions came to him in order to give him an opportunity to be able to reveal the matter of faith above reason. If he has no questions, he cannot know that he is going above reason. But when he sees the questions and does not want to provide answers, which reason mandates doing, he says, "Now that these questions came to me, I can observe the commandment of faith, which is above reason, and I want to take the opportunity."

Accordingly, we can understand why if the Creator knows that these are tough questions, which a person cannot answer with reason, why does He send them? The answer is as it is written, "And God made it that He would be feared." That is, specifically through these questions, a person can observe the commandment of faith, called "fear of the Creator." That is, specifically now he has an opportunity to observe the *Mitzva* of faith above reason.

Our sages said, "A *Mitzva* that falls into your lap, do not miss out on it." We should interpret that "A *Mitzva* that falls into your lap" is the *Mitzva* of faith, which "comes into your lap" through the "Who" and "What" questions. "Do not miss out on it," but rather accept it right away and do not argue with these questions and think about answering the questions. Rather, take the questions as they are, since now you have an opportunity to observe the *Mitzva* of faith, so "Do not miss out" accepting it as is, with all the toughness of the questions.

This is so because anything that conflicts with the intellect, with what the intellect argues, that it is not worthwhile to walk on this path, faith above reason and intellect is greater. This is why they said, "Do not miss out on it," do not miss out on the opportunity that you received through their questions.

Therefore, through the "What" question, which is the question of the wicked, who says, "What is this work for you," that you want to work only in order to bestow? He asks, "What will you gain from this? You should work only for your own benefit." This is a *Kli* [vessel], meaning a deficiency for the Creator to give him in the place of deficiency, since the wicked's question interrupts him from having the power to work in order to bestow, which is called "being rewarded with a second nature," called "in order to bestow." This is the meaning of "Reply unto your heart," meaning that the evil inclination, too, will work in order to bestow.

Through Pharaoh's questions, who said, "Who is the Lord that I should obey His voice?" when he overcomes this question, he is rewarded with permanent faith, which is called what *The Zohar* says, meaning after he has been rewarded with "Reply unto your heart." At that time, he comes to the degree of "The Lord, He is God."

What Is, "For I Have Hardened His Heart," in the work?

Article No. 17, Tav-Shin-Nun-Aleph, 1990/91

We should ask about the verse, "for I have hardened his heart," why did the Creator not harden Pharaoh's heart right in the beginning, but we see that only after Pharaoh admitted and said, "The Lord is the righteous one, and I and my people are the wicked," then the verse says, "for I have hardened his heart"? Also, all the interpreters ask, Why did the Creator deny Pharaoh the choice?

It is known that the order of the work is that we begin the work in order to receive reward. To the extent that the body hears that it will be rewarded, and if it does not suffer, this leads a person to work in observing Torah and *Mitzvot* [commandments/good deeds]. That is, to the extent that he believes in reward and punishment, he receives motivation so as to be able to observe Torah and *Mitzvot* in all its details and precisions.

What Is, "For I Have Hardened His Heart," in the work?

In this way, a person sees that he is advancing each day, and therefore enjoys his work, since he sees progress in the work. This follows the rule that one cannot do any work unless he sees progress in the work. It is like a person learning a profession and sees that he is not advancing in this profession, so he looks for something else to do, an easier job for him. But without progress, it is impossible to do anything. This stems from the matter, "which God has created to do." For this reason, there must be progress in everything.

This is like the horse that circles the grindstones and walks in circles all day long. Because it constantly walks in the same place, its eyes must be covered so it does not see the truth, but will think that it is walking to a different place each time. That is, even animals must see progress in what they do, and any progress in the work is seen only when we work in order to receive reward.

But when we begin to work in order to bestow, when we want to achieve *Dvekut* [adhesion] with the Creator, which is equivalence of form, a person cannot look at the things he does. That is, although he sees that now he is doing more than he did while he was working in order to receive reward, but now he has a different measurement, which is to what extent he aims his actions to be in order to bestow and not for his own sake. At that time, he sees that he is far from it. Although he has many ascents, meaning he ascends in his degree, and now he wants to do everything for the sake of the Creator, it is only because he has received an awakening from above. Then he wants to annul before Him, as a "candle before a torch."

But afterward, he descends from this state and falls once more into self-love. Then he sees that he has become worse; that is, he sees that each time he is farther from the work of bestowal, to the point that many times he comes to a state of "pondering the beginning."

A person asks himself, "Why when I worked in order to receive reward, I had a good taste in the work, and I prayed and learned willingly, but now that I want to make more efforts than I did while I worked in order to receive reward, I see that I do not have the flavor that I had then?" The person asks, "Now that I want to work for the sake of the Creator, it stands to reason that I should have felt more closeness than while I was working for my own sake, but now I see the opposite! Not only am I not advancing in the work, but I am going backwards!"

The answer is as Baal HaSulam said, that one must believe that everything he feels now, that he is farther from the Creator, comes from above. That is, it is the hardening of the heart that the Creator gives in order for one to discover the real need, meaning to feel that without the help of the Creator, a person cannot emerge from the control of the will to receive for himself, but only the Creator Himself can help. That is, as the Creator gave him the nature of the desire to receive for himself, He should now give him a second nature called "desire to bestow," since there is no light without a *Kli* [vessel], which is called "deficiency." That is, the lack puts the taste in the filling.

Thus, if a person is given a filling but he has no need for it, he cannot taste the real taste in the filling. If he is given the filling before he has a need, he will not be able to use the filling, to elicit from the filling what is in it. It follows that the lack is part of the filling, since one without the other does not work. It follows that as one is given a filling from above, so one should be given a lack. It turns out that when a person sees that now he is farther from the work of bestowal, he is given this from above because the lack is part of the filling. Therefore, as the upper one gives the filling, so He gives the lack.

By this we can interpret the two questions we asked: 1) Why specifically after Pharaoh said, "The Lord is the righteous one, and I and my people are the wicked," the Creator hardened his heart, and not before? 2) Why did He deny him the choice, as it is written, "for I have hardened his heart"?

The answer is that in the beginning, when starting the work, a person must see that everything depends on him. This is so as long as he is working in order to receive reward. At that time, a person can say, "The Lord is the righteous one, and I and my people are the wicked." Hence, when one wants to work in order to bestow, meaning achieve *Dvekut* with the Creator, he must see the truth: It is not within man's hands, since it contradicts the nature with which he was born. Only the Creator can give him a second nature, but without a lack, there is not real flavor in the filling. Hence, the Creator gives the hardening of the heart so that the person will feel the deficiency to the fullest.

This explains why only afterward did the Creator harden his heart, meaning after he began to work for the sake of the Creator and not before. Also, why did he need the hardening of the heart? It is for another reason, that if one does not feel the real lack, one cannot receive the real filling, since there is no light without a *Kli*. It follows that the hardening of the heart was not to his detriment, to remove him from the Creator. On the contrary, the hardening of the heart was in order to bring him to *Dvekut* with the Creator. We therefore see that the lack that a person feels when he is distant from the Creator, that, too comes from above and not by a person's awakening.

By this we can interpret what our sages said (*Avot* 2:5), "In a place where there are no people, try to be a person." We should interpret this in the work. When one begins the work, he begins in order to receive reward. Afterward, he sees that there are no people here, since in the work, we learn everything in one person. It follows that he saw that there was no quality of people in his heart, but only that of beasts—who do not know anything more than their own benefit. And he thinks about himself, how can it be said about the chosen people, as it is written, "You have chosen us from among all the nations; You have loved us," that there is nothing more than a beast's desire in the heart of the chosen people? Our sages said about this, "In a place where you see that there are no people in your heart, do not look at how the rest of the people behave. Rather, try to be a person."

In other words, since you have come to see the truth, that one must be a person and not a beast, while the rest of the people have not achieved this awareness—that there are no people in their hearts—since they have not received this awareness, it is a sign that they still do not belong to the work of the individual, which is the work of bestowal. This is the meaning of the words, "In a place," meaning in a place where the knowledge comes that "there are no people," meaning that this person who received this awareness must try to be a person and not a beast.

Hence, for the most part, a person feels that he is complete. He prays, he learns Torah, and he observes *Mitzvot*. He thinks that he should only increase the quantity, but in terms of the quality of the work, he has nothing to examine because he thinks that he is doing everything for the sake of the Creator.

It therefore follows that when one feels deficient, that he is immersed in self-love, and that he is far from the matter of bestowal, this does not come from the person, but rather by an awakening from above. That is, from above, he was notified his real state, that he is removed from the Creator and does not want to annul before Him. That is, when one feels his own lowliness, he must believe that it came to him from the *Kedusha* [holiness]. This is similar to what is written about Moses (Exodus 2:11-12), "He went out to his brethren and saw their suffering, and he saw an Egyptian man striking a Hebrew man, one of his brethren, and he saw that there was no one."

In the work, we should interpret that precisely when a person has the quality of Moses, called "Torah," he can see how an Egyptian man, meaning the will to receive for himself, he says that it is called "a man," and with this force, called "Torah," he sees that it strikes the Hebrew man. That is, for the Hebrew, a "man" is one who does not do what a beast does, meaning that a man is one who does not use the desires of beasts, as it is written, "and he saw that there was no one," meaning that "a man" will never emerge from him by itself. This is so because that person has the quality of Moses, who is the quality of "faithful shepherd" (who shepherds the faith for the whole of Israel), and that force awakens a person to see the truth, that he will never achieve the quality of "man" by himself. This is the meaning of the verse, "and he saw that there was no one." This causes him to ask the Creator to give him faith in the Creator, by which he will achieve *Dvekut* with the Creator.

What Is, "For I Have Hardened His Heart," in the Work?

However, once a person has been rewarded with faith, it is still incomplete, for although now he is called "man," and not "a beast," he should also achieve the quality of Torah, for specifically through the Torah, a person achieves his wholeness, since he should achieve the state of "the Torah, the Creator, and Israel are one." This is called "the quality of speaking," as it is written about Moses, who said, "And Moses said to the Lord, 'Please, Lord, I am not a man of words.'"

In the work, we should interpret that he asked that it was not enough that he was already in the quality of "man," but he wanted to be a "man of words," to be rewarded with the quality of "speaking," called "Torah," for specifically the quality of "speaking," which is the Torah, is regarded as wholeness.

However, we must not forget that in the work, there is the matter of "right," which is the opposite of "left." That is, just as on the path of the "left," the more deficiencies a person sees in him, the better, since a lack is called "a *Kli* [vessel]," so a greater lack means a bigger *Kli*. The same is true for the "right": The more complete one feels, the bigger is his *Kli*. That is, the more a person sees that he is full of deficiencies, the bigger is the prayer that he can pray compared to one who is not so deficient, and whose prayer is therefore not as wholehearted. Thus, specifically the lack determines the measure of the prayer.

Also, the path of the right is considered that a person must feel that there is wholeness. Here, too, to the extent that he feels wholeness, to that extent he can thank the Creator. That is, the wholeness that one is in determines the measure of the gratitude to the Creator. Hence, a person must seek advice how to see that he has wholeness. However, he must see that his wholeness is not built on falsehood. We should ask, If a person sees that he has no need for spirituality, and he is immersed in self-love, how can he tell himself that he has wholeness?

First, we must appreciate the connection we have with the Creator, meaning that one must believe that the state where one feels that he is empty and destitute, when he feels that in his heart, there is no need for spirituality, who gave him that feeling? Usually, a person worries about what he lacks, and he does not worry about what he does not need. Thus, we should ask, Who gave him the worry for that which he does not need?

The answer is that in truth, he does have an inner desire, he does need nearness with the Creator, but that lack is still not revealed within him to an extent that he will need to seek advice how to satisfy his lack. For this reason, a person must be glad that at least he has a need for spirituality, whereas the rest of the people have no interest in spirituality whatsoever.

When a person appreciates this, although it is not important to him, he does appreciate it and tries to thank the Creator for this. This causes him to acquire importance for spirituality, and from this a person can be happy. By this, a person can be rewarded with *Dvekut*, since as Baal HaSulam said, "The blessed clings to the Blessed." In other words, when a person is happy and thanks the Creator, he feels that the Creator has blessed him by giving him a little something of *Kedusha*, then "The blessed clings to the Blessed." Through this wholeness, one can achieve real *Dvekut*.

Baal HaSulam said that a person should depict to himself, even when he is in utter lowliness, when he thinks that if the Creator had illuminated for him a great awakening as he once felt during the ascent, he would certainly be willing to do the holy work. But now that he does not feel anything, how can he deceive himself that he has wholeness? At that time, he must believe in the sages, who said to us that one must depict to himself as though he has already been rewarded with feeling the existence of the Creator in all his organs, and how he would thank and praise the Creator. Likewise, now he should thank and praise the Creator as though he has already been rewarded with the real wholeness.

What It Means that We Should Raise the Right Hand over the Left Hand, in the Work

Article No. 18, Tav-Shin-Nun-Aleph, 1990/91

The *Zohar* asks (*Yitro* [Jethro], Item 1), "'And Aaron raised his hands.' It writes 'His hands' without a *Yod* [in Hebrew], which means one hand, since he had to raise the right over the left." This means that if the right is above the left, it indicates that the right governs the left. Hence, it is regarded as one hand.

We should understand what are "right" and "left" in the work, and that we must raise the right over the left.

It is known that "right" means wholeness, meaning that a person feels about himself that he is a complete person and is not deficient in corporeality or spirituality, since he is content with little. For this reason, this person can be grateful to the Creator for completing all his needs, and for behaving with him with the quality of mercy. That is, he sees that he does not deserve all that he has, and when he looks at other people, he sees that they have far less than he, and he says that he certainly does not deserve more than the rest of the people. That person is always happy and can be grateful to the Creator for what He has rewarded him, and he feels that the Creator loves him and he loves the Creator. He is always high spirited because the Creator loves him, and he always wants to cite psalms and praises to the Creator. And the more he thinks about the Creator, the more he enjoys, since he feels that He is a soulmate and this gives him high spirits, and he has no concerns over deficiencies, and he feels that he lives in a world that is all good. He always yearns to speak with the one who loves him, meaning he always feels the Creator's love, and he regards other people in his surroundings as pitiful, since he sees that they are all living a sorrowful life, appreciating meaningless matters as though they were the most important thing in their lives. And since they cannot be satiated, they have nothing with which to be happy. He has nothing in common with them because when he begins to speak with them, they do not understand him. He cannot do anything for them other than to ask for mercy for them.

However, we should know that a person should also walk on the left line. "Left" means criticizing one's actions, whether or not they are fine. That is, on one hand, he is content with little. But on the other hand, he needs to see what he is doing for the purpose of creation, for His desire to do good to His creations was not about being content with little. Rather, He wants to give to the created beings abundant delight and pleasure, and in this respect, he sees that he is bare and destitute. At that time, he has no other choice but to pray to the Creator to bring him closer and give him vessels of bestowal. Through them, he will be rewarded with *Dvekut* [adhesion] with the Creator and will also be rewarded with the Torah as in "The Torah, and the Creator, and Israel are one." But as long as he has not received the vessels of bestowal, and he sees how immersed he is in self-love and is inherently incapable of emerging from this governance, but only the Creator can help him in this, and he sees more, that not only did he not advance in

What It Means that We Should Raise the Right Hand over the Left Hand

the work, he regressed! And sometimes, he comes to a state where he wants to escape the campaign.

It follows that this left is truly opposite from the right, called "wholeness." At that time, he should ask, "What should I do?" That is, since now he sees that the one line he had before, meaning wholeness, now that wholeness is regarded as "right," since there cannot be "right" if there is no "left," it follows that this "left" has made for him the previous situation of wholeness as "right," and now he has "right" and "left." That is, each one contradicts the other.

However, we must know that a person can walk forward only on two legs, and not on one leg, as the ARI says (in the poem "I will Sing the Praises"), "Right and left, and in between a bride." We should interpret that through the "right" and the "left," we are rewarded with the bride, who is called "The installing of the *Shechina* [Divinity]." But a person cannot walk on one leg.

Therefore, a person should raise his hands, meaning both hands, where raising a hand means raising the hand to look what he has in the hand, meaning what he has acquired from all the work that he engages in the work of the Creator. However, a person must know that when he looks at the left hand and sees how far he is from the Creator, it causes him separation from the Creator, since when he sees that he is not all right, in that state he is regarded as "cursed," and "The Blessed does not cling to the cursed." For this reason, one must shift to the right line, where a person works in a state of wholeness.

However, wholeness cannot be built on a lie, but on truth. Hence, when a person raises the left hand and sees there that he is full of faults, how can he then say that he is a complete man and thank the Creator for his good situation?

The answer is that by being content with less and saying, "I am happy that I have some grip on the work, even though it is *Lo Lishma* [not for Her sake], and even though he cannot overcome and labor as befits one who wishes to serve the King, and he thanks the Creator for rewarding him with grip in the work, to the extent that he appreciates it, to that extent he is considered a complete person. However, he should know that this "right," that he is content with little, is after he walked on the left line. Then it can be said that he is content with little, meaning that the left made him see how full of faults he is, so when he is content with little, it is considered complete because he appreciates small things in the work as important. From this, he can ascend because he is saying the truth by being content with less. Conversely, one who has only one line is not regarded as being content with little. Rather, he thinks of himself as complete and not as settling for little.

This is similar to a person having guests and giving each of them 300 grams of bread. There are people there who are used to eating 200 grams of bread, and there are people there who are used to eating 400 grams of bread. Certainly, we cannot say that those who are used to eating 200 grams of bread settle for little, that they should suffice for the little bread that they are given, since for them, 100 grams of the bread are already redundancies. Rather, only those who are used to eating 400 grams of bread can be said to suffice for less, since they need more but have none. Then it can be said that they suffice for little and are thankful to the landlord for the bread that he has given them, as though the bread filled their entire need.

The lesson is that when a person walks on one line, he suffices with whatever grip he has on the work and understands that he is whole, meaning that he does not need more. Instead, he sees that he is in a state of wholeness, while other people around him are inferior compared to him. It follows that he sufficed for less because he saw that he had more possessions than other people.

But when he raises his left hand, meaning looks at the value of his possession in the work and begins to understand that we must walk on the path toward achieving *Dvekut* [adhesion] with the Creator, called "equivalence of form," he sees that he is far from it. So how can he be happy that he is serving the Creator, when he sees how immersed he is in self-love? Sometimes he falls into a descent where he sees that he is so low that he does not even want the Creator to help him emerge from the governance of the will to receive. Thus how is it possible to work in the right, called "wholeness," and for this wholeness not to be built on falsehood?

The answer is that the person believes in faith in the sages and says that the sages told us that the order of the work is that a person should walk on the right line, meaning wholeness. Therefore, he grows stronger and observes the faith in the sages, who said, "Who is rich? He who is happy with his share." In other words, he is content with little and says that he is grateful to the Creator for rewarding him with doing something in the work, although it is all *Lo Lishma*, but only for his own sake.

At that time, he does not want to work for the sake of the Creator, and yet he is content with his share even though it is *Lo Lishma*. Out of this joy, because he observes faith in the sages, he can be rewarded with achieving *Lishma* [for Her sake], meaning that the Creator will help him and give him the second nature called "desire to bestow."

It follows that in order for one to be able to appreciate the work of Torah and *Mitzvot* [commandments/good deeds], it is only by being content with little. That is, a person must appreciate it if he has some small grip on spirituality, and regard it a as a fortune. Therefore, when one walks on one line, he still does not need to appreciate the little grip he has, since he does not feel that this is regarded as "little." On the contrary, he feels more or less like a complete person and only sees that others are in lowliness. But he, thank God, feels that he is serving the Creator and he is happy about it and rejoices, and can thank the Creator for this. Hence, on one hand, one who walks on one line, it is very good, since he does not have complaints or demands to the Creator, and he is happy and high spirited.

For this reason, such people must not be told that there is any fault in their work, since there is a rule that it is forbidden to reveal a deficiency in one's friend's work if his friend does not feel the deficiency himself, or at least that his friend has revealed to him that he is dissatisfied with the work. Then it is possible to tell his friend the truth, that we must do the holy work in order to achieve *Dvekut* with the Creator. Otherwise, it is considered that a person is shown a lack while a person is capable of working only in the manner of the general public and not in the manner of individuals. It follows that we are giving a grip to the *Klipot* [shells/peels]. Hence, when he walks on one line he is fine. This is regarded that this person belongs to the "still of *Kedusha* [holiness]."

However, to be a "vegetative of *Kedusha*," meaning to have progress in the work, requires that one walks on two lines, which are called "right and left." We need the right because it is forbidden to reveal any deficiency, since where there is a deficiency in *Kedusha*, there is a grip to the *Sitra Achra* [other side], as the ARI says, "In *Ibur* [impregnation], we need the depicting force and the detaining force." *Ibur* means that this is the beginning of man's entrance into *Kedusha*. The depicting force shows the truth, meaning a depiction of the work, meaning if he has a good depiction about the situation he is in and the work shines for him, meaning what form he has when he looks at his work, whether he is in wholeness or not, whether he is working in order to bestow or does he want to nonetheless work in order to bestow.

The detaining force is considered that when the depicting force shows him the truth, that during *Ibur*, called "beginning of the work," he certainly sees deficiencies and there can be a grip to the *Sitra Achra* [other side]. Therefore, there must be a detaining force so the fetus is not aborted, meaning falls into the *Sitra Achra*. In order to prevent a miscarriage, although there is a lack, as the depicting force indicates what is form of this work, the detaining force is called "right" because he shifts to wholeness. That is, he believes in the sages who said that a person should be happy with his share, meaning whatever grip he has on Torah and *Mitzvot* he regards it as a great privilege, since he sees that there are people to whom the Creator did not give even the thought or desire for the little bit of grip that I have. This is called the "detaining force," so he will not fall off from the work and will also be born later, meaning that from this work of keeping himself in *Ibur* at the beginning of the work, he will have two lines, right and left, and he will be rewarded with birth and with being in *Yenika* [nursing] of *Kedusha*. Thus, through the depicting force and the detaining force, a complete newborn will emerge in *Kedusha*.

Accordingly, we should interpret what *The Zohar* says, that the reason why it is written about Aaron, "'And Aaron raised his hands' with a missing *Yod* [in Hebrew], which means one hand, it is because we must raise the right over the left." We asked what this teaches us in the work. According to the above, we should interpret that the fact that a person should walk on the left, he should be careful that the right is always higher than the left. That is, while he is walking on the left and looks at the depiction of the work, whether or not it is complete, he should see that he can immediately return to the right, meaning that the right will always be of higher importance, and that he needs the left only in order to help the right, meaning to have room to always be in wholeness and on the path of truth. That is, he should be happy with his share, and this is called the "detaining force," since we must be careful that the person does not use the left for long, since when one raises the left, he sees his fault. And according to the rule, where there is a lack in *Kedusha*, there is immediately a grip to the *Sitra Achra*. It follows that the person is placed under the *Sitra Achra* and should therefore remember that when he enters the state of "left," he does not intend to remain in the left, but for the left to serve the right. It follows that then the left does not merit its own name because the aim is not only the left, for the purpose of the left, but that the left is required for the purpose of the right. For this reason, the left does not merit a name. This is regarded as having only one hand, since it is annulled before the right. This is why *The Zohar* says that "we must raise the right over the left," and this is regarded as "his hand," one, which is why it is written with a missing *Yod*.

According to the above, we should interpret what we say in the prayer, "How good are your tents, Jacob, Your dwellings, Israel." It is known that Jacob is called *Yod-Akev* [Hebrew: Yaakov (Jacob), *Yod-Akev* (*Yod*-heel)], which means *Katnut* [smallness], heels, the end of *Kedusha*, as it is written in *The Zohar*, "That *Yod* that Esau threw to the back, Jacob took to the head." We should interpret in the work that *Yod* is called *Malchut*, which is the kingdom of heaven, called "faith." Esau does not want to use it; it is regarded as dust, something tasteless, which he considers dust. Rather, he wanted only to work in a manner that he will see what comes out from his work, what benefits he gets from his work. When he prays, he is willing to pray in a manner that he will receive what he is praying for immediately. When he is told, "You must believe that the Creator hears the prayer of every mouth," meaning that a person must not say that the Creator hears only the prayer of an important person, but if an unimportant person prays, the Creator does not hear his prayer, this, too, is regarded as not believing that the Creator hears the prayer. This is as Baal HaSulam said, that one should believe what is written, "For You hear the prayer of every mouth of Your people Israel with mercy." This means that anyone asking for the Creator's mercy should believe that the Creator hears the prayer of every mouth, even if he is the lowliest.

It follows that if he says that the Creator does not hear every mouth, this is considered that he does not believe. Hence, even when a person sees that his prayer was not accepted, he should believe above reason, and this is called *Yod*, meaning the kingdom of heaven. A person should take upon himself this faith, the work that Esau threw to the back.

But Jacob placed it in the head. This is why it is *Yod-Akev*, where the *Yod* is before the *Akev* [heel], meaning that heel is considered "end" and "lowliness," that which a person tramples with his heels. This means that it is something unimportant, and the person takes this as his head, meaning values it, and this is work where a person considers himself whole in that he has been rewarded with something. That is, in prayer, when he prays as much as possible, a person should depict to himself and believe as though he feels the existence of the Creator although he sees that the body is not impressed by what a person thinks.

What It Means that We Should Raise the Right Hand over the Left Hand

Still, when he grows stronger and believes in the sages that this small contact that he has with spirituality, he appreciates it and believes in the sages that the Creator has more contentment from this work than from other works that a person thinks, that precisely when one thinks that the body agrees to the work, the Creator derives contentment from this. Yet, a person believes that precisely when one must use the above reason, this work is important to the Creator. Hence, he must work a lot in order to be able to appreciate work of lowliness, when the body disagrees with the work. This is so because when a person walks on the left and understands that he must achieve the degree of "And you shall love the Lord your God with all your heart," which our sages said, "with both your inclinations," meaning that the evil inclination should also agree to be a servant of the Creator, and naturally, when a person sees that the body does not agree to the work, he says that in any case, there is no point to this work, so why should he exert for nothing? And yet, he believes that this is important work.

This is as Baal HaSulam said (Essay, "Faith in the Rav," *Tav-Shin-Gimel*, 1943), that before a person is rewarded with the singular authority, meaning when he no longer has multiple authorities, which is two desires, meaning a desire to bestow, but he also wants to use the will to receive for himself, a person cannot know the importance of his work. That is, he might think that his work is in descent, when this is not the truth. Also, sometimes a person thinks of his work as an ascent, which is also not true. Instead, one must believe with faith in the sages, who said that one should walk on a path where he feels wholeness in the work even if it is of utter lowliness. However, we should also walk a little bit on the left, to the extent that it serves the right.

According to the above, we should interpret what is written, "How good are your tents, Jacob." It means that one should see and try to appreciate and thank the Creator when he is inside the "tent of *Yod-Akev*," meaning in a state of "heels," which is the end of *Kedusha*, and say, "How good." In other words, he does not have sufficient intellect to value this state and say that it is a good state, and thank the Creator. Afterward, by appreciating the "tent of *Yod-Akev*," he will be rewarded with the "dwellings of *Yashar-El* [Israel]," where Israel is already regarded as *Rosh* [head]. It follows that through the degree of *Yod-Akev*, he will be rewarded with *Gadlut* [greatness] and the *Rosh* of the degree, called "Your dwellings, Israel."

What Is, "Rise Up, O Lord, and Let Your Enemies Be Scattered," in the Work?

Article No. 19, Tav-Shin-Nun-Aleph, 1990/91

The Jerusalem Talmud says, "The Tanna Rashbi says, 'If you see people whose hands have given up on the Torah, stand firm and reinforce yourself in it, and you will receive everyone's reward.'"

We should understand the meaning of people giving up on the Torah. Giving up has to do with a person who has made great efforts to obtain something but saw that all his efforts did not help him and he still did not obtain that thing. At that time, a person comes to despair. It follows that if a person sees that people have given up on finding the Torah, it must be that they have made efforts, so how can it be said, "Stand firm and reinforce yourself in it"? After all, we see that the labor did not help them, so with what can we reinforce ourselves?

It is known that in the work, we learn everything within one body. It follows that seeing people whose hands have given up on the Torah is in one person. Thus, what does it mean that he sees that they have given up on the Torah? We should understand why he says that their hands have given up on the Torah. It is known that "hands" means that which we take with our hands. Thus, what does it mean that "their hands have given up"? It means that they saw that it is impossible to receive in their hands from the Torah what they want to receive. Thus, we should know what it is they wanted to receive from the Torah but have given up.

It is known that man was created with the evil inclination and the good inclination. The evil inclination was created as soon as one is born. A person does not need to work to acquire this desire, since the Creator created man with this nature, called "desire to receive delight and pleasure." Therefore, since it comes by nature, it is very strong and needs no assistance. Wherever one sees that he can enjoy something, he immediately does all that he can to obtain that pleasure. Accordingly, we should ask, "If it tries to bring one pleasures, why is it called "evil inclination"? After all, it is concerned with bringing pleasures, not bad things, to a person.

The answer is that since the purpose of creation is to do good to His creations, in order not to have the matter of shame, there was a correction that the abundance does not reach the vessels of reception. This is called "the correction of the *Tzimtzum* [restriction]." Only a very thin light shines into the vessels of reception. This is the meaning of what the ARI interprets, that *Malchut* sustains the *Klipot* [shells/peels], as in "Her legs go down to death," and the corporeal world is nourished by this.

Yet, the real delight and pleasure, of which He thought, does not shine into the vessels of reception. It therefore follows that the evil inclination, called "will to receive for one's own sake," cannot receive the real delight and pleasure. Hence, since the will to receive for oneself is the disruptor, it is called "evil inclination," as it disrupts a person from receiving the abundance.

For this reason, since man was created with a nature of wanting to receive for himself, how can he have the power to emerge from the control of the evil inclination? The answer of our sages to this is "Thus the Creator said to Israel: 'My sons, I have created the evil inclination, and I have created for it the spice of Torah. And if you engage in Torah, you will not be given into its hands'" (*Kidushin* 30).

This means that only through the Torah can we emerge from the control of the evil inclination. That is, when one learns Torah, he should always see whether he has taken from the Torah the subjugation of the evil inclination. Hence, if one learns Torah, he sees that he did not receive from the Torah the cure of the Torah, which subdues the evil inclination.

It follows that to the extent of the time and effort that one has given to learn Torah, and yet did not move at all from his evil, but sometimes sees the opposite, that he has retreated, and each day he thinks that he is a new creation, meaning that each day he thinks, "Perhaps today I will be rewarded with the Torah giving me the cure to persuade the evil inclination," but since he sees that he is not succeeding, he falls into despair. Then he says that although our sages said, "I have created the evil inclination; I have created the Torah as a spice," this might be so for a person who was born with good qualities. Yet, he sees his own lowliness, that he cannot achieve this level. Thus, he must leave the campaign since it is not for him, and he is wasting his time working in vain. This brings him to a state called "pondering the beginning."

This is the meaning of what is written, "If you see people whose hands have given up on the Torah," meaning that all those days when he engaged in Torah with the aim to obtain from the Torah the cure of annulling the bad, and since each day was a new creation for him, it follows that he has many creations within him. Now, their hands have given up on the Torah because he is in a state where he will never receive this cure from the Torah. Yet, in this way, he is under the control of the will to receive. Hence, what should he do now? Normally, when one gives up on something that he wants to obtain, he quits it and runs from it. Thus, he should escape the campaign.

Rashbi says about this, "Stand firm and reinforce yourself in it, and you will receive everyone's reward." We should understand what Rashbi says and adds, "You will receive everyone's reward." Why is it not enough that he says that he should believe what he is saying, "Stand firm and reinforce yourself in it"? In other words, we must believe in the sages that we must not give up, and believe that the Creator hears the prayer of every mouth. Why does he add and say, "and you will receive everyone's reward"? If he does not receive everyone's reward, should he not reinforce himself and not give up?

We should interpret what he says, "and you will receive everyone's reward," that this is the reason why he must not give up on receiving the cure from the Torah that brings to us the cancellation of the evil inclination. The thing is that we must believe that when one begins the work of bestowal, he sees each time that he is more immersed in self-love. Each day he adds in the work, which is regarded as a new creation, as our sages said, "A gentile who became a proselyte is like a newborn child," which means in the work that each day when one takes upon himself the burden of the kingdom of heaven, he becomes "Israel," and this is called "A gentile who became a proselyte is like a newborn child."

It follows that man consists of many creations. And the more creations there are, he sees that he has still not been rewarded with permanent faith and he is still far from the Creator due to disparity of form, which causes separation from the Creator. This is called that he sees that the creations have given up on the Torah, meaning that they have given up on receiving the medicine called "annulment of the evil."

The question is, Why does the Creator not give them what He promised us, as He said, "I have created the evil inclination; I have created the Torah as a spice"? Why does He not give the spice to those people who want to work in order to bestow?

The answer is, as we explained in previous articles, that "There is no light without a *Kli* [vessel], no filling without a lack." Since one is not shown more lack than he can receive, meaning to the extent of the good within him, meaning since he engages in overcoming the bad and does things in order to cancel the bad, therefore, he is shown a greater lack each time, according to the value of his work, and how far he is from the desire to bestow.

It follows that in truth, the Creator does hear a prayer, but the answering of the prayer is not the way the person thinks he needs it, meaning the filling, since what man really needs is the lack, meaning a real desire, to want to be rewarded in his life with only a desire to give contentment to the Creator. But in the beginning of his work, a person thinks that he needs a little bit desire to bestow, meaning that he still does not have a need to be able to bring contentment to the Creator. It is not a big desire because he is not as materialized with self-love.

Rather, he thinks that whenever he wants to work in order to bestow, he will be able to do so. Thus, he still does not have a real need to feel how far he is from doing anything not for his own sake. This is why this is still not regarded as a real need for the Creator to satisfy.

Hence, the beginning of answering the prayer of a person who wants to walk on the path of bestowal is that the Creator shows him each time a greater lack, that he is removed from the work of bestowal. It follows that the fact that one sees that the Torah is not giving him the spice is for his sake, since by this he receives a *Kli*, called "lack," for the Creator to later give him the filling for the lack.

Thus, to the extent that each time he receives a greater lack for the desire to bestow, he thereby receives more *Kelim* [vessels] that can receive the filling of the lack. In other words, if he has a big desire to obtain the desire to bestow, it follows that the increase in desires is called "increase in the *Kelim* for the reception of the filling," called "desire to bestow." That is, he receives a big desire to bestow, according to his *Kelim*. This means that according to the measure of the lack, to that extent he can receive the spice from the Torah. It follows that according to the increase in the *Kelim*, to that extent he receives light.

Accordingly, we should interpret what we asked, What does Rashbi add to us when he says that he takes everyone's reward? We should interpret that when one sees that the creations have given up on the Torah, that they see that they are not receiving into their hands the spice that the Torah is meant to give them, namely the annulment of the evil inclination, but on the contrary, Rashbi says about this, "Know that all the rejections you feel, that each time, you are pushed farther away from nearing the Creator, from equivalence of form called '*Dvekut* [adhesion] with the Creator,' it is in order for you to acquire *Kelim* in which to receive the spice."

It follows that now that you have many *Kelim*, which come from many rejections, now all the *Kelim* will receive reward, meaning the filling, and this is called that he will receive reward for everyone, for all the rejections, since these rejections are *Kelim* in which to receive the filling called "reward."

It follows that by seeing that one is in thoughts and desires of the will to receive, which are called "wicked," since they harm a person so he cannot achieve the delight and pleasure that is in the thought of creation, which is to do good to His creations, we must know that they are also called "enemies of the Creator" because they obstruct the Creator and He cannot carry out His plan to do good to His creations. Because of the will to receive for one's own sake, the Creator cannot bestow upon them because it will all go to the vessels of reception, which are the *Sitra Achra* [other side]. Thus, these wicked, the desires of reception that have accumulated within man, are considered "the enemies of the Creator and the enemies of man."

Now we can interpret what is written (Psalms 34), "I sought the Lord and He answered me." The RADAK interpreted "I sought," since while in their hands, he sought the Creator in his heart and begged before Him in his heart to save him from them.

In the work, we should interpret that David saw that when he was in their hands, under the rule of thoughts and desires of the will to receive, his heart sought the Creator. That is, although he saw that they controlled him, his heart demanded of the Creator to save him from them. In other words, even though on the outside they governed him, within the heart he protested their governance and begged the Creator to save him from them. In his heart, he demanded and begged the Creator to save him from them and did not give up because they controlled him on the outside. This is as our sages said (*Berachot* 10), "Even if a sharp sword is placed on his neck, he should not deny himself mercy." Thus, the descents, too, cause the filling of the lack.

According to the above, we should interpret what we asked, "What is 'Rise up, O Lord, and let Your enemies be scattered, and let those who hate You flee before You'?" In the work, we should interpret who are the Creator's enemies in the work, who do not let one work for the sake of the Creator. These are the desires within us to work only for our own sake. These desires are called "enemies of the Creator and enemies of man."

Being unable to work for the sake of the Creator is called "enemies of the Creator." Yet, it is not that the Creator needs to be served. Rather, by working for Him, they receive *Dvekut* with the Creator, called "vessels of bestowal," and in these *Kelim* the Creator can give them the delight and pleasure that was in the thought of creation. Since these desires of self-reception interrupt this, it follows that they are disrupting the desire to do good to His creations from being carried out.

Thus, they are also called "man's enemies," since the desires to receive interrupt people from being able to receive the delight and pleasure that the Creator wants to give them. These desires for reception for themselves can receive only from the light called "very thin light," which shines into the *Klipot* [shells/peels]. This thin light can illuminate to the vessels of reception that belong to the *Klipot*.

But on the real light, there was a *Tzimtzum* [restriction] so it will shine only in vessels of *Kedusha* [holiness] called "vessels of bestowal," meaning specifically on the desire to bestow contentment to one's Maker and not for one's own sake. This is why we ask, "Rise up, O Lord, and let Your enemies be scattered," since all the power in the will to receive is because the *Shechina* [Divinity] is in the dust, the *Shechina is in exile*. That is, since the *Kedusha* is concealed and hidden, and we do not see its importance, the enemies of the Creator and the enemies of man raise their heads and want to rule.

But this is not so if the Creator helps us during the concealment, when *Malchut* is regarded as dust, when the creatures do not feel the existence of the Creator but the *Klipot* stand before us and the *Kedusha* is concealed and we do not see its importance. At that time, the enemies of the Creator and the enemies of Israel are the rulers.

As is said in *The Zohar* about *Malchut*, she is the tree of knowledge of good and evil. If he is rewarded, it is good, meaning that the bad is covered and not seen outside. Naturally, the evil does not rule because it is concealed. If he is not rewarded, it is bad, meaning that the good is concealed and the bad is revealed outward. At that time, the bad rules because the bad is revealed and the good is concealed.

Hence, a person sees that sometimes he understands that man's purpose is to work for the sake of the Creator. He has no doubt about it and thinks that it is natural, that it cannot be otherwise. Afterward, after this state when he understands that what matters is only to do the holy work and not to follow the majority, and moreover, sometimes when he looks at the general public, he cannot understand how intelligent people can be so immersed in superficial things and not engage in the holy work.

Afterward, the person himself falls into all kinds of foolish penchants that he previously ridiculed and could not comprehend. Now, he is in there himself.

We should understand how such a thing can happen. The answer is that later, when one has come to a state of "not rewarded," the good disappears from him and the bad becomes revealed in him.

What Is, "Rise Up, O Lord, and Let Your Enemies Be Scattered"?

Hence, he is taken after what is revealed outside, which is the bad. He has no choice; he does only that which is revealed outside.

This is the meaning of the words "*Malchut* is called 'the tree of good and evil.'" However, the whole matter of choice is about what is revealed, namely the choice to be "rewarded" or "not rewarded." It follows that man must do only one thing—to pray to the Creator that the bad will be covered and the good will be revealed. Then, he will consider working for the sake of the Creator as labor, since he will not be able to understand otherwise than to work for the sake of the Creator. At that time, he will have no effort annulling himself before the Creator, since he will think that this is natural. Hence, everything he previously thought was impossible, now he sees that it is natural and he wants to annul before the Creator like a candle before a torch. And all this is because the bad is concealed and the good is revealed outside.

This is the meaning of the words "Rise up, O Lord, and let Your enemies be scattered." We pray that the Creator will "rise up," the way we pray and say, "The Merciful One will raise for us the fallen hut of David," where the "hut of David" is *Malchut*, which is the *Shechina* in the dust. We ask the Creator to raise her from her falling and that she will rise, meaning upright.

Naturally, each one will cancel his self and will want to work only for the sake of the Creator and not for himself. Through "Rise up, O Lord," the "Let Your enemies be scattered" will happen. In other words, the desires in the creatures, which are the enemies of the Creator and the enemies of man, will be scattered, "and let those who hate You flee before You." That is, when there is "Rise up, O Lord," when the *Kedusha* is in the state of *Panim* [anterior/face], then "and let those who hate You flee before You" will come true, meaning that all the enemies and haters will flee.

Concerning "Rise up, O Lord, and let Your enemies be scattered," we should know that scattering the enemies is not the end of the work, although it is the heart of it, as it is written, "And you shall uproot the evil from the midst of you." However, this is only the correction of creation, and not the purpose of creation. The purpose of creation is for the lower ones to receive delight and pleasure, which is called "Torah," as in "the names of the Creator."

It follows that the first discernment is "faith," the kingdom of heaven, and then comes the Torah. This is the meaning of the verse "For the Torah shall come forth out of Zion." Man must be rewarded with the quality of the Torah, which is the names of the Creator, namely the delight and pleasure that was in the thought of creation.

However, we must not forget that man should primarily exert to walk on the "right," called "wholeness," and believe in the sages, who said that one should be happy that the Creator has awarded him the ability to observe Torah and *Mitzvot* [commandments/good deeds] even if *Lo Lishma* [not for Her sake]. That is, when a person sees that everything he does is only for his own sake, and that he cannot do anything for the sake of the Creator, this is also a great thing. One should be happy about this and thank the Creator for it. It is as Baal HaSulam said, that the *Lo Lishma* that one does is more important to the Creator than the importance a person ascribes to the *Lishma* [for Her sake]. Clearly, the *Lishma* is more important, but the *Lo Lishma* is also important to the Creator. Hence, one should be happy even with the *Lo Lishma*.

What Is, "There Is Nothing that Has No Place," in the Work?

Article No. 20, Tav-Shin-Nun-Aleph, 1990/91

Our sages said (*Beresheet Rabbah* 68:9), "Why is the Creator called 'Place'? It is because He is the place of the world, and the world is not His place. From what is it written? 'Here is a place with Me.' Thus, the Creator is the place of the world, and His world is not His place." It was also said (*Avot* 4:3), "There is nothing that has no place." We should understand what this comes to teach us in the work.

In the work, a "place" is a place of deficiency. That is, if a person has some lack, we should say that he has a place in which to receive a filling for the lack. But if he has no lack, it cannot be said that it can be filled, since there is no one to fill. For example, if one is not hungry, he cannot eat. This is considered that he has no place to fill his hunger. Or, if he is not thirsty, he cannot drink water, since he has no place in which to receive the filling.

According to the above, we should interpret the difference between "the place of the world," and "Blessed is the place," meaning the place of the Creator. In the work, we should interpret that the Creator is the place of His world. That is, the correction of creation is that the place of the Creator, meaning the lack, called "the place of the Creator," is that the Creator wants to bestow, meaning the deficiency.

The deficiency that can be said about the Creator is that He wants to do good to His creations. That desire to bestow, when the world is deficient because they want to bestow like the Creator, at that time the world will exist in wholeness. At that time, the Creator will be able to bestow upon them delight and pleasure. Why? Because the reception of delight and pleasure will be in a manner of correction.

However, His world is not His place. That is, the deficiency, meaning the desire that is in the world, is the very will to receive. This does not belong to the Creator, since from whom would He receive? Hence, He, meaning the desire to bestow that the Creator has, is what His world must take upon themselves, and not use the nature of the will to receive, the lack with which creation—which is called "existence from absence"—was born. This is called "the place of the world."

Man's work is only about how to emerge from the nature of the desire that is in the world and acquire a different desire, which is the desire to bestow. This is hard work, and it can be obtained only through the Torah, as our sages said, "I have created the evil inclination; I have created the Torah as a spice." Specifically through the Torah can we emerge from the control of the will to receive for ourselves and obtain the desire to bestow, since this is a second nature, to which only the light of Torah helps.

It follows that He, meaning the Creator, is the place of the world, meaning that the world must obtain the deficiency of the Creator, who is the desire to bestow. However, His world, which is the will to receive, meaning the lack that is in the world from the perspective of creation, which is the will to receive for oneself, this is not the Creator's lack.

This is why we say, "Blessed is the place." That is, when one has been rewarded with receiving the lack of the Creator, which is the desire to bestow, the person thanks the Creator for giving him His place, meaning the desire to bestow, which is what the Creator has. A person should achieve this degree of having the desire to bestow. This is why we say, "Blessed is the place," for giving us the place, meaning His deficiency, which is the desire to bestow, for with this desire of the Creator, the Creator can satisfy it with delight and pleasure.

Accordingly, we should interpret what we asked, What is "There is nothing that has no place" in the work? It means that this thing that a person wants to obtain, meaning the desire to bestow, which is what a person feels he lacks, a person must first work so that the thing he wants to obtain, namely the desire to bestow, must first have a place, meaning a real lack.

This is expressed in two ways: 1) to feel deficient, 2) to feel that only the Creator can help him, and the person himself is utterly unable to emerge from the governance of the will to receive for himself.

This is the meaning of "There is nothing that has no place." It means that the order of the work is that one must first prepare the place, meaning the lack, and then the Creator gives the filling of the lack.

However, we should know that although the heart of man's work is to come to know that he lacks the desire to bestow, and to pray for the Creator to satisfy his lack and give him that desire, one should also walk with the right line, which is regarded as wholeness. That is, a person should feel himself as whole, in order to be able to thank the Creator, for when one prays for something, that the Creator will satisfy his deficiency, he is considered "cursed," and "The cursed does not cling to the Blessed."

This is why our sages said (*Berachot* 32), "One should always establish the praise of the Creator and then pray," since when one establishes the praise of the Creator, it is certain that if a person sees the praise of the Creator and praises Him, in that state he is in a state of wholeness, meaning that man is in a state of blessing, and naturally, "The blessed clings to the Blessed." At that time, a person can extend the blessing from above.

The order should be that one should find within him something good that the Creator has given him. Although now he is deficient, he should invoke within him *Reshimot* [recollections] of something good he had from the Creator, and for which he can be grateful to the Creator. It does not matter what one enjoys, but only that he enjoyed it and thanks the Creator for it. Then he is in a state of wholeness.

In other words, then he was at peace with the Creator because He delighted him, so he can already be in gladness from what he had, and now he can come to the Creator to help him because now he is not in a state of sadness, where he feels that he is worse off than all other people, a state called "cursed," and "The cursed does not cling to the Blessed." Rather, now he is in a state of "blessed." Hence, a person should look within him for something that will enable him to be thankful to the Creator.

This is the meaning of the verse, "And none shall appear before Me empty-handed." We should interpret that when one comes to ask for something from the Creator, he should not be empty-handed, meaning that he has nothing. Rather, one should first try to find within him something that the Creator gave him and for which he blesses the Creator.

Afterward, he can ask of the Creator because he is thinking about what he received from the Creator. Thus, he already has connection with the Creator, for the Creator has given him something, whatever it is, but what matters is that he can thank the Creator for it, and already has a connection with the Creator in that he is pleased with the Creator for bestowing upon him.

Hence, since now he is in wholeness with the Creator, it is a *Segula* [remedy/cure/virtue] for the Creator to grant his wishes. This is as Baal HaSulam said, that by this, "The blessed clings to the Blessed." Hence, one must be very careful not to fall into the

Klipa [shell/peel] of sadness, for then one is apart from the Creator, unlike when he is in a state of "blessed."

And most important, a person should try to be in a state of "rewarded," meaning to pray to the Creator that he will be rewarded, for when one is in a state of "rewarded," he has a yearning for Torah and prayer, and he likes everything he sees in *Kedusha* [holiness]. This gives him high spirits because he feels the taste of life in everything that pertains to *Kedusha*.

But when he is "not rewarded," it is the complete opposite—he has no desire for Torah or prayer. Anything he does in *Kedusha* is forced on him, and when he introspects, he says about everything that pertains to *Kedusha* that it is to him as the potion of death, that he wants to quickly run away from all those things around him.

Although he sees that people around him engage in Torah and *Mitzvot* [commandments/good deeds] and have high spirits in the work that they do, his body excuses itself by saying that if the people had the same taste that he is feeling, they would not be any better off than he is. Sometimes, he does not even contemplate explaining why they can and he cannot. That is, their enthusiastic engagement in Torah and prayer is not enough to give him a yearning in the work. In truth, we should say that since this person is in a state of "not rewarded," his Torah becomes to him a potion of death.

According to the above, we should interpret what our sages said (*Yoma* 72), "Rabbi Yehoshua Ben Levi said, 'Why is it written, 'This is the law that Moses set.' If he is rewarded, it becomes to him a potion of life; if he is not rewarded, it becomes to him a potion of death.'"

We should interpret in the work, that if a person is rewarded, his Torah becomes to him a potion of life. This means that he feels the taste of life in the Torah and in prayer, and in everything of *Kedusha*. And if he is not rewarded, his Torah becomes to him a potion of death, meaning that he feels in the Torah and in the work the potion of death, meaning the taste of the potion of death, and wants to escape the campaign and the work, and all that he does is by compulsion.

However, we should know that the order of man's work is in two ways: 1) *Lo Lishma* [not for Her sake], 2) *Lishma* [for Her sake], meaning in order to bestow. As he says in the "Introduction to The Book of Zohar" (Item 29), "Know that our work during our seventy years is divided to four divisions:

"The First Division is to obtain the excessive will to receive without restraints, in its full, corrupted measure from under the hands of the four impure worlds ABYA. If we do not have that corrupted will to receive, we will not be able to correct it, for 'one cannot correct that which is not in him,' for the *Klipot* [shells/peels] will dominate it and give it of their lights, to provide one with all the material he needs to work with and correct." This is until the completion of thirteen years.

"The second division is from thirteen years and on. At that point, the point in his heart, which is the *Achoraim* [posterior] of the soul of *Kedusha* [holiness] that is clothed in his will to receive since his birth is given strength. However, it only begins to awaken after thirteen years (for the above reason), and then one begins to enter the system of the worlds of *Kedusha*. The primary intensification of the will to receive is only in spirituality. And yet, it is a much more important degree than the first, since this is the degree that brings one to *Lishma*, as our sages said, 'One should always engage in Torah and *Mitzvot Lo Lishma*, as from *Lo Lishma*, one comes to *Lishma*.' And the final degree in this division is to fall passionately in love with the Creator, until the object of passion remains before one's eyes all day long and all night, as the poet said, 'When I remember Him, He does not let me sleep.'

"The third division is work in Torah and *Mitzvot Lishma*, in order to bestow and not to receive reward. This work cleanses the will to receive for oneself in him and replaces it with a will to bestow. To the extent that one purifies the will to receive, he becomes worthy of receiving the five parts of the soul called NRNHY."

We therefore see that first we must work in *Lo Lishma*, meaning to obtain the desire and yearning for the light of pleasure that is

What Is, "There Is Nothing that Has No Place," in the Work?

dressed in Torah and *Mitzvot*. This work, which one should do only for his own sake, meaning to engage in the work in order to delight that will to receive with greater pleasures than corporeal pleasures. It follows that this work, called *Lo Lishma*, is because he works only in order to derive emotional satisfaction, and not in order to bestow contentment upon his Maker. In other words, he works in observing Torah and *Mitzvot* for his own sake and does not think about the benefit of the Creator.

When one begins to work in *Lo Lishma*, in order to obtain emotional fulfillment, he begins to feel a good taste in Torah and work, and he has high spirits and begins to feel the love of the Creator. At that time, he has the grace of *Kedusha*. Yet, when he wants to begin the work of bestowal, meaning to work for the sake of the Creator and not for his own sake, the taste he felt while working only for his own benefit is taken away from him.

This is so in order for him to accustom himself to work for the sake of the Creator and not for his own sake. Since he was used to feeling the taste of the work in the state of the second division, and now he does not feel that same taste of sweetness he felt while working *Lo Lishma*, he thinks that he does not feel a good taste in the work as he did before he began the work of *Lishma* because he has become worse than he was then. Therefore, he says that he sees that this work is not for him, and he wants to escape the campaign.

But in truth, a person should believe that the fact that he does not feel a good taste in the work is not because now he has descended from the degree he had before. Rather, it is that now he is being guided from above to accustom himself to work for the sake of the Creator, and not notice himself—whether he enjoys this work. Rather, he should accustom himself to work for the sake of the Creator. It is as Baal HaSulam said (in "The Order of the Work, by Baal HaSulam"), that one should believe that when he attributes his work to the Creator, the Creator accepts his work, regardless of the form of his work.

It follows that when one does not feel a good taste in the work, he should say that now he has an opportunity to work only for the sake of the Creator, meaning for the Creator to enjoy his work, since now he does not feel any flavor in the work, that he can say that he is attracted to the flavor.

However, when one overcomes and works in order for the Creator to enjoy his work, he should try to enjoy having a place to work only for the sake of the Creator, and from this one should derive high spirits. It was said about this work, "Serve the Lord with gladness." That is, when one sees that he has work, meaning when he sees that he has a place to overcome, since the body wants specifically for the will to receive to enjoy his work, he should overcome and work specifically because the Creator will enjoy his work, since now he does not feel taste in the work, to say that the flavor draws him. This is called "work."

From this work, a person should derive joy, from seeing that now he has a chance to perform work that will be only in order to bestow contentment upon his Maker. Yet, here begin the ascents and descents, since each time, a person is made to feel the truth of why he is remote from the Creator, since it is against nature.

But we should ask, Why did the Creator make it so that man will be unable to overcome his vessels of reception by himself, but will need the help of the Creator? Baal HaSulam said about this, that if a person did not see that he cannot overcome the evil in him without the help of the Creator, he would remain outside of *Kedusha*. He said that the reason is that if man could overcome the evil in him, he would naturally taste a good flavor in the work and would be content with little. That is, he would feel "Thank God, I engage in Torah and *Mitzvot* [commandments/good deeds]," and he would feel that he is doing everything for the sake of the Creator, so what else does he need? Therefore, he does not see what else he needs to add, since he really is working for the Creator. And since one cannot work without a lack, he would remain in *Katnut* [smallness/infancy] of *Kedusha*.

But if a person sees that he cannot overcome and work for the sake of the Creator, and each time he has descents and ascents, by

What Is, "There Is Nothing that Has No Place," in the Work?

which he sees that he needs the help of the Creator, and the help that the Creator gives is as *The Zohar* says about what is written, "He who comes to purify is aided," it asks, "With what is he aided?" and he replies, "With a holy soul."

That is, each time, he is rewarded with a higher soul, according to the help for which he asks—initially the light of *Nefesh*, then *Ruach*, until he is rewarded with the *NRNHY* of his soul. It therefore follows that the ascents and descents that one experiences come from above on purpose, so that through them, he will attain what pertains to his soul.

However, while one is still in *Lo Lishma*, and even when he has not obtained the *Lo Lishma* in the manner of the great passion for the Creator, as in the second division, as in "When I remember Him, He does not let me sleep," he should still begin with the work of bestowal and not wait until he achieves the state of *Lo Lishma* called "When I remember Him, He does not let me sleep," since one might remain in this state forever. But once he has achieved the state of *Lo Lishma* and feels a good taste in the work, he is given from above an awakening to want to work in order to bestow. At that time, the real work begins, until from above he is given the desire to bestow.

What Does It Mean that We Read the Portion, *Zachor* [Remember], Before Purim, in the Work?

Article No. 21, Tav-Shin-Nun-Aleph, 1990/91

The verse says, "Remember what Amalek did to you along the way when you came out from Egypt, what happened to you along the way. Blot out the memory of Amalek from under heaven; do not forget."

We should understand why we must remember what Amalek did to us in order to observe "Blot out the memory of Amalek." That is, this means that if we do not remember what he did to us, we cannot blot out, but rather precisely as much as we remember of him, this we can blot out, and not more. We should understand what it means in the work that he says, "Blot out the memory of Amalek," and if we have no memory then we cannot blot out. Therefore, first we were given the *Mitzva* [commandment/good deed], "Remember what Amalek did to you," and then we have the memory of Amalek, and we can carry out the *Mitzva* of blotting out Amalek.

It is known that there is no light without a *Kli* [vessel], no filling without a lack. Hence, a person cannot do anything if he has no need for that same thing. Therefore, how can we blot out Amalek if we have no need to blot him out? That is, a person does not know what is Amalek or why we need to perform the action of blotting him out. Therefore, first we must know what is Amalek and what troubles he had done to us. Afterward, to the extent that we understand that he is causing us troubles, to that extent we are ready to observe "Blot out the memory of Amalek."

In other words, according to one's memory of the troubles he had done to him, to that extent a person is willing to blot him out. That is, precisely according to what he remembers that he had harmed him, to that extent he wants to remove him from the world. If a person does not remember that he had done to him many troubles, then he has no need to blot him out. Hence, to the extent that he remembers, he can blot him out, and not more.

It follows that it is impossible to observe the blotting out of Amalek, but only to the extent that he remembers the troubles that he did to him. For this reason, the preparation for blotting out Amalek should be that one must know what is Amalek, meaning what is the role of Amalek against the people of Israel. It is about this that the verse says, "Remember what Amalek did to you along the way when you came out from Egypt, what happened to you along the way."

To the extent that a person feels the "what Amalek did to you," he can carry out "Blot out the memory of Amalek." That is, if a person does not remember that Amalek harmed him, he has no reason to blot him out. When a person introspects and wants to see who is his enemy and does him only harm, it is the will to receive for one's own sake, which is called the "evil inclination," since it prevents a person from receiving the delight and pleasure that the Creator wants to give him.

Therefore, when one looks at it, to the extent that he feels that the will to receive is his enemy, to the extent of the preparation to know and to feel the suffering it causes him, only to that extent is one willing to obliterate it from the world. This is the meaning of what is written, "Blot out the memory of Amalek." That is, this implies that we should know that we can blot out only to the extent that we remember what is the measure of the bad that he had done to us.

Accordingly, we can understand why we read the portion *Zachor* [remember] before Purim. First we must understand what is Purim in the work. The importance of Purim is explained in the words of the ARI (*The Study of the Ten Sefirot*, Part 15, Item 220), "This is the meaning of what is written, 'Their memory shall not fade from their descendants.' That illumination is on the days of Purim each and every year. Therefore, in the future, all the occasions will be cancelled except for the scroll of Esther. The reason is that there has never been such a great miracle, not on Sabbaths and not on good days, for such an illumination to be. In this respect, there is a big merit to Purim over all other days, even Sabbaths and good days."

In the commentary *Ohr Pnimi*, he interprets that that light, which was in the days of Purim, can shine only at the end of correction and not before. This light is called "the light of the purpose of creation." That is, it is light of *Hochma* that is clothed in vessels of reception, meaning he wants to receive the delight and pleasure that is there, which comes from the purpose of creation. This light of the purpose of creation, called *Ohr Hochma*, cannot shine without clothing, and it dresses in the light of the correction of creation, called *Ohr Hassadim*. Before the end of correction, this light of *Hochma*, called *Gadlut* of *Hochma*, cannot shine together with light of *Hassadim*.

At that time, there was a miracle because of the fasting and the outcries, which extended *Ohr* [light] *Hassadim*, and then *Ohr Hochma* could dress within the *Ohr Hassadim*, and this is considered that there was a miracle when the light shone before the end of correction, since by nature, that light can shine only at the end of correction, which is called "in the future." The miracle was that it illuminated before the end of correction. This is why our sages said, "All the occasions will be cancelled except for the scroll of Esther, since the light of Purim is the light that will shine in the future.

It is written (*Shabbat*, p 88), "'And they stood at the bottom of the mountain.' It means that He forced the mountain on them like a vault and said, 'If you accept the Torah, very well. But if you do not, there will it be your burial.' Raba said, 'Although the generation received it in the days of Ahasuerus, as it is written, 'they kept what they had already received.'"

We therefore see the importance of Purim, that they accepted the Torah willingly, whereas until then, it was only by coercion. By this we can interpret what we asked, What is the meaning of the portion *Zachor* being before Purim? The reason is that there is no light without a *Kli*. Hence, first we must remember what Amalek did, for Amalek in the work is called "the evil inclination," and remember the troubles he caused the people of Israel. Afterward, once we have a *Kli*, meaning a lack, it is possible to pray, as then it was fasting and crying out, and then they were rewarded with "kept and received willingly, for the love of the miracle."

It follows that we must prepare for Purim. We must say that the preparation is for the need and the *Kli* [vessel] for the reception of the light. This means that by feeling the lack, we can receive the filling. As there are six workdays before we can come to the state of Shabbat [Sabbath], as our sages said, "He who did not toil on the eve of Shabbat, what will he eat on Shabbat?" meaning that only when there are six workdays, then when Shabbat comes there is rest.

Therefore, one who works on Shabbat is regarded as "desecrating the Shabbat," meaning he desecrated the rest. Likewise, the preparation for Purim is also the feeling of the evil of Haman, who wants to destroy and to kill and annihilate all the Jews, from youth to old, infants and women, in one day.

Therefore, one must pay attention to the Haman in his heart, how he wants to destroy anything related to *Kedusha* [holiness], meaning anything that can yield something that is regarded as *Kedusha*.

Regardless of the measure of the matter, even if it is the smallest, he wants to destroy it. He regrets that he hasn't the power to overcome the sensation of evil of Haman, who wants to destroy all the Jews.

We should interpret that "all the Jews" means anything that has some relation to "for the sake of the Creator," this he wants to destroy. This is called "recognition of evil," which is a *Kli* and a lack. Afterward, we can receive a filling for it, called "light," which comes to fill the lack that is in the *Kli*. Hence, afterward, Israel were rewarded with "and it was turned to the contrary, so that the Jews governed their enemies," and they were rewarded with receiving the Torah willingly and not forcefully.

But the heart of the miracle is that "the Jews governed their enemies." That is, when the quality of "Jews" in one's heart governs, the work of the Creator can be done willingly and not by force. It follows that the heart of the miracle is when he was in a state where Haman controls and wants to destroy the entire quality of the Jews. But when the Jews control one's heart, they can observe willingly and not forcefully.

This is as our sages said, "Tyre was built only out of the ruin of Jerusalem, and vice-versa, when one rises, the other falls." Hence, the heart of man's work is to pray to the Creator to give him the desire to bestow, as this is the heart of the prayer, as it is written, "He who comes to purify is aided." When the Creator gives him the desire to bestow, this is the heart of the miracle, and this is called "a second nature," and it is in the hands of the Creator to give him a second nature.

This is why we read the portion *Zachor* before Purim. But before the portion *Zachor*, we read the portion *Shekalim* [pl. of shekel]. This comes to tell us that in the work, as *The Zohar* says, "*Shekalim* means *Even* [stone] with which to weigh." This is so because one must weigh the order of one's work, to see whether or not it is for the sake of the Creator. That is, it is impossible to blot out Amalek before one knows the power of the bad within him, and how it causes all the distancing from the Creator.

Therefore, when weighing the work in order to see if they are fine or not, we can come to the recognition of evil. Then, the extent to which we feel the bad and cannot overcome it, meaning that we see that we cannot prevail over it, this is still not regarded as "recognition of evil." However, this means that he sees the losses that the evil causes him and he wants to get rid of the evil but cannot. This is called "recognition of evil," meaning the sensation of the evil. In other words, when he sees the losses that the evil causes him, this is called "recognition of evil."

This feeling comes to a person through labor in Torah and *Mitzvot* [commandments/good deeds], when the light in the Torah makes him feel that the situation he is in is very bad because it causes him to be far from *Kedusha*. But if he does not feel that he is immersed in self-love, it harms him (and this is called recognition of evil). Precisely through Torah and *Mitzvot*, when he tries to obtain through them assistance in the work, the Torah reveals to him the bad in him. The first assistance he receives is the recognition of evil, meaning to recognize that the bad, meaning the will to receive for oneself, is bad and harmful to spirituality. It follows that the meaning of recognition of evil is to recognize that the bad, meaning the will to receive, is what is harmful to man. And when one feels that it is harmful, he can pray from the bottom of the heart.

However, we must understand why there should be a prayer from the bottom of the heart. The answer is that since one cannot feel the real taste of anything unless he has a yearning for it, from above they want that when he asks for something, that his request be answered, there must be a real lack. This is called "a prayer from the bottom of the heart," and it is known that "heart" means "desire."

Hence, when one prays to be given some filling, he must have a lack for the filling. For this reason, if one has another desire in one's heart, it is a sign that he does not have a big desire, since his desire splits into two desires. It follows that neither are great. But if he has but one desire in the heart, this is considered that what he asks is from the bottom of the heart. That is, he does not have any desire in between. He might have a desire to learn Torah but also a desire to rest and not exert. This, too, is considered two desires and is already not considered that the fact that he wants to learn Torah is one desire, since he also wants to enjoy rest.

Therefore, we read the portion *Shekalim* before the portion *Zachor*, since first we must know that the will to receive is called "bad and harmful," and then we can say, "Remember what Amalek did to you," when he enthroned the will to receive over the people of Israel in both mind and heart. And since we know that he did a bad thing, we want to obliterate Amalek.

We should know that in the order of the work, we must make several discernments:

1) When a person begins to enter the work of observing Torah and *Mitzvot*, he does not feel deficient, since he knows that he is more or less observing Torah and *Mitzvot*. Hence, he has no reason to say that he has bad.

2) When he begins to examine his actions, he begins to feel that he has bad in him, and he is wicked, but not a complete wicked, since he sees that there are worse people than him. Therefore, he is called "incomplete wicked."

3) When he wants to work in order to bestow, he sees how far he is from this work. Hence, the wicked comes to him with the "Who" and "What" questions. At that time, he comes to a state where he sees that he is a "complete wicked" in both mind and heart.

4) When he is in a state of ascent, he thinks of himself that he is righteous, meaning that he will remain in a state of ascent forever. Yet, afterward, another descent comes to him and he sees that he is wicked. Therefore, he does not know what to say about himself, whether to say that he is a complete wicked, since he sees that he has ascents when he appears to himself as righteous, or to say that he is righteous, since he sees that during a descent, he is wicked.

Since a person is close to himself, he accepts a bribe from the body, which he loves, and says that in truth, he is righteous, but an "incomplete righteous." In other words, since the body will enjoy more if he justifies himself, he says about himself that he is an "incomplete righteous." Because he has descents, at which time he is in a state of "wicked," and he does not say that he is "wicked" because of the descent, for the above reason that he accepts a bribe from the body, so he chooses to say that he is righteous, but an incomplete one, as it is written (Deuteronomy 16:19), "A bribe blinds the eyes of the wise and distorts the words of the righteous."

We can see an example of this in the manner that the world behaves. We see that many people buy lottery tickets in order to win the draw. Each one thinks that he will win the grand prize in the lottery, although there could be a million participants in the lottery and only one winner. Nevertheless, he participates in the draw and thinks that he might win. That is, although it is doubtful, he thinks that he might still win.

Conversely, we see that when those who buy the lottery want to go some place by car, we see that one out of a million has a car accident, and people are hurt. But that person who bought the lottery ticket is not afraid that he might have an accident. He does not say, as when he comes to buy a ticket, that he might have an accident.

The reason for this is that since a person is close to himself, he cannot see anything bad about himself. If there is something bad, it will probably happen to others, and not to him. Although he has hopes about winning the lottery, with a car accident, someone else will "win" this, and not he, although based on what does he determine that there is a difference between the lottery and an accident. And yet, "A bribe blinds the eyes of the wise and distorts the words of the righteous."

Therefore, when one sees that he has ups and downs, he says that in truth, he is righteous, so why is he having descents, for then, during the descent, he sees that he is wicked? As a result, he says about himself that he is righteous, albeit incomplete.

5) When he is rewarded with complete faith and can aim his work in order to bestow, but only in vessels of bestowal, it can be said that he already has love of the Creator, although only with the

good inclination. But the vessels of reception, which pertain to the evil inclination, those are still outside of *Kedusha*.

6) When he achieves "repentance," meaning when he is rewarded with love of the Creator "with both your inclinations," as it is written, "And you shall love the Lord your God with all your heart," meaning with both your inclinations, the good inclination and the evil inclination. This is considered that one has repented, meaning that the bad in him, which are the vessels of reception, have also entered the *Kedusha* [holiness], and he can work with them in order to bestow. This is why our sages said, "In a place where they who repent stand, complete righteous do not stand." This means that complete righteous cannot stand in *Kedusha*, meaning that complete righteous cannot use *Kelim* [vessels] of the evil inclination, which are vessels of reception for self-benefit, so they are corrected and are in *Kedusha*, meaning that they work for the sake of the Creator.

It follows that everything follows the order of degrees, from light to heavy. Hence, the order of the work is that we begin in *Lo Lishma* [not for Her sake], and then we achieve *Lishma* [for Her sake]. Accordingly, we should interpret what our sages said about the words "received and kept, kept what they had already received." That is, thus far it was by force, as it is written, "And they stood at the bottom of the mountain," and they explained, "He forced the mountain on them like a vault and said, 'If you accept the Torah, very well. But if you do not, there will it be your burial.'"

It follows that thus far it was by force, and now, on Purim, they accepted it willingly. This is called "the order of the work." That is, the beginning of man's work should be by force. By nature, when a person wants to work for the sake of the Creator, his body objects to it. This means that in truth, we begin in *Lo Lishma*, when the body does not object so much, since when it believes that it will be rewarded for relinquishing small pleasures and receive in return great pleasures, meaning he promises the body that it will receive a greater reward in return for his work in Torah and *Mitzvot*, this is not against nature. Hence, this is truly the first beginning.

But afterward, when he begins the work in order to bestow, the body resists it as it contradicts the nature with which it was born, which is to think only about its own benefit. At that time, the work is coercive. That is, he must not look at the body, whether it agrees to work for the sake of the Creator. Rather, one must do everything by force, even if the body disagrees.

This coercion that a person does is regarded as "a prayer," since a person wants to observe "love the Lord your God," but sees that he has no love for the Creator, for there is a rule that where there is love there is no coercion. Rather, specifically where there is no love, and a person wants to work for someone for whom he has no love, he can work for Him.

Thus, we should ask, If a person has no love for the Creator, why does he work for Him? That is, Why should one work coercively? The answer is that we were given faith. A person must believe that through the coercion that he forces himself, and he truly wants to love the Creator, this is a prayer. By this he will be rewarded with "accepted willingly, for the love of the miracle." That is, the Creator gave them the second nature, which is the desire to bestow, and they were rewarded with the love of the Creator and received everything willingly.

What Is "A Lily Among the Thorns," in the Work?

Article No. 22, Tav-Shin-Nun-Aleph, 1990/91

It is written in *The Zohar* (*Ki Tissa*, Items 31-32), "'As a lily among the thorns, so is my wife among the daughters.' The Creator wished to make Israel similar to what is above, so there would be one lily in the earth that is like the lily above, which is *Malchut*. And the fragrant lily, finer than all the lilies in the world, is only one that grows among the thorns. This one smells as it should, which are seventy souls, and brought them among the thorns, which are the Egyptians. At that time, the lily blossomed among them. When the Creator wished to pick out the lily from among them, the thorns dried out and were thrown away and were corrupted until they were regarded as nothing."

We should understand what it implies to us in the work when a person must be similar to the upper lily, and why specifically when one is among the thorns, he is regarded as more select and finer than the rest of the people, as it is written, "This is why seventy souls went down to Egypt, so as to become finer."

What Is "A Lily Among the Thorns," in the Work?

Baal HaSulam said, Why is *Malchut* called "a lily"? It is because a person can assume the burden of the kingdom of heaven only by overcoming the will to receive in him, since it comes and asks a person when he wants to work in order to bestow, meaning for the sake of the Creator and not for himself, "What is this work for you?" That is, "What will you get out of wanting to work for the sake of the Creator?"

It is written in the Passover Haggadah [narrative], "The answer is, 'Blunt his teeth.'" This means that we must not argue with it, but blunt its teeth, meaning we have to overcome it by force. That is, when it comes with its questions (we must remember that it comes with these questions precisely when one wants to work in order to bestow; then there is room to ask "Why?" But when a person works in order to receive reward, this wicked one has nothing to ask), we must not reply or contemplate what to answer it. Instead, we must know that it is a waste of time to want to find answers to its questions. Rather, when it comes and asks, a person should immediately treat it with force and overcome it with force, and not by arguments.

Since each time, even once a person has overcome it, it is still not impressed by it, and each time a person wants to do something for the sake of the Creator it comes with its questions, there are numerous "blunt its teeth" here. This is why *Malchut* is called "a lily." In other words, when a person wants to be rewarded with the kingdom of heaven, called "faith," he must undergo a process of many "blunt its teeth," which is why *Malchut* is called "lily." He said that this is the meaning of "To the victor on lilies," meaning that the victory comes specifically through lilies.

According to the above, we can interpret the meaning of "as a lily among the thorns," and why it is that specifically when she is among the thorns, she is finer than other lilies. We should know what thorns are in the work. In corporeality, the thorns prick the lily, but what does this imply in the work? It means that when the wicked comes and asks "What is this work for you?" with these questions, it pricks man's thoughts and heart, and makes a person suffer. As thorns prick in corporeality, so the questions prick the person.

He suffers torments, meaning that these questions distance him from the work, since one cannot always overcome his questions and he begins to see that he is declining from the *Kedusha* [holiness], since normally, these questions come during an ascent, when a person understands that it is worthwhile to work in order to bestow.

But suddenly, he comes with his questions and one must overcome it. At that time, a person comes and asks for help from the Creator to help him, since he sees that by himself, he cannot overcome it. It follows that he always needs heaven's mercy.

As it is written in *The Zohar*, the help that comes from above is regarded as a soul that he receives each time. This is regarded that the help he receives from above is light that gives one the power to overcome the evil in him. It was said about this, "He who comes to purify is aided."

By this we can interpret the words "As a lily among the thorns," and a lily that is more fragrant and finer than all the other lilies in the world is only one that grew among the thorns. In other words, because she is among the thorns, they prick her, meaning the kingdom of heaven. When a person takes upon himself to work in order to bestow, this is called "a lily."

At that time, the wicked comes with his questions of "What is this work for you?" and pricks the kingdom of heaven in his heart. Each time, he must overcome and pray and ask for help. By this, the lily becomes fragrant, for fragrance is as it is written, "And they smelled in the fear of the Creator," which is finer than all the lilies in the world, who have no thorns to prick them. Those lilies are not as fine as the lily that is among the thorns.

This comes to teach us that one should not be alarmed when the wicked keeps coming to him and asks the question, "What is this work for you?" and he cannot overcome it. It is not as one sometimes thinks, that these thoughts come to him because he is unfit for the work of the Creator. On the contrary, the fact that the wicked comes to him is because from above, they want to help him attain upper *Kedusha* [holiness]. This is why he is given these disturbances, so as to have a need to ask for help.

Therefore, when one sees that he is unfit by nature to be able to work in order to bestow, his work at that time is to increase his prayers to the Creator to help him from above, so he can work in order to bestow.

Conversely, an ordinary lily—meaning other people, who observe Torah and *Mitzvot* [commandments/good deeds] in order to receive reward—although this is also regarded as a lily, meaning that the body does not agree to observe Torah and *Mitzvot* even in order to receive reward, and it requires labor and effort, since we must believe in reward and punishment, to which the body objects, but because it is not against nature, since his work is for his own benefit, the lily in his heart, which is called "kingdom of heaven," is not regarded as feeling that there are thorns that prick her.

Therefore, although *Lo Lishma* [not for Her sake] is an important thing, this is called a mere "lily," since she does not suffer pricks from the thorns. Therefore, he has no need to pray to the Creator to help him overcome. Naturally, he also does not extend *Kedusha* from above, by which he will receive help from above. For this reason, he is called a mere "lily."

But a "lily among the thorns" is finer than all the other lilies in the world because the pricks, meaning the sufferings she suffers from the wicked, cause him to receive new powers from above each time, and by this his soul grows. This is why she is finer than all the lilies in the world.

It follows that one should be careful not to say when he sees the wicked always coming to him with questions called "thorns," which prick the lily in his heart, he should not say that this is a sign that he is unworthy of this work of bestowal because it is not for him, since he sees that he hasn't the strength to overcome the evil.

Rather, one should believe that every person has the strength to work and achieve *Dvekut* [adhesion] with the Creator, as our sages said, "One should always see oneself as half guilty, half innocent." That is, according to the measure of the good within him, so is the measure of bad. Otherwise, a person cannot subdue the bad, as it is more than the good. We must believe in our sages, who said so, and it is so precisely so that one will be able to decide to the side of merit. Therefore, always, in whatever situation, the bad does not have more power than the good within him. This is why they said, "If he performs one Mitzva [sing. of Mitzvot], happy is he, for he has sentenced himself and the whole world to the side of merit."

Accordingly, we should interpret what is written, "The rich shall not give more and the poor shall not give less than half a shekel." We should understand what this implies to us in the work. We must know that we were given the choice, as it is written, "Behold, I have set before you today life and good, and death and bad, and you shall choose life, so that you and your descendants will live."

It is known that choice means that a person can decide which is better for him. This can be said when both are equal and he does not know which to choose. At that time, we are given the commandment to choose, as our sages said, that one must see oneself as "half guilty, half innocent," and then we can talk about choice.

This means that one who sees that he is not succeeding in the work and wants to escape the campaign since he sees that he cannot work for the sake of the Creator because he was born with worse qualities than others, and he also sees that he has a weak character and therefore hasn't the strength to overcome the evil in him, the text teaches us about this that one has no more bad in him, but according to the measure of the good.

In other words, if a person sees that he has a weak character or worse qualities than another person, he must know that the bad in him does not have more power than the good in him; they are ever equal, fifty-fifty. Therefore, if he sees that one person has better qualities than his, he should not say that it is easier for him to work than for him, and this is why the other one is working. Rather, one should know that every person has bad according to the measure of the good that he has. Hence, if the other has better qualities, he also has worse qualities than the other, since the bad and the good are ever equal in strength.

The verse says about this, "The rich shall not give more and the poor shall not give less than half a shekel, to give a donation to the Lord, to make atonement for your souls." "The rich" means that even if one is rich in knowledge and good qualities, he will not give more than half a shekel because "half" means a lack, which one gives as a contribution to the Creator, so that He will satisfy his lack, as was said, that "a prayer makes half." He cannot say that he gives more powers than half by having good qualities, but rather precisely half, for the above reason that corresponding to the good that he has, he also has more bad than another person. It follows that one never gives more than half.

Likewise, "The poor shall not give less." This means that one who is poor in knowledge and in good attributes, and he prevails and does not escape the campaign, the Creator helps him. He, too, should not say that he makes less efforts than another person, since he sees that he is poor in knowledge. Therefore, when the Creator helps him and brings him closer to Him, he should not say that he has given less than half the forces of the work in order to overcome the bad in him. Rather, he, too, gave half, since the bad in him was also not so powerful that it was said that the filling was more than the lack of the forces in the bad.

Rather, it is always fifty-fifty, as it is written, "The poor shall not give less than half a shekel." That is, the good and the bad are always equal. Therefore, a person cannot say that he is incapable of this work, since he should give more powers than others. Rather, a person never gives more than half a shekel.

This is the meaning of what is written, "to give a contribution to the Lord." That is, the contribution that one should give to the Creator is only half, meaning the lack that a person feels that the Creator will help give the filling. What is the filling? Answer: The filling is always that which a person needs. Hence, when one begins the work, he should obtain a lack for the Creator to help him have the desire to bestow, as this is the heart of the work, to obtain this desire.

It follows that half means the necessity for the matter, to feel how much he needs to obtain this desire, meaning to obtain suffering at not having the desire to bestow, to know the loss at not having the desire to bestow. To the extent that he knows what he is losing, to that extent he can feel how happy he would be if he had the desire to bestow.

By this he obtains half a thing, meaning the *Kli* [vessel] for the Creator to satisfy his lack by giving him from above a second nature called "desire to bestow." This is the meaning of what is written, "half a shekel, to give a contribution to the Lord." In other words, a person should know that he can only give half, as in "a prayer makes half." One must know that he cannot give a full shekel, which is light and *Kli*, meaning the need for the desire to bestow, and to be able to do everything in order to bestow.

Rather, the half shekel belongs to man's work, to give only the deficiency, while the filling belongs to the Creator. This is the meaning of what is written, "go give a contribution to the Lord, to make atonement for your souls." In other words, by giving a contribution to the Lord, which is the half, the Creator gives the other half, called "desire to bestow," which is a second nature, and by this a person makes atonement for his soul, by being able to do everything for the sake of the Creator.

Therefore, after one is rewarded with the Creator giving the desire to bestow, a person is rewarded with permanent faith, as it is written ("Introduction of The Book of Zohar," Item 138), that we must be thankful to the Creator for rewarding us with nearing Him. This is as it is written (Psalms 68:32-33), "Sing to God, kingdoms of the earth, sing praises to the Lord, Selah. To Him who rides upon the highest, ancient heavens; He will speak forth with His voice, a mighty voice."

We should interpret that the "kingdoms of the earth" are those who have been rewarded with faith, called *Malchut*, and the quality of "Earth." "Sing to God," they should sing for the Creator awarding them with the quality of faith. Also, *Malchut* is called God, as it is written, "Sing praises to the Lord, Selah. To Him who rides upon the highest, ancient heavens; He will speak forth with His voice, a mighty voice."

We should understand why they must sing to the Creator and thank Him. Does the Creator need flesh and blood to thank Him? The answer is that the created beings should know that all that they have is what the Creator gave them in order to thereby achieve the love of the Creator. Through love of the Creator, they will always be in *Dvekut* with the Creator, as it is written ("Introduction of The Book of Zohar," Item 138), that then they attain Him as doing good. And if they do not attain Him as doing good, then they must be under the governance of heresy, since "It is a law that the creature cannot receive disclosed evil from Him, for it is a flaw in the glory of the Creator for the creature to perceive Him as an evildoer, as it is unbecoming of the Complete Operator."

This is the meaning of what is written, "He will speak forth with His voice, a mighty voice." In other words, the creatures must sing and thank Him for letting them hear the voice of the Creator. That is, by feeling that the Creator has given them the quality of *Malchut*, called "permanent faith," by their feeling that it comes from the Creator, this adds to them the love of the Creator, as it is written, "He will speak forth with His voice." And what will He say with His voice? Answer: "a mighty voice." The RADAK interpreted that He will speak forth against the enemies with His voice, which is a mighty voice. It is known that in the work, the enemies are the will to receive that awakens each time to receive in order to receive. They are man's enemies because they prevent a person from receiving the delight and pleasure.

Therefore, one should believe that the fact that one has been rewarded with faith in the Creator comes from the Creator. By this he is rewarded with the voice of the Creator subduing the enemies, meaning that the will to receive surrenders and in its stead comes the desire to bestow, and now he wants to work for the sake of the Creator. This comes from the voice of the Creator, as it is written, "The voice of the Lord is powerful" (Psalms 29:4). We should interpret that the voice of the Lord gives power to man to subdue the enemies.

This is the meaning of what is written (there), "Give strength to God." The RADAK interprets "Give strength"—with words. Give Him the strength since His strength has done your vengeance against the enemies, and not by your own force.

We should interpret his words, "with words," meaning they said that all the strength of the force, the Creator alone did it. That is, the fact that you see that your enemies, meaning the will to receive has surrendered before you, it is not man's force, but only the force of the Creator. This is as the RADAK says, "His strength has done your vengeance against the enemies, and not by your own force."

This is the meaning of what is written, "over Israel, His pride and His strength is in the skies." As the RADAK says, "The pride and greatness of the Creator is seen and apparent over Israel, since He fights the enemies for them with pride and strength." It is as *The Zohar* says, "When the Creator wished to pick out the lily from among them, the thorns dried out and were regarded as nothing." That is, he did this by the might of the Creator, meaning surrendered all the enemies. In other words, the fact that the will to receive surrendered and now the desire to bestow governs the person, this is "over Israel, His pride."

In other words, the pride and greatness of the Creator is seen and apparent over Israel, meaning that the desire to bestow controls, and this does not come by man's power, but by the power of the Creator. This means that it is apparent that it came from the Creator in that His help comes by being rewarded with greater light each time, that His help, says *The Zohar*, is as "a new soul." Thus, now it is evident that it came from the Creator.

We should interpret the reason that a person cannot achieve the vessels of bestowal by himself. The answer is that if a person could achieve vessels of bestowal by himself, he would be content with little and would feel himself as a complete human being. He would remain in his *Katnut* [infancy/smallness], since he would have no need to go forward because he really is doing everything for the sake of the Creator.

There is a rule that there is no light without a *Kli*, meaning a need. But when a person himself cannot obtain vessels of bestowal and must ask the Creator to help him, the person needs His help. By this, he receives from the Creator new help each time, and all her help is part of his soul. By this he is rewarded with receiving the NRNHY in the root of his soul.

A person must be cautious to take upon himself the burden of kingdom of heaven unconditionally. This is called "unconditional surrender." That is, one need not say, "If the Creator gives me a good taste in Torah and prayer, I will be able to do the holy work. Otherwise, I cannot be a servant of the Creator."

This is as it is written in *The Zohar* (*Truma*, Item 710), and we learned that this is the meaning of the verse, "'Lift up a song for Him who rides through the prairies,' which are *Netzah* and *Hod*, which are thighs. They do not bear fruit; it is all like the willows in the palm branch."

It is known that the willows in the *Lulav* [palm branch used festively on *Sukkot*] imply that the work should be done in the manner of willows. Although the willows have neither taste nor smell, as Baal HaSulam said of what is written (in *Hoshaana*), "To entertain You with the willows of the brook." That is, even if he feels no flavor in the work, and it is like the willows of the brook, devoid of taste or smell, during the work, they should be to man as great entertainments. This is called "unconditional surrender," and this is the meaning of what is written, "rejoice before Him," meaning be happy as though they have great attainments. This is the meaning of entertainment before the Creator, and thus we should believe.

What Is the Meaning of the Purification of a Cow's Ashes, in the Work?

Article No. 23, Tav-Shin-Nun-Aleph, 1990/91

RASHI interprets, "This is the statute of the law": "Because Satan and the nations of the world taunt Israel, to say, 'What is this *Mitzva* [commandment/good deed] and what is its reason,' therefore, it is written about it, 'It is a statute, a decree before Me; you have no permission to doubt it.' 'And have them take for you': It will always be named after you. 'A red cow': This can be compared to the son of a maidservant who soiled the king's palace. They said, 'Let his mother come and clean up the feces.' Similarly, let the cow come and atone for the calf."

We should understand what the matter of the burning of the cow, whose ashes purify, implies to us in the work. Also, we should understand the matter of answering those who ask questions about the point of this red cow. Normally, when someone asks a question

What Is the Meaning of the Purification of a Cow's Ashes, in the Work?

he receives an answer that the asking person can accept. Yet, here he asks, what is the point of the cow, and the answer is "statute," "decree." Is this answer acceptable? And we should also understand why he says that it is a statute and then gives the allegory about the cow, "Let his mother come and clean up her son," which implies that there is already a reason for it, which is that the mother will clean up her son.

We should understand all this in the work. It is known that the purpose of creation is to do good to His creations, and this is why the Creator created in the creatures a desire and yearning to receive pleasure. However, in order for the creatures not to feel shame while receiving delight and pleasure, since if they are ashamed, the pleasure will be incomplete, there was a correction that a person does not receive the delight and pleasure for man's own pleasure, meaning in order to enjoy the King's gift. Rather, it is to the contrary—it is for the Creator to enjoy His will being done by their receiving pleasure from Him. In other words, since the Creator wants to do good to His creations, he observes the commandment of the Creator. Otherwise, for himself, he would relinquish the pleasure. It follows that there is no matter of shame here since everything he does is for the sake of the Creator and not for his own benefit.

However, Baal HaSulam gave another explanation concerning why we must do everything in order to bestow, since by nature, when a person is in high spirits and enjoys life, he has no need to make efforts and obtain more than he has, if the property that he has gives him complete satisfaction. Hence, since spiritual pleasures satisfy a person, and even the smallest degree in spirituality provides more satisfaction than any corporeal pleasure, a person would be content with little and would have no need to obtain the *NRNHY* in his soul.

But when a person works in order to bestow, when all his work is only in order to bring contentment to his Maker, it follows that when one obtains some spiritual degree and takes that pleasure because the Creator will enjoy it, he cannot say, "Master of the world, I do not want a higher degree than I have, since all the pleasures I am receiving are only because I want to please You, and I have given you plenty of pleasures already, and I do not want You to enjoy too much; I have given You enough, and I do not want to give You any more."

We should know that when one receives in order to bestow, he receives a continually greater taste in bestowing contentment upon his Maker. As a result, a person cannot say, "I do not want to receive any more pleasures because I am settling for little." It turns out that working for the sake of the Creator causes one to have to receive a higher degree each time, since he cannot say to the Creator, "I have already given You plenty of pleasures and I cannot give You any more." This is why we must work in order to bestow.

There is another explanation why we must work in order to bestow: It is because of disparity of form. In spirituality, equivalence of form is called "unification," *Dvekut* [adhesion], and disparity of form causes "distance" and "separation." And since the main thing that one should strive for in life is to cling unto Him, since man should depict to himself that there is nothing more important in the world than to be in the King's palace, through equivalence of form, as our sages said about "cling onto His attributes," "As He is merciful, so you are merciful," by this a person enters the King's palace and is rewarded each time with speaking with the King.

It follows that on the whole, there are three reasons why we need to work for the sake of the Creator and not for our own sake. It is written about it, "Blessed is our God, who has created us for His glory." We should understand why we thank the Creator for creating us for His glory and not for ours, since it makes sense that if He had created us for our glory, all creations would have blessed Him. Yet, the verse says that we must thank Him for creating us for His glory. What is our benefit in this?

The answer is that we must know that the Creator does not need us to give Him anything; the whole purpose of creation is only for the sake of the created beings, as it is written, "His desire to do good to His creations." In order for the creatures to be able to receive the abundance for the three above reasons, for they can prevent the purpose of creation from being fully achieved, 1) because of shame, 2) in order for man not to settle for little, but each one should obtain the NRNHY in his soul, 3) because of *Dvekut*, which is equivalence of form, one should work in order to bestow, like the Creator.

It follows that the Creator created us and gave us the Torah and *Mitzvot* [commandments/good deeds] by which we can come to do everything in order to have the glory of the Creator. It follows that when we bless Him for creating us for His glory, it means that He has guided us and gave us the means by which to be able to work for His glory. By this we can achieve the purpose of creation, called "His desire to do good to His creations." This is as our sages said, "The Creator said, 'I have created the evil inclination; I have created the Torah as a spice.'" These are the means by which we can come to do everything for His glory. This is why we thank Him for it and say, "Blessed is our God, who created us for His glory."

In order for one to be able to work in order to bestow, meaning to do things not for his own benefit, we were given work in mind and in heart. "In mind" means that one should go above what the mind and reason obligate him to do. This is called "above reason," meaning that he believes although his intellect and reason disagree with what he wants to do. That is, we were given the *Mitzva* [sing. of *Mitzvot*] of faith above reason, which says that what reason tells us to do, we do not obey, and the faith, where we are commanded to believe what the Torah says, this is what we do, and we say that faith is of the utmost importance, and what reason and intellect obligate us to do are of inferior importance. Certainly, we should follow the one who is more important, and this is called "faith above reason."

But in faith, too, we should make three discernments:

1) For example, if a person gives to his friend $1,000, and the person accepts it, and he is completely sure and believes, since this man is my friend, and a meticulous person, so if he gives the money, there must be $1,000 there, and there is no need to count. This is called "faith below reason." In other words, he believes him because his reason does not object to what he believes, meaning there is no

contradiction between believing him and the reason. It follows that to him, faith is below reason, and the reason is more important. That is, he believes him because reason does not object. However, if this is in contrast to reason, he will probably not believe. This is still not regarded as faith above reason.

2) He tells him, "Here is $1,000." The receiver counts it three times and sees that there is the stated amount there and says to the giver, "I believe you that there is that amount here, as you say." Certainly, this does not count as faith.

3) He counts the $1,000 three times and sees that one dollar is missing, but he says to the giver, "I believe you that there is $1,000 here. Even though the reason and the intellect say that there is less here, he says that he believes. This is called true "above reason." However, maintaining faith above reason, meaning saying, "I annul my reason, and the fact that I counted three times does not matter, but I believe with faith above reason," meaning that the faith is more important than the reason, this is hard work.

By this we will understand that the faith that one should have in the Creator where he annuls his reason and what it tells him, by saying, "My reason will be as annulled as the dust of the earth," this is considered that he annuls his view from before the view of Torah. This called "the work of the mind."

Also, there is the work of the heart. The heart is called "desire." Since man was created with a nature of desire to receive for one's own sake, meaning to enjoy life, when he is told that he should work for the sake of the Creator, it is against nature, so why is this needed? A person needs to do everything for the sake of the Creator for the three above reasons, and this is why it is special work, for by this a person knows that the fact that he wants to do everything for his own sake, since man was born with a nature of will to receive for himself, he must divide his work in two manners: 1) in the mind, which is that one should pay attention to the state of his faith. Yet, in faith, a person can work in order to receive reward, meaning to observe Torah and *Mitzvot* because it will later reward him, meaning that he will have benefit for himself from this, and he will therefore remain separated.

Hence, there is another special work called "heart," which is "love of others." If he works only on love of others, he will still remain outside of *Kedusha* [holiness], since love of others is not the purpose of creation, for the purpose of creation is to do good to His creations, meaning for the creatures to receive from the Creator the delight and pleasure. But if they have no faith, how can they receive anything from the Creator when they have no faith in the Creator? Hence, the work must be in two ways.

However, Baal HaSulam said that the fact that we must go with faith, and the Creator does not let us serve Him by the way of knowing, is also in order for the work not to be for one's own sake, since if He were revealed to the creatures and they would not need faith, it would be impossible to do anything for the sake of the Creator. We can see how difficult it is to receive corporeal pleasures only in order to bestow, and it is much more so with spiritual pleasures, for in a spiritual pleasure, even a small bit has more pleasures than corporeal pleasures, so he will certainly not be able to receive in order to bestow. Hence, there is work in two ways: 1) in mind, 2) in heart.

Accordingly, we should interpret what we asked, What is the meaning of the purification of a cow's ashes, in the work? Our sages said, "Because Satan and the nations of the world taunt Israel, to say, 'What is this *Mitzva*?'" the answer is that this is why he wrote about it, "It is a statute." We asked, What is the answer that can be accepted, since they are asking why this is so, and it makes sense that we must answer so that the one who is asking will understand why. But what is the answer? "It is a statute, a decree before Me; you have no permission to doubt it."

The thing is that since the order of the work is that we must begin the work in the mind, meaning take upon ourselves faith above reason, therefore, if the nations of the world do not ask, What is this *Mitzva*? but only that he takes upon himself faith, that he believes above reason, this is regarded as faith of the first kind, which we said above was like a person who gave him $1,000 and he believes him that the sum is as stated and does not count them.

But when they come and ask, What is this *Mitzva* and what is its reason, it is similar to faith of the third kind, of which we said that it is when he does count them, and his counting falls short, yet he believes him above reason, meaning he cancels his reason and intellect before the giver. This is called "faith above reason." Hence, precisely when the nations of the world in one's body ask what is this *Mitzva* and what is its reason, since the body feels no taste in that which is above the intellect and reason, hence, the true and correct answer is to reply to the body that he believes that these questions were sent to him from above so that now he will be able to observe the *Mitzva* of faith above reason. Hence, the correct answer is specifically because it is a statute and decree. At that time, it is forbidden to give the body reasonable answers about why he wants to work for the benefit of the King.

It follows that precisely through the reply of statue and decree, he can advance in the work of the Creator. Although he sees that he cannot overcome the arguments of the nations of the world, he should believe above reason about that, too, that the fact that he cannot overcome is not because he has a weak character and this is why he cannot overcome, but rather that this is what is desired above—that he will not be able to overcome.

And the reason is specifically that by being unable to overcome, he now receives an opportunity to pray that the Creator will help him overcome. The benefit of this is that specifically through the help from above, it is possible to be rewarded with the NRNHY in his soul, since each time he receives help, it is by receiving an illumination from above. It follows that now he has an opportunity to be rewarded with the *Gadlut* [greatness/adulthood] of the soul because he has a need for the Creator to help him. It is known that *The Zohar* says, that His help is in giving him from above a soul.

What Is the Meaning of the Purification of a Cow's Ashes, in the Work?

Therefore, one should be careful when the body comes and asks, "Why must you exert in Torah and *Mitzvot* if you see that you feel no taste in them?" A person should not think of ways to answer intellectually, but rather tell the body, "I am thankful to you for approaching me with these arguments, since I am saying that reasonably speaking, you are correct, meaning that from the perspective of common sense, I should be sitting still. Yet, I am working above reason, and although you are not letting me overcome, I do want to overcome as much as I can. Therefore, I am asking for the help of the Creator so I can prevail over you. This must be the best opportunity, for by this I can be awarded entry into *Kedusha* and to do everything in order to bestow. It follows that the reply, "It is a statute, a decree before Me," is the real answer in order for a person to advance in the work and achieve permanent faith, for the Creator to help him be rewarded with mind and heart.

According to the above, we can interpret what we asked, that on one hand, he says that a cow is a statute without any reason, but then our sages give a reason through the allegory about "the son of a maidservant who soiled the king's palace. They said, 'Let his mother come and clean up the feces.' Similarly, let the cow come and atone for the calf." Thus, they do give a reason for the red cow, and the answer is that the mother will come and clean up her son. This is the answer to the red cow being a statute without reason. It means that the sin of the calf was as it is written in *The Zohar* ("Introduction of The Book of Zohar," Item 14), "Those who sinned with the calf said about, 'These [ELEH] are your gods, O Israel,' since they blemished that clothing and the abundance went out to other gods." This means that they wanted to receive the light of *Hochma* without a clothing of *Hassadim*, which is regarded as not wanting to accept the clothing of *Hassadim*, called "faith above reason."

Hence, it is about this that the commandment of red cow comes, which is all statute and decree, entirely above reason, for this cow is called "mother," and if he corrects the sin of not wanting to go with faith above reason, by this the sin will be corrected. It follows that there is no reason for the red cow itself. On the contrary, since the matter of the red cow is entirely above reason, this will correct what they wanted with the sin of the calf, that it will all be within reason, when they said, "These are your gods, Israel." It follows that the matter of the red cow is completely above reason, which indicates the matter of faith, which purifies the impure, since *Tuma'a* [impurity] comes from the will to receive for one's own benefit, and the correction of exiting the will to receive is by accepting the work of faith above reason, for then one asks for the help of the Creator and by this, he emerges from the rule of the will to receive. This is called "the exodus from Egypt," for only the Creator Himself delivered them from Egypt, as it is written, "I and not a messenger."

It follows that the meaning of a red cow, whose ashes purify, ash indicates something that was cancelled, such as after the burning of the cow, when only ashes remain, implying the annulment, once a person has annulled his reason and his will before the will of the Creator. At that time, a person is rewarded with the will of the Creator, which is to bestow. When a person has the desire to bestow, he is called "a pure man," for he does not do anything unless it brings contentment to his Maker.

According to the above, we should interpret what is written (in *Yotzer*, for the portion, "Cow"), "to purify the impure, to defile the pure with saying, 'holy.'" We should understand how there can be two opposites in the same subject. In the work, we should interpret that when one begins to prepare oneself to take upon himself faith above reason, he is immediately defiled. That is, before he began this work, when he worked in order to receive reward, he felt that he was righteous. That is, he saw that he was observing Torah and *Mitzvot* and did not find within him any flaw. Hence, he knew that he was pure and did not have any *Tuma'a*. He was only concerned about others—that they are not walking in the path of the Creator, and he wanted to give the faith, but they would not listen. But concerning himself, he knew that he had enough faith to dispense to several people, if they only wanted to receive.

What Is the Meaning of the Purification of a Cow's Ashes, in the Work?

But when he begins the work of bestowal and to believe in the Creator above reason, he sees the truth, that he is immersed in self-love and is devoid of faith. It follows that now he has become impure. This is called "to defile the pure." But afterward, he is rewarded with "to purify the impure."

What Does It Mean that One Should Bear a Son and a Daughter, in the Work?

Article No. 24, Tav-Shin-Nun-Aleph, 1990/91

It is written in *The Zohar* (*VaYikra*, Items 94-95), "This is why He created him male and female, so he would be whole, such as above. And a son and daughter came out of him and his wife, and then he is a whole man, such as above, and completes below like the upper, Holy Name. This is so because *Yod-Hey* are *AVI* and *Vav-Hey* are son and daughter. At that time, he is called by the name of the upper, Holy Name. A man who does not wish to complete the Holy Name below, meaning to bear a son and a daughter, it would be better for him that he were not born, for he has no part at all in the Holy Name."

We should understand what it implies to us in the work, that if he does not have a son and a daughter, it is better for him not to be born. It is known that we should discern two things in the world: 1) The purpose of creation, which is "to do good to His creations," meaning for the creatures to receive delight and pleasure. This is why He created in the creatures a nature where they have a desire and yearning to receive delight and pleasure. If the creatures receive from Him the delight and pleasure, this brings contentment to the Creator that they are doing His will and are enjoying Him. 2) The correction of creation. In order for the creatures not to feel shame when receiving the pleasures, the creatures must receive the pleasures only in order to delight the Creator and not for their own sake. This means that the reason they want to enjoy life is that the Creator wants it, while for themselves, they would relinquish the pleasures, since they want to adhere to the Creator, which is called "equivalence of form."

Therefore, we discern two kinds of *Kelim* [vessels] within us: 1) "Vessels of bestowal," and the light that is drawn into them is called "light of *Hassadim*." This light is called "male light," since the *Kli* [vessel] in which the light dresses is a *Kli* of bestowal and a male is called "bestowing."

The light that dresses in vessels of reception is called "light of *Hochma*" or "light of life," and the *Kli* to receive the light of *Hochma* is called "female," meaning a receiver. This means that since this light is called "the light of the purpose of creation," which is "to do good to His creations," meaning that the Creator is the Giver and wants the lower ones to receive, so the *Kli* for reception is called "female," which receives from the Creator, and the Creator is the Giver.

It is the opposite in vessels of bestowal—the lower one bestows upon the upper one. This is why the lower one is called "male," since he bestows and the upper one receives, as our sages said (*VaYikra*, Item 98), "Israel provide for their father in heaven."

It therefore follows that the order of the work is that since man was created with a nature of a desire to receive for his own sake, the beginning of man's work is to try to come to a state where everything he does is for the sake of the Creator. And here one begins to do all that he can, meaning he observes Torah and

Mitzvot [commandments/good deeds] in order to thereby achieve "recognition of evil," meaning that he wants reward for the Torah and *Mitzvot* he is observing, and the reward is that he will have recognition of evil, meaning that he will know and feel that the will to receive for oneself is bad and harmful to his life, that because of it, he cannot be awarded spiritual life. This is his reward, which is called "recognition of evil," that now he knows that the will to receive for himself is the harm-doer and his angel of death.

Hence, if a person says that he still does not feel that the will to receive is the angel of death, he should know that this stems from the fact that he needs more light, so as to see the truth, since in the dark, we cannot see. The light is called "Torah," as it is written, "And the Torah is light." Hence, he should exert in the Torah with the aim to receive light from the Torah, so as to show him the truth of who is his enemy and angel of death, who denies him real life which is spiritual life.

Therefore, when one sometimes comes to a state called "Days of no desire," meaning that he has no energy to do anything, neither in thought nor in speech or in action, the reason is that the Creator created man in order to do, as it is written, "Which God has created to do." Thus, when one sees that he is not advancing in the work, he loses the tools for work, meaning he has no motivation. At that time, the question is, What should one do when he is in such a state?

The answer is that at that time, one should believe "above reason" that this state, too—when he has no desire awakened within him, and which can be filled, but that now he wants to accept the situation he is in—this came from the Creator and was sent to him deliberately. And the reason is, "as the advantage of the light from within the darkness."

In other words, when a person sees that he is in a decline, afterward, when he is rewarded with emerging from that state he will know how to appreciate the importance of the state of ascent. That is, at that time he will be able to discern between light and darkness and will be able to thank the Creator for bringing him closer to spirituality. Then, when he appreciates the importance of the matter, he will have the power to extend the light of Torah, since then, "the blessed clings to the Blessed." To the extent that one appreciates one's wholeness, how blessed he is with his lot, that the Creator has brought him closer, to that extent he can extend the blessing, as it is written, that "the blessed clings to the Blessed."

Therefore, if one has no darkness, he cannot appreciate the light. Hence, one is not as delighted over being able to receive closeness to the Creator as he would be if he knew how to appreciate the state of ascent. Therefore, they are proportional: To the extent that he thanks and praises the Creator for bringing him closer to Him, and the person feels blessed by the Creator, to that same extent he can extend abundance from above. It follows that it seems as though the amount of abundance that one can draw is proportional to the level that one is in a state of "blessed."

When a person prevails and asks for help from the Creator, after he has decided that he has a harm-doer in his heart, called "will to receive," and that he cannot emerge from it, meaning after going through several ascents and descents, he finally sees that he has remained bare and destitute. At that time, his prayer is from the bottom of the heart. That is, he sees that if the Creator does not help him, he cannot overcome it.

Although one can say that he believes above reason that only the Creator helps him, within reason, he does not feel this, since he knows that he himself made the efforts and the labor to obtain something in spirituality. But when one sees that after all the exertions, he cannot emerge from the governance of the will to receive for himself, then he sees within reason that only the Creator can help him.

It follows that what our sages said, "Man's inclination overcomes him every day, and were it not for the help of the Creator, he would not be able to overcome it," he does not need to believe in this above reason, the way ordinary workers of the Creator who observe Torah and *Mitzvot* believe "above reason" that this is so, that the

Creator helps them. Rather, those people who want to work in order to bestow, for them, it is within reason, to the point that they must believe above reason that the Creator can help them emerge from the governance of the will to receive.

This is as it is written in *The Zohar* about the spies, who said that the landlord cannot save his own vessels. Baal HaSulam said about this that it means that the spies, who slandered the land of Israel, refer to *Eretz* [land], which is *Malchut*. The spies said that the Creator, too, cannot help save His own *Kelim* [vessels], meaning the *Kelim* of *Kedusha* [holiness], meaning vessels of bestowal. It follows that everyone knew that it was not within man's power to emerge from the control of self-reception, but that we must believe that the Creator can help.

At that time, a person falls into doubt whether it is true that the Creator can help in this, since he says that he has already asked the Creator several times to help him and give him the desire to bestow, and award him love of the Creator, but he received no answer to his prayers. At that time, it is difficult for him to believe that the Creator will help him. But after all the efforts he has done, without escaping the campaign, he is rewarded with obtaining the desire to bestow, and then he sees within reason, that "were it not for the help of the Creator, he would not be able to overcome it."

It follows that now that the Creator has helped him and granted his prayers, when he asked the Creator to help him, it is as is said, "He will open our hearts with His law [Torah] and will place in our hearts the fear of Him and the love of Him, to do His will and to serve Him wholeheartedly." How he praises the Creator for granting his prayers and how he values the blessing he has received from the Creator. Now a person is truly called "blessed." And accordingly, we say, "The blessed clings to the Blessed," and then he can receive a great illumination because his quality of "blessed" is great.

However, once a person has been rewarded with vessels of bestowal, he is considered to have borne a son, meaning a male. That is, he has obtained "vessels of bestowal," which is considered that he has been rewarded with the correction of creation, which is *Hesed* [mercy/grace], meaning to serve the Creator with vessels of bestowal, which extends from above (from *Zeir Anpin*, from which the *Hassadim* are extended, for ZA is called "male," who bestows *Hassadim*).

It follows that the preparation is called "father," for the preparation for something is called "the reason," and the result is called "offshoot." This is considered that the person bore a male child, that he has now taken upon himself the desire to bestow, which is the correction of creation, by which he will be able to receive the delight and pleasure.

It follows that once he has a son called "correction of creation," comes the time when one needs to try to obtain the purpose of creation, which is "His desire to do good to His creations." This is considered that the abundance comes from above downward, meaning that the lower one is the receiver. This is considered that now the quality of a daughter was born, who receives the light of the purpose of creation. This is a female, who receives from the Giver, and this is called *Malchut*, the last *Hey* of the name *HaVaYaH*.

In other words, now that he has a son and a daughter, which imply the *Vav-Hey* of the name *HaVaYaH* (since the name *HaVaYaH* are the letters *Yod-Hey-Vav-Hey*, where *Yod* is *Hochma*, the first *Hey* is *Bina*, from which the quality of ZA is extended, called *Hesed*, which receives *Hassadim*. *Malchut*, too, is extended from the *Yod-Hey*, for she receives *Hochma*, called "daughter"). Hence, when one is rewarded with bearing the qualities of "son" and "daughter" through his work, that person is considered to have completed the holy name.

If he did not bear a son and a daughter through his work, it means that he has not completed the holy name. This is why *The Zohar* says it would be better for him if he were not born, since man is born in the world in order to perform corrections and complete the holy name, as our sages said about the verse (Exodus 17:16), "The Lord has sworn; the Lord will have war against Amalek." They said, "The Creator has sworn that His name is not complete and His throne is not complete until He blots out the name of Amalek."

We should interpret that the name *Yod-Hey*, called *HB*, should illuminate for the *Vav-Hey*. This comes through man's work, who bears a son and a daughter, meaning a male, which are vessels of bestowal in which light of *Hassadim* shines, and also to extend to *Malchut*, called "daughter," which are vessels of reception, in which light of *Hochma* illuminates. At that time, through one's work, one complements the holy name, called *Yod-Hey-Vav-Hey*, and this comes by blotting out Amalek, meaning by engaging in Torah and *Mitzvot* in order to complete the holy name. And then he will reveal the wholeness called "He is one and His name, One."

It follows that one who did not complete the holy name, who did not bear a son and a daughter, meaning did not correct the vessels of bestowal, in which light of *Hassadim* shines, which is considered a male, and even if he did bear a son, called a "male," but has not completed his work of bearing a "female," too, meaning vessels of reception, which will enter *Kedusha*, in which the light of *Hochma* shines, called "female," which is the light that shines from above downward to the creatures, for the receivers of the abundance are called "female," we are told that he still did not complete his work. Hence, it is better for him if he were not born because he has no part at all in the holy name.

This is as was said above, that he did not draw the *Vav-Hey*, for drawing the light into the *Vav-Hey* depends on the actions of the lower ones. This is the meaning of "Which God has created to do," that the lower ones must draw through their good deeds. This is as the ARI says, that "All the works of the lower ones, whether good deeds or bad deeds, concern only the *Vav-Hey*, which are called ZA and *Malchut*."

According to the above, we should interpret what is written, "This month is to you." We should interpret in the work that "There is nothing new under the sun" [*Hodesh* (month) comes from the word *Hidush* (renewal)]. Thus, what is the meaning of renewal, of which it is written, "This month is to you"? The answer is "to you," since all the novelties and changes are specifically "to you," meaning for you. In other words, with regard to the Creator, it is written, "I the Lord do not change." This means that with regard to the Creator there are no changes. Rather, all the many degrees and changes are only from the perspective of the receivers.

But why are there changes with respect to the receivers? After all, there are (no) changes in spirituality. The answer is that since it is impossible to receive any light, but only according to the size of the clothing, the clothing affects changes in the light, so that according to the value of the clothing, so is the attainment in the light.

And what is the clothing in which the light dresses? That clothing is *Ohr Hozer* [Reflected Light]. This means that since there was a correction where in order to avoid shame while receiving delight and pleasure, there was a *Tzimtzum* [restriction] and concealment so we cannot see the light but only to the extent that one can receive in order to bestow. In other words, to the extent that one can aim to bestow, the light is revealed to him.

It follows that the *Kli* that can receive light is essentially the extent to which he can bestow upon the Creator and does not do anything unless for the sake of the Creator. Since the matter of working in order to bestow is against nature, this work is very slow. To the extent that he overcomes, that he prevails in order to work in order to bestow, to that extent he dresses and attains the light. Naturally, many degrees are made according to the value of the work of the receivers, though from the perspective of the Giver, there are no changes. This is the meaning of the words "This month is to you," meaning all the changes are for you, meaning it is your work, for you, for the lower ones.

And the main work is that we need additional overcoming, which is "faith above reason," meaning that any renewal in the work comes from "faith above reason." Conversely, those who work with "faith within reason," have no renewals. This is the meaning of the words "There is nothing new under the sun," meaning specifically under the sun there are no renewals, but above the sun, there are renewals.

We should understand the meaning of "sun" in the work. The sun shines during the day. A "day" means as it is written (*Pesachim* 2), "'The murderer arises at dawn; he kills the poor and the indigent.' Does that mean that light is day?" The meaning is that if the matter is as clear as day to you, this is called "sun," meaning knowing. Conversely, "night" means doubt. It follows that "There is nothing new under the sun" means that if the sun, which is knowledge, is of superior importance, meaning that one's reason is the cause of the actions, in that respect, there is no renewal in the work, for when the work does not object to reason, there are no renewals there.

But if a person wants to work above the sun, meaning above reason, then he has renewals in the work, since each time, the wicked comes to him and asks Pharaoh's question and the wicked's question, which are called "Who" and "What," and a person should answer them. This work belongs to you. Out of these questions and answers, novelties always emerge, as it is written, "There is nothing new under the sun," but above the sun, meaning above reason, there are novelties.

The work above reason should be unconditional surrender. That is, one should take upon himself the burden of the kingdom of heaven above reason. A person should say, "I want to be a servant of the Creator even though I have no idea about the work and I feel no flavor in the work. Nevertheless, I am willing to work with all my might as though I have attainment and feeling and flavor in the work, and I am willing to work unconditionally." At that time, a person can go forward, and then there is no place for him to fall from his state, since he takes upon himself to work even when he is placed right in the earth, since it is impossible to be lower than the earth.

This is as it is written (Ecclesiastes 1), "A generation goes and a generation comes, and the earth forever stands." We should interpret that in the work, "A generation goes and a generation comes" means ascents and descents. The fact that one yearns for knowledge, meaning he does not want to work above reason, but specifically within reason, meaning that he says that if the body understands the benefits of working and observing the *Mitzvot* [commandments/good deeds] of the King, he is willing to labor and work. But to believe above reason, to this the body does not agree. Instead, he stands and waits for the body to understand it, but otherwise, he cannot do the holy work. Sometimes, he does overcome these thoughts and desires, and this causes him the ascents and descents.

Yet, if one decides that he wants to work as "dust," meaning even if he tastes the taste of dust in the work, he says that it is very important for him to be able to do something for the sake of the Creator, and for himself, he does not care which taste he feels, and says that this work, in which one tastes the taste of dust, meaning that the body mocks this work, he says to the body that in his view, this work is regarded as "raising the *Shechina* [Divinity] from the dust."

In other words, although the body tastes dust in this work, the person says that it is *Kedusha* and does not measure how much flavor he feels in the work. Rather, he believes that the Creator does enjoy this work, since there is no mixture of the will to receive here, since he has nothing to receive because there are no flavor or scent in this work, as there is only the taste of dust here. For this reason, he believes that this is the holy work, and he is delighted.

Accordingly, we should interpret that "A generation goes and a generation comes" means ascents and descents. "A generation goes" means that the state of ascent has parted from him, and "a generation comes" means that another ascent has come to him. This is endless. However, "the earth forever stands." The earth is regarded as "dust," when a person feels that he is placed in the earth, that there is no lower state than the one he is in. If a person works in the manner of "earth," meaning that he agrees to work even in a state of "dust," this is "forever stands," when he has no falls because he is already placed in the earth, and sanctifies the earth.

What Does It Mean that One Who Repents Should Be in Happiness?

Article No. 25, Tav-Shin-Nun-Aleph, 1990/91

It is written in *The Zohar* (*VaYikra*, Items 109-113), "Rabbi Yehuda started and said, 'Serve the Lord with gladness.' We learned that any work that a person wishes to do for the Creator should be done with gladness, willingly, so that his work will be whole. If you say that this is not possible, since that man has breached his Master's commandment, and repented before his Master, with what face will he rise before Him? Certainly, with a broken spirit, meaning he should be with a sad spirit. Thus, where is the joy? These joy and singing are absent. Indeed, by what are they corrected? It is by those priests and Levites. Joy exists in the priest because he is always far from the judgment, and singing is in the Levites. Now that no offering has been found (since the Temple was ruined), how does one sustain the joy and singing? We learned that the praising that one praises one's Master and the joy of the Torah, as well as the singing of the Torah, this is joy and singing. Thus, we learned

(*Berachot* 8), 'One should always enter the measure of two openings and pray his prayer.' Can you imagine, actually two openings? Rather, say, the measure of two openings, called *Hesed* and fear, meaning *Gevura*, and they are everlasting openings."

We should understand what it tells us in the work that the priest is in gladness and the Levites are in singing, and also what is written, that the joy is in the heart and the singing is in the mouth, and that specifically by those two, the offering is corrected. The thing is that it is known that the order of the work is that we begin to work in Torah and *Mitzvot* [commandments/good deeds] in order to receive reward, and the reward is always what a person wants to receive but there is no desire to give him, but he rather pays what is required of him, and this is the reward for which man works.

Naturally, every person has a passion for that which his body demands. This is why there are differences among people, among children, and between children and grownups. For example, we see that sometimes, when little children do not want to eat, they are told, "If you eat you will get a prize," such as buying them toys. It follows that by eating, they make concessions in order to receive toys. They make an effort by eating in order to obtain toys. Grownups are told, "If you work, we will let you eat." That is, each one has a special thing that he calls "a reward."

Therefore, when coming to speak of the work of the Creator, that the Creator commanded us to observe Torah and *Mitzvot*, this is certainly regarded as exertion, since by nature, a person loves rest, and if he is requested to do something and give up the rest, he promptly asks, "What will I gain more?" meaning "What greater pleasure will I have than the pleasure I get now from resting?" When he hears that the pleasure he can receive from the labor is less than the pleasure he enjoys from the rest, he will certainly not do it.

Therefore, when a person begins to do the holy work, he has no idea what is pleasure, except that which the will to receive for himself understands that it will receive pleasure from this work more than the will to receive for himself enjoys the rest. Therefore, he is promised a reward that he will receive for his work, as it is written in

The Zohar, that he is promised that he will have "abundant pleasures of this world," as well as a reward in the next world. To the extent that he believes in this, to that extent he is willing to work, meaning to the extent that he believes in reward and punishment.

This is regarded as "working on one line," which is in order to receive reward for his own benefit. This is called "work in practice." That is, he must believe in the Creator, that He has commanded us through Moses to observe Torah and *Mitzvot*, in return for which we will be rewarded, and if not, we will be punished. Those two compel us to observe Torah and *Mitzvot*.

In the words of our sages, this is called "fear and love," as our sages said, "Fear is needed because one who fears does not kick, and love is needed because one who loves does not hate." However, understanding the term "in order to bestow" is impossible while one is still in *Katnut* [smallness] of the mind. He cannot understand that there is a matter of bestowal. Rather, one can understand that we must bestow only in order to receive reward in return for the bestowal he is giving.

However, this, too, is considered a high degree, although it is in order to receive. This is called the degree of *Lo Lishma* [not for Her sake], about which our sages said, "From *Lo Lishma* we come to *Lishma* [for Her sake] because the light in it reforms him." Therefore, a person must be careful while serving the Creator even *Lo Lishma* to appreciate the work. One must be grateful to the Creator for giving him a desire and yearning to observe the Torah and *Mitzvot*. And the first state of entering the real work, by which he is called "a servant of the Creator," is to work without any reward but only for the sake of the Creator.

Conversely, when a person works in order to receive reward, he is regarded as "working for himself," meaning for his own benefit, and not for the sake of the Creator. However, a person should see that he appreciates the work and does not slight it but thanks the Creator for rewarding him with observing Torah and *Mitzvot* in practice.

However, afterward a person must work for reward and punishment in a different manner, as in the allegory about the grownups and children, where the reward should be that he has been rewarded with bestowing upon the Creator, meaning that now he can aim in order to bestow, by which he achieves *Dvekut* [adhesion] with the Creator. This is the reward that one should demand for his labor in Torah and *Mitzvot*.

However, since a person is accustomed to do everything for his own sake, although he believes what is written, that one should do everything "for the sake of the Creator," since the body resists this, as this is against nature, a person cannot determine that this is truly a great thing, meaning to bestow, and that it is so important that it is worthwhile for a person to observe Torah and *Mitzvot*, that this thing, meaning in order to bestow, will be his entire reward for his work in Torah and *Mitzvot*.

Since the matter of bestowal is not so important to a person, he has no need to pray to the Creator from the bottom of the heart to give him a desire to bestow as a gift from the Creator. It follows that although one understands that it is worthwhile to work in order to bestow, for a person to feel the necessity of it, he does not have this. This is why a person must work so the Creator will illuminate for him the necessity of the matter, how the desire to bestow will bring a person to the purpose of creation, which is the obtainment of the delight and pleasure that are found in the purpose of creation. For this reason, a person must ask the Creator to let him feel the need, meaning that he needs the desire, to ask the Creator from the bottom of the heart to give him the desire to bestow, since there is no filling without a lack.

Afterward, he should ask the Creator to give him the filling, since many times a person comes to a state where he has no desire whatsoever for the Creator to help him make the will to receive loathsome in his eyes and to feel the lowliness in the will to receive. Rather, he wants the opposite, that the Creator will satisfy all that the will to receive demands. Therefore, when one comes to a state of lowliness, he must ask the Creator to give him the necessity for the need for the desire to bestow, and for the prayer to be from the bottom of the heart. At that time, the awakening from above comes to him.

However, when one comes to a state where he sees that he is in utter lowliness, when one sees one's lowliness, he is broken and shattered, so how can he be in gladness, as *The Zohar* says, "If you say that this is not possible, since that man has breached his Master's commandment, and repented before his Master. Certainly, with a broken spirit, where is the joy?"

We should ask about this, If it makes sense that when a person sees that he is in lowliness, he should be sad, why must he be in gladness? The reason is that it is written, "Serve the Lord with gladness." This, too, we should understand, why a person is demanded something that is impossible, since they are two opposites in one subject.

Baal HaSulam said that when a person is in a state of "bare and destitute," he is considered "cursed," and "The cursed does not cling to the Blessed," as it is written in the article "Faith in His Rav." Therefore, a person cannot receive a blessing from the Creator because there is no blessing on an empty thing. For this reason, *The Zohar* replies that the offering is corrected by those priests and Levites, for joy is present in the priest, and singing is present in the Levites. And the reason is that "priest" is *Hesed* [mercy], and he is far from judgment.

We should know what it means in the work that the priest is *Hesed*. The thing is that *Hesed* is bestowal, meaning that he does not need anything for himself, but only to bestow upon others, and one who is in a state of *Hesed* is content with his share does not need anything. It follows that he has no lack, so he can be in gladness, since "judgment" indicates a lack because the whole matter of deficiency that there is in the creatures is because there was a judgment that it is forbidden to use the vessels of reception, but only the vessels of bestowal, for only there is the place where the abundance may be received.

Therefore, when we say that there are judgments in the world, it means that the delight and pleasure has no place in the world where it can expand, since the world is immersed in vessels of reception on which there were *Tzimtzum* [restriction] and judgment. For this reason, a priest, who is *Hesed*, which is vessels of bestowal, has no connection to judgment. This is the meaning of what is written, that joy is present in the priest because he is ever far from judgment. That is, the vessels of bestowal are far from the vessels of reception, which are judgment.

Conversely, a Levite is considered judgment, where there is singing, meaning a song. This is as our sage said (*Berachot* 35), "One does not chant except over wine." It is explained in *The Zohar* that wine means "the wine of Torah," which is illumination of *Hochma*, called "left line." Singing means "sweetening of the judgments," since judgments are as said above, vessels of reception, on which there was a judgment that it is forbidden to use them because they are in disparity of form, which causes separation. For this reason, that place of judgment remains without abundance.

Conversely, when correcting the vessels of reception to work in order to bestow, the abundance comes and fills the vessels of reception. It follows that the judgments, meaning the vessels of reception that previously worked in order to receive, was a state of bitterness, since they were without light, whereas now that they have received the correction of working in order to bestow, the light of *Hochma* shines there, which is the light of the purpose of creation, and the purpose of creation is to do good to His creations. Thus, that which was bitter has now become sweet, as it is written, "One does not chant except over wine," which is *Hochma*.

This is the meaning of the words "Singing is in the Levites." And so it is because the Levites are ever on the song, and those priests and Levites stand on it and in them, the work of the Creator is completed. That is, through them, the work of the Creator is completed, which is the correction of the three lines: *Hesed* [mercy/grace], *Din* [judgment], and *Rachamim* [mercy]. In other words, through the right and the left, the person is completed by the offering, meaning that by this a person draws near to the Creator.

Also, we should interpret what is written, that now that the Temple is ruined, how are there joy and singing? He replies that the praises he praises his Master and the joy of Torah and singing of the Torah are joy and singing. We should interpret that "a priest" implies the work of the right line, where "right" means wholeness, and wholeness engenders gladness.

We should understand the answer that "right" means wholeness, and for which he will take the wholeness of the right when he wants to make an offering, meaning when he wants to draw near to the Creator because he feels how remote he is from the Creator in mind and in heart, and he is broken and sad.

The Zohar replies that the praises he praises his Master bring him joy. We should ask, What praise and gratitude can he give to the Creator when he feels that he is a sinner? However, the thing is that we must know that we should discern two sides in everything: 1) On one hand, a person is now broken and shattered because he sinned against the Creator and he is sad because he feels that he is bare and destitute in *Kedusha* [holiness]. 2) There is the other side of the coin here, which is that until now, he did not think at all about spiritual matters. Rather, he was immersed in worldly matters and did not remember at all whether there is the matter of spirituality in the world. But now he has come to another world, where he does not think at all about worldly matters, but all his concerns are over why he is so materialistic. Hence, in that respect, he has now risen in degree, meaning that his reward and punishment are not in corporeal matters, but in spiritual ones.

It follows that according to the rule that if a person ascends in degree, he must be glad because now he has been endowed with a desire to serve the Creator, so even when he sees how far he is from the Creator and it pains him that although he was born "Jewish," he is not using it to do things that befit a Jew, meaning to have faith in the Creator as is fitting for a Jew, but all his concerns are to satisfy the needs that the body demands, like all other bodies, meaning the needs of the created beings. He even demands what Jews do not demand, as it is written, "And they mingled with the nations and learned from their actions," meaning his body demands all the needs of the gentiles.

Hence, now that he has attained and feels a little bit that there is spirituality in the world, called "*Dvekut* with the Creator," and he is far from it and it breaks his heart and he wants to make an offering, meaning he wants to draw near to the Creator, which is called "making an offering," on one hand he should be broken because he feels far from the Creator. On the other hand, he should be happy that now he wants to come closer to the Creator.

Therefore, in that respect, a person can observe "Serve the Lord with gladness." But why should he be glad? It is in order to praise the Creator for bringing him closer. But how does one know that the Creator has brought him closer? The answer is that a person should know that the Creator has brought him closer by feeling that he is far from the Creator.

This is similar to what happens in the corporal world, when one does not know that he is far from something unless he sees it from afar. That is, if he sees something, he can say that this is far from him or near him. But if the thing is so far from him that he does not see it whatsoever, how can he say whether it is far or near? Likewise, here in the work, when one feels that he is far from the work of the Creator, and thereby comes to the breaking of the heart because of the remoteness from the Creator, and he wants the Creator to bring him closer, this is called "wanting to make an offering," meaning to bring himself closer to the Creator, and it is certain that the Creator has come near him.

The evidence of this is that he sees Him from afar, meaning he feels that he is far from the Creator. In that sense, a person should receive "joy" from the fact that the Creator has come near him and he sees the Creator from afar. This joy causes a person importance from the work of the Creator. That is, even though he feels remoteness from the Creator, he says that the Creator is somewhat close to Him, and in that respect, when a person says that he has wholeness from this, he is already considered "blessed." At that time, he can truly be rewarded with the Creator bringing him closer, meaning that he will be rewarded with feeling that he is close to the Creator, since "the blessed clings to the Blessed."

However, when one has no need to emerge from his state of *Katnut* [smallness/infancy], then even though the Creator wants to give him a higher degree, so he will emerge from his *Katnut*, when he is in a state of wholeness because he engages in the state of "right" and he is content with his lot, how can he be given something, since he has no *Kelim* [vessels] for it, meaning no need to emerge from his *Katnut*, since he is happy with his lot.

For this reason, he must walk on the "left," as well, which is the quality of "Levites," *Gevura*, fear. That is, he criticizes his actions and sees that he lacks the quality of "mind" and the quality of "heart," and he is afraid that he will remain forever in the state of *Katnut*, and will remain in disparity of form from the Creator, since the Creator is the Giver, while man is completely immersed in self-reception. And each time he wants to overcome, he sees that it is not within man's power. Hence, by this he become needy of the Creator to help him.

This is the meaning of the words, that the praises he praises his Master, and the signing of the Torah, are joy and singing. That is, the offering comes from the quality of "right" and "left," meaning that by both, the person approaches the Creator because a person receives the *Kelim* and the need from the left, for then he needs the Creator to help him and give him the strength from above, called "a soul," where each time he wants to overcome he receives help.

But the answering of the prayer is when a person is in a state of joy, when he is content with his share and has no need to receive a higher degree. Rather, in the state he is in, he is content and feels that he is blessed by the Creator. At that time, "The blessed clings to the Blessed," and then is the time when he can be rewarded with *Dvekut*, since he already has *Kelim* for it from the left.

Then, when he can say that he is content with his share, although he is deficient to the point that he feels deficiency and pain at being

What Does It Mean that One Who Repents Should Be in Happiness?

removed from the Creator, this is considered that he is "happy with his lot." And since only in the manner that he is deficient can we say that he is "happy with his lot," whereas when he has no lack, it is not regarded as "happy with his lot," since "happy with his lot" means that he settles for little, and if he has no deficiency then he is not regarded as "settling for little," since he has no need for more than he has.

This is as Baal HaSulam interpreted what our sages said (*Megillah* 12), "The drinking is according to law, no coercion." What is "according to the law"? It is according to the law of Torah. What is the law of Torah? It is eating more than drinking.

He said that the "law of Torah" is "no coercion," meaning he has no necessity for it. Rather, he may eat also without drinking, for drinking means "faith above reason," where he believes that the Creator leads the world in a manner of good and doing good. Although he does not see this, meaning that although reason denies it, he still believes it. At that time, he is rewarded with "drinking," called "wine of Torah," which is *Hochma*, the light of the purpose of creation, which is His desire to do good to His creations.

We can understand this by what our sages said, "One should always enter the measure of two openings and pray his prayer." That is, in order for his prayer to be granted, meaning to be rewarded with an "offering," considered nearing the Creator, it is known that a prayer is in the place of the offering, meaning that in order to be rewarded with nearing the Creator, he must walk on the right and on the left. The two openings mean that we need two things: 1) To know what he is missing, and by this he receives a lack and a need, called *Kelim*, that the Creator can fill his lack. But if he has no lack, it is impossible to fill. 2) A time to receive the filling. When a person is deficient, this is not the time to fill him, since "the cursed does not cling to the Blessed." Hence, we need a time of wholeness, for then is the time to receive the filling. For this reason, we need two legs—right and left.

What Is Revealing a Portion and Covering Two Portions in the Work?

Article No. 26, Tav-Shin-Nun-Aleph, 1990/91

We should understand this matter of "revealing a portion." This means that previously, a portion was covered here, and then one came and revealed a portion but concealed two portions. Thus, now it became more concealed than before he revealed. This means that he came and made a greater concealment now than before. Would it not be better if he did not reveal the portion?

We should interpret that when he comes and says, "I revealed a portion and I covered two portions," he comes and tells us that there is a place of scrutiny here, to examine what he revealed, since the matter should not be revealed to all, but only to those who need to know. For this reason, he had to cover two portions so that people who have no need to know would not exert in order to understand the matters, while those who feel that they are lacking

What Is Revealing a Portion and Covering Two Portions in the Work?

this knowledge in order to complete themselves will exert in order to reveal the matter that he concealed.

By this we should interpret in matters of work, which is man's engagement in Torah and *Mitzvot* [commandments/good deeds] in order to achieve completion, and for which man was created. We should make two discernments here:

1) The purpose of creation. The purpose of creation is for the creatures to come to a state where they receive delight and pleasure from the Creator.

2) The correction of creation. The correction of creation is to achieve *Dvekut* [adhesion], called "equivalence of form," meaning that all their actions will be only in order to bestow contentment upon the Creator. Therefore, when there is some revelation and a person cannot receive it in order to bestow, he blemishes it. For this reason, everything must be in concealment until a person can receive it in order to bestow.

Hence, when he says, "I revealed a portion and I concealed two portions," it means that those who have no need for the matter will not exert to work and reveal, while those who do have a need, when they are told, "I revealed a portion and I concealed two portions," they are willing to work until they attain the portion he revealed, since the Creator helps them. When a person gives the awakening from below, he receives help from above.

It follows that He did reveal the matter to those worthy of them. Who is worthy? Those who make an effort. To them, the portion they revealed is revealed to them. That is, those who do not have the quality of the correction of creation cannot receive anything from the purpose of creation, which is to do good to His creations.

Yet, this matter of revealing a portion and covering two portions applies also during the preparation for the work. In other words, it applies even in the beginning, when a person wants to begin the work, since those who have been rewarded from above are shown some illumination that shines for them, and they begin to work with great enthusiasm and power.

This is so because they received a revelation from above and they see that the most important thing in life in this world is spirituality and not corporeality. They feel confident that soon they will be rewarded with entering the King's palace and will be rewarded with *Dvekut* with the Creator and the flavors and secrets of the Torah. A person feels all this by the revelation of the portion that has been revealed to him from above.

However, after some time, when it is seen above that the person has begun the work of bestowal, in order for him to grow on his own toward nearing the Creator, and also to feel what it is like to be remote from *Kedusha* [holiness], so he will discern "the advantage of the light from within the darkness," subsequently, a person comes into a state of "covering two portions."

One cannot understand why at first, when he did not know what the work of bestowal was like, spirituality illuminated for him as a revelation, and in his mind, he understood that after this revelation he should advance and go forward, but in the end he sees that now he is worse than before he began the work of bestowal. A person cannot provide answers to these states.

But the answer is that in order for him to begin to work, he had to be given from above the revelation, to give him the strength to emerge from the state he was in before he began the work. This is called "an awakening from above." Afterward, this revelation was taken from him so that now he would be able to give the awakening from below.

This is the meaning of what the ARI says, that on Passover night, when the Creator had to deliver the people of Israel from Egypt, a great light appeared upon them in a manner of an awakening from above. For this reason, at that time *Mochin* of *Haya* illuminated, and all by the power of the awakening from above. But afterward, they all fell once more to their places, meaning that afterward, the people of Israel had to work in a manner of an awakening from below in order to continue in the manner of *Gadlut* [greatness/adulthood] of the *Mochin*.

Similarly, here we should interpret that when a person begins the work, he is shown a portion. Namely, he is shown from above some illumination, and that illumination gives him the power to serve the Creator. He begins to feel that this is the goal for which man was created in this world, and that feeling comes to him as a revelation from above in order to give him momentum for the holy work.

Therefore, afterward, when a person sees that he is not advancing but regressing, and now he is even far from the state he was in before he revealed to him a portion of the holy work, that person thinks that it is because he was thrown out from the work.

Therefore, a person must know that such is the work, that in order to admit a person into the work, there is such a correction called "awakening from above," which is given to a person who is capable of entering the holy work, meaning that afterward he will be able to work by an awakening from below, since a person obtains the real *Kelim* [vessels] specifically through the awakening from below. This is why afterward he loses the light of confidence he had in the beginning of his work.

Accordingly, we should discern concerning the words "revealing a portion and covering two portions":

1) In the beginning of his work, he is in a state of "still of *Kedusha*," meaning he only acts and does not contemplate the thought.

2) He is shown a portion from above. At that time, he begins to feel that there is a new world, meaning that he feels that if he makes an effort, he will be rewarded with entering the King's palace and will be granted attainment of Godliness. At that time, he will see that his confidence is so strong that he will achieve real wholeness. When he looks at other people, how they engage in Torah and *Mitzvot* in the "still" manner, he says about them that they are acting as beasts—doing without reason, and that they have no feeling of what is within the Torah and *Mitzvot*. All this is built in him on the basis that he was rewarded with revealing a portion.

3) Afterward, meaning after the work, when he begins to advance in the intention, through the power of the awakening from above, he comes to a state of "covering two portions." That is, he falls into a descent. This is on purpose, so that now he will give the awakening from below, since specifically from this work he receives *Kelim* for the light.

In other words, it is impossible to discern any flavors in the light before we taste the taste of darkness, as it is written, "as the advantage of the light from within the darkness." This means that although anyone can tell between light and darkness, to enjoy the light as it is possible to enjoy, this is impossible, as we see in corporeality.

We must believe that all this extends from spirituality as a "branch and root," as we can see for ourselves. We walk on our legs and use our hands. Although we are glad that we are well, at the same time, we cannot rejoice over the fact that we are healthy. However, if we visit a hospital where there are patients with paralyses, some in their legs, some in their hands, if someone went in there and gave them a cure so they would regain their health and would be able to use their hands and legs, what joy would they have at being healthy?

It follows that the darkness they are suffering from not being able to use their hands and legs is the cause of their joy. This is the meaning of "as the advantage of the light from within the darkness." In spirituality, the light does not only add joy to them. We must know that in spirituality, the joy is used only to obtain the light. Put differently, the joy is a dressing for the spirit of the Creator.

In other words, attainment of Godliness dresses in many names. In general, this is called "Torah" or *Hochma* [wisdom]. That is, spiritual pleasure is not merely pleasure; it is the revelation of the names of the Creator. We are awarded this through the lack, called *Kelim* and "a need." This is why we need an awakening from below, for specifically by our work in Torah and *Mitzvot* we obtain those *Kelim* called "the need for the light of Torah."

Therefore, a person must be careful not to be alarmed by the descents he suffers, since from this he learns how to appreciate the importance of nearing the Creator, as in "the advantage of the light from within the darkness." It follows that the meaning of "revealing a portion and covering two portions" in the work is that we must make three discernments in the work until we achieve *Dvekut* with the Creator: 1) When he is in a state of "still of *Kedusha*," working only in action. This is called one line. 2) When he is shown one portion, meaning he is shown from above, as Surrounding Light, what there is to attain in Godliness. By this he gains confidence that he will achieve great attainments and understand that this is worth living for, and his life will not be like those of the rest of the people, who are living aimlessly. 3) Afterward he comes to the third state, which is a descent. This is when he is required to show an awakening from below. That state is called "covering two portions." In other words, not only has the state of revelation been concealed from him, but now even the "still" state has been concealed from him and it is difficult for him to engage in Torah and *Mitzvot* even in actions without the intention.

It follows that now he has two covers: 1) the state of revealing the portion, 2) the state of the still, when he engaged in Torah and *Mitzvot* with enthusiasm. That state has also disappeared from him.

Why is all of this? Why is there is a need for it to be more covered now than even in the first state, called "still of *Kedusha*"? The answer is that it is so that now he will not be content with less and will remain in a state of "still." It follows that the whole revelation of the portion was for nothing, meaning he did not do any action of nearing the Creator. But now that he cannot do anything unless by coercion, so he must think and find ways to be able to do the holy work once more. For this reason, now he must be twice as covered.

However, a person must be careful not to look down on the forced work, although during the coercion the body finds no taste in this work. We can learn about the importance of work in coercion from what we understand and see in the way the world behaves in corporeal matters.

Let us take eating, for example, which is something that applies to both grownups and children. There is love in this, and there is fear, meaning fear of punishment. We see that there are little children who do not want to eat. What do the parents do? Sometimes the parents tell the children nice stories to make the children eat. Because the children want to hear nice stories, they eat. And sometimes, when the parents have no patience, they hit the children to make them eat. And sometimes, when a person has no appetite, he forces himself to eat, also because of fear, since he is afraid that if he does not eat for several days he will grow weak, and if he does not eat for a long time he might even die.

It follows that he is eating by coercion, out of fear. No one will say that it is not good that he is eating by coercion, although it would certainly be better if he ate from love. But it is good if he can at least eat by coercion. However, sometimes, a healthy man must eat later for some reason. In that state, he eats with love. It is so much so that sometimes he regrets that when he begins to eat, the love departs from him. In other words, to the extent that he begins to eat, after every bite he eats the love for eating wanes in him because the satiation drives out the love of eating. Still, it is clear to all that a person must eat whether from love or from fear.

The same applies to the work of the Creator. In the things a person does when he observes Torah and *Mitzvot* there is also the matter of love and fear. That is, sometimes he enjoys engaging in Torah and *Mitzvot* and is high spirited, and the reasons do not matter. This means that a person has a good mood from observing Torah and *Mitzvot*, since by this he will later be rewarded, called *Lo Lishma* [not for Her sake].

Or, another reason, he is happy that he is serving the King. We should separate the reasons from the actions. In other words, we take into consideration what a person feels and not the reason that caused him the feeling.

That is, the fact that a person is happy is regarded as "working from love." That is, he is happy because he will later be rewarded, or because he is serving the King, but first of all, he is happy. This is called "working from love."

Sometimes a person works out of fear. That is, he is afraid that he will suffer punishments in this world, or that he will suffer punishments in the next world. At that time, a person is not happy with this, since he does everything by coercion. "Coercion" means that a person would be happier if this did not exist, and he would not be punished for it.

We therefore see that actions work on the body in corporeality even when we do them out of fear, meaning compulsively. We should learn from this and believe that so it is in the work, as well, meaning even by coercion. This means that even when a person does not find any flavor in Torah and prayer, he should do this by coercion because the act does its thing. As in the corporeal act, when he acts compulsively, it works whether for better or for worse even when he works out of coercion. So it is in the work. Even though he observes Torah and *Mitzvot* by coercion, it works within the person.

However, there is certainly a difference in the work whether he does it from love or from fear. Yet, we should know that even in work he does out of love, there is a difference between working from love and saying "The Creator needs me to observe Torah and *Mitzvot*, but I have no need that I can say that I am observing the Torah and *Mitzvot* for myself." He says that he does not see for what purpose he must observe them, since he says, "What will it give me if I observe Torah and *Mitzvot*?"

However, a person believes in the reward he will receive for this, and this is why he observes Torah and *Mitzvot*. This follows the rule that one who needs to be given something for his needs should pay. Therefore, he works from love because the Creator will certainly pay him for his work.

But if a person observes Torah and *Mitzvot* because the Torah and *Mitzvot* will correct him, meaning that he feels that he needs correction, this is as our sages said, "The Creator said, 'I have created the evil inclination; I have created the Torah as a spice.'" It follows that one should observe Torah and Mitzvot for oneself. He certainly cannot ask the Creator to pay him for observing Torah and Mitzvot, since he is not observing Torah and Mitzvot in order to benefit the Creator, since the Creator does not need the lower ones to observe Torah and Mitzvot for the Creator. Rather, this is for the sake of man. It follows that he is working out of love, for by this he will be a complete person, a corrected person. In that case, it cannot be said that the Creator should reward him for his work in observing Torah and Mitzvot.

It follows that his observing Torah and Mitzvot out of love is not because he will later be rewarded. Rather, he thanks and praises the Creator for giving him a cure to correct the body. As in corporeality, one who gives someone a cure, the recipient of the medicine pays the doctor, and the doctor does not pay the patient for taking the medicine.

However, we should ask, What evil is there in man that should be corrected by observing Torah and Mitzvot? meaning that without Torah and Mitzvot he will remain with his evil and will suffer. Otherwise, why should he mind if he remains with the bad within him? This means that he must remove the bad in him, or he will suffer from the bad and will not be able to live in the world and will have to die. But through the merit of Torah and Mitzvot, the evil will depart from him and he will have a good life and peace at home.

The answer is the will to receive with which man was created. This desire cares for its own benefit, and has no feeling or perception of the benefit of others. A person can understand working for the sake of others only when the will to receive for his own sake gains from this. This is called "bestowing in order to receive."

For this reason, people go to work, Jews for gentiles and gentiles for Jews, all according to the reward that the will to receive for himself will receive. But actually for the sake of others? A person has no feeling that there can be such a thing in reality. A person can only believe that there is such a thing as working for the sake of others, but we should ask why indeed should one work for the sake of others.

What Is Revealing a Portion and Covering Two Portions in the Work?

To this comes the answer that there is the matter of the purpose of creation and the correction of creation. The purpose of creation is that His desire is to do good to His creations, meaning for the creatures to receive delight and pleasure. Hence, the general name of the Creator is The Good Who Does Good. However, there was a correction so there would be no shame while receiving that good, that a person must receive in order to bestow. Since man was created with a nature of reception and not with a nature of bestowal, he must correct himself so as to be able to work in order to bestow.

Before he has this desire, he is left bare and destitute due to the disparity of form between the Creator and the created beings. This is called "evil," meaning the will to receive for himself. If he does not correct it to work in order to bestow, he will remain in the dark. For this reason, a person must observe Torah and *Mitzvot* in order to correct his evil and acquire a second nature, which is in order to bestow.

It follows that a person observes Torah and *Mitzvot* for his own sake. That is, by observing Torah and *Mitzvot*, which is the spice, he will achieve the purpose of creation: to do good to His creations.

By this, man will be rewarded with "peace at home." "Home" is man's heart, as it is written in *The Zohar*, which says, "A handsome abode is his heart." Man's heart is not at peace with the Creator, since he has complaints to the Creator that He is not satisfying all his wishes. But the reason is "disparity of form." Therefore, when a person corrects himself to work in order to bestow, he receives the delight and pleasure from the Creator, and then peace is made. This is called "peace at home."

What Is, "If a Woman Inseminates First, She Delivers a Male Child," in the Work?

Article No. 27, Tav-Shin-Nun-Aleph, 1990/91

Our sages said (*Berachot* 60), "If a woman inseminates first, she delivers a male child. If a man inseminates first, she delivers a female child, as was said, 'If a woman inseminates, she delivers a male child.'"

We should understand what this implies to us in the work, so we will know how to behave.

It is known that the work that is given to us, to observe Torah and *Mitzvot* [commandments/good deeds], is in order to cleanse Israel, as it is written in the essay, "Preface to the Wisdom of Kabbalah," "It is known that 'cleansing' is derived from the [Hebrew] word 'purifying.' It is as our sages said, 'The *Mitzvot* were only given for the purification of Israel.'"

What Is, "If a Woman Inseminates First, She Delivers a Male Child"?

Since the creatures were created with a nature of a desire to receive for oneself, since the purpose of creation is to do good to His creations, for this reason, He created in the creatures a desire to receive delight and pleasure. Since this is in disparity of form from the Creator, who is the Giver, we were given work, where we must equalize in form with the Creator, so we, too, must correct ourselves so that all that we do will be in order to bestow.

We see that there are things we do that are giving, and there are things we do that are receiving. For example, we engage in *Mitzvot* between man and the Creator, and *Mitzvot* between man and man, which are usually called "acts of bestowal." Also, we perform acts of reception such as eating and drinking, and we were given the work of equivalence of form, meaning that both acts of bestowal and acts reception, we must perform them in order to bestow.

It is known that there is an inverse relation between *Kelim* [vessels] and lights. That is, there are lights that are called "male," and there are lights that are called "female." "Male" means wholeness, and "female" means lack, when the degree is not in wholeness with the light that it received.

There are two kinds of light: 1) the light of the purpose of creation, which is called "complete light," 2) the light of the correction of creation, which is only a clothing for the light of the purpose of creation. This is a female, meaning incomplete, but only a means to achieve wholeness.

The first light is called "light of *Hochma* [wisdom]" or "light of life," and the second light is called "light of *Hassadim* [mercies]," usually referred to as *VAK* [*Vav-Kzavot* (six edges)]. This means that it still lacks the first three *Sefirot*.

Therefore, if a person uses the female *Kelim*, namely vessels of reception, meaning that the person has awakened to use the vessels of reception in order to bestow, then "she delivers a male child." That is, from this work, light of *Hochma* is born, a complete light, the light of life, called "male," since this light belongs to the purpose of creation, since the Creator created the vessels of reception, called "will to receive," for the light of the purpose of creation.

It is written, "If a woman inseminates first, she delivers a male child." But if a person works with the vessels of bestowal, meaning only with acts of bestowal, he can work in order to bestow, for vessels of bestowal are called "male." Then, only female light is born out of it, since light of *Hassadim*, which is revealed over vessels of bestowal, can engender only the light of *Hassadim*, called "VAK without GAR [first three]," indicating the absence of GAR. The light of *Hassadim* is called "clothing light," meaning that within the light of *Hassadim*, the light *Hochma* will dress later. This is the meaning of the words "If a man inseminates first, she delivers a female child."

The Zohar says (*Tazria*, Item 60), "Come and see, when the Creator is with the assembly of Israel, which is *Malchut*, and she evokes the desire for him first, and attracts him to her with much love and yearning, *Malchut* is filled with the *Hassadim* of the male from the right side. And when the Creator evokes love and desire first, and *Malchut* awakens later, then everything is in the form of female, which is *Malchut*."

We should understand what this tells us in the work. It is known that the creatures extend from *Malchut*. Hence, *Malchut* is called "the assembly of Israel," and the people of Israel extend from *Malchut*. Therefore, *The Zohar* says that as the order is above, so it extends to the corporeal branches. Accordingly, we should interpret that when a person awakens to the Creator, when he wants the Creator to bring him closer to Him, meaning he wants to adhere to Him, which is called "equivalence of form," it means that a person wants to do everything for the sake of the Creator but he cannot. Therefore, he asks the Creator to give him the strength, called "desire to bestow."

When one yearns for this force, since he has a lack, meaning he does not have the power to do everything for the sake of the Creator, through this work he awakens to ask the Creator to give him this power. At that time, he is given from above the power of the desire to bestow, which is a second nature. This is called "she delivers a male child," meaning a desire to bestow, called "male." This is considered that the upper one has given the lower one the light of *Hassadim*, where *Hesed* [mercy] means bestowing.

In other words, the work of yearning, where the lower one feels its deficiency, this is called "a prayer." That is, he asks the Creator to fulfill his deficiency. At that time, the satisfaction of the lack is called "male." It is written, "and she evokes the desire for him first," meaning her desire, *Malchut*, called "will to receive."

In other words, her desire for him, to adhere to him, which is called "equivalence of form," when he asks the desire to bestow, this is called *Dvekut* [adhesion]. This is the meaning of the words "*Malchut* is filled with the *Hassadim* of the male from the right side." By this we can interpret "If a woman inseminates first, she delivers a male child," meaning that the awakening came from the person.

However, this can be precisely where a person initially did not have a desire to draw near to the Creator, meaning he received the awakening from above, since there is the matter of will to receive for spirituality, meaning we can feel pleasure in observing Torah and *Mitzvot*. We already said in previous articles that there are three discernments to make in this pleasure of receiving reward:

1) He will be rewarded in this world and will be rewarded in the next world. That is, he observes Torah and *Mitzvot* because he will be rewarded, paid. In other words, he finds no taste in the things he does, but he observes Torah and *Mitzvot* because he will be rewarded later, so he enjoys it now.

2) He feels a good taste while observing the *Mitzvot*, since it illuminates for him, he enjoys serving the King, and this is his reward. He believes what he heard from books and from authors that there is pleasure in Torah and *Mitzvot*, and he also received some awakening from above and began to feel that there can be good taste in observing Torah and *Mitzvot* more than in the pleasures of this world.

3) He sees what our sages said about *Dvekut*: "Cling unto Him, cling unto His attributes. As He is merciful, so you are merciful." For this reason, he awakens to work as a giver and sees that this is out of one's hands. At that time, he begins to yearn for the Creator to give him the power to be able to do everything in order to bestow. This is considered that the person feels that he is regarded as a woman, a female, meaning immersed in self-love, and at that time he receives from above the quality of "male," and he is rewarded with a second nature called "desire to bestow." This is the meaning of the words "If a woman inseminates first, she delivers a male child." That is, from above, he is given *Hesed*, which is male.

But "If a man inseminates first, she delivers a female child." It is written, "And when the Creator evokes love and desire first, and *Malchut* awakens later, then everything is in the form of female, *Malchut*." Similarly, it is written, "If a woman inseminates first, what is the reason? We learned that it is because the lower world is akin to the upper world, and one is like the other."

We should interpret this in the work, that if the man inseminates first, she delivers a female. The Creator is called "man," and the man is called "female," since he derives from *Malchut*. For this reason, if the awakening comes from above, meaning that when the Creator brings a person closer, the person begins to feel the greatness and importance of the Creator. At that time he feels that if he is connected to the Creator, he will feel pleasure when near the Creator. Then, a person begins to engage in Torah and *Mitzvot* because he feels some vitality in this. It follows that the whole cause that obligates him to engage in Torah and *Mitzvot* is the pleasure he feels now by the awakening of the "man," meaning the Creator.

This is the meaning of "If a man inseminates first, she delivers a female child." That is, from this work, when a person works because he received an awakening from above, only a female can be born. It is known that a female in spirituality means "receiving and not bestowing." We should interpret here in the work that then a person builds his work on the basis of receiving pleasure from this work, and this is what causes him to work.

This is called "female," meaning that then a person works on the basis called "will to receive spirituality." However, he does not have the strength to work in order to bestow, since his entire basis is built on the pleasure he received from above by the awakening from above. At that time, a person is born with the quality of a female, which is the desire to receive spirituality in order to receive. However, he cannot work in order to bestow, as it is written, "If a man inseminates first, she delivers a female child," meaning receiving and not giving.

Therefore, if a person is rewarded, he is shown from above that man must work in order to bestow, but he cannot work in order to bestow. For this reason, he suffers a descent because he is still unable to work on the basis of bestowal. That is, when he sees that he should work in order to bestow and not for his own sake, he suffers a descent because he sees that this is not for him.

Sometimes, this descent causes him to escape the campaign. If he is rewarded, he recovers and begins to see what it means that one must work in order to bestow. He sees that it is out of man's hands, and then he begins to pray to the Creator to help him emerge from the control of self-love with which man was born, and asks the Creator to help him.

This is regarded as a person having to ask for the exile of the *Shechina* [Divinity], meaning how to work for the sake of the kingdom of heaven. This is difficult, as it extends from the governance of the nations of the world over man's personal quality of Israel. And also, one should pray for the general public, that all of Israel will be able to work for the *Kedusha* [holiness], called "kingdom of heaven." This discernment, when one works for *Malchut*, is called "If a woman inseminates first, she delivers a male child." But "If a man inseminates first, she delivers a female child."

For this reason, one should not sit and wait to receive an awakening from above. Rather, in any state one is in, he should start and awaken, so the Creator will help him.

Concerning the prayer, we should know that when a person prays to the Creator to help him, we should discern between prayer and request. A "prayer" means that a person prays the order of the prayers that our sages have arranged for us. A "request" is when a person asks privately. This is how prayer and request are interpreted.

We can explain this, since what our sages established, a person should say with his mouth. That is, even if he does not mean that the Creator will hear what he says in the phrasing of the prayer, it is still considered a prayer, since we say what they said, and to them, these were holy words. For example, after the Eighteen Prayer, a person says a prayer, "My soul shall be as dust to all." Certainly, a person does not want the Creator to grant his prayer.

Nevertheless, a person says it in the phrasing of the prayer as a *Segula* [virtue/merit/remedy]. That is, as a *Segula*, saying "My soul shall be as dust to all" can help even for obtaining sustenance, and so forth. This is so because all the prayers that our sages established are holy names, which is a *Segula* for everything, meaning it helps with everything.

But the meaning of the words that a person thinks, which is according to what one thinks, he should know that these prayers are above our mind. Rather, they are all holy names. We use them as *Segula*, for by them we have connection with the Creator. This is why we have to say all the prayers with the mouth, since in the heart, we do not understand. Therefore, when we say this with the mouth, we have connection with what they said, since what they said was all with the holy spirit, and they are founded on the holy names.

Baal HaSulam said that although it is customary that when we want to pray for a sick person, the order is that in the Eighteen Prayer, when we say, "Heal us, Lord, and we will be healed," it is because the general public can understand only according to the meaning of the words, but in truth, he said that we can mention the sick person, that the Creator will send him a cure, even in the blessing, "And to the slanderers," since all the blessings in the Eighteen are holy names. This is why he said that when we say the prayers that they said, we have a connection with them, meaning with their prayers, namely connection with their intentions.

What Is, "If a Woman Inseminates First, She Delivers a Male Child"?

This is not so with a request. This is when a person feels what he is lacking. This is specifically in the heart, meaning that it does not matter what he says with his mouth, since "requesting" means that a person asks for what he needs, and all of man's needs are not in the mouth, but in the heart. Therefore, it does not matter what a person says with his mouth. Rather, the Creator knows the thoughts. Hence, what is heard above is only what the heart demands and not what the mouth demands, since the mouth has no deficiency that must be satisfied.

Hence, when a person comes to pray he should prepare for the prayer. What is this preparation? It is written "Prepare for your God, Israel" (*Shabbat* 10). He says there that preparation is something each one does according to his understanding. We should interpret that concerning the preparation that each one does, it is in order to know what to ask, since one must know what to ask. That is, a person has to know what he needs.

This means that a person can ask for many needs, but normally, we ask for what we need the most. For example, when a person is in prison, all his concerns are about the Creator freeing him from imprisonment. Although sometimes a person has no income, and so forth, he still does not ask the Creator for income, too, although he needs it, since then he suffers most from being in prison. For this reason, a person asks for the thing he needs the most, meaning he asks about that which pains him the most.

Therefore, when a person comes to pray to the Creator to help him, he should first prepare and examine himself to see what he has and what he needs, and then he can know what to ask of the Creator to help him. It is written, "From the depths I have called upon You, Lord." "Depth" means that a person is at the very bottom, as was said, "at the bottom of Sheol," meaning that his lack is below and he feels that he is the lowliest of all humans.

In other words, he feels so far from *Kedusha*, more than everyone else, meaning that no one feels the truth, that his body has nothing to do with *Kedusha*. For this reason, those people, who do not see the truth of how far they are from *Kedusha*, can be content with their work in holiness, while he suffers from his situation.

Therefore, this person, who criticized himself and wants to see the truth, this person can say, "From the depths I have called upon You, Lord," meaning from the bottom of the heart. This is called "a prayer from the bottom of the heart," on the part of the receiver. That is, he examined himself and saw his fault.

However, when the person prepares himself for prayer, he must pay attention to the Giver. This is the hardest, since there is a rule that anything that depends on faith, the body does not agree to it. Since a person prays to the Creator, he must believe that the Creator "hears the prayer of every mouth," even when the person is unworthy of the Creator granting his wishes.

This is as we say in the prayer between man and man. Normally, there should be two conditions when one asks a favor from another: 1) His friend must have what he wants, so if he asks him, he will be able to give him because he has it. 2) His friend must have a kind heart. Otherwise, his friend might have what he asks, but will not want to give it because he is not a merciful person.

Likewise, between man and the Creator, these two conditions must be met, as well, as our sages said (*Hulin* 7b), "Israel are holy. Some want and do not have, some have and do not want." We should interpret this in the work. The Creator has what he wants, meaning what a person asks—that the Creator will bring him closer and give him the privilege of serving Him. In other words, a person wants the Creator to give him the desire to bestow. At that time, he believes that the Creator has the power to give man the desire to bestow.

However, the Creator does not want, since He sees that the person is still incapable of it because he still does not have a real desire for it, since he thinks that he has already prayed many times to the Creator to satisfy his wish and give him the filling, namely the desire to bestow.

But because "as the advantage of the light from within the darkness," the person's awakening from below is still incomplete, and the person must still labor in order to understand the great gift called "desire to bestow," which he is asking of the Creator. This is called "He has but He does not want to give." However, the person is considered holy because he is asking the Creator to take him as a servant of the Creator.

Sometimes, a person asks the Creator to bring him closer and give him a good taste in Torah and in prayer. Then, if he tastes sweetness in Torah and work, he will agree to serve the Creator. But to learn and pray and observe all 613 *Mitzvot* with all their details and precisions just like that, when he feels no taste in this? A person says he cannot do this.

Therefore, he asks the Creator to grant his wish. To the Creator, this is called "Israel are holy. Some want and do not have." This means that the Creator wants to give to the person the flavors of Torah and *Mitzvot*, but "He does not have." That is, these things do not exist in the Creator, in vessels of reception, that it is possible to give this to a person in his vessels of reception.

This is the meaning of "the Creator cannot give him," since the Creator has no vessels of reception. Rather with the Creator, everything is in vessels of bestowal. Since a person wants the Creator to give him everything in man's vessels of reception, since he claims that he wants to enjoy Torah and *Mitzvot*, and this is why he asks the Creator to satisfy his deficiency, to the Creator, this is called "He wants to give to the man what the man wants, and He wants to give because of His desire to do good to His creations. But because the person asks the Creator to give him everything in man's vessels of reception, the Creator does not have this." Rather, the Creator has only the desire to bestow.

For this reason, although a person cannot receive from the Creator, he is still called "holy," since he wants to engage in Torah and *Mitzvot*. Hence, when a person comes to pray, he should first prepare in order to know for what to pray.

What Are Holiness and Purity, in the Work?

Article No. 28, Tav-Shin-Nun-Aleph, 1990/91

It is written in *The Zohar* (*Kedoshim*, Item 13), "The Torah is called 'holy,' for it is written, 'for I the Lord am holy.' This is the Torah, which is the upper, Holy Name. Hence, one who engages in it is purified and then sanctified, as it is written, 'You will be holy.' It does not say, 'were holy,' but 'will be holy,' will be indeed. That is, it is a promise that through the Torah, you will be holy."

We should understand what it means when it says that through the Torah you will be holy, and then says, "Hence, one who engages in it is purified and then sanctified." Therefore, we should understand why he begins by saying that through the Torah, he will be holy, and then says that through the Torah he will have purity, and only afterward will the Torah bring him *Kedusha* [holiness]. Also, we should understand what are the promises that he will certainly achieve *Kedusha*, meaning what is the cause and the reason for the certainty that it will bring him to *Kedusha*.

It is known that the purpose of creation is that His desire is to do good to His creations. Accordingly, the created beings should have received the delight and pleasure. Yet, we must understand that the delight and pleasure that the Creator wishes to give to the created beings is not the same delight and pleasure that is appropriate for beasts, but what is appropriate for humans. We must believe what the ARI says, that all the corporeal pleasures extend only from what fell through the breaking of the vessels (that were in the world of *Nekudim*), when holy sparks fell from there into the *Klipot* [shells/peels]. But the main pleasures are in *Kedusha*, and they are called "the holy names."

In order for the creatures to be able to receive the delight and pleasure, and in order not to have shame while receiving the pleasure, a correction was placed on it. The correction was a *Tzimtzum* [restriction] and concealment on the upper light. That is, before one receives the correction on the will to receive, which is the aim to bestow, there is no disclosure of the upper light. The *Mitzvot* [commandments/good deeds] that we observe, where we should have tasted the flavor of delight and pleasure, we cannot feel this taste because of the above-mentioned reason, so there will not be shame while receiving the pleasure, for which there was a correction that when we receive the pleasure, we must aim to bestow. Otherwise, there are concealment and hiding on the actions.

Hence, we must observe the Torah and *Mitzvot* so it will bring us purity, where purity means purification of the *Kelim* from the will to receive for oneself, which is called "dirt," since it is in disparity of form from the Creator, who is all to bestow. For this reason, before we clean the *Kelim*, it is impossible to place within them anything good, for anything we might place in a dirty *Kli* [vessel] will be spoiled.

Hence, we must receive good advice, things that will purify our *Kelim* [vessels], which is called "making kosher [fit to be eaten according to Jewish laws]" and "preparation" so we can receive the delight and pleasure. Because of this, we were given 613 *Mitzvot* [commandments/good deeds], which *The Zohar* calls "613 counsels," namely counsels about how to purify ourselves from the filth of our vessels of reception.

This is as it is written in the "Introduction of The Book of Zohar" ("General Explanation for All Fourteen Commandments and How They Divide into the Seven Days of Creation," Item 1): "The *Mitzvot* in the Torah are called *Pekudin* [Aramaic: deposits], as well as 613 *Eitin* [Aramaic: counsels]. The difference between them is that in all things there is *Panim* [anterior/face] and *Achor* [posterior/back]. The preparation for something is called *Achor*, and the attainment of the matter is called *Panim*. Similarly, in Torah and *Mitzvot* there are 'We shall do' and 'We shall hear.' When observing Torah and *Mitzvot* as 'doers of His word,' prior to being rewarded with hearing, the *Mitzvot* are called '613 *Eitin*,' and are regarded as *Achor*. When rewarded with 'hearing the voice of His word,' the 613 *Mitzvot* become *Pekudin*, from the word *Pikadon* [Hebrew: deposit]."

We should interpret his words, that in order for one to be able to receive the delight and pleasure and that they will be in a manner of *Dvekut*, which is equivalence of form, since man was created with a desire to receive for oneself, man should cleanse himself from self-reception. But this is not within man's power, as it is against nature. Hence, we need His help, to give us this power called "desire to bestow." And how do we receive this desire? This is done through the Torah, as our sages said, "The Creator said, 'I have created the evil inclination; I have created the Torah as a spice.'"

It follows that the fact that we observe the Torah and *Mitzvot* is with the aim that the Torah and *Mitzvot* will bring us purity. This is called "613 counsels." The 613 *Eitin* are counsels concerning two things—the light and the *Kli*, called a "need." In other words, it is impossible to receive something unless there is a need for it.

Therefore, a person must learn the Torah so as to feel the bad and understand that the will to receive for oneself is bad. Put differently, he should ask the Creator to give him the need to obtain the desire to bestow, since the fact that one understands that he must obtain the desire to bestow is still not considered a need. Rather, first one must know why he needs the desire to bestow, meaning what he loses by not having the desire to bestow. If he does not see the great loss from not having this desire, he certainly cannot ask from the bottom of the heart that the Creator will give him the desire to bestow.

Moreover, sometimes a person does not want the Creator to give him that desire, and how can one pray for something that he is not certain that he needs? And the evidence that he does not need it so much is that many times he does not even want to be given that desire. It therefore follows that one should pray to the Creator to make him feel the need for this desire, meaning to yearn for the Creator to give him that desire, since he does not always understand the need for this desire.

By this we can interpret what is said in the supplementary prayer (for *Rosh Hashanah* [beginning of the year] and *Yom Kippur* [Day of Atonement]), "And be in the mouths of Your people, the house of Israel, who are standing up to ask. Inform them what to ask." In other words, the Creator should give them, the messengers of Your people. That is, each person is a community in itself and has a messenger of the public, meaning a person who is going to pray for himself. It is known that man is called "a small world in and of itself." Hence, first we must ask the Creator to send him what to ask, meaning that one should first ask to feel the need for the desire to bestow, and only the Creator can give him that need.

It follows that the beginning of his work is the recognition of evil, meaning that a person asks the Creator to feel how bad is the will to receive. This awareness that the will to receive is called "bad," only the Creator can make him feel. This is considered that through the Torah, a person can achieve recognition of evil, meaning to understand how much his will to receive is bad, and then he can ask to replace the will to receive and give him instead the desire to bestow.

Yet, if he has no lack, meaning torments at the fact that he is dirty and immersed in the filth of the will to receive for himself, then he asks the Creator to satisfy other desires for him, which pain him, meaning whose absence of feels. He wants the Creator to satisfy all that his heart desires. Although a person does not say verbally to the Creator to satisfy all his wishes, it is as we said in the previous article, that the request is not that which one says with his mouth, for a request of the Creator is only a lack, and a lack is recognized in the heart, and not in the mouth. Thus, we should know that we do not need to say out loud what we are asking of the Creator, for only that which is in the heart is regarded as a request. Therefore, even if one does not say to the Creator, "Satisfy all my heart's wishes," the demand within the heart is already considered a request.

Therefore, one must know that the Creator takes into consideration only that which is in one's heart. And since man cannot live without pleasure, because His desire is to do good, if a person cannot receive pleasure from *Kedusha*, the body must receive pleasure from corporeal lusts. And if a person is accustomed to sometimes receive pleasure from Torah and *Mitzvot*, then during the descent, when he does not feel the lack for spirituality, he should work in order to obtain that lack, so he will suffer at not having the need for spirituality. Then a person receives a greater need for corporeal lusts, to complement what he was used to occasionally receive from Torah and *Mitzvot*.

Hence, during the descent, one must be mindful that he engages in Torah and *Mitzvot* so that the light of the Torah will shine for him and he will feel its absence, meaning that he will suffer at not having love and fear of the Creator. In order for one to feel suffering in the heart from being far from *Kedusha*, we can receive this feeling by engaging in Torah and *Mitzvot*, so it brings us to feel the truth about what one needs. By this he will be able to achieve wholeness. At that time, a person receives through this the Torah, and this is called that he receives the need from above, meaning through the power of the Torah. Afterward, a person receives the filling, which is the light, meaning the power of the desire to bestow, which is a second nature. This is regarded as receiving purity, where by the desire to bestow that he received, he is now in a state of "purification of the *Kelim*."

According to the above, we should interpret what we asked concerning what *The Zohar* says, that through the Torah you will be holy, and afterward it says, "Hence, one who engages in it is purified and then sanctified." The answer is that the Torah does two things: 1) Purifies, meaning gives the *Kli*, namely the lack. 2) Afterward, the Torah gives him the light.

There is a rule that when a person is told, "I will give you something good," first he is told what is the good thing, and then he is given details. This means that first, one is told, "You will be awarded *Kedusha*," and then he is given details, meaning that you cannot enjoy from the *Kedusha*, for you should know that this is something very important. Hence, first the Torah must give you the *Kli* to receive the *Kedusha*." Before a person has the *Kli*, he cannot receive the filling. It follows that the Torah gives the light, as well as the *Kli*. But at first, we do not speak of the *Kli*, but of the light, and then we also speak about the *Kli*. This is why it is written, "You will be holy."

Now we can understand what we asked, "What is the guarantee that 'You will be holy,' for he says, 'You will indeed be holy,'" meaning that through the Torah you will be holy. We should interpret that since His desire is to do good to His creations, but because of the disparity of form there was a correction of *Tzimtzum* [restriction] and concealment, where the light does not shine to the lower ones before they have *Kelim* that are fit to receive, meaning that the *Kelim* have the correction of the aim to bestow, which is called "purity," since through the Torah they will receive purification, as our sages said, "I have created the evil inclination; I have created the Torah as a spice." It follows that the *Kelim* can be purified by the Torah, since "the light in it reforms him."

Hence, if they have pure *Kelim*, they will certainly be rewarded with the light, and the light is called *Kedusha*. There is no shortage of lights; only *Kelim* are missing. Thus, purity is called a *Kli*, meaning the correction of receiving in order to bestow, and the work of the *Kelim* is an order in and of itself, meaning that all the work that one must do is only *Kelim* that are fit to receive. This is as it is said, "More than the calf wants to eat, the cow wants to feed." It follows that the most important is the purification of the *Kelim*.

For this reason, once a person engages in Torah and the Torah brings him to purity, as it is written, "I have created the evil inclination; I have created the Torah as a spice," he will certainly be rewarded with *Kedusha*, which is called "light," which is the names of the Creator. This is why he says that the Torah is called *Kedusha*, as it is written, "for I the Lord am holy."

This is the meaning of what he says, "It does not say, 'were holy,' but 'will be holy,' will be indeed. That is, it is a promise that through the Torah, you will be holy." And at that time one is rewarded with wholeness and he can observe "And you shall love the Lord your God with all your heart," meaning with both your inclinations—the good inclination and the evil inclination, due to the *Kedusha* that he received from above. At that time, the whole body annuls before the *Kedusha*. It follows that the evil inclination, too, agrees to work for the sake of the Creator. By this we should interpret what our sages said (*Berachot* 35b), "When Israel do the Creator's will, their work is done by others."

That is, when one has been rewarded with doing the Creator's will, meaning that as the Creator wants to bestow, so man wants to bestow upon the Creator. At that time, their work, meaning one who wants his work to be in wholeness, which comes to him from working with the good inclination, once he has been rewarded with the desire to bestow, the work of heaven is done by others. Who are the others? It is the evil inclination, who is the "other" of *Kedusha*, meaning the other side, which is against *Kedusha*. However, when one works for the desire of the Creator, which is the desire to bestow, the other, too, the evil inclination, also does the Creator's work.

However, before one has been rewarded with being among the people who do the Creator's will, the good inclination is also unable to work, since the evil inclination controls it. For this reason, the evil inclination is called "an old and foolish king." It is called "a king" because it controls the person and each time, thoughts and desires of every kind in the world come to a person. Hence, when a good thought or desire comes to a person, he should believe that it came to him from above, and he should be thankful to the Creator for it, since by thanking the Creator for it, spirituality becomes more important to him each time.

A person should know that in spirituality, exile means that the importance of *Kedusha* has departed from him. This is called "*Shechina* [Divinity] in the dust." It follows that by thanking the Creator for a small thing in *Kedusha*, regardless of the quantity, since this gives some assistance to spirituality, he should be thankful to the Creator. According to the above, we should interpret what our sages said (*Avot*, Chapter 1:15), "Welcome every person with a bright face."

Therefore, since thoughts and desires always come to a person, whether beastly or human, meaning that a thought and desire that do not pertain to the beastly level, normally a person weighs its benefit, meaning that one weighs which is preferable to which. In other words, a person can repel beastly lusts in order to receive lusts that are suitable for the human level. But the person says, "I want to relinquish beastly lusts, but in return, receive the status of a great and important person. That is, if by conceding corporeality, I will feel a good taste in Torah and prayer, it is worthwhile for me to relinquish." But on the level of a small person, meaning that he does not feel any flavor in Torah and *Mitzvot*, and for this, I must relinquish corporeal needs and be happier than with beastliness? About this, a person says that it is not worth relinquishing.

Our sages said about this, "Welcome every person with a bright face." That is, when a thought and desire to be human comes to a person, which is considered that now he received the quality of "man," one should not say, "First, I want to see the greatness of this person and what he promises me." The answer to this is "every person," meaning that he should not distinguish between a great and important person or a simple person. "Every" means every person, without distinctions, as long as he is in the quality of "man," meaning if the thought and desire belong to being human, we should welcome it with a bright face, meaning be happy with it, with this thought and desire, as though he feels it as a great man.

He must be thankful to the Creator for sending him this desire, and by thanking the Creator, it is not because He needs gratitude. Rather, it is because by focusing one's thought when he thanks the

Creator, he has some *Dvekut* [adhesion] with the Creator, since it is impossible to thank someone unless we love that person.

Since we normally thank one who has done something good for us, by nature, the one who receives the benefit loves him. It follows that this causes love of the Creator when a person thinks about the gratitude he gives to the Creator; hence, the measure and importance of the quality of man that he received is not important (but we must remember that the quality of "man" means what our sages said, "You are called 'man,' and not the nations of the world"). Rather, "a bright face" expresses the joy he has when receiving the quality of man. This means that one should exert to be able to have the strength to broaden the importance of the matter. He must believe that the Creator sent him this desire, so he must depict in his mind as though the Creator speaks to him and tells him, "My son, behave as I am telling you."

However, when a person wants to appreciate the thought and desire that came to him, and wants to execute it, the desires and thoughts about the seventy nations that are in his body come to him and laugh at him: "For such a small taste that you feel that there is something in spirituality, you want to betray corporeal needs?" They tell him, "Do you want to lose all importance for self-benefit for such a small and worthless thing?"

Then the person begins to say, "I hope and believe in the words of our sages, who said, "A *Mitzva* [commandment/good deed] induces a *Mitzva*." Therefore, I am certain that by this, I will be rewarded with achieving wholeness, as this is what I hope." The person should overcome and say as it is written (in the litany following the Eighteen Prayer), "Look from above and see that we have been the laughingstock of the nations." "Nations" means the seventy nations within one's body. They mock the person when he wants to do the holy work, and he must ask for the Creator's help.

According to the above, we should interpret what our sages said, that one should not be ashamed of people who mock him in the work of the Creator. It means that man consists of the whole world.

Hence, there are discernments within man that mock a person wanting to appreciate small words and actions that a person wants to do, and say about such small actions, meaning about a *Mitzva* on which he cannot make any intentions, that it is not worth exerting in order to do them. Therefore, the sages said that they should not be ashamed from those who mock. Rather, one should believe that anything pertaining to the work of the Creator is important, and certainly, if one can aim while performing the *Mitzvot*, it is even better. Nevertheless, even the smallest act is priceless and one cannot evaluate it.

We already said that Baal HaSulam said that one should believe that according to man's view, who knows that an act *Lishma* [for Her sake] is a great thing above, he should believe that an act *Lo Lishma* [not for Her sake] is even greater and more important above than one thinks that the *Lishma* is great and important. Hence, we must exert and believe in the sages in everything we do, that we are rewarded with performing acts of *Kedusha*. Even without any intention, that, too, is a great and important thing, and we should thank the Creator for it.

What Does It Mean that a High Priest Should Take a Virgin Wife, in the Work?

Article No. 29, Tav-Shin-Nun-Aleph, 1990/91

The *Zohar* says (*Emor*, Item 38), "It is a *Mitzva* [commandment/good deed] for the high priest to marry a virgin. This is the meaning of what is written, 'A widow, or one divorced, or a profaned woman, or a harlot, these he shall not take, but a virgin of his own people shall he take for a wife.' He asks, 'Why is it necessary to take only a virgin, without a flaw?' He replies, 'A woman is a cup of blessing. If it is tasted, it is flawed.' This implies to *Malchut*, who is called 'a cup of blessing,' and the priest, who offers a sacrifice before the Creator, must be perfect and flawless, since the flaws blemish the priests. Perfect in his body, perfect in his *Nukva*, by which to observe, 'You are all beautiful, my wife, and there is not a flaw in you.'"

We should understand what a "high priest," a "virgin," a "widow," a "divorcee," a "profaned woman," and a "harlot" mean in the work, and that he should take only a virgin, who is without a blemish, meaning that a virgin is unblemished. What does it imply that a virgin has no blemish in her, and what is the connection, in that he says that a woman implies a cup of blessing, which is *Malchut*?

The ARI says about *Malchut*, that each day she becomes a virgin once again (*The Study of the Ten Sefirot*, Part 12, Item 144), which is regarded as only a dot, and must be rebuilt until she obtains *Gadlut* [greatness/adulthood]. It is written in *Shaar HaKavanot* (Part 2) that each day is separate, and "There is not a single prayer since the world was created through the end of the world, that is similar to another whatsoever. And each day, new sparks are sorted, which have never before sorted until that time."

We should understand this in the work. *Malchut* is called the "kingdom of heaven," which man must take upon himself each day anew. It is not enough that he took upon himself the kingdom of heaven yesterday, but rather each day is a new discernment in and of itself. Hence, we must believe that each time we take upon ourselves the kingdom of heaven, it is considered that we sort out sparks that were outside of *Kedusha* [holiness], which is called (in *Shaar HaKavanot*) that "These sparks were previously captive among the *Klipot* [shells/peels], and they were raised to *Kedusha* by accepting the kingdom of heaven and by engaging in Torah and *Mitzvot* [commandments/good deeds]."

It is as we say in the prayer (Master of the World, after the *Omer* count), "By this, great abundance shall flow in all the worlds." For this reason, it is said in the holy books that a person, while accepting the kingdom of heaven during the *Shema* reading, should take upon himself the kingdom of heaven and intend that the acceptance of the kingdom of heaven will be with devotion. And since each day is a new discernment, and we must build the *Malchut* so she is in *Gadlut*, each time it is renewed.

This is why there is the intimation about the high priest. In the work, one who is a servant of the Creator, who wants to draw near to the Creator in *Gadlut*, is called "high priest." When he comes to take a "wife," called "kingdom of heaven," he must take a "virgin," since a virgin means that she has not been blemished. A virgin is as it is written, "a virgin soil," which is a moniker for land that has never been cultivated, as it is written, "It was virgin soil," which man has never tilled (*Avoda Zara* 32).

In other words, a person should take upon himself the burden of the kingdom of heaven as though he never had the kingdom of heaven and it is a new thing for him. Naturally, now he must think that he is going to do something new that he has never known about. It follows that this acceptance that he takes upon himself requires extra scrutiny, to know what is the acceptance of the kingdom of heaven, and what it requires so that the fear of heaven will be upon him.

This means that one should reflect on what he should do so that this will be a perpetual thing for him. That is, what does the Creator require of a person who has taken upon himself the burden of the kingdom of heaven. The verse says, "What does the Lord your God require of you but to fear Me," and to reflect on what is fear. But if a person stops remembering about the matter of accepting the kingdom of heaven, regardless of the reason, and then reawakens to accept the kingdom of heaven, he does not need to continue the acceptance of the kingdom of heaven upon him in the manner he did prior to losing it, and to say, "I must go and awaken the kingdom of heaven," meaning that it will be continual. Rather, he must begin the work anew.

We should compare this to a person who died and had valuable things, and his children come and want to receive the inheritance that their father bequeathed them. Our sages said about that (*Avot*, Chapter 2:17), "Prepare yourself to learn Torah that has not been bequeathed to you." We should interpret that if a person comes to a state where he has forgotten everything, meaning he suffered a descent, it is as though he is dead. That is, previously, he was alive, meaning that he had the kingdom of heaven, which is considered being adhered to the Life of Lives. When it stops in him, he is considered dead, as was said, "The wicked in their lives are called 'dead.'"

In spirituality, cause and consequence are called "father and son." It follows that now he is called "a son" and wants to take upon himself of what is left after the demise of his father. We should interpret that "this is not your inheritance." Rather, one must turn to a new page in the work of the Creator, as though he was born now, and now he wants to take upon himself the burden of the kingdom of heaven and has no one from whom to inherit.

Accordingly, we should interpret what we asked, What do "high priest" and "plain priest" imply to us in the work? We should interpret that a "priest" is one who serves the Creator. Some workers belong to the general public. These are called "plain priests." And some want to work in the individual manner, to achieve *Gadlut*, which is to work in truth. These are called "high priests."

Among high priests, there is a completely different order of work than that of the general public—when a person engages in Torah and *Mitzvot* in practice and relies on the general public as far as the intention is concerned. Conversely, there are people who want to work also with the intention, meaning they want to aim all their actions for the sake of the Creator.

In other words, a "plain priest" means that his work is in the manner of the general public, and a "high priest" means that his work is in the manner of individuals. By this we can interpret what *The Zohar* says, "'Why is it necessary to take only a virgin, without a flaw?' He replies, 'A woman is a cup of blessing. If it is tasted, it is flawed.'" We should interpret that a high priest, meaning one who wants to be a true servant of the Creator, must not take a wife, meaning the kingdom of heaven, that has already been flawed in him, meaning to continue the kingdom of heaven that he had prior to the descent he suffered, for this one is no longer "a virgin," since he had this kingdom of heaven previously, and she was blemished.

That is, like the cup of blessing, "If it is tasted, it is flawed," meaning that this *Malchut* was already tasted before he suffered the descent. This is the meaning of "If it is tasted, it is flawed," since he already suffered a descent. It follows that he already blemished this

Malchut, so he must take upon himself a new kingdom of heaven as though he never tasted the taste of the kingdom of heaven, and must turn to a new page in the work.

According to the above, we can interpret what we asked about what is written, "A widow, or one divorced, or a profaned woman, or a harlot, these he shall not take." We should interpret that a widow is after he suffers a descent, he is regarded as dead. It follows that the previous wife, which is the kingdom of heaven that he had prior to the descent, is regarded as that person's widow.

Likewise, what is a divorcee in the work? It means that he divorced her because he did not like her, since the minute a person does not agree to work for her, since he does not feel her importance, this is considered that the man divorces the wife. Although she does not want to divorce, since she has mercy on him, meaning *Malchut* sees that he is immersed in self-love and feels sorry for him, but he divorces her against her will.

This is the meaning of the judgment being that a woman is divorced against her will, since as soon as he does not like her, it is considered that he has divorced her. Therefore, a servant of the Creator, who is called a "high priest," will not return and take that woman who is a divorcee. Rather, now he must begin to accept the burden of the kingdom of heaven anew and not take what happened into consideration.

Also, we should interpret "profane," that he must not take a profaned woman. When a person wakes up once again to the work of the Creator, if it is in the manner of a high priest, it means he wants to work on the greatness of the Creator. That is, it is known that when one works in order to receive reward for his work, he does not look at who is giving, whether he is an important person or not. Rather, he looks at the reward. This means that if the owner is a simple person but pays twice as much as an important person who has some factory and pays salaries, he will certainly work for the one who pays higher wages.

But if a person works without a salary, but because he wants to serve an important person, that person always looks to see who is the most important and wants to work for him. It follows that one who wants to work in *Gadlut*, meaning that his work is built on the greatness of the Creator, since he wants to work without any reward, he is called "high priest," since a priest is one who serves the Creator, who wants to approach the Creator. It is as we interpret the verse, "Should a man from among you make an offering to the Lord." It is interpreted that "from among you" means that the offering is "from within you, yourselves," meaning that the person who offers himself to the Creator is called "high priest."

That person must not take a profaned woman. This means that whenever he comes to take a wife, he will always take a virgin, one who has never had a husband, meaning that he never used this *Malchut*. Rather, it must always be a new wife. Conversely, if he already used this *Malchut* before and had a descent, and stopped the acceptance of the kingdom of heaven, this is because he profaned her and did not behave with her as one should honor the kingdom of heaven, and dealt with her in contempt. Hence, he will not receive that discernment once again, since he already desecrated her.

Rather, a high priest should try to always take a virgin woman, meaning to depict to himself that now he is beginning to do the holy work, and what he had until now does not interest him. Rather, he says he hopes that henceforth, he will keep her and respect her. This is the meaning of the words "He shall take a wife in her virginity."

We should also interpret what is written, "A widow, or one divorced, or a profaned woman, or a harlot, these shall he not take, but a virgin of his own people shall he take for a wife." We should interpret what is a harlot in the work. The thing is that when the high priest wants to assume the burden of the kingdom of heaven, he must take a virgin, meaning "virgin soil," which is a moniker for a land that has never been cultivated. Naturally, such soil cannot be expected to yield crops for food. This means that a person cannot sustain himself from this soil. Only after he cultivates it and gives it all that it needs, he will be able to sustain himself from that soil, and not before.

It follows that when a person accepts the burden of the kingdom of heaven, which is called "a wife," he must be careful not to want the woman to be a *Zona* [harlot], from the words *Zan uMefarness* [nursing and sustaining]. That is, if the acceptance of the burden of the kingdom of heaven will sustain him, meaning he will have nourishments from her while he engages in Torah and *Mitzvot*, then he is willing to take her. Otherwise, he will not agree to take this woman, and this is called "a harlot woman" in the work.

Rather, he must accept the kingdom of heaven as a burden, meaning "as an ox to the burden and as a donkey to the load," unconditionally. This is regarded as a "virgin woman," which is a "virgin soil," which bears no fruit. If a person agrees to these conditions, he will be rewarded with being a high priest, namely bring himself closer to the Creator.

According to the above, we should interpret what our sages said (*Kidushin* 70a), in the work: "Anyone who marries a woman for wealth has unworthy children, as was said, 'They have betrayed the Lord, for they have borne foreign children.'" We should understand what is marrying a woman for wealth. It means that a woman, in the work, is called "kingdom of heaven," and he takes upon himself the burden of the kingdom of heaven because he heard that she has great wealth, and wealth means that she will provide for him, meaning that through the kingdom of heaven, he will have good taste in the Torah and in the prayer. Otherwise, it is enough for him to continue the same path that he received by education.

And why does he now need to take upon himself the burden of the kingdom of heaven and exert, if the kingdom of heaven does not add to his provision, so he can sustain himself more affluently, whereas what sustains him now, all the nourishments he currently finds in the pleasures of this world do not satisfy him, so he wants to receive the kingdom of heaven?

This is called "marrying a woman for wealth," meaning his only reason for accepting the kingdom of heaven is to satisfy self-love. This is also called that he marries an unworthy woman, since it is written in all the holy books that the acceptance of the kingdom of heaven should be with devotion, and there are many interpretations about it.

According to what we learn, the meaning is that he accepts the kingdom of heaven for the sake of the Creator and not for his own sake. This means that by taking upon himself the kingdom of heaven, he wants that His great name will grow and be sanctified, and not for his own sake. It follows that if he accepts the kingdom of heaven for his own sake, it is considered an "unworthy woman." This is called "for wealth," since "wealth" means that from this he will be able to sustain himself, meaning that through the wealth, he will be satisfied in life. Instead, one should try to take a woman for the sake of the Creator, meaning that the kingdom of heaven, called "woman," will be for the sake of the Creator and not for his own sake.

Now we can understand why a person should accept faith above reason. It is so because usually, a person always considers the profit. If he does not see that he will gain something from the work, he chooses to stay at rest and does not want to make any movements unless he gains something.

Hence, when one is told that he should accept the kingdom of heaven for the sake of the Creator, meaning to sanctify His name, the body asks, "What will I get out of taking upon myself the kingdom of heaven? What is my gain in this?" It is told, "There are no words that the body can understand. Rather, you must believe that this is a great thing for you that you have the privilege of serving the King." This is called "above reason," since there are no words to tell the body so it can understand that it is worthwhile.

Therefore, when one does not see the profits within reason, it is considered that the labor is greater than the reward, since he does not know what is the reward, but he sees the labor and does not need to believe concerning the labor. Thus, as long as one has not been rewarded with fear of the Creator, he always looks at the labor, since he cannot understand the benefit from the work, but only believe above reason. Hence, this work is called "hard work," and requires heaven's mercy.

By this we can understand what is written (Deuteronomy 25:18), "when you were faint and weary, and he did not fear God." It means that since he sees that he is making the effort, but he still does not see the benefit from this work, and he must only believe. It follows that one becomes faith and weary, and all because he has still not been rewarded with fear of God.

One should know that faith is the *Kli* [vessel]. When the *Kli* is properly completed and is fit to receive, the abundance immediately fills the *Kli* of faith, which is above reason. The abundance is called "fear of heaven," and a person obtains this light after he has provided this *Kli*, called "faith above reason." Before one is rewarded with fear of the Creator, he suffers the labor because the light does not shine for him.

It follows that one who wants to assume the burden of the kingdom of heaven must work above reason, meaning that it will not be for his own sake but for the sake of the Creator. This is called "above reason," since the body does not agree to it, since it does not understand anything but that which is to its own benefit.

Now we can interpret what our sages said, "There is no poor public." It is known that "poor" means one who is "poor in knowledge," as our sages said (*Nedarim* 41), "There is no poverty except in knowledge." Baal HaSulam said that *Malchut* is called "public." By this we should interpret that "There is no poor public" means that one who accepts the burden of the kingdom of heaven above reason, it does not mean that he has no reason and he is poor, and this is why he accepts the burden of the kingdom of heaven. It is to the contrary; he stands at a degree that is above reason, meaning even more important than reason. In the work, "above" and "below" mean that "above" means being of superior importance, and "below" means being of inferior importance.

"There is no poor public" means that one who takes upon himself the kingdom of heaven above reason is not regarded as "poor," meaning one who has no reason. It follows that the heart of the work is to work above reason, since when a person wants to work for the sake of the Creator, it is called "above reason," namely against the view of the body. However, one must know that we also need the Torah, as our sages said, "I have created the evil inclination; I have created the Torah as a spice."

This is as he writes in the book *A Sage's Fruit* (Letters, pp 115-116), "The purpose of the soul when it comes in the body is to attain returning to its root and to cleave unto Him, while clothed in the body, as it is written, 'To love the Lord your God, to walk in all His ways, to keep His commandments, and to cleave unto Him.' Yet, who knows the ways of the Creator? Indeed, this is the meaning of 'Torah that has 613 ways.' He who walks by them will finally be purified until his body will no longer be an iron partition between him and his Maker, as it is written, 'And I will take away the stony heart from your flesh.' Then he shall cleave to his Maker. Thus, it is best to yearn for the commandment of the Upper One (meaning the Torah), for 'He who does not know the ways of the Upper One and the commandments of the Upper One, which are the secrets of Torah, how will he serve Him?'"

We therefore see that one should try to exert to obtain the Torah. In order to obtain the Torah, one should accept the kingdom of heaven above reason. That is, against one's view, meaning that for himself, he does not need anything, but only for the sake of the Creator. By this we should interpret what is written (Genesis 28:14), "And your descendants will be as the dust of the earth." "Your descendants" means *Banim* [sons]. In the work, *Banim* means *Havanah* [understanding] in Torah and *Mitzvot*. The Creator promised Jacob that understanding in Torah and *Mitzvot* can be obtained only when one agrees to be "as the dust of the earth," meaning that he agrees to observe Torah and *Mitzvot* even if he does not feel any feeling in it and tastes only the taste of dust in Torah and *Mitzvot*, since he says, "I am working for the Creator. If He wants me to work for Him in this manner, I agree." Then he is rewarded with *Gadlut* [greatness] and understanding.

What Does It Mean that One Who Was On a Far Off Way Is Postponed to a Second Passover, in the Work?

Article No. 30, Tav-Shin-Nun-Aleph, 1990/91

The *Zohar* says (*BeHaalotcha*, Item 66), "Rabbi Yosi said, 'man, man' twice. Why? He replies, 'A man who is a man, fit for reception of a high soul, but has blemished himself because he caused himself to be blemished.' 'Man, man' means he is worthy of being a man, 'or on a far off way,' since a person who defiles himself is defiled from above. And since he is defiled above, he is on a far off way from that place and that road to which the descendants of Israel grip. Rabbi Yitzhak said, 'It is written, 'If [any one of you] becomes impure for a soul or on a far off way,' which is the meaning of the word 'or.'" Rabbi Yosi said, 'Here, when it says 'impure for a soul,' it means before he is defiled from above. But when it says here, 'a far off way,' it means after he was defiled from above and fell to a far off way, which is the *Sitra Achra* [other side]. This means that both will be devoid of *Kedusha* [holiness] above, and will not do the Passover when Israel do it.'"

Our sages said (*Shabbat* 104), "When one comes to defile, it is opened for him; when he comes to be purified, he is aided." We should understand what is written here, that "when a person who defiles himself is defiled from above." He does not say that it is opened for him, but that he is defiled from above. Also, we should understand why it is opened for him, since "the Creator does not complain against His creations." RASHI interprets that the Creator does not slander His creations (*Avoda Zara* 3), so why is he given from above some assistance that is to man's detriment? On the contrary, he should have been assisted, as it is written, "He who comes to be purified is aided." If he is not given help for his benefit, at least they should not do above an act that is to his detriment.

There are certainly many explanations in the literal, but we should interpret this in the work. It is known that when one observes Torah and *Mitzvot* [commandments/good deeds] in the manner of the general public, meaning to receive reward, and does not pay attention to the issue of the aim to bestow, he sees that each day he advances in the work, since this is the truth. In the practice, everything a person does is registered to his name, and in that state, called *Lo Lishma* [not for Her sake], one cannot see that it is *Lo Lishma*, meaning that he cannot see that there is a matter of deficiency here, that it should be *Lishma* [for Her sake], while he is working *Lo Lishma*. Instead, the things he does generally illuminate for him.

As a result, a person cannot see any deficiency in himself. That is, in terms of the general public, there is a correction that the things he does illuminate for him as Surrounding Light, which is a correction on the level of actions. Hence, one must be careful not to slight the practice of Torah and *Mitzvot*, even if it is only in action and without any intention. That is, even if a person does his deeds by coercion, it is still considered a great thing.

Hence, people who still cannot work with the aim to bestow have a correction that they do not find any fault in the things they do, so they will be happy with their work, as it is written, "Serve the Lord with gladness." Conversely, when a thought and desire come to a person and he begins to feel that there must be the matter of intention in observing Torah and Mitzvot, and he awakens to act not in order to receive reward, but in order to bestow, then begins a new order.

The order is that at that time, a person shifts to working on the left, when he begins to criticize his actions, whether they are in order to bestow, and he enters the work called Tuma'a [impurity] and Tahara [purity]. This means that he begins to work on the purification of the Kelim [vessels].

It is impossible to work on purity before we know what is Tuma'a. That is, it is not enough that it is written that there is the matter of Tuma'a, but one must feel what losses the Tuma'a causes, what he loses by knowing that he is defiled, meaning what he would gain if he were not impure, and what he loses now that he has been defiled.

In other words, although before he began the work of bestowal he knew that there was the matter of impurity and purity, he did not know why impurity was bad and purity was good. Therefore, one must engage in recognition of evil, meaning to try to grasp that the will to receive for oneself is called Tuma'a. That is, this Tuma'a removes him from Kedusha [holiness], meaning from the Creator, as it is written, "You will be holy, for I the Lord your God am holy." This means that you will be removed, meaning that as the Creator gives, so man should try to make all his actions be with the quality of bestowal, and this is called Kedusha. The opposite of this is called Tuma'a.

A person should ask the Creator to help him grasp the evil that is found in the will to receive for oneself, meaning that the Creator will help him feel the loss that the will to receive for oneself causes him, and how much he could gain if he had the power of the desire to bestow. In other words, great Tuma'a or small Tuma'a and great Kedusha or small Kedusha are not measured by the size of the Tuma'a or Kedusha, but by the measure of harm that the Tuma'a brings, and the measure of importance that the *Kedusha* brings, meaning how much he suffers when he knows that he is impure and how much pleasure he would feel when he knows that he is in *Kedusha*.

According to the above, we should interpret what we asked about what our sages said, "He who comes to defile, it is opened for him." We asked, "The Creator does not complain against His creations," so why is it "opened for him"? This implies that he is shown that he can go further into the *Tuma'a*, whereas before he came to defile, the place of *Tuma'a* was closed, and only when he came to defile it was opened for him. From above, there should have been mercy on that person, as it is written, "And His mercies are on all of His deeds."

We should interpret the meaning of "He who comes to defile." It means that one who wants to begin the work of bestowal cannot work in order to bestow unless he knows the loss of working in order to receive, which is why he now comes to know the measure of the bad that exists in the will to receive for oneself, meaning what is the measure of the bad that is found in the will to receive, which is called *Tuma'a*, which is the opposite of *Kedusha*. He asks the Creator to let him know the measure of the bad that is found in the will to receive that is called "impure," meaning impure for the soul. When he asks the Creator to help him, the answer to that is "it is opened for him" to see the bad that exists in the *Tuma'a* of the will to receive.

There are two discernments: 1) coming to defile, 2) seeing that he is already impure and wanting to see more than he sees now. If he asks to see more, he is helped from above, as it is written here in *The Zohar*, "A person who defiles himself is defiled from above." In other words, once it is opened for him and he sees that he has been defiled, and he asks for more, to be shown the truth—that he is so far from *Kedusha*—then he is defiled from above. That is, he receives help from above by being shown the loss that is found in the will to receive for oneself. This is regarded as arriving at a state of "recognition of evil." At that time, a need is born in him, called a *Kli* [vessel] that the Creator will help him and give him the purity, as it is written, "And I will sprinkle on you pure water."

By this we can interpret what we asked, Why does *The Zohar* say, "A person who defiles himself is defiled from above"? After all, the Creator does not complain against His creations! The answer is that being defiled from above is help, meaning he is assisted from above to see the truth of how the will to receive is bad and impure, since now he is asking for this help because he wants to see the truth about what is evil.

Accordingly, we should interpret what Rabbi Yitzhak asks about Rabbi Yosi, who says about the verse, "If a man, man, is impure for a soul or on a far off way," that a far off way is also regarded as *Tuma'a*, but when he is defiled from above it is called "a far off way." It is written, "or on a far off way," meaning that they are two things, meaning that a far off way is not *Tuma'a*. Rabbi Yosi explains, "When it says, 'impure for a soul,' it means before he is defiled from above. And here, when it says, 'on a far off way,' it means after he has been defiled above and fell to a far off way, which is the *Sitra Achra*."

We should interpret that there are two discernments in *Tuma'a* in the way of the work: 1) He who comes to defile, meaning comes to see if the will to receive is *Tuma'a*, meaning that it inflicts stupidity of the heart. At that time, it is opened to him to see the evil. But before a person comes to defile, meaning to see the bad in him, there is a correction from above that a person cannot see the evil, since there is a rule that one is not shown more than one can correct in oneself. It is as in corporeality, when one is not told one's true illness if the illness is incurable.

For this reason, precisely He who comes to defile, who want to see the truth, it is opened for him. If he wants to advance and prays to be shown the true measure of the bad that is found in the will to receive for oneself, he is assisted from above, meaning he is defiled from above. That is, he is shown from above the harm in *Tuma'a*. At that time, he begins to pray from the bottom of the heart that the Creator will give him the desire to bestow instead of the will to receive that he has by nature, and to be given a second nature, which is a gift from above.

By this we should interpret what is written, "This means that both will be devoid of *Kedusha* above, and will not do the Passover when Israel do it." In other words, both when a person is in the first state, when he comes to defile, and when he is in the second state, when he is on a far off way, when he is shown from above how far he is from *Kedusha*, he cannot do the Passover when Israel do it.

We should interpret that "Israel" means that he is already in the quality of "Israel," meaning that he is already in a state of *Yashar-El* [straight to the Creator], implying that all his actions are directed straight to the Creator. This is regarded as being in the right line, which is purity, meaning purity of the *Kelim*, when all his actions are for the sake of the Creator. This is called *Lishma*, as was said, "Rabbi Meir says, 'He who learns Torah *Lishma*, the secrets of Torah are revealed to him." We should interpret that when a person is rewarded with the quality of "Israel," this is the time to make the Passover offering. Israel means purity, and when a person is purified, this is the time to sacrifice the offering to the Creator, where sacrificing the offering is regarded as wholeness.

This is as it is written in *The Zohar* (*VaYikra*, Item 109), "Rabbi Yehuda started and said, 'Serve the Lord with gladness.' If you say that such is the work of the offering, this is not possible. Since that man has breached his Master's commandment, the commandment of the Torah, and repented before his Master, with what face will he rise before Him? Indeed, by what are they corrected? It is by those priests and Levites who complete the joy and singing for Him."

He interprets there in the *Sulam* [Ladder commentary on *The Zohar*] that this matter will be corrected by an order of three lines. This is why when speaking of the Passover offering, which is the matter of the exodus from Egypt, there must be the intimation in our work that first we must achieve purity, and then comes the nearing and we are rewarded with *Kedusha*. However, a person must believe that when he is awakened to enter the work, that it comes to him from above, meaning he is brought closer from above, so he will have connection with the *Kedusha*.

Certainly, he must be thankful to the Creator for pulling him out from the state of lowliness and elevating him to the domain of *Kedusha*, meaning that he began to feel that there is a higher place from which to receive provision, that his provision should not be as that of animals, but that he should receive provision from the "speaking" level. And the more he is grateful, the more he increases that feeling.

Yet, at the same time, he must know that he should ask the Creator to raise him to an even higher state than the one he is now, to be rewarded with the Torah. That is, although he depicts to himself that the state he is in is very important, meaning that he cannot imagine greater importance in the world, he should still say, "As much as I depict my current state as very important, I still cannot depict the real importance. As much as I depict a state of greatness, I should say that although I am as thankful to the Creator as can be, above reason, I still believe that there is a higher state than the one I am in now, and I am asking You to give me a greater gift."

By this we should interpret what is written (Psalms 71), "I will always long," meaning that there are higher degrees than what I can picture to myself. Although one should know that as much as he appreciates the current state, it is truly more important because a person cannot grasp the value of a tiny moment of spirituality. Still, above reason, he believes and asks for it.

This is the meaning of the words "I will always long," meaning that I will be able to depict that there is more greatness than I can depict. This is the meaning of what is written, "And I will add to all Your glory." This means that although now I praise you, I am asking to be able to praise You more than I can, and I want to add to Your glory.

However, when one should reflect on his spiritual state, and the person is brought before the judge within his heart, so he would give the verdict, whether one is guilty or innocent, meaning that sometimes, the judge acquits him because he cannot pay the debts that he must pay. At that time, a person needs mercy. That is, at times, the judge within his heart belongs to the wicked, those who condemn their Maker and not themselves. It follows that these judges cause a person to go to the prison of the criminals against the King, as it is written (Psalms 107), "Dwellers of darkness and the shadow of death, prisoners of poverty and iron, for they rebelled against the words of God And spurned the counsel of the Most High."

Although there might be good judges, they are taking a bribe. That is, the judge in his heart is concerned with his own benefit; therefore, he always sides with man's detriment. Then, a person has no other choice but to ask the Creator for mercy and to give him a real judge. The person sees that there is no real judge but the Creator.

In that regard, we should interpret what King David said (Psalms 82), "Arise, O God, judge the earth, for You will inherit all the nations," meaning that the Creator will be the judge. At that time, a person receives the strength from the Creator, "for You will inherit all the nations," for then one inherits all the nations in his heart.

The order of the work should be primarily about one thing: to work against man's reason. That is, when a person is told that he must work for the sake of the Creator and not for himself, this is against man's reason. After all, it is written, "And lives by them, and not that he will die." It follows that this contradicts the purpose of creation, which is to do good to His creations.

We can interpret this through Abraham's trial. On one hand, the Creator told him, "for through Isaac your descendants shall be named," but then it is written, "Take now your son, your only son, and offer him there as a burnt offering." We should interpret this in the work. "Your *Ben* [son]" comes from the word *Bina*, meaning *Havanah* [understanding]. "Your only one," meaning the only understanding that there is in man, which man guards with his heart and soul so that no harm will come to it, namely the will to receive for his own sake. "And offer him as a burnt offering," meaning slaughter the will to receive for one's own sake, cancel it, and work only with the desire to bestow and not with the will to receive.

Afterward, He said, "Do not stretch out your hand against the lad." We should interpret that we should not say that he should revoke the will to receive. Rather, one should work so he can use the will to receive in order to bestow, and the parts that he cannot direct in order to bestow are forbidden to use. We can interpret this by what He said to him, "and Abraham went and took the ram instead of his son." "Ram" is called *Bina*, as it is written in *The Zohar*, where he asks, "Why a ram and not a horn"? And he answers that a ram is regarded as *Bina* and a horn is *Malchut*. We should interpret that *Malchut* is "the will to receive." Therefore, the vessels of reception that we cannot aim so they work in order to bestow are forbidden to use. Instead of them, we use the *Kelim* of *Bina*, which are called "vessels of bestowal."

Accordingly, we can understand that when a person feels that he is not all right, that he is a sinner, it does not come to him because he did many bad deeds, since there is a rule, "transgressing and repeating, it becomes to him as permitted." Hence, many sins do not make one feel his fault. Rather, the size of the sin is measured by man's feeling of how far he is from the Creator. In other words, to the extent that one feels and believes in the Creator, to that extent he feels how far he is from the great King.

This means that when he feels that he is a sinner, he must know that the Creator let him feel a little bit, that there is a King in the world. This feeling, which he received from above, causes him to feel that he is a sinner. But when he has no connection to the Creator, how can he feel that he has sinned before the Creator and did bad things, which are against the Torah, when he does not know that there is the Giver of the Torah in the world? Rather, the sensation of sin is according to the measure of his faith in the greatness of the King, to that extent he can feel the measure of the sin. This means that the sin is measured in the one who flawed.

This is as our sages said (*Baba Kama*, Chapter 3), "The matter of shame is all according to the one who shames and the one who is ashamed." We should interpret that if the one who shames is smart, he can know that if one shames one who is great, it is a grave sin.

That is, the one who shames has the intellect to appreciate the size and importance of the one who is ashamed. It follows that he has committed a grave sin.

However, if the one who shames does not have the intellect to appreciate the importance of the one who is ashamed, it cannot be said about him that he has committed a grave sin and needs great atonement for the flaw that he has flawed in someone. Therefore, according to the sensation of the greatness of the King, so is the sin. Thus, if a person is righteous and has some understanding of the greatness of the King, his flaw is certainly greater than that of an ordinary person.

It follows that we always measure the importance of the King that a person has according to the person's feeling. Therefore, if one feels that he has sinned, it must be that he was given from above some nearing to *Kedusha*, and this is why he feels that he has sinned. It is as Baal HaSulam said about what our sages said, that the Creator is meticulous with the righteous as a hairsbreadth, as it is written, "And round about him was very stormy." He asked, Why do they deserve more punishment than others? He said that one who is righteous, says that the Creator is meticulous with him as a hairsbreadth. Therefore, when one feels that he has sinned, he should not be alarmed. On the contrary, it is a sign that he is being brought closer from above. Therefore, he must overcome and take upon himself the burden of the kingdom of heaven, and he will succeed.

What Does It Mean that Charity to the Poor Makes the Holy Name, in the Work?

Article No. 31, Tav-Shin-Nun-Aleph, 1990/91

It says (*BeHukotai*, Item 20), "'I will give your rains in their season.' Each one will give his strength over you. Who are they? It is that correction that you made, unifying that Holy Name. That unification of law and ordinance will bestow upon you. It is written, 'Keep the way of the Lord, to do righteousness and justice.' Since it is written, 'Keep the way of the Lord,' why does it need to write, 'To do righteousness and justice'? He replies, 'Since one who keeps the ways of Torah, it is as though he does righteousness and justice. And what are righteousness and justice? It is the Creator.' Rabbi Shimon wept and said, 'Woe unto people who do not know and do not consider the glory of their Master, for who makes the Holy Name every day? One who gives alms to the poor. One who makes this awakening from below, meaning gives alms, it is as though he made the Holy Name in completeness: As one does below, so it awakens above.'"

We should understand the connection between alms and the unification of righteousness and justice. Also, what is the connection between righteousness and justice and making the Holy Name? We should also understand what it means that a person makes the Holy Name, since we understand that the Holy Name makes man and not that man makes the Holy Name.

We should interpret this in the work, what this comes to teach us. It is known that the essence of our work in Torah and *Mitzvot* [commandments/good deeds] is to be able to receive the delight and pleasure that He contemplated giving to the created beings. The whole delay is in that we haven't the *Kelim* [vessels] to receive the abundance that comes from the Giver to the creatures, meaning for the creatures to have equivalence of form, called "As He is merciful, so you are merciful," meaning for the creatures to also have vessels of bestowal like the Giver.

Therefore, when a person takes upon himself the kingdom of heaven, the body asks, "What will you get out of this work of accepting the kingdom of heaven?" Our sages said about this (*Pesachim* 50), "One should always engage in Torah and *Mitzvot* even if *Lo Lishma* [not for Her sake], since from *Lo Lishma* he comes to *Lishma* [for Her sake]." This is as it is written in *The Zohar*, that there is the matter of fear when he observes Torah and *Mitzvot* in order to be rewarded in this world and in the next world. But the fear that is important is "because He is great and ruling," meaning not in order to be rewarded, but because he says that he has the privilege of serving a great King, and this is why he wants to observe the Torah and *Mitzvot*.

Although a person understands that there is the matter of serving the King, man's body is created with a nature of a desire to receive delight only from things that benefit itself. The body cannot understand serving someone else, so that the other will enjoy, meaning that he will enjoy someone else enjoying his work.

That is, it is unnatural for an employee, who works for the owner, and the owner really benefits from the work of the employee, that the employee will tell the owner, "I don't want you to pay me; it is enough for me that you enjoy the things I fixed for you because you regretted the broken tools you had. But now that I fixed them, you are enjoying this and I don't want any payment for my work." This is against nature. On the contrary, if you are enjoying my work, you should pay me more than I requested for my work.

Accordingly, we can understand how it is possible for a person to have the strength to work for the sake of the Creator without any reward. The first state is when a person wants to observe Torah and Mitzvot so it will bring him the cure, which is "the light in the Torah reforms him." That is, through them, he will obtain the second nature called "desire to bestow." Then, he will be able to serve the King without any reward, and his only reward will be that he is delighting the King. *The Zohar* calls this time, when he observes Torah and *Mitzvot* in order to obtain the desire to bestow, "613 *Eitin* [Aramaic: counsels]."

The second state is after he has acquired the desire to bestow. This is the state of receiving the delight and pleasure that are in the 613 *Mitzvot*, which *The Zohar* calls "613 *Pekudin* [Aramaic: deposits]." This means as it is written in the *Sulam* [Ladder commentary on *The Zohar*], that the delight and pleasure are there as a deposit.

For this reason, man's work when he takes upon himself the burden of the kingdom of heaven is to make it as a "charity for the poor." It is known that *The Zohar* calls *Malchut* "poor and meager." We should interpret this as not wanting to receive any return. This is similar to giving charity to a poor person and not asking him for anything in return. That is, we do not even want the poor person's gratitude, since real charity is called "concealed giving," which means that he does not see to whom he gives. Therefore, giving the charity was devoid of any gratitude from the poor.

It follows that when a person accepts the burden of the kingdom of heaven above reason, he does not hope for the Creator to thank him for it. Thus, the body asks, "Why are you taking upon yourself the burden of Torah and *Mitzvot*?" In that state, when he wants to take upon himself to observe Torah and *Mitzvot* without any reward, a person needs the Creator to give him the strength to overcome the body's question, and have the strength to do the holy work gladly.

It follows that precisely when one works in order to come to work that is purely holy, without any mixture of waste in there, he becomes needy of the Creator's help. Each time he wants to reassume the burden of the kingdom of heaven, he must work anew. A person must believe the words of the ARI, who says, "Each and every day, new discernments that have fallen into the *Klipot* [shells/peels] are corrected, and one day is not like the next, or one moment like its following."

Therefore, assuming the burden of the kingdom of heaven anew corrects new discernments into *Kedusha* [holiness]. For this reason, when a person wants to take upon himself the kingdom of heaven anew, the body asks, "What will you get out of working for the sake of the Creator?" And there is no other way but to ask the Creator to give him the power of faith above the reason of the body. In the words of our sages, this is called "Had the Creator not helped him, he would not overcome it."

According to the above, we should interpret what we asked about the relation that *The Zohar* explains about the verse, "Keep the way of the Lord," why it had to be written, "to do righteousness and justice." He replies that "one who keeps the ways of Torah, it is as though he does righteousness and justice." As said above, since man does not have the strength to assume the kingdom of heaven above the reason of the body, but only by the *Segula* [merit/quality/power] of Torah and *Mitzvot*, which is the way of the Creator, the ways of Torah, by which a person is rewarded with giving alms to the poor, since "the light in the Torah reforms him," then he will be rewarded with doing "righteousness and justice."

This is the meaning of what he says, that by keeping the way of the Lord, they will achieve the degree of doing "righteousness and justice." Yet, what are "righteousness and justice"? That is, what is this unification that *The Zohar* says is called "making the Holy Name?" In other words, what does it mean that by giving alms, he makes the Holy Name?

As said above, "righteousness and justice" mean that the Creator is called "justice" and *Malchut* is called "righteousness," which is the quality of judgment, on which there was a judgment, since *Malchut* is called a *Kli* [sing. of *Kelim*] that receives the abundance from the Creator. There were *Tzimtzum* [restriction] and concealment on the vessels of reception in order to receive, meaning a judgment that it is forbidden to use the vessels of reception as they are due to disparity of form between the receiver, who is called *Malchut*, and the Giver, who is called "the Creator." It follows that there is separation above where the abundance cannot spread to the creatures because of the disparity of form.

For this reason, there was a correction for the lower ones to give "alms to the poor." In terms of the work, when they take upon themselves the burden of the kingdom of heaven without anything in return, but rather as one gives charity to the poor and does not want to receive anything in return for this, each one causes at the root of his soul, above in *Malchut*, that it will also work only in order to bestow. It follows that they cause the unification of the Creator and His *Shechina* [Divinity]. This means that by a person doing everything in order to bestow, alms, called "justice," extend from the Creator to *Malchut*. In other words, through the abundance that *Malchut*, called "*righteousness*," receives, she is now called "charity," due to what she receives from the Creator.

In other words, by the lower ones giving alms to *Malchut*, the Creator, too, gives alms to *Malchut*. At that time, *Malchut* receives the name "charity." This is the meaning of the words "One who gives alms to the poor, it is as though he made the Holy Name complete, as it should be," meaning connects her with the Creator, who gives her everything, as though he made the Holy Name in completeness, "As one does below, so it awakens above."

What Does It Mean that Charity to the Poor Makes the Holy Name?

This means that the kingdom of heaven is called "poor" because she has nothing to give to the creatures. If the creatures come to her with vessels of reception, then she is poor and meager, since the creatures cause in *Malchut* the reception that exists in the quality of *Malchut*, and this causes separation between *Malchut* and the Creator, who is the Giver. Hence, the name is not complete because in terms of the name, the Creator is called The Good Who Does Good. Since they cause the reception that there is in *Malchut*, at the root of their souls, and there was a *Tzimtzum* of the abundance on the quality of reception, by this they prevent the abundance from spreading to the lower ones.

But if the creatures give alms, meaning do their actions in order to bestow, they cause a desire to bestow at the root of their soul, and then they cause equivalence of form above, and the abundance flows to the created beings. Then, the name The Good Who Does Good is revealed to the lower ones and this is considered that they make "the Holy Name in completeness." In other words, everything comes by directing their actions to be in order to bestow.

It follows that there are two states to man: 1) At the beginning of the work, we must begin in *Lo Lishma*. That is, everything he does is in order to receive reward in this world and in the next world. At that time, the Creator is called for him "King of the Nations," as it is written, "Who will not fear You, King of the Nations."

In the work, we should interpret that when one works for one's own benefit, he is regarded as "gentiles." He has still not achieved the quality of "Israel," where his actions are *Yashar-El* [straight to the Creator]. It follows that the person is serving a king who is called "King of the Nations." Thus, what sort of greatness of the King can there be in a person who is in a state of "gentile," although he has fear, as it is written, "Who will not fear You, King of the Nations"?

We should know that this is very important. That is, a person must know that any contact he has with the Creator is very important. Therefore, when a person works for a reward, we must not slight these works, although there is certainly a greater degree than the degree of "King of the Nations." This means that when a person is rewarded with the quality of "Israel," certainly in his current attainment, when he is at the degree of "Israel," he has a better understanding of the greatness of the Creator, to the point that he is delighted that he is serving a great King and he has no need to receive anything in return for his work.

Concerning work for the sake of the Creator, we should interpret what our sages said (*Midrash Tanchuma*, p 235b), "'If your brother becomes poor and stretches out his hand,' the writing says, 'Do not rob a poor, for he is poor.' What is 'Do not rob a poor'? Is there a person who robs the poor? What does one rob of someone who has nothing? However, if you were accustomed, if you were used to sustain him and you retracted and said, 'How long will I provide for this one?' and you refrain from giving him, if you did so, know that you are robbing him. This is 'Do not rob the poor, for he is poor.'"

According to the above, we should interpret that charity to the poor refers to *Malchut*, who is called "poor and meager" because she has nothing to give back to man. If a person works for the sake of the Creator and wants nothing in return, but works only for the sake of the Creator, but sometimes, in the middle of the work, thoughts come to him that he is always working for the sake of the Creator and wants nothing in return, he will certainly be rewarded for this with a higher degree, meaning feel more flavor in Torah and work, since he has already done his part, meaning he says that he is assuming the kingdom of heaven without any reward, meaning he is not even receiving a flavor in Torah and *Mitzvot* in return for his work, so if his intention is already for the sake of the Creator, called "*Dvekut* [adhesion] with the Creator," he should have felt vitality in his work. Yet, he does not see any progress in the work; therefore, he wishes to stop this work of bestowal and work like the rest of the people—in order to receive reward.

The text says about this: "Do not rob a poor, for he is poor." The Midrash asks, "Is there a person who robs the poor? What does one rob of someone who has nothing? However, if you were accustomed to sustain him and you retracted and said, 'How long will I provide for this one?' and you refrain from giving him, know that you are robbing him."

It follows that the text warns us that one should not say, "I have already worked a lot on achieving the aim to bestow, and I did not obtain the delight and pleasure one should obtain when working with the intention to bestow, called "alms to the poor." Also, I was promised that I will nonetheless obtain the light, called "power," to be able to do everything in order to bestow, which is the light that is revealed when a person observes Torah and *Mitzvot* in the manner of "613 counsels," in order to obtain vessels of bestowal, called "the light for the completion of the *Kelim*," so they can work with the *Kelim* in order to bestow." He did not obtain that force, either, although the whole time he engaged in Torah and *Mitzvot* it was with this intention. "Therefore," says the person, "I have given You many exertions but I have acquired nothing, so I want to stop this work."

This is the meaning of saying, "How long will I provide for this one?" In other words, I have given You much, but I have received no spiritual progress in return. "Therefore," says the person, "How long will I have to work in a manner of 'alms to the poor'?" At that point, a person wants to escape the campaign and return to working like the general public, when he was working in the manner of "Who will not fear You, King of the Nations?" As said above, when a person works in observing Torah and *Mitzvot* for the purpose of self-love, there is no place for working for the sake of the Creator. This is regarded as the king whose Torah and *Mitzvot* a person observes is called "King of the Nations" and not "King of Israel," since then a person is not regarded as "Israel" but as a "gentile."

The text warns about this, "Do not escape the campaign; do not rob the poor, for he is poor." We should interpret "Do not rob the poor." It means that you should not stop the alms that you are giving him, meaning the acceptance of the kingdom of heaven without any reward, for although you claim that you have already given him many alms, know that this is incorrect. The meaning of "for he is poor" is that as long as you think that *Malchut*, who is poor, should give you anything, you are not saying she is poor. That is, if a person demands of *Malchut* to reward him, he blemishes the name of *Malchut*, who is called "poor and meager," since you are demanding something of her.

Rather, a person should pray to the Creator to give him the strength to be content and happy from being able to work for *Malchut* even when she hides herself and does not show him any nearing, and his taste in the work is as if he has now begun anew, meaning that he cannot say that he feels any flavor of which he can say that for this flavor he is working and laboring in assuming the kingdom of heaven.

That is, he has no support or basis that he can say, "This is why I engage in Torah and *Mitzvot*." This is called "hanging the earth on nothing," and it is called "completely above reason." Although it is completely against the body's nature, he prays to the Creator for this, to give him this power. This is the meaning of what is written, "Do not rob the poor, for he is poor." One should always want to stay, take upon himself the kingdom of heaven, and his basis is "for he is poor."

This is as Baal HaSulam said about what is written (in the poem, "A Woman of Valor"), "Charm is deceitful and beauty is vain; a woman who fears the Lord, she shall be praised." He said that when one assumes the burden of the kingdom of heaven, sometimes the kingdom of heaven is graceful, and sometimes he feels that there is beauty in the kingdom of heaven. The writing says about this: "It is all a lie." That is, this whole basis on which he builds his kingdom of heaven is a lie.

However, a "woman," who is the kingdom of heaven, that a person takes upon himself, should be because of the fear of the Creator, meaning that his fear will be as it is written in *The Zohar*, "The essence of fear should be because he is great and ruling" ("Introduction of The Book of Zohar," Item 191), as it is said, "Fear, which is the most important, is when one fears one's Master because He is great and ruling, the essence and the root of all the worlds, and everything is considered nothing compared to Him, and he will place his will in that place."

It therefore follows that prayer is the most important. A person should pray to the Creator to give him the required force for anything that concerns the work, both in Torah and in prayer. Hence, one should ask of the Creator to give him the need, meaning a desire for the work. Sometimes, a person comes to a state where he has no desire for anything, meaning that he does not see anything good before him that he should want, that will bring him vitality, that will give him a need to exert in order to obtain something. Rather, the person stays without any desire of which he can say that it is worth laboring in order to obtain it. He does not see this.

At that time, he must ask the Creator to give him some desire for something, meaning that this thing will give him desire to work. According to a person's understanding, the request will be that the Creator will let him see something that will bring him delight and pleasure. This is as our sages said, "The eye sees and the heart covets." That is, if the Creator lets him see something for which it is worthwhile to work, the coveting in the heart will make him seek ways by which to obtain the matter. It follows that the prayer that a person prays now is only for the purpose of desire, called a *Kli* [vessel].

This means that the first prayer that a person should pray is for a desire and lack that the Creator will give him to ask for a deficiency, so that if he obtains the satisfaction of the deficiency, that satisfaction will fill man in completeness. That is, the Creator will notify him what is the wholeness he should achieve, so as to know what it is he truly needs. And in order to know what he truly needs, this is done through the Torah, where by the *Segula* of the Torah, the light in it reforms him, meaning that the Torah lets him know what he is missing.

However, a person should demand this of the Torah, meaning for the Torah to guide him toward attaining the truth. Also, a person should find the connection between him and the Torah, for his desire to know his connection with the Torah is already regarded as a prayer. This means that by this he already connects himself to the Creator when he learns Torah, since he is asking the Creator—when he engages in Torah—to understand the connection between the Torah and the person who is learning the Torah. And once he has prayed for the Creator to give him the deficiency, he must ask the Creator to give him the satisfaction of the deficiency, meaning to be rewarded with achieving the degree of man's completeness.

What Are Banners in the Work?

Article No. 32, Tav-Shin-Nun-Aleph, 1990/91

Midrash Rabbah says about the verse (Numbers, Portion 2), "Each man by his own banner." "It is written, 'We will sing in Your salvation and in the name of our God we will set up our banners.' Israel said to the Creator, 'We sing in Your salvation, which You did for us in Your name; we will sing in Your salvation, and in that day, the Lord will save Israel.' It is written, 'will save,' as though Israel are saved and as though He is saved. 'And in the name of our God we will set up our banners,' for the Creator established His name in our name and made us banners, as was said, 'Each man by his own banner.' Rabbi Issachar says, 'And his banner over me is love.' Even a person who sits and engages in Torah, and skips from rule to rule and from verse to verse, the Creator says, 'I am fond of him and his banner is over Me is love, and his skipping is over Me with love.'"

We should understand the following:

1) What does it mean that the Creator established His name in our name?

2) Why is it written "will save," as though Israel are saved and as though He is saved (concerning what is written, "will save," it is interpreted that the meaning is "and will be saved").

3) "Skipping from rule to rule." It is known that the name of the Creator is The Good Who Does Good. That is, He always wants to bestow upon the creatures delight and pleasure, for which He created in the creatures the desire to yearn to always receive delight and pleasure. Accordingly, there is a question, Why are the creatures not feeling the delight and pleasure, but rather the whole world suffers from lack of pleasure and satisfaction in life, for every sensible person asks, "What is the meaning of our lives?"

The answer is that the Creator made a correction so that when we receive the delight and pleasure from the Creator, we will not feel shame about it, which stems from the disparity of form between the receiver, who is the creature, and the Creator, who is the giver. The correction is that before a person has the desire to bestow, which is in order to be in equivalence of form, it is impossible to receive the real abundance that the Creator wants to impart upon the creatures.

And since the desire to bestow is against human nature, we learn that there are seventy nations of the world within man. In other words, each person is a small world, as it is written in *The Zohar*, and the quality of Israel in man is under the governance of the nations of the world. This is regarded as the people of Israel being in exile among the nations, when they haven't the strength to go against the desire of the nations of the world. For this reason, the people of Israel ask the Creator to deliver them from the exile they are in among the nations, meaning to be able to work for the sake of the Creator.

Also, our sages said, "Israel who exiled, the *Shechina* [Divinity] is with them." We should interpret this the way Baal HaSulam said about what our sages said, "A disciple who is exiled, his teacher is exiled with him." He said that this means that when the disciple is in exile, meaning suffers a descent, in his eyes, his teacher is also in descent. That is, when a person is in descent, he has no taste in Torah and prayer, it is because his teacher exiled with him, meaning that all the matters of *Kedusha* [holiness] are in decline in him, as well, and he looks at everything as though there is no importance to anything spiritual. This is considered that spirituality is also in exile.

By this we should interpret that when Israel are in exile, meaning in descent, and the nations of the world control the person—and the nations of the world are generally called "will to receive for one's own benefit"—then the Creator is also in exile for them. In other words, they have no importance of the Creator, since if they had importance of the greatness of the Creator, they would not be able to rule over the Israel in him.

As is known, Israel means *Yashar-El* [straight to the Creator], when all of one's actions are straight to the Creator. But by their control, they make all of one's actions be only for his own sake. This is called "for the sake of the will to receive and not for the sake of the Creator." It follows that when the quality of Israel is in exile, the Creator is in exile with them, too, meaning that the desire to bestow is in exile, and the one to whom they want to bestow is in exile, as it is written about what Pharaoh said, "Who is the Lord that I should obey His voice?" That is, he denied the greatness of the Creator and did not allow to believe in the greatness of the Creator, so the quality of Israel is in exile within them.

According to the above, we can interpret what we asked, Why does he say that it is "as though Israel are saved and as though He is saved"? That is, what is the connection between the redemption of Israel and the redemption of the Creator? According to the above, it follows that the exile of Israel and the exile of the Creator are the same, since when a person attains and feels the greatness of the Creator, the nations of the world have no control and they are annulled before Him. Hence, it follows that the whole exile is that we do not know His greatness.

In the matter of concealment that one feels, which causes him to be in exile, a person should know that he must correct his actions so they are in order to bestow. Otherwise, there will be shame. Hence, there must be concealment and hiding on the upper light. To the extent of the sensation of evil, when one sees how immersed he is in self-love, to that extent he sees that he is far from *Kedusha* [holiness]. That is, he sees that he is far from doing anything for the sake of the Creator, and he is under the governance of the nations of the world, while the quality of Israel in him is completely powerless to emerge from their exile.

For this reason, when the Israel in him emerges from exile and is rewarded with redemption, the Creator, too, who was covered from him during the exile because of the governance of the nations, now appears and the greatness of the Creator becomes revealed. This is so because now there is no longer a need for the *Tzimtzum* [restriction] and concealment, since the *Tzimtzum* has been lifted from him, following the rule, "To the extent that one wants to aim to bestow, to that extent the *Tzimtzum* and concealment are removed from him." This is the meaning of the verse, "We will sing in Your salvation, and in that day, the Lord will save Israel. It is written, 'will save,' as though Israel are saved and as though He is saved."

Also, we should interpret what we asked, What does it mean that it is written, "We will sing in Your salvation," since we sing in Your salvation that You did for us in Your name"? And what is the name of the Creator, who created creation? His name is The Good Who Does Good, whose desire is to bestow. Because of it, He created in the creatures a desire to receive, or the creatures would not be able to taste the taste of delight and pleasure, since we see that without desire and yearning it is impossible to enjoy anything.

Yet, at the same time, the Creator wanted that there will be no shame while receiving the delight and pleasure. For this reason, He wants us to receive everything in order to bestow. Since this is against the nature He created in us—a desire only to receive and not to bestow—when we want to work in order to bestow, we are powerless to do so. Hence, when we receive this power, called "the name of the Creator," meaning that we, too, can work in order to bestow upon the Creator, it is considered that the Creator has given us a second nature (as Baal HaSulam said about this, that when the Creator gives one the desire to bestow, it is called "a second nature").

This is the meaning of the verse, "Israel said to the Creator, 'We sing in Your salvation, which You did in Your name.'" That is, we sing with the salvation that You gave us the desire to bestow, which is called "the name of the Creator," who is the Giver. He has given us this name, meaning that now we, too, can perform acts of bestowal.

It is written, "And in the name of our God we will set up our banners," for the Creator established His name in our name and made us banners." This means that now we support the name of the Creator, whose name is "desire to bestow." This is our salvation, that the Creator established His name, which is the desire to bestow, in our name, for the Creator is implied in the name, Israel, too, meaning *Yashar-El*, meaning that all of Israel's actions are straight to the Creator and not for self-benefit. This is considered that the people of Israel support the name of the Creator, and this is the salvation of the people of Israel.

According to the above, we should interpret what is written, "Rabbi Issachar says, 'And his banner over me is love.' Even a person who sits and engages in Torah, and skips from rule to rule and from verse to verse, and his skipping is over Me with love." We should interpret that the meaning of skipping is that man was created with a desire to receive and cannot work in order to bestow. This is why our sages said, "One should always engage in Torah and *Mitzvot* [commandments/good deeds] even if *Lo Lishma* [not for Her sake], since from *Lo Lishma* he comes to *Lishma* [for Her sake]" (*Pesachim* 50b).

It follows that one is compelled to work in *Lo Lishma* as he was born this way in his nature. And yet, the Creator skips his state of *Lo Lishma* and lets him into *Lishma*. It follows that through assistance from the Creator, there is the matter of skipping here, meaning that a person skips over everything that is in his nature—to do everything for his own sake—and begins to work for the sake of the Creator. This is called "and his skipping is over Me with love," where because of the love that the Creator loves us, He has given us banners. In other words, from rules that a person engages in *Lo Lishma*, the Creator gives us the power to skip the degree of *Lo Lishma* and achieve the degree of *Lishma*.

This is the meaning of the words "from verse to verse," meaning that the person begins the verse in *Lo Lishma* and promptly skips the *Lo Lishma* and achieves the degree of *Lishma*. It is written, "I am fond of him and his banner is over Me is love, and his skipping is over Me with love." This means that because of the love, the Creator gives him the power to skip the *Lo Lishma* and arrive at *Lishma*.

This love is considered that a person begins to work in *Lo Lishma*, and the people of Israel craved to work for the sake of the Creator but could not. Hence, with the desire that they wanted to work for the sake of the Creator but could not, that desire evoked love above, and the Creator gave them the power to work *Lishma*. This is the meaning of what is written, "The Creator said to them, 'As you craved to make banners, verily, I grant your wishes.'"

This means that the people of Israel craved the discernment of "banners," meaning to be able to skip the work of *Lo Lishma* and achieve *Lishma*, and saw that they could not achieve this by themselves. Hence, they made an awakening from below, which is that they craved it, and said, "When will we be able to skip the work for our own benefit and come to work for the sake of the Creator?" With this yearning, they evoked love above, and this is why it is written, "The Creator said to them, 'As you craved to make banners, verily, I grant your wishes.'" Because they craved banners, meaning to skip the work for their own benefit, the Creator granted their wishes.

It therefore follows that the heart of man's work is to come to work for the sake of the Creator, although we must begin to work in *Lo Lishma*. However, we must yearn for the Creator to help us and give us the power to work *Lishma*, meaning that all his actions will be in order to bestow contentment upon his Maker. That is, one must accept the burden of the kingdom of heaven without hoping to receive reward from it, namely not to demand of it, that it needs to give us some nourishments in return, so we can say that in return for receiving from it, it is worthwhile to work for it.

Rather, everything is above reason, as it is a law. Put differently, *Malchut* is called "a law," and we cannot understand how it is possible to work without a reward, meaning without receiving any nourishments from it. If so, from where will we have nourishments?

How can we work without receiving anything in return, to feed us and allow us to sustain ourselves?

The answer is also above reason, meaning we must ask the Creator to give us the power to live, and to have the power to work gladly in order to bestow and not receive any return. But how can such a thing be done, since it is inconceivable for us to understand two opposites in the same subject?

On one hand, we do not want anything in return. Rather, we accept the kingdom of heaven without it giving us any nourishments. But how can we live without any vitality, since we are not asking for any nourishments?

On the other hand, we want the Creator to sustain us. But with what do we want Him to sustain us if we do not want anything for our work? The answer is that it is true that we want nothing in return, but we want the Creator to give us the power to work so that we cannot receive any reward.

How can this be? This thing belongs to You. That is, You will make us a miracle so we can work without any reward. Because it is above reason, we have no idea what to tell You about how You should sustain us. Rather, You will sustain us above our reason, and we want to go above reason, although no such thing exists within man's intellect.

It follows that our work is above reason, and we want our nourishment to also be above reason. Above reason means by a miracle. It turns out that we are asking the Creator to sustain us in a miraculous way, and not in the natural way. In the natural way, when a person works, he wants provision for the effort. But here, in the work, the person wants to be given provision not because of his work, but because of a miracle, meaning not in the natural way.

Accordingly, we should interpret what our sages said (in the beginning of *BaHar*), "On Mount Sinai means, what is the connection between the *Shmita* [remission of land cultivation every 7th year] and Mount Sinai"? In the work, we should interpret that it is known that *Malchut* is called *Shmita*, and *Malchut* is also called

Eretz [land], since *Malchut* is the seventh *Sefira* (for the world begins with *Hesed*, as it is written, "For I said, 'A world of *Hesed* [mercy] shall be built,'" and *Malchut* is the seventh *Sefira* from *Hesed*).

This means that it is forbidden to ask of *Malchut* to yield fruit. That is, it is forbidden to till the land so it will yield fruit. "Tilling the land" means work when we want it to yield fruit; otherwise, who would till the land without it bearing fruit? In other words, work means that a person labors, and in return for the labor, he is rewarded. That is, he does not enjoy the labor. But if so, if he does not enjoy the work, why does he work? It must be that he wants to receive reward.

For this reason, if a person takes upon himself the burden of the kingdom of heaven and does not want any reward, it is a sign that he is not tilling the land, since he does not want *Malchut* to somehow reward him. This is called *Shmita* [remission], meaning that he is not tilling the land so as to receive reward.

But when he does work in order to receive reward, this is called "tilling the land." In the work, this is considered doing "remission of soil," meaning that he does not even touch the soil at all. To him, the soil is regarded as "the land shall have a Sabbath [rest/stillness] to the Lord." This implies that the whole earth, meaning the kingdom of heaven, is all for the Creator, and the will to receive has no contact with *Malchut*, called *Eretz* and *Shmita*.

By this we can explain the question, "What is the connection between the *Shmita* and Mount Sinai?" This means that all the *Mitzvot* [commandments/good deeds] must be observed in a manner of *Shmita*, meaning that the intention in observing *Mitzvot* should be as in *Shmita*, which is in the manner of "the land shall have a Sabbath to the Lord." In other words, we observe the *Mitzvot* of the Creator with the aim not to receive any reward for the work, but rather that the whole of the kingdom of heaven that one takes upon oneself, and for which he observes the *Mitzvot* of the Creator, will all be in a manner of *Shmita*, meaning that it is with the aim to bestow, and not to receive any return.

According to the above, we should interpret what is written (Leviticus 25:20-21), "And if you say, 'What will we eat on the seventh year, and I will order My blessing for you in the sixth year.'" We should interpret the question in the work. Because we must accept the kingdom of heaven without any reward, meaning that a person does not say, "I take upon myself the kingdom of heaven on condition that You will give me a good taste in work and in prayer, as well as in observing the *Mitzvot*, and if I receive a reward in return, I am willing to do the holy work."

But if it is all for the Creator, how can we work above taste and above reason? From where will we eat? That is, from where will we receive nourishments to live in a work where we have nothing in return? This is opposite from our intellect! In our intellect, we understand that if *Malchut*, called *Eretz*, gives us some flavor in the work, by this taste that we will feel, we will have something to eat. In other words, this flavor that we feel is called "nourishments." But while we are forbidden to work on the seventh, meaning we are forbidden to demand reward from this work, from where will we take something to eat?

The answer is, "I will order My blessing for you in the sixth year." The sixth *Sefira* is *Yesod*, called "righteous *Yesod*." "Righteous" means bestowing. By working only in order to bestow, as well, there will be equivalence of form between *Malchut* and *Yesod*, and from this the blessing will extend. But if it is to the contrary, and you receive the *Malchut* in order to receive, you will cause separation at the root of your souls, which is *Malchut*, called "the assembly of Israel," the collection of all the souls, making it separated. Therefore, the *Yesod* will not be able to bestow upon *Malchut* because of the disparity of form between them.

Thus, precisely by keeping the *Shmita*, meaning only in this manner, I am telling you, "I will order My blessing for you in the sixth year." In other words, only when you keep the *Shmita* and have no desire to receive for yourselves, but rather specifically in order to bestow, there is room for equivalence of form between *Yesod*, who is the giver, and *Malchut*, who is also corrected by the lower ones who observe the matter of *Shmita*, so as not to receive for one's own benefit. Then there is equivalence of form and the blessing can expand to *Malchut*.

It follows that when one wants to work in order to bestow and without any reward, the body asks, "From where will we take vitality for the work, if we agree to work for no return?" The answer should be that we are going above reason. Within reason, we do not want to answer, but our work is above reason, and the nourishments we need for sustenance during the work, are also above reason, meaning as a miracle, since anything that is against nature is considered "miraculous."

Thus, the whole basis of our work when we want to work in order to bestow is without any basis of provision, since we do not know from where we will get the strength to work so as to have with what to sustain ourselves, meaning to have nourishments and vitality while he engages in Torah and prayer if he does not want anything for his own sake. It follows that he is asking the Creator to give him nourishments to live in Torah and *Mitzvot* above reason, and above reason means against nature, and anything that is attainment against nature is regarded as working miracles, without any basis on which to rely.

It follows that those who want to work in order to bestow must know that when the body asks "What will we eat?" as it is written, "And if you say, 'What will we eat?'" The body must not be given an answer within reason. Rather, the reply should be that the Creator will give us the blessing, as it is written, "and I will order My blessing," and any blessing is considered a miracle, since when everything is in order, in the best way, there is no need for blessings.

But the body comes and asks, "Our sages said (*Pesachim* 64b), 'One does not rely on miracles,' and our sages also said (*Pesachim* 50), 'A miracle does not happen every day.'" It follows that all the answers that we must reply to the body are above reason, meaning to tell the body, "Within reason, you are correct, but I am going above reason."

What Does It Mean that the Creator Favors Someone, in the Work?

Article No. 33, Tav-Shin-Nun-Aleph, 1990/91

Our sages said (*Midrash Rabbah*, Chapter 11:7) about the verse, "The Lord will turn His face to you [favor you]": "One verse says, 'The Lord will favor you,' and another verse says, 'who does not turn His face [favor].' How can these two verses be reconciled? When Israel do the Creator's will, 'The Lord will favor you.' When they do not do the Creator's will, 'who does not favor.'"

We should understand this. If Israel do the Creator's will, why is being favored needed? To understand what they explained, we first need to understand what is the "will of the Creator" and what is the "face of the Creator." We learn that the Creator's will is to bestow, as it is written, that the purpose of creation is His desire to do good to His creations, meaning to bestow upon them delight and pleasure. The face of the Creator is called "revelation of the face," when one is rewarded with attaining open Providence, that the Creator leads the world as The Good Who Does Good.

It is written ("Introduction to The Study of the Ten Sefirot," Item 83), "The first degree of the revelation of the face is the attainment of the Providence of reward and punishment in utter clarity. This comes to a person only through His salvation, when one is awarded the opening of eyes in the Holy Torah in wonderful attainment, and becomes 'a flowing spring.' In any *Mitzva* [commandment/good deed] in the Holy Torah that one has kept of his own labor and choice, one is granted seeing the reward of the *Mitzva* intended for him in the next world, as well as the great loss in the transgression."

According to the above, we should interpret what we asked about what is written here, that "Those who do the Creator's will, He favors them," if they are doing the Creator's will, why do they need "The Lord will favor you"?

The thing is that the face of the Creator is revelation of His guidance as a guidance of good and doing good. Since there was a correction that before one corrects the will to receive so as to work in order to bestow, there will be concealment and hiding on His Providence. Hence, before one achieves the state of "doers of His will," meaning that as the Creator's will is to bestow, so man should come to want to bestow.

When there is equivalence of form, the Creator can give him the revelation of His face, which is the opening of the eyes in the Torah, and he is rewarded with the attainment that the Creator leads the world in a manner of good and doing good. But this can be only after one does the will of the Creator, meaning that one has been rewarded with desire to bestow, for specifically then the *Tzimtzum* [restriction] and concealment are lifted.

Before Israel do the Creator's will, when they rather want the Creator to give them everything in vessels of reception, which is the opposite of the Creator's will, whose desire is to bestow, there must be guidance in a manner of "who will not favor," but in the manner of *Achoraim* [posterior], called "the concealment of the face of the Creator." This is regarded as "who will not favor," and it is because of the correction that there will not be the matter of shame.

Likewise, we should interpret the above verse in relation to the time of the beginning of the work, before one has been rewarded with being among those who have been rewarded with "doing the Creator's will." We should interpret "doers of His will" to mean those who are walking on the path to achieve being among those who do the Creator's will, since when they walk on this path, they are already named after the road on which they walk. This is as Baal HaSulam said about what is written, "will give wisdom to the wise." He asked, "It should have said, 'will give wisdom to the fools.'" And he said that this refers to those who already want wisdom; they are already called "wise" because they are walking on the path toward obtaining wisdom. And since they are giving an awakening from below, they are given wisdom from above.

It is likewise here: When they want to achieve the power of the desire to bestow, this is regarded as doing the Creator's will. According to the rule, "He who comes to purify is aided," they are given help from the Creator. For this reason, the writing tells them "The Lord will favor you," meaning the Creator shines His face to them, namely helps them.

And what is the help? This is as it is written in *The Zohar*, "He who comes to purify is aided." He asks, "With what?" The reply is "with a holy soul," which is called "the face of the Creator," as it is written, "For by the light of Your face you have given us the law [Torah] of life and the love of mercy [*Hesed*]." In other words, through the light of the face, they receive the love of *Hesed*, which is bestowal. That is, the Creator gives them the strength to love *Hesed*, meaning to love being a giver.

This is called "The Lord will turn His face to you [favor you] and will give you peace." Peace means as it is written (Psalms 85), "I will hear what the Lord God shall speak, for He shall speak peace unto His people, and let them not turn back to folly." It follows that "peace" means that the Creator says "peace," that he will not sin again, and he is rewarded with being at peace with the Creator. This is the meaning of "When they do the Creator's will," they receive the assistance of the Creator, as it says, "The Lord will favor you."

But "when they do not do the Creator's will," when they are not walking on the path toward achieving the desire of the Creator, which is the desire to bestow, it is said about them, "who does not favor." That is, He cannot help them by satisfying their wish, since their wish is the opposite of *Kedusha* [holiness], so how can He give them something that contradicts the Creator's will, since all that one should do in the work is correct his actions so they are in order to bestow? If the Creator favors them, meaning that they receive help so they work for the will to receive for themselves, it is as though the Creator is failing them. Hence, the Creator helps them by not favoring them, so they do not remain in self-love. It was said about this, "He who comes to defile, it is opened for him," but he is not helped, unlike when he comes to purify, who is assisted.

Now we can understand the meaning of repentance. What should one reply, since *Teshuva* [repentance/answer/returning] means that he received something and must (return) what he received? The thing is that since man is born with a nature that is the will to receive for his own benefit, when he wants to work only for man's sake, meaning that he wants the Creator to fill his vessels of reception, a person should repent on this, meaning do everything for the sake of the Creator. In other words, what he receives, he does not want to receive for his own sake, but rather all that he receives is in order to bring contentment to the Creator. Since the Creator wants man to receive, as it is written, "His desire is to do good to His creations," it follows that all that he receives is only in order to return. Otherwise, he does not want to receive. This is *Teshuva* [to return], meaning he returns everything that he receives.

This is as it is written in *The Zohar* (Nasso, Item 28), "Anyone who repents, it is as though he returned the letter *Hey*, which is *Malchut*, to the letter *Vav*, which is ZA, who is the son of *Yod-Hey*, completing the *HaVaYaH*. This is certainly repentance, for it is the letters of 'The *Hey* shall return to the *Vav*.'"

And in *The Zohar* (Nasso, Item 31), it says, "This repentance, which is *Malchut* and the *Hey* of *HaVaYaH*, is called 'life,' as it is written, 'for from it is the offshoot of life,' which are the soul of

Israel, the offshoot of *Malchut*, who is called 'life.' She is a *Hevel* [mouth/breath] that goes out and into a person's mouth without toil and without labor, which is the *Hey* of *BeHibaram* [when they were created], for the letter *Hey* is expressed by the mouth more easily than all the letters, and it was said about it, 'And the image of the Lord does he behold,' since *Malchut* is called 'the image of the Lord.' Also, 'Only in the shadow shall one walk,' and because it is on the man's head, he must not walk four cubits bareheaded, since if it departs from over man's head, life immediately departs from him."

We should interpret the words of *The Zohar* when it says that repentance means the return of the *Hey* to the *Vav*. The thing is that all of our work is to take upon ourselves the burden of the kingdom of heaven although it is concealed and hidden. That is, although the thought of creation is to do good to His creations, there was a *Tzimtzum* and concealment on the kingdom of heaven so there would be room for choice, meaning that man would be able to say that he does not accept the burden of the kingdom of heaven out of self-love, but in order to bring contentment to his Maker. If the King were revealed, man would accept the revelation of the King because of self-love, since we must believe that there is no greater pleasure in the world than to see the King's face. It follows that at the time of the acceptance of the kingdom of heaven, man was compelled to be separated due to disparity of form, as it is known that disparity causes separation in spirituality.

It follows that this concealment causes that it is difficult for us to assume the burden of the kingdom of heaven and believe that His guidance is in a manner of good and doing good. Only when one walks on the path toward achieving equivalence of form, meaning that all his actions will be for the sake of the Creator, to the extent that his aim is to bestow, to that extent the concealment and *Tzimtzum* [restriction] are removed from him. At that time, a person can obtain the delight and pleasure, since then he receives in the manner of *Ohr Hozer* [Reflected Light], meaning that he enjoys only because he wants to bring contentment to his Maker.

Hence, the reception of pleasure does not inflict separation. In that state, a person receives the abundance, according to the rule, "More than the calf wants to eat, the cow wants to feed." Then, a person has no more work to obtain anything because the upper one can already give because he already has the *Kelim* [vessels] of equivalence of form. It follows that the heart of man's work is to obtain vessels of bestowal.

According to the above, we should interpret what is repentance, when he says, "the *Hey*, which is *Malchut*, shall return," as she is separated from the name *HaVaYaH*. That is, *Malchut*, which is the totality of the souls and should provide for all the souls. If the created beings work (as) they must, meaning doing everything in order to bestow, each of them causes a desire to bestow at the root of his soul. At that time, *Malchut* receives equivalence of form with the Creator, who is the Giver.

It follows that the abundance pours down to the creatures without any toil and labor, as in the words of *The Zohar*, since the giving of the abundance belongs to the Creator. He will give, and man will have no work to obtain it. Rather, all of man's work is on the *Kelim*, so they will have equivalence of form. This is called "the work of the earth," meaning that the work is for their kingdom of heaven to work in order to bestow.

This is as it is written (*Berachot* 33), "Everything is in the hands of heaven but the fear of heaven." We should interpret that "everything" means the filling that the Creator gives. There are many kinds in the abundance, but in general, they are called *NRNHY*, or *Hochma*, or *Hassadim*. The Creator gives all those without any labor on the part of man, other than fear of heaven, where fear means that one must work to have fear that he might not be able to work in order to bestow. This pertains to man's work.

In other words, a person is afraid he might not be able to aim in order to bestow. We attribute the matter of not receiving to man, and the matter of giving, we attribute to the Creator. It follows that fear of heaven means he is afraid to receive, since he might thereby come to separation from the Creator. This work, (we) attribute to man. That is, all of man's work is to obtain vessels of bestowal, but it is not upon man to seek advice how to obtain abundance, since we need not worry about this. Rather, all our worries should be how to obtain the desire to bestow, since *Malchut*, who is called "life," from her are the offshoot of life.

This is after one has obtained the vessels of bestowal, by returning the *Malchut*, called "the receiving *Kli*," to now be as a "giving *Kli*," meaning that the created beings have corrected at the root of their souls, which is *Malchut*, that she will work in order to bestow and not to receive. At that time, *Malchut* bestows upon them life, as it is written, "for from it is the offshoot of life." This, one receives without toil and without labor, which is the meaning of the *Hey* of *BeHibraam* [when they were created]. In other words, once a person has corrected the *Malchut*, which is the final *Hey*, into equivalence of form with the *Yod-Hey-Vav*, the abundance extends to the man who has corrected her without toil or labor.

This is the meaning of saying "It was said about her, 'and the image of the Lord does he behold,'" since *Malchut* is called "the image of the Lord." We should interpret that he wants to tell us that all the work is only on "fear," meaning not to receive the abundance, lest he will not be able to aim in order to bestow. This is as it is written about Moses (*Berachot* 7), "'And Moses hid his face for he was afraid to look.' They said, in return for 'Moses hid his face,' he was rewarded with 'the image of the Lord does he behold.'"

In other words, the labor is on the fear, as it is written, "for he was afraid to look," after which came the reward without toil or labor, when he was rewarded with seeing the image of the Lord, which is *Malchut*, as it says, "for *Malchut* is called 'the image of the Lord.'" It follows that all of life came from *Malchut*, as he says, "*Vav-Hey* of *HaVaYaH* is called 'life,'" which comes without toil or labor.

This is the meaning of "Only in the shadow shall one walk." Baal HaSulam said that "shadow" means "shade," and shadow is where the sun does not shine, which is concealment. In other words, once a person accepts the kingdom of heaven as concealment above reason, he is rewarded with knowledge of *Kedusha* [holiness]. This is the meaning of what is written, "Only in the shadow shall one walk," precisely when one takes upon himself the kingdom of heaven as a "shadow" by which one can ascend the rungs of holiness. This is the meaning of "shall one walk."

Also, we should interpret what is written, "One must not walk four cubits bareheaded." "Head" means knowledge and intellect. Covering the head means that he covers the intellect and does not look at it, but goes above reason. "Four cubits" are the man; this is his height. It means that one is forbidden to walk without faith above reason. If he does walk within reason, meaning "bareheaded," "Life immediately departs from him." Rather, specifically by covering the head, he will be rewarded with the knowledge of *Kedusha*.

However, this work of faith above reason should be with a sound mind, for only then can one understand what is above reason. Otherwise, a person is mistaken with the meaning of above reason. This is as our sages said (*Avot*, Chapter 4:23), "Do not appease your neighbor while he is angry." Hence, when one is angry, when he is dissatisfied with the situation he is in and begins to introspect, he falls into mistakes and cannot calculate truthfully, as our sages said (*Sifrei Matot*), "Once he comes by anger, he comes by every mistake."

Man's main anger at himself is expressed in work in sadness at the state he is in. Hence, all the calculations he does are wrong, since he himself is in a state where there is no peace of mind in him. In that state, he should not make any calculations but take upon himself the kingdom of heaven without any calculations. Only once he has taken upon himself the burden of the kingdom of heaven by force, and when his anger has subsided, can he calculate, to know what is above reason and what is below reason, and what is within reason.

We should know that when a person is angry at something, he feels that he is in an uncomfortable situation. At such a time, it is impossible to believe in private Providence, that the Creator leads

What Does It Mean that the Creator Favors Someone, in the Work?

the world in a manner of good and doing good. Hence, in that state he slanders the guidance of the Creator, and naturally becomes separated from faith, since there is a correction from above, which our sages called "One does not sin unless a spirit of folly has entered him." This means that the spirit of *Kedusha* that he had has departed from him. This is done in man's favor, since when he does not have the spirit of *Kedusha*, he cannot blemish what he does not have.

Hence, when one falls into a state of sadness, meaning he has nothing from which to derive joy, he becomes separated from the *Kedusha*. At that time, there is only one advice, to take upon himself, by force, the burden of the kingdom of heaven, and pray to the Creator to help him so that this coercion that he has taken upon himself, the Creator will help him make it with joy, as it is written, "Serve the Lord with gladness." Since now this work is compulsory for him, from where will he take joy?

For this reason, one must pray to the Creator to help him be able to observe what is written, "Serve the Lord with gladness." Also, at that time, one should overcome in the manner of "an awakening from below," and believe that it is a great privilege that he was able to overcome his situation and be able to do something against the intellect, which is called "above reason."

Also, he should believe, once he has overcome above reason, this is regarded that he is a servant of the Creator. That is, this overcoming that he is now doing is called "work of the Creator," since now he is working with faith above reason. In other words, only now is he considered "working," since the body does not agree to this work.

It therefore follows that when one comes to a state where the body does not want to do the holy work, and a person is in a state where he has no spirit of life, this is the time when a person is regarded as having no faith in the Creator, since faith in the Creator brings joy. Hence, when he is irritated and angry with himself to the point that he cannot stand anything around him, he is considered to be an "idol-worshipper."

This is as our sages said, "Anyone who is angry, it is as though he is committing idol-worship." This is so because he has no faith. Hence, a person should try to be thankful to the Creator for every contact that he has with spirituality, and then he unifies the connection with the Creator. In other words, even if he is in a state where the body rejects anything of *Kedusha*, he can maintain contact with the Creator even over this, meaning that a person must say at that time, "the fact that I feel that I have no desire for work, this, too, is called 'contact.'"

That is, a person sees that he does not always think about work, whether or not he wants to work. Rather, he should think and worry about other matters, which have no connection to spirituality. Hence, now that he has contact, he is thankful for it, and by this he can reenter the work and begin to live a life of *Kedusha*.

Although there are many discernments in the connection that one connects oneself to the Creator, any contact is a great thing. It is written about it (Psalms 48:11), "As Your name, God, so is Your glory." This means that as much as one can appreciate the greatness and importance of the Creator, to that extent he can thank and praise the Creator. Clearly, the more one can depict to oneself the greatness and importance of the Creator, he will be able to give greater praises to the Creator. However, by overcoming and praising the Creator over something, regardless what it is for which he thanks the Creator, this act already gives connection to the Creator, and by this he can come to do the holy work in truth. Hence, in every situation, only prayer helps.

What Is Eating Their Fruits in This World and Keeping the Principal for the Next World, in the Work?

Article No. 34, Tav-Shin-Nun-Aleph, 1990/91

It is written in *The Zohar* (*BeHaalotcha*, Items 140-144), "Rabbi Aba said, 'The evil in the heart, which clings to all organs of the body, does that to them. 'There is evil which I have seen under the sun, and it is heavy upon men.' This evil is the force of the evil in the heart that wishes to dominate the worldly matters and does not watch over the matters of that world at all.' He asks, 'Why is the heart evil?' And he replies, 'The following verse proves it, as it is written (Ecclesiastes 6), 'A man to whom God has given wealth and possessions and honor, whose soul lacks nothing of all that he desires, and God has not empowered him to eat from it, for a foreign man shall eat it.'"

"This is a perplexing verse, since it is written, 'whose soul lacks nothing of all that he desires,' why will God not empower him to eat from it? After all, his soul lacks nothing. He replies that a person walks in this world and the Creator gives him wealth so he will be rewarded with the next world by it, and will remain with a principal of his money. What is a principal? It is that money that exists forever. This is why he must keep this principal after him, and he will receive this principal after he departs from this world. Because this principal is the tree of life of that world, which ZA, there is nothing of it in this world but the fruits that come out of it. This is why a man who has been rewarded with these fruits in this world eats them, while the principal remains for him in that world, to be rewarded by it with the upper life, above.

"And one who defiles himself and is drawn after self-benefit, and lacks nothing for his soul or his body, God does not empower him to eat from it and to be rewarded with that wealth."

We should understand what it means in the work that he eats their fruits in this world and keeps the principal for the next world. Also, What is "to whom God has given wealth and possessions and honor," in the work? of which he said, "God has not empowered him to eat from it, for a foreign man shall eat it."

It is known that in the work, we have the matter of "doing," as it is written, "Which God has created to do." This means that the Creator created man with a desire to receive delight and pleasure. To the extent of one's desire and yearning for something, so is his ability to enjoy it. Hence, we were born with a desire to receive for our own sake, and we attribute this to the Creator.

Yet, He has given us to make other *Kelim* [vessels], which are opposite from the *Kelim* that the Creator has made. In other words, the *Kelim* that the creatures should make are a desire to bestow upon the Creator. This means that the *Kelim* that the Creator made are for the creatures to receive delight, and the *Kelim* that the creatures should make are for the Creator to receive delight. However, if man was born with a nature of a desire to receive, how can that nature be changed?

The answer is that there is a *Segula* [remedy/power/virtue], and with this *Segula* they can receive a second nature from the Creator. Our sages said about this, "The Creator said, 'I have created the evil inclination; I have created the Torah as a spice,'" since "the light in the Torah reforms him." That is, through the light in the Torah, they will ultimately receive the second nature, which is the desire to bestow contentment upon the Maker. At that time, they will be rewarded with *Dvekut* [adhesion], called "equivalence of form."

However, before we obtain the desire to bestow, one must go through several degrees:

1) First, one must understand that we must obtain this desire, since when we come to do something, we go and see how people behave, if the people around us also think that we should do everything for the sake of the Creator. Naturally, a person goes to see among those who engage in Torah and *Mitzvot* [commandments/good deeds], and sees that no one around him is concerned with finding ways by which to obtain the desire to bestow.

The reason he does not see it in others is simple: They are not on the path toward obtaining the intention to bestow. At that time, he sees the truth. However, those who do engage in Torah and *Mitzvot* in order to bestow are probably working in concealment, since if their work were revealed outside, externality would become involved in their work, since by nature, when one sees that others are looking at what he does, he thinks that the other appreciates his work. This gives him strength for the work not because the Creator mandates his work, but the other person, by looking at him, obligates him to work in Torah and *Mitzvot*. Hence, those who want to work for the sake of the Creator conceal their work from others. This is why it is impossible to see if someone is working in order to bestow.

Therefore, one has a lot of work before he comes to feel that he is deficient of the desire to bestow. Although sometimes, he begins to understand that he does need the desire to bestow, but he sees that many people are engaging in Torah and *Mitzvot*, and they are respectable people, and he does not see that they have any deficiency, that they suffer because they haven't the desire to bestow. Thus, the first work is to try to obtain the need to be rewarded with the desire to bestow.

2) Once he has obtained the need for the desire to bestow, he does not receive the filling as soon as he begins to obtain the deficiency. This is so because the feeling of deficiency depends also on the measure of the suffering he feels from not having the desire to bestow. But when a person begins to feel how much he needs it, and above there is a desire that he will have a real deficiency, then he receives help from above to feel the lack. That is, he is shown how far he is from it, meaning he sees how difficult it is to obtain the desire to bestow, which causes him a great deficiency.

Yet, why do we need a great deficiency? The reason that when something is unimportant, we do not know how to keep from losing it. Hence, before one has a real lack, he is not given the matter from above, for the lack and the yearning make the thing important.

But in the work, when one sees that it is hard to get what he wants, he escapes from the work. He says, "I believe that there are people who have been rewarded and to whom the Creator gave the desire to bestow. But this was because they were more gifted than I am. But a person like me, with worse qualities than others, has no chance of meriting this." Hence, he escapes the campaign and begins to work like the general public.

Only those who say that they want to escape from the work but have nowhere else to go, since nothing satisfies them, those people do not walk out from the work. Although they have ups and downs, they do not give up. This is as it is written, "And the children of Israel sighed from the work, and they cried, and their cry went up to God from the work." In other words, they cried out from the work because they were not advancing in the work of the Creator, so they could work in order to bestow contentment upon the Maker. At that time, they were rewarded with the exodus from Egypt. In the work, this is called "emerging from the control of the will to receive and entry into the work of bestowal."

It therefore follows that the beginning of man's work is to take upon himself the kingdom of heaven, meaning that where he used to care only to satisfy the desire of an old and foolish king, meaning that all his work was only for his own sake, he has taken upon himself a different King, called "kingdom of heaven," when he crowns the Creator over all his organs, meaning that all his organs will serve the Creator. This is called in the work, "exodus from Egypt," exodus from the governance of self-benefit, and taking upon oneself to serve the Creator, as it is written, "I am the Lord your God, who brought you out from the land of Egypt to be a God unto you." We should interpret that He brought them out from the governance of the will to receive for oneself and gave them the desire to bestow. This is called "to be a God unto you," meaning that I gave you the desire to bestow so you can work for My sake. This is called "I gave you the power to feel that I am the Creator."

However, how does one acquire this feeling that the will to receive is something bad? Who notifies him that he should correct his actions? He writes in the *Sulam* [Ladder commentary on *The Zohar*] (*Beresheet Bet*, Item 103), "Hence, the Creator has imprinted bitter and harsh afflictions in self-reception, instilled in man from the moment of his birth—bodily pains and pains of the soul—so that if he engages in Torah and *Mitzvot* even for his own pleasure, through the light in it he will still feel the lowliness and the terrible corruptness in the nature of receiving for oneself. At that time, he will resolve to retire from that nature of reception and completely devote himself to working only in order to bestow contentment upon his Maker, as it is written, 'All the works of the Lord are for His sake.' Then the Creator will open his eyes to see before him a world filled with utter perfection. Then, he partakes in His joy as at the time of the creation of the world (for our sages said, "There has never been such joy before Him as on the day when heaven and earth were created")."

It follows that this light of Torah gives one the lack, so he will have the need to ask the Creator to give him the power to take upon himself the burden of the kingdom of heaven, and all his actions will be in order to bestow. Afterward, when he has been rewarded with the kingdom of heaven, there is another degree, called "Torah," which is the names of the Creator. This is regarded as "The Torah and the Creator and Israel are one."

According to the above, we should interpret the words of *The Zohar*, "Because this *principal* is the tree of life of that world, which is ZA, and there is nothing of it in this world but the fruits that come out of it, so a man who has been rewarded with its fruits eats them in this world, while the *principal* remains for him in the next world."

We should interpret what is written, "And the *principal* remains for the next world," which is ZA, since ZA is called "Torah," and this is called "that world," meaning "the next world," which comes after this world, since this world is called *Malchut*, and the next world comes afterward. *The Zohar* calls that world ZA, which is the tree of life, the Torah.

It is known that the order of the work is that first, one must be rewarded with the kingdom of heaven, that it will be in order to bestow. But how can one be rewarded with bestowal? This is the meaning of "I have created the evil inclination; I have created the Torah as a spice." It follows that it is through the Torah, meaning through the light that reforms in it. Thus, the Torah is to him as *Eitin* (counsels) by which to achieve the kingdom of heaven, for *Malchut* [kingdom/kingship] is called "this world," and the light that reforms is called "fruits." In other words, a person sees fruits in his work, meaning he exerted in the Torah and yielded fruit from it, and the fruits are the reward from the work. Hence, we should interpret that he eats "fruits from the Torah," meaning that he has been rewarded through the Torah with the desire to bestow, which "reforms him." This is called "613 counsels."

Afterward, comes the matter of the 613 *Pekudin* [Aramaic: deposits], which is already the actual Torah, as in "The Torah and the Creator and Israel are one." This is called "actual Torah." This is as it says, "ZA is the tree of life, which is Torah," and this is his principal for the next world, which is regarded as the Torah.

This is called "the principal that is the actual Torah." Conversely, the kingdom of heaven, which is considered this world, there the Torah is only as fruits, meaning that it is only the light of Torah that reforms him, while ZA is called "the principal that is the actual Torah." This is regarded as "their fruits in this world," which is called *Malchut*, meaning permanent faith. Afterward comes another degree, called "the next world," meaning it comes after *Malchut*. This is regarded as ZA, the land of the living, the actual Torah.

According to the above, we should interpret what he asks, "Why is the heart evil?" He replies that it is as it is written, "A man to whom God has given wealth and possessions and honor, whose soul lacks nothing of all that he desires, and God has not empowered him to eat from it, for a foreign man shall eat it." He asks, "Since it is written, 'He lacks nothing for his soul of all that he desires,'" why has God not "empowered him to eat from them"? After all, "He lacks nothing for his soul." He replies about this that a person eating their fruits in this world refers to the kingdom of heaven. When the light in it reforms him, this light is called "fruits." Afterward, he comes to a state of "the principal exists for him for the next world," meaning that he is rewarded with the "actual Torah," and this is called "wholeness."

By this *The Zohar* explains that "One who defiles himself and is drawn after self-benefit, and lacks nothing for his soul or his body," then "God does not empower him to eat from it" and be rewarded with that wealth. We should interpret that "wealth" pertains to "There is none who is poor except in knowledge," meaning that he has been rewarded with learning Torah and knowing all the rules, and he has possessions, meaning he knows that thank God he has great possessions of Torah and *Mitzvot* and good deeds, and he has honor, and everyone respects him because of the glory of the Torah. And yet, "God does not empower him to eat from it."

The reason is that although he has wealth and honor and good deeds, because he is drawn toward self-benefit, meaning for his own sake, as it is written, "He lacks nothing for his soul," meaning that all his concerns are that there will be no deficiency in self-benefit, naturally, he has nothing to eat from *Kedusha* [holiness], but it all goes to the *Sitra Achra* [other side].

This is the meaning of what is written, "a foreign man shall eat it." That is, the *Klipot* [shells/peels] took everything because all his work was for the will to receive, which is the authority of the *Klipot*. It follows that all the wealth, when he thought he had knowledge of the Torah, and possessions, which are the possessions of Torah and *Mitzvot*, are all in the domain of the *Klipot*.

By this we will understand what he asks, "Why is the heart evil?" We should interpret what is the evil that exists in the will to receive. He replies about this, "The following verse proves it, as it is written, 'A man to whom God has given wealth and possessions.'" That is, although the Creator let him do many things in *Kedusha*, since it was all for self-benefit, it all went into another authority. This is the meaning of the words, "for a foreign man shall eat it," meaning the *Klipot*, since he worked for them and not for the *Kedusha*. However, we must know that when one corrects one's actions, he elicits everything from the *Klipot* and everything returns to the *Kedusha*, as it is written, "He has swallowed down riches, and he shall vomit them out."

According to the above, there is the matter of "fruits in this world," with respect to "the light in it reforms him," from which he receives the kingdom of heaven, where the work is in order to emerge from the governance of the will to receive and do everything in order to bestow. Afterward, there is the matter of "keeping the principal for the next world," which is the meaning of Torah, as in "the names of the Creator."

We can interpret what *The Zohar* says (*BeHaalotcha*, Items 26-27), "It is written, 'And to Zebulun he said: Rejoice, Zebulun, in your going out, and, Issachar, in your tents.' This teaches that they were joined together. One went out and waged war, and the other sat and engaged in Torah. One gives to the other a share of his spoils, and the other gives to the one, a share of his Torah. Issachar is *Tifferet*, and Zebulun is *Malchut*. This is why Zebulun inherited going to war, since he is regarded as *Malchut*, meaning abundance through wars. And the share of Issachar is the Torah. This is why they joined together, so that Zebulun would be blessed through Issachar, for the blessing in the Torah is a blessing for all."

We should interpret that the partnership between Issachar and Zebulun in the work are in one body. That is, the work should be arranged in two manners: 1) It is in the manner of the kingdom of heaven, at which time there is the war of the inclination, to emerge from the control of self-love, and take upon oneself that all his actions will be in order to bestow. At that time, through the wars, he takes spoils. That is, he takes forces of the will to receive and replaces them with the desire to bestow. This is considered that through the war, he subdues it, and the will to receive must do everything according to his will, meaning that all his actions will be only in order to bestow. But from where does the quality of Zebulun take the powers to win the war? He takes it from Issachar, meaning from the Torah of Issachar.

This is as it is written, "I have created the evil inclination; I have created the Torah as a spice." This is why it says, "and the other gives to the one, a share of his Torah. Issachar is *Tifferet*." From the Torah of Issachar, Zebulun has the power to win the wars. This is considered that he "eats their fruits in this world," meaning he sees the fruits that the Torah brings him. That is, he sees that through the light in the Torah, he has been rewarded with the desire to bestow, as fruits are called "profits from the work."

This is regarded as 613 *Eitin* [Aramaic: counsels], and it is considered that Issachar "gives to this one, a share of his Torah," from which he eats fruits. This is the meaning of saying, "and one gives a share of his spoils." Through the spoils that Zebulun gives him, he sits and engages in Torah, meaning that had Zebulun not given him of his spoils, he would not have been able to be rewarded with the Torah.

We should interpret that here we are speaking from the perspective of the Torah, which is the names of the Creator, from the 613 *Pekudin* [deposits], which is the actual Torah. As was said, it is impossible to be rewarded with actual Torah before one is rewarded with faith, the kingdom of heaven, in order to bestow, at which time the will to receive surrenders and the desire to bestow governs.

Hence, when *Malchut* has the desire to bestow, a desire that *Malchut* has won by wars, this is considered that she took spoils from the war. When she gives him the desire to bestow, he can "sit in the tent of Torah," and she calls this discernment *Tifferet*, ZA. But if there is still no desire to bestow in the degree, there is no place for the actual Torah. This is called "the partnership between Issachar and Zebulun" in the work, meaning when *Malchut* goes out to war, and ZA, called "Torah," gives to *Malchut* of his Torah.

In other words, we should discern two manners in the Torah: 1) "The light in it reforms him." From this, a discernment of "fruits" extends to *Malchut*. 2) The "actual Torah," which is called "keeping the principal for the next world." This comes specifically after the quality of *Malchut* has the desire to bestow, with which she has been rewarded through the "light of Torah," regarded as "fruits."

This is as our sages said, that the hand *Tefillin* [phylacteries] comes before the head *Tefillin*, since a hand *Tefillin*, says *The Zohar*, is considered *Malchut*, the weaker hand, since it needs strengthening, since in the kingdom of heaven there are all the wars required in order to subdue the will to receive. Afterward comes the head *Tefillin*, regarded as the Torah.

What Is the Meaning of "Spies," in the Work?

Article No. 35, Tav-Shin-Nun-Aleph, 1990/91

It is written in *The Zohar* (*Shlach*, Item 82), "Rabbi Yosi said, 'They took upon themselves a counsel, to slander everything. What is 'everything'? It is the earth and the Creator. Rabbi Yitzhak said, 'The earth, this is true. But the Creator? How do we know?' He told him, 'This is the meaning of the verse, 'Nevertheless, strong is the people,' meaning Who can overcome them, for 'strong is the people'? In other words, even the Creator cannot overcome them. Thus, they slandered the Creator."

We should understand how such a thing can be said in the work, about the Creator, since we are speaking of people who want to draw near to the Creator. How can it be said that they do not believe that the Creator is almighty? It is written in *The Zohar* (Item 63), "'And they returned from touring the land.' 'Returned' means that they returned to the side of evil, and returned from the path of truth, saying, 'What did we get out of it? To this day we have not seen good in the world. We have toiled in Torah and the house is empty. Who will be awarded that world? It would have been better had we not toiled so. We labored and learned in order to know the part of that world. That upper world is good, as we know in the Torah, but who can be rewarded with it?'"

We should understand what is the sin of the spies, if they said that everything is true, "but who can be rewarded with it?" In other words, they were saying that they are unworthy of the good, as it is written, "That upper world is good, as we know in the Torah, but who can be rewarded with it?" Thus, why is the sin so grave?

In *Midrash Rabbah* (*Shlach* 15:7), he says, "Rabbi Yehoshua says, 'What were they (spies) like? Like a king who arranged for his son a fair woman, from a good and wealthy family. The king told his son, 'She is a fair looking woman and she is from a good and wealthy family.' The son replied, 'I will go and see her,' for he did not believe his father. Promptly, the matter perplexed and irritated his father. His father said, 'What should I do? If I tell him, 'I will not show her to you now,' he will say that she is ugly, and this is why he does not want to show her.' In the end, he said to him, 'See her, but because you did not believe in me, I swear that you will not see her in your house, for I will rather give her to your son.'"

This is perplexing, for it implies that the Creator showed that the land is good, but the spies did not see the good land, since they said that they did not see there any good. Instead, they said that they saw there only bad things, for they said, "It is a land that devours its inhabitants." Thus, what is the allegory about the king's son?

To understand the above, we must understand what we learn, that we have two things before us: 1) to receive delight and pleasure, which is the purpose of creation, 2) how to obtain the delight and pleasure.

Because we see that although everyone agrees that we should receive delight and pleasure, without labor, one does not attain anything. The labor is that we must offer some payment to the landlord so he will want to give us what we want. In the work, this is called "desire to bestow," for only in vessels of bestowal can we receive abundance of *Kedusha* [holiness], which is as we learned,

"You will be holy for I am holy," meaning that everything must be in order to bestow.

Before one obtains the vessels of bestowal, he is placed under the *Tzimtzum* [restriction] and the concealment that were placed on the upper guidance, so that man is unable to see the truth. That is, a person is unable to see His guidance, the way He behaves with the creatures in a guidance of good and doing good, as Baal HaSulam said (in the book *Shamati*, essay, "Faith in the Rav") about what is written, "They have eyes but they will not see," that one must believe in his rav [teacher] about what the rav arranged for us—an order of work on the "right." At that time, a person should depict to himself as though he has already been rewarded with complete faith in the Creator, and he already feels in his organs that the Creator leads the whole world in a manner of good and doing good, meaning that the whole world receives from Him only good.

And even though when he looks at himself, he sees that he is bare and destitute, he should say about this, "They have eyes but they will not see," where "they" means that as long as one is under multiple authorities, called "they," "they will not see" the truth. And what is multiple authorities? It is two desires.

This means that man has a will to receive for his own sake, which is a different desire from that of the Creator, whose desire is to bestow, and a person wants only to receive for his own sake. Hence, when one is going to criticize what the Creator gave him, he sees only suffering and pain, since there are two desires in the world.

Therefore, when one must thank the Creator and say, "Blessed is He who said, 'Let there be the world,'" to praise and be thankful that the Creator gave us a world filled with abundance, yet, now he sees the opposite, then one must exert and go above reason and say that everything he sees is not the truth, and believe what is written, "They have eyes but they will not see" the truth.

It follows that every work and labor that one must give is in order to obtain the desire to bestow, for only then can one see how the Creator created a world so filled with abundance that our sages said, "There has never been joy before Him as on the day when heaven and earth were created." This is so because to the Creator, there is no issue of time. Hence, He immediately saw the wholeness of creation at the end of its correction, since the purpose of creation was as it is written, "His desire to do good to His creations," and to Him, past and future are all the same. Naturally, at that time He saw the delight and pleasure that the creatures are receiving.

However, when one begins to work in order to obtain the desire to bestow, begins the order of ascents and descents, since in everything there are things that are good for one and bad for the other. However, everything must be balanced. For this reason, often, a person does not keep to the middle road between them, but leans to one side more than to the other, and spoils everything.

It is known that in the work of bestowal, a person must walk on two lines, called "right and left." "Right" means wholeness, and "left" is called in the work, "a path that requires correction." Because of it, we have two orders in the work:

1) Songs and praises, which pertain to the state of wholeness. That is, when one is satisfied with the guidance of the Creator, with how He behaves with him, he thanks the Creator for the good that the Creator has given him.

2) Prayer and litany, which pertains to when one sees that he has deficiencies and wants the Creator to satisfy his needs. At that time, a person asks the Creator to grant him his wish. However, since they are opposite from one another, meaning when a person thanks the Creator, and certainly when a man is thankful, one should try to give to the Creator many thanks, for the gratitude should be evaluated according to the measure of the good that the Creator has given him. Thus, it is upon man to depict to himself the greatness and importance of the matter.

In other words, a person says that he does not deserve this good that the Creator has given him. Thus, how can he then say that he is deficient? Certainly, a prayer must be from the bottom of the heart, meaning to feel his need in all his organs or the prayer will not be from the bottom of the heart. Thus, how is it possible can it be said, once he has thanked the Creator for all the good that he has received, that he is deficient, and pray and cry to the Creator to grant him his wishes?

Therefore, those two things cause descents and ascents, since each one cancels the other. Yet, we should understand why we need both, and why prayer or gratitude is not enough, but rather both are required, but since they cannot be in the same carrier at the same time, we arrange them consecutively.

In other words, first we thank the Creator because He chose us from among all the nations, although we are lowly and inferior compared to His greatness, yet He chose us out of every nation. This is as our sages said, "One should always establish the praise of the Creator and then pray." Thus, when one thanks the Creator because He has been good to him, meaning certainly when the Creator gave him all that is needed, how is there a place to then pray for the things he is missing, and for the prayer to be from the bottom of the heart?

The answer is that on one hand, one should receive vitality during the work. When one does not have anything from which to live, he is distraught and cannot observe the Torah and *Mitzvot* properly, as it is written, "These words, which I am commanding you today, shall be on your heart. You shall teach them diligently to your sons and you shall speak of them when you sit in your home, and when you walk on the way, and when you lie down, and when you rise."

Thus, there is a complete order in observing Torah and *Mitzvot*. If one's mind is not settled, his work cannot be done in the order that it should. Hence, when one praises the Creator and depicts to himself the greatness and importance of the Creator as much as he can, from this one can derive vitality and feel the importance of the Creator, that the Creator gave him a thought and desire to speak with Him. From this, one should derive contentment.

One should imagine what mood he would be in if the greatest in the generation, whom the whole world praises, if that great man gave him permission to speak with him, how elated he would be, since when he feels this pleasure of being able to speak with him, he would not feel that he needs anything in the world. The pleasure that one feels more than usual makes him forget all his worries and his whole body gives itself up to the pleasure he is receiving now. That is, if during the reception of the pleasure, he can think about anything other than the pleasure he is receiving now, it is a sign that the pleasure he is receiving now is incomplete.

Hence, when one depicts to himself that the Creator permitted him to speak with Him, it does not matter what he says, but the importance that he has an opportunity to speak to the Creator, from this one should derive delight and pleasure that he has such a privilege. It follows that the work of the right is that one should believe that he is speaking with the Creator and that he does not need anything right now.

However, one should know that anything that depends on faith, the body does not agree to this work, especially because this work is considered a correction, and anything that pertains to correction invokes the body's resistance. This extends from the breaking of the vessels that occurred in the world of *Nekudim*. Therefore, there is much work on this.

Baal HaSulam said about the work of the right, when a person begins to slight it because he begins to work on a line that is contradictory to the right, which is the left line—that the work of the right is work in wholeness and truth, meaning that one must believe that the Creator is great and important, and man is utterly base. It follows that both are true. It is hard to walk on this line, and the body objects. He said that in the state of the right, a person is considered "blessed," since he is happy with his share and does not need anything. At that time, a person is fit to receive abundance from above by way of "The blessed clings to the Blessed." In this quality, he has *Dvekut* [adhesion] with the Creator. Hence, precisely in that state, a person can rise in degree.

However, we must also walk on the left line, which is the way to see how one sees the faults that need correcting. In other words, in the right, the work is only to depict the greatness of the Creator and believe in His greatness and importance. But the quality of the left is specifically to look at oneself and see the faults in him, in order to correct himself so there is no flaw in him. But the main flaw that one should see is the bad within him, meaning what is the essence of the evil that we must find, meaning that we must search and find.

Certainly, each person knows that there is evil in him. The thing is that we must know the root of evil, which is what prevents one from being able to receive the good that there is in the world.

The world was created for a purpose, and it was said that the purpose of the creation of the world was His desire to do good to His creations. Since man suffers torments in the world, and asks, "Why does it seem to us in this way?" For this reason, one must believe in the sages, who said that one should know that there was a correction on the purpose of creation, so as not to have the matter of shame upon the reception of the pleasure. This can be only if during the reception of the abundance, it will be in order to bestow. In that state, there is no place for shame.

Hence, only then, when he believes in the sages that we must obtain vessels of bestowal, otherwise it is impossible to obtain the good that the creatures should receive, then one realizes that all the bad is only the will to receive for one's own sake, and man should do everything to root it out and receive in its stead the desire to bestow, called a "second nature." At that time, he will be rewarded with the delight and pleasure that was in the thought of creation.

According to the above, we should work in two manners:

1) On the path of the right, which is the time when one works so as to feel that he has wholeness and he is content with his situation, and he can thank the Creator for it. This is the time when he can receive from above abundance and advance in the rungs of *Kedusha* [holiness]. However, although this is time to receive abundance from above, he does not lack anything, meaning he has no *Kelim* [vessels] to receive the abundance, so he must shift to the other line, called "left."

2) This is the path of the "left," by means of criticism that one passes on himself. The right line means that one looks only at the Creator, meaning to understand and to learn about the measure of the greatness of the Creator, and not about himself, to see what he is missing. Rather, he wants to look at what he has, meaning what the Creator gave him, and be thankful to the Creator for this.

However, the path of the left is to examine oneself, how much bad he has and what is the bad within him, and to try to correct it. At that time begins the matter of the spies who slandered the earth. "Earth" means the kingdom of heaven, as they said, that this matter of the kingdom of heaven is not for them.

According to the above, we should interpret what is written, "Rabbi Yosi said, 'They took upon themselves a counsel, to slander everything. What is 'everything'? It is the earth and the Creator. 'This is the meaning of the verse, 'Nevertheless, strong is the people,' meaning who can overcome them?' In other words, even the Creator cannot overcome them. Thus, they slandered the Creator."

They said that "We were born with a nature of doing everything for ourselves, so how can we accept the burden of the kingdom of heaven with the aim to benefit the Creator, meaning to do everything in order to bestow? After all, we began the work many times and in our view, we have done all that we could. But not only did the Creator not help us advance at all toward the aim to bestow, but we have even gone backwards. Thus, we must determine that even the Creator cannot help us emerge from the control of the will to receive. Otherwise, we would have moved a little bit forward. But after all the labor we have given in order to obtain the desire to bestow, in our view, it has all been in vain. Therefore, we are in a state where we have neither the corporeal world nor the spiritual world."

This is why it is written, "What did we get out of it? To this day we have not seen good in the world. We have toiled in Torah and the house is empty. Who will be awarded that world?" That is, they saw that they were not advancing in the work. But what was the sin? It was that they should have had faith in the Creator that all those descents that they felt in the work were not because they did not go forward, but that each time a person sees that he is far from the goal, it is in order for him to find a real need for His salvation. And the need is called "a *Kli* [vessel] to receive the filling." Yet, what was missing there and for which they could not continue and wanted to escape from the campaign was the lack of the right line.

The meaning of "right" is that one must have vitality during the work, and we receive vitality specifically from wholeness, which we can obtain precisely when we are not looking at ourselves, but at the Creator, and all the effort is to think about the greatness of the Creator and not about ourselves, meaning what we acquired, some progress in the work. Rather, we should think what a privilege we have that we have some contact with the Creator.

This means that when he performs a commandment or says a blessing, he should say, "I am happy that I believe that I am doing the Creator's will by observing His commandments. Although I understand that we must observe the commandments of the King with more importance than I ascribe to observing the *Mitzvot* [commandments/good deeds], I cannot appreciate the importance of the act, even though the act is incomplete. Still, I am happy that the Creator has given me a desire and yearning to do something in observing Torah and *Mitzvot*, even if these actions are not so important. Yet, it is important to me, since now I can say that I am doing the Creator's will."

From this, one should derive vitality and joy because it is the truth that the Creator is great. Hence, when one has a desire to do something in the work, this is very important. A person should believe that even when a person does things by coercion, it is still important, since in terms of the action, there is nothing to add and the act does its thing.

Therefore, since the spies did not go on the right, as well, they wanted to escape the campaign and said that even the Creator cannot help them. That is, they understood that the Creator should bring them closer in the way that they understood, not in the way that the

Torah obligates us, as it is written, that there are two writings that deny one another until the third wiring comes and decides between them. For this reason, the spies, who strayed to walk on the left line and abandoned the right, saw that they could not come and inherit the land. It was all because they went by the wrong path, as Moses had arranged for them.

This is the meaning of what is written about a king who arranged for his son a wife and said, "I will show her to you (but) I swear that you will not see her in your house, for I will rather give her to your son." We asked, But the spies did not see her, that she is fair and comes from a good and wealthy family?! We should interpret that in the work "father and son" are "cause and consequence." The present is called "father," and the future is called "son." In spirituality, "seeing" means attainment. Since they took the wrong path, they could not see it "in your house," meaning in the state they were in, in vessels of reception. Rather, "to your son," meaning after you repent, when you are rewarded with vessels of bestowal, you will be able to see all the merits that there are in the inheritance of the land that the Creator promised to our forefathers.

What Is, "Peace, Peace, to the Far and to the Near," in the Work?

Article No. 36, Tav-Shin-Nun-Aleph, 1990/91

The *Zohar* says (Korah, Items 5-8), "Korah went by way of dispute. What is a dispute? It is removing and repelling above and below. One who wishes to repel the correction of the world is lost from all the worlds. A dispute is removing and repelling of the peace. One who disagrees with peace disagrees with His Holy Name, since His Holy Name is called 'Peace.' The world stands only on peace. When the Creator created the world, it could not exist until He came and established peace upon them. And what is it? It is the Sabbath. Hence, one who disagrees with peace will be lost from the world. Rabbi Yosi said, 'It is written, 'Those who love Your Torah [law] have much peace.' The Torah is peace, as it is written, 'And all her ways are peace.' Korah came to blemish the peace above—the Torah, meaning the middle line, which is called 'Torah,' which makes peace between right and left—and below, of

Moses. This is why he was punished by upper and lower, by fire and the mouth of the earth.'"

We should understand why he says that the world can exist only on peace because His Holy Name is "Peace." It follows that the reason that the world cannot exist is that the Creator is called "Peace."

We should understand the connection to the name of the Creator. In simple terms, everyone understands that if there is a dispute, there cannot be an existence to the world. But how does this concern the name of the Creator? Also, we should understand why he says, "And what is peace?" He says that peace means Shabbat [the Sabbath], and Rabbi Yosi says that peace is called "Torah." Thus, how is it expressed that the Shabbat and the Torah indicate peace?

First, we must repeat two tenets that we have spoken of many times: 1) the purpose of creation, 2) the correction of creation, meaning what we should do in order to achieve the purpose of creation.

It is known that the purpose of creation is for the creatures to receive delight and pleasure, as he says, "His desire to do good to His creations." For this purpose, He created in the creatures a desire to receive pleasure. In other words, if there is no yearning for something, we cannot enjoy it. If we sometimes see that wherever one can enjoy something, he cannot stop himself and not want to receive the pleasure. If we sometimes see that a person does relinquish a pleasure, this must be for some special reason for which it is worthwhile for him to relinquish, since one cannot go against the nature of the will to receive. Hence, if there is a good enough reason, a person will give up pleasures that he wants to receive.

This can happen for two reasons: 1) Because of a reward, meaning that if he relinquishes the pleasure that he wants now, he will receive greater pleasure instead. 2) Because of punishment. That is, if he does not relinquish this pleasure, he will suffer great torments for it, and he sees that it is better for him to give up this pleasure in order not to suffer.

What Is, "Peace, Peace, to the Far and to the Near," in the Work?

It follows that the fact that a person has now relinquished the will to receive pleasure, this concession is not because he does not want to work for his own benefit. Rather, he sees that if he does not concede what he wants now, it will harm his self-benefit, and this is why he gives it up. For this reason, we do not say that by giving up a pleasure, he did something against nature, meaning that he blemished the will to receive. Rather, all he did was according to the method of the will to receive.

In other words, we should not look at what people do, for sometimes they relinquish something, but it is not a sign that this person is working. Rather, we must see the aim, as well.

For example, a person might give up the lust for food. If he knows that someone might see that he is a person who renounces pleasures, it is a sign that he is a servant of the Creator, and there are people who will respect him for this. Then, a person has the power to overcome because he will receive a greater pleasure, which is respect. This is usually the case.

But there are also exceptions. There are those who can degrade themselves, meaning relinquish respect in order to obtain a lust. Also, there are those who do not relinquish lusts, but not because of respect, but on the contrary, meaning that if one works in concealment, he can eat much, for example, and people are bound to see how he is eating and will despise him in their hearts. He relinquishes the respect in order to gain from this the ability to work in concealment, since through this work he can be rewarded with an even greater pleasure, since one who is humble is rewarded with *Dvekut* [adhesion] with the Creator.

This means that he does not want to be satisfied with people respecting him, since there is a rule that when people think that he is above them they respect him, and respect takes over, so one who develops a passion for respect cannot come out of it and must work and toil in order to obtain the respect. Then, he cannot do anything for the sake of the Creator. Therefore, we were given the counsel to do everything in concealment, and thereby not be given respect. By this he can be saved from falling under the governance of respect. At that time, he can accustom himself to work in order to bestow.

Accordingly, we see that one who relinquishes small pleasures and instead receives a big pleasure, it is not that he flawed the will to receive. Sometimes, he receives the big pleasure from satisfying some passion, and sometimes the great pleasure comes through respect, and so forth.

Sometimes, he receives a small pleasure, meaning a small passion, since he knows that by this he is giving up a big pleasure, which is respect. The question is, Why would he want to relinquish a big pleasure? It is because in return for relinquishing a big pleasure, he wants to receive a higher degree. For example, by relinquishing respect, he wants to be rewarded with *Dvekut* with the Creator.

In this manner, we do not say that he received a small pleasure, such as eating, and gave up a big pleasure, which is respect. Rather, we should say that he also does not relinquish the small pleasure, but only in the eyes of people who are looking at him and say that this person is not smart, since he does not want to relinquish a small passion, for if he gave up that passion he could receive a greater pleasure, but he does not even have the power to overcome a small passion. It follows that it is impossible to know the truth about a person whose way is concealment.

Now we return to what we discussed concerning the correction of creation, that one should come to do everything in order to bestow. Since man was created with a nature of receiving only for his own benefit, how can he be told to go against nature, since the body asks, "What will I get out of this?" Certainly, we should tell it, "You will get out of this, that if you work in order to bestow, you will be rewarded with the delight and pleasure that are found in the purpose of creation."

Thus, the answer is that the will to receive will obtain a greater pleasure than he can receive now, in the will to receive without the aim to bestow. At that time, the body claims, "So you are saying that then I will benefit, as well. That is, I see that if I work in order to bestow, I will get self-benefit from this." In that case, a person says that he does not see anything that one can do without yielding some benefit for himself from it.

The answer is that with the intellect, it is impossible to understand how one can do something against nature. Therefore, a person is told, "What you are saying is correct; by nature, it is impossible for man to understand what is in order to bestow." Therefore, our sages said, "One should always engage in Torah and *Mitzvot Lo Lishma* [not for Her sake], since from *Lo Lishma* he will come to *Lishma* [for Her sake]." Then, when he learns *Lo Lishma*, "the light in it reforms him," as it says in the *Sulam* [Ladder commentary on *The Zohar*] (*Beresheet Bet*, Item 103), "If one engages in Torah and *Mitzvot* [commandments/good deeds] even for his own pleasure, through the light in it he will still feel the lowliness and the terrible corruptness in the nature of receiving for oneself. At that time, he will resolve to retire from that nature of reception and will completely devote himself to working only in order to bestow contentment upon his Maker. Then the Creator will open his eyes to see before him a world filled with utter perfection without any deficiencies whatsoever."

According to the above, we see that man cannot understand what it means to work in order to bestow and not for his own sake. We can begin to understand it specifically by engaging in Torah and *Mitzvot* even *Lo Lishma*. Nevertheless, the light in it can make him see that there is the matter that it is worthwhile to work only for the sake of the Creator and not for one's own sake.

But without the remedy in Torah and *Mitzvot*, man's intellect cannot understand that it is possible to do something unless it yields pleasure with which one can please his will to receive. Hence, when a person is told to do everything for the sake of the Creator, and he sees that he cannot understand such a thing, the answer is that it is true that it is impossible to understand it with the external mind that was given to man, but he is told, "You must know that you are wasting your time waiting and saying that if he learns it, he will understand how to engage in it in order to attain the desire to bestow, and in the meantime he will wait with praying for the Creator to give him that desire. Before he understands that he needs this thing, how can he pray to the Creator to give him something if he does not know he needs it? He can say that he wants the desire to bestow, but how can he pray from the bottom of the heart that this is what he needs?

There is no way to understand this with the external mind, but one who wants to walk on the path toward achieving the goal for which he was created must believe in the sages, who said that one should do everything in order to bestow and not for his own sake. That is, the fact that he must walk on a path where all his actions are in order to bestow, a person cannot take this desire. Only the Creator can give him that second nature, as well as the belief that he will receive the need for this from observing Torah and *Mitzvot* even *Lo Lishma*, because "the light in it reforms him."

Hence, we see here two things that the Creator gives: 1) The need for one to understand that he needs the desire to bestow, and he receives this through the light in the Torah. Later, he also receives the light, which is the power to do everything in order to bestow.

Accordingly, we should interpret what we asked, What is the reason that the world stands only on peace, since the name of the Creator is "Peace"? We asked, What is the connection between them?

The answer is that since it is impossible to make peace where there is no dispute, for only where there is a dispute, there can be peace, for this reason, first we must know what is the dispute that there is in the world, for which we must make peace, since the Creator is called "Peace," and only then the world exists.

It is known that the Creator's desire is to do good to His creations. Hence, all the creatures feel that they should receive delight and pleasure from the Creator. It follows that when they are not receiving delight and pleasure, they are disputed with the Creator over why is He not giving them delight and pleasure. Since there was a correction that in order to prevent the shame, everything must be done in order to bestow, the Creator is in dispute with the created beings over why they are unwilling to work in order to bestow.

It therefore follows that there are two opposite opinions here: 1) The creatures say to the Creator, "Let us enjoy; satisfy our desires, meaning our will to receive, with abundance, so we can say, 'Blessed is He who said, 'Let there be the world,'" since we feel the abundance that we have and we enjoy it." 2) The Creator said, "I, too, want to enjoy the world that I created, and all My joy is that you are enjoying, as this was My purpose in creation, as it is written, 'His desire to do good to His creations.' However, I want your pleasure to be complete, without any unpleasantness, called 'shame.'"

For this reason, once the creatures feel the dispute, they want to make peace with the Creator, since otherwise the world cannot exist. That is, the world must exist only for the purpose for which it was created. If the goal cannot be achieved, then why do they need the world, for the world was not created so that the creatures would suffer torments?

Hence, the name of the Creator is "Peace" because it is impossible to reveal the name of the Creator, as His general name is The Good Who Does Good, but how can the name The Good Who Does Good be revealed when there is a dispute between the Creator and the creatures?

We therefore see that precisely by peace, the world can exist. Peace means that through peace, it is possible to feel that the Creator is good and does good, since they are receiving the delight and pleasure from the Creator, once peace has been established, meaning when the creatures accept the desire of the Creator, who wants the creatures to do everything for the sake of the Creator.

This is called "resembling the desire of the Creator," whose desire is only to bestow upon the creatures. Likewise, now the creatures become similar to the desire of the Creator in that they, too, want only to bestow upon the Creator. Then, through equivalence of form, it is possible to reveal the delight and pleasure that exist in the thought of creation, and then it becomes revealed that the name of the Creator is The Good Who Does Good.

By this we will understand what we asked about peace being specifically where there is a dispute, so why did the Creator create the world with a dispute to begin with? The answer is that a dispute exists wherever there are opposite things. Since the world was created with a *Kli* [vessel] of a desire to receive, since otherwise, if there is no desire to receive something, it is impossible to enjoy it; therefore, creation emerged with a nature of wanting to receive for oneself. Afterward, in order to correct it so there will not be the matter of shame in it, the creatures must acquire a second nature, meaning to acquire the desire of the Creator, whose desire is to bestow. For this reason, a dispute emerged from this.

It follows that the dispute is necessary. That is, if the creatures do not understand the matter of the dispute, they can never achieve the purpose of creation, which is to do good to His creations, since it is impossible to correct anything if we do not know what is missing. Hence, once we know the dispute between the desires, we can make peace between them.

According to the above, we can interpret what we asked, "What is peace?" He says that peace is Shabbat. Rabbi Yosi says that peace is Torah, meaning that through the Torah, a person comes to feel the dispute, since the Torah, even in *Lo Lishma*, the light in it makes him see that there is the need to work in order to bestow. It follows that through the Torah, he first comes to the dispute, and then he knows what needs to be corrected. Afterward, by being rewarded with "Torah *Lishma*," the Torah makes peace, meaning gives him the power of the desire to bestow, which is the meaning of doing everything for the sake of the Creator. It follows that through the Torah, he achieves two things: the *Kli*, which is the lack, and the light, which is the power to be able to do everything in order to bestow.

When it says that peace is called Shabbat, it does not dispute the interpretation that peace is called Torah, since our sages said (*Avoda Zara* 3), "The Creator said to them, 'He who toiled on the

What Is, "Peace, Peace, to the Far and to the Near," in the Work?

eve of Shabbat will eat on Shabbat. He who did not toil on the eve of Shabbat, from where will he eat on Shabbat?'"

We should understand this saying in the work. It means that since Shabbat is called "peace," how can one be rewarded with peace if there is no dispute there? And what is the dispute? It is as our sages said, "One should always anger the good inclination over the evil inclination." RASHI interprets that he should make war with it (*Berachot* 5). The war means that since the good inclination is to have the same desire as the Creator, namely a desire to bestow, and the evil inclination is called the will to receive, a person should try to make a dispute, meaning that they are two opposing desires. At that time, Shabbat comes and makes peace.

But if there is no dispute, how can we say that Shabbat makes peace? This is why he says, "He who did not toil on the eve of Shabbat, from where will he eat on Shabbat?" It follows that the toil is the dispute, meaning to fight against the evil inclination, which is the will to receive.

However, why is Shabbat called "peace"? It is as *The Zohar* writes, "What is Shabbat? The name of the Creator" (brought in *The Zohar* on the Shabbat morning meal). It is known that the name of the Creator is "Torah," as our sages said, "The whole Torah is the names of the Creator." It follows that both Shabbat and Torah make peace. This means that through the revelation of the Torah in the manner of the "name of the Creator," peace is made between the creatures and the Creator, for the creatures enjoy being rewarded with receiving the delight and pleasure, and the Creator enjoys the purpose of creation being achieved. In other words, the desire to do good to His creations is revealed in full.

According to the above, we should interpret the words of *The Zohar*, which says that Korah "went by way of dispute," and one who wants to repel the correction of the world will be lost from all the worlds. We should interpret that the correction of the world was for everything to work in order to bestow. Korah went by way of dispute, and had to later achieve peace, which is correction. But Korah wanted to stay in the dispute. It follows that he repelled the correction of the world. This is why it says, "One who disagrees with peace disagrees with His Holy Name, since His Holy Name is called 'Peace.'"

This means that since His name is peace, meaning that peace was done between the Creator and the creatures, meaning that the name of the Creator, that He is good and does good, becomes revealed, and through the dispute, called "disparity of form," the good cannot be revealed, it follows that the creatures are disputed with the Creator. But when peace is made from the perspective of the *Kelim*, meaning from the perspective of the desires, when there is one desire in the world, called "desire to bestow," then all the delight and pleasure in the world becomes revealed.

What Is the "Torah" and What Is "The Statute of the Torah," in the Work?

Article No. 37, Tav-Shin-Nun-Aleph, 1990/91

It is written in *The Zohar* (*Hukat*, Item 2), "It is written here, 'This is the statute of the Torah.' It is also written, 'This is the Torah,' and it is not written, 'The statute of.' 'This is the Torah' is to show that all is in one unification. For this reason, it is written, 'And this is the Torah,' indicating ZA and *Nukva* in one unification. But 'this' without the added *Vav* is the statute of the Torah, *Malchut*, which is called 'statute,' coming from ZA, who is called 'Torah.' Yet, not the Torah herself, which is ZA, but only the *Din* [judgment] of Torah, the decree of Torah, which is *Malchut*."

We should understand the difference in the work between the "statute of the Torah" and the Torah herself. The statute of the Torah relates to *Malchut*, and the Torah relates to ZA. Also, we should understand what is written about a red cow "on which a yoke has never been placed." We see what our sages said (*Avoda Zarah* 5b), "Tana de Bei Eliyahu, 'One should always take upon himself the words of Torah as an ox to the burden and as a donkey to the load.'" This means that one who takes upon himself a burden, it is a good thing. Certainly, this pertains to the burden of Torah, as our sages said (*Avot*, Chapter 3, 6), "Anyone who takes upon himself the burden of Torah, the burden of *Malchut* [kingship] is removed from him." Therefore, concerning a red cow, of which it says, "on which a yoke has never been placed," and which comes to purify the impure, why is it written, "on which a yoke has never been placed"?

We should understand what is a burden [in Hebrew, *Ol* means both "yoke" and "burden"], of which they said, "One should always make himself as an ox to the burden and as a donkey to the load." We see that a "burden" means "coercion," which is work above reason. This ox, on which the owner places the yoke so it will till the land, does not understand why it needs to work for the owner. Also, we cannot say that the ox works for him because he loves the owner since he lets it eat and drink. If this is because the owner has a kind heart, and this is why he gives the ox all its needs, the ox probably knows that if the owner could work with the ox without having to provide for its needs, he would certainly do so. But the owner knows that if he does not provide the ox with all its needs, the ox will not have the strength to work. Therefore, he gives everything to the ox so he can work with the ox, and not because he wants to delight the ox. In other words, he knows that if he does not give the ox everything that the ox needs in order to have the strength to work, the owner will not be able to yield crops and produce from the land. It follows that he draws all the wealth from the strength of the ox. Therefore, when the owner feeds the ox, it is not because he loves the ox, but in order for the ox to have the strength to work. Likewise, the reason why the ox works for the owner is compulsory, and when the ox sees that the owner is not looking at it, it immediately stops working. This is called coercion.

Now we can understand what is the burden of the kingdom of heaven and the burden of the Torah that one should assume, which is coercion. A person's body is like an ox or a donkey, and we must work with the body as one works with an ox or a donkey. By working with his body, through the work of the body, the person will be rewarded with wealth and spiritual properties. Also, a person must be considerate with the body as with an ox, as we place on the ox the yoke to work in coercion although the ox and the donkey do not want to work. No one takes into consideration the ox's view; whether it wants to or not, it is used for work.

However, we should also be considerate with the body, meaning to give it what it needs, what the body demands. But when we give to the body what it needs, it should not be because he loves the body, meaning his will to receive. Rather, it is because otherwise the body will not be able to work. It follows that the only reason a person examines the body so as to satisfy its needs is not because of love, but like an owner who provides for the needs of the ox, only because of the benefit of the owner, and not for the love of the ox.

Also, a person should aim while satisfying the desires of the body, that it will not be because he loves it, but that by this he will then be able to make his body till the land and yield fruit, as it is written, "much produce by the strength of the ox." This means that one should be careful while working with the body as while working with the ox. That is, the reason why he satisfies the needs of the ox, he would certainly be happier if he could work with the ox without having to provide for the ox's needs.

Likewise, a person must come to understand that he would be happier if he did not have to do something for the needs of the body, and satisfy the needs of the body, but would dedicate all his time to holy work and would devote all his time to increase the glory of heaven, and the body would work without any disturbances. Yet, what can one do if the Creator wants man to see and to tend to the needs of the body?

According to the above, we already know the meaning of "the burden of the kingdom of heaven" and "the burden of Torah," meaning to work with the body coercively, even if it disagrees with the work. It should all follow the example of the ox to the burden and the donkey to the load. However, it is a lot of work for a person to have the strength to overcome the body and work with the body coercively, as with an ox. From what source can one derive this strength? Our sages said about this, "The Creator said, 'I have created the evil inclination; I have created the Torah as a spice.'" That is, only through the Torah that a person engages in, even if *Lo Lishma* [not for Her sake], and he aims that he wants to engage in the Torah so as to thereby receive the light of the Torah, which will give him the strength to force the body when it disagrees with the work.

The resistance of the body appears primarily when he wants to do everything for the sake of the Creator and not for his own sake. Here the body resists with all its might, since it argues, "Why do you want to put me and my domain to death? You come to me with having to work only for the sake of the Creator and not for one's own sake, which is truly annulment of the will to receive from everything. You tell me that our sages said, 'The Torah exists only in one who puts himself to death over it,' meaning to put to death all the domain of self-benefit and care only for the benefit of the Creator, and before this, a person cannot be rewarded with the Torah." Yet, a person sees that it is unrealistic that he will have the strength to go against nature.

At that time, one has no choice but to turn to the Creator and say, "Now I have come to a state where I see that unless You help me, I am lost. I will never have the strength to overcome the will to receive, as this is my nature. Rather, only the Creator can give another nature."

A person says that he believes that this was the exodus from Egypt, that the Creator delivered the people of Israel from under the governance of Egypt, as our sages said (in the Passover *Haggadah* [story/narrative]), "And the Lord brought us out from Egypt, not by an angel, and not by a messenger, but the Creator Himself; I am the Lord, it is I and not another."

Now, he, too, sees that only the Creator can deliver him from the governance of the will to receive and give him a second nature. In other words, just as the Creator gave the first nature, there is no one who can give the second nature but the Creator Himself. Therefore, at that time a person prays wholeheartedly, from the bottom of the heart, and this is the time for the reception of the prayer.

However, we should ask, Why does one need to work coercively, against the will to receive? The answer is that it is because there was a correction so there would not be shame when receiving the delight and pleasure. Therefore, two things are needed here: 1) On one hand, a person yearns to receive delight and pleasure. Otherwise, if there is no passion for the pleasures, a person is unable to enjoy. 2) He should receive delight and pleasure with the aim to bestow.

It follows that we need both. That is, first we begin to work with the will to receive, which is called *Lo Lishma*, and then a person is taught to work in order to bestow. In other words, by observing Torah and *Mitzvot* [commandments/good deeds], a person wants to come to be a giver, meaning to thereby be rewarded with a second nature, that the Creator will give him this power, as it is written, "The light in it reforms him," and afterward, he is rewarded with "receiving in order to bestow."

This is as it is written (*Avot*, Chapter 6), "Rabbi Meir says, 'Anyone who engages in Torah *Lishma* [for Her sake] is rewarded with many things. Moreover, the whole world is worthwhile for him, and the secrets of Torah are revealed to him.'"

It follows that later, a person comes to a state where he receives the delight and pleasure, and then there is no more need for coercion because the period of coercion was only in order to obtain the vessels of bestowal, by which there would be reception of the pleasure without any unpleasantness, since by this, the issue of shame would be corrected, so he can do everything for the sake of the Creator.

According to the above, we should interpret what we asked, Why is it written about the red cow, "on which a yoke has never been placed"? We asked, what does it imply that the red cow should be without a yoke? According to the above, we should interpret that the meaning of the red cow is that it purifies the impure. And what do they obtain through purification? It is known that the whole matter of *Tuma'a* [impurity] implies the will to receive. We must work with the will to receive, called "body," coercively, "as an ox to the burden and as a donkey to the load." This coercive work is only before one is rewarded with purity. After one has been rewarded with purity, which implies to us the matter of the red cow, he is rewarded with work, "on which a yoke has never been placed." At that time, his work is no longer coercive, and he serves the Creator from love.

Therefore, we should discern two times:

1) Before one is rewarded with purification of the *Kelim* [vessels], so they work in order to bestow. At that time, his work is compulsory, and this is called "a law." That is, if the body comes and asks, "What is this work for you?" we tell it, "You ask questions according to the mind of the will to receive. I have no answer to this, and you are right. Yet, I do not want to answer within reason," meaning so that the will to receive will also understand it. It would mean that I am working for the will to receive, or it would never agree to work.

Therefore, at that time, a person says, "You are right when you ask, 'What will I have,' meaning the will to receive, 'from this work?' So I am telling you that I do not want to work for you. Why? It is because I believe in the sages that we must work for the sake of the Creator above reason although the body does not understand, and I accept this work 'as an ox to the burden and as a donkey to the load,' meaning by coercion."

2) A person says, "But once I am rewarded with purity, my work will be by way of love, and not by way of coercion. However, I do not mean that now I am working coercively so that afterward I will work out of love." That would be as though it is also for the will to receive, since afterward he will receive the delight and pleasure. Rather, when he says that afterward he will be rewarded with love, it is for a different reason: It will only be a sign for him by which to know whether he is truly working for the sake of the Creator and not for his own sake.

What Is the "Torah" and What Is "The Statute of the Torah," in the Work?

This is so for because the Creator wants to give delight and pleasure, but we still have no *Kelim* to receive, since we are not working in order to bestow. Hence, this is a sign whether he is working in order to bestow. That is, if he still did not receive delight and pleasure, it is a sign that he is still under the governance of the will to receive. However, his aim is not to receive the delight and pleasure, but to know whether he is truly working in order to bestow.

The Sayer of Duvna said about the verse, "You did not call upon Me Jacob, for you labored in Me, Israel." He said that if you labor while observing Torah and *Mitzvot*, it is a sign that you are not working for Me, meaning for the sake of the Creator, for one who works for the sake of the Creator has no labor in Torah and *Mitzvot*. On the contrary, he feels pleasure when he knows that he is serving the King. It follows that he wants to work out of love and not by coercion not because he wants to please the will to receive, but in order to know for certain that he is working for the sake of the Creator.

By this we should interpret the words, "on which a yoke has never been placed." It means that before he took her, there was no yoke on her. We should interpret that in the work, this implies to us why it has to be one "on which a yoke has never been placed," implying that through the red cow, by which one is purified, by receiving purification from a red cow, he will be rewarded with working in a state of love, and not by coercion. In other words, the body, which resisted working for the sake of the Creator, by being purified, the body agrees to work for the sake of the Creator, for at that time he will observe, "And you shall love the Lord your God with all your heart," with both your inclinations. This means that the evil inclination, too, agrees to serve the Creator, meaning to work in order to bestow.

According to the above, we should interpret why he says that *Malchut* is called "the statute of the Torah" and not "the Torah," and ZA is called "the Torah." Because assuming the kingdom of heaven should be above reason, like a law, this is why *Malchut* is called "statute." But afterward, we are rewarded with the Torah, called ZA, and they are united. This is called "the unification of the Creator with His *Shechina* [Divinity]." In other words, by accepting the kingdom of heaven as a law, completely mindlessly, above reason, as our sages said, "Because Satan and the nations of the world taunt Israel, to say, 'What is this *Mitzva* [commandment/good deed] and what is its reason,' therefore, it is written about it, 'It is a statute, a decree before Me; you have no permission to doubt it.'"

Hence, when a person takes upon himself the burden of the kingdom of heaven, he is rewarded with the Torah. This is the meaning of saying, "'This is the law' is to show that all is in one unification." This means that in the end, everything becomes united, and then it is evident that the thought of creation, which is to do good to His creations, becomes revealed, since the will to receive has united with the desire to bestow, and equivalence of form is achieved. Then, there are no longer two desires, but one: the desire to bestow of the Creator to the creatures. And the will to receive of the created beings is annulled and included in the Creator's desire to bestow, and this is considered that there is only one authority in the world. This is called "singular authority," and then the delight and pleasure are apparent in the world.

However, the work should be done in two lines—right and left. "Right" means "completeness," and "left" means "incompleteness," and a correction is needed there. When one engages in the manner of "the statute of the Torah," meaning he wants to assume the burden of the kingdom of heaven but the body objects to it and fights him, that state is called "left line," since then a person feels his deficiency, how far he is from the love of the Creator. This is when the body comes with the "Who" and "What" questions. At that time, he has nothing from which to derive vitality, since a person cannot live on a lack.

This work is called "depart from evil," meaning that a person should depart from the bad that is within man, called "will to receive," whether in mind or in heart. Although this work is necessary, since this is the first foundation, that one should assume the burden of the kingdom of heaven, but at the same time, the writing says, "There is more to do, meaning the work of the right, called "completeness."

The work of the right is called in the verse, "and do good." We should interpret that a person should engage in the good, and good is called "completeness." In other words, a person should calculate how much good he has, which is called "and do," meaning work and calculate how much good he has. That is, a person should regard everything of *Kedusha* [holiness] as a great fortune and believe that any grip he has on *Kedusha*, although it is a small grip, he should believe that the Creator has given him some desire and yearning to have a grip on *Kedusha*, and even if it is *Lo Lishma*, it is still a very important matter. He should thank the Creator for the little bit of good that he has, and from this, a person can derive vitality and be in high spirits. From this, a person can receive what is written, "Serve the Lord with gladness." It follows that a person should maintain the right and the left, and this is the meaning of the verse, "Part from evil and do good."

However, a question arises in a person. For example, he has been busy all day and did not have time to remember that there is a reality of the work of the Creator in the world. Afterward, he remembers that he went through the whole day in matters that have no connection to the work. What should he do now? Should he be sorry for not engaging in the work the whole time, or should he introspect and say, "Who reminded me now that there is the matter of a spiritual reality in the world, and that we must do something for the *Kedusha*? It must be the Creator who gave me this thought now. Therefore, I must thank the Creator and be happy that the Creator is calling me to Him." Should he be happy about this and thank and praise the Creator, or regret that all day long he was removed from the work altogether? It is true that he was removed from the Creator the whole day, and it is also true that now the Creator has given him an awakening so he will know the state he is in. So the question is, "What should he do?"

According to what Baal HaSulam said, "Where a person thinks, there he is." Thus, if a person thinks about the time when he was removed from the Creator and regrets it, then he is attached to the state of remoteness from the Creator, when he thought about trivial matters that he was engaged in all day long. It follows that the *Dvekut* of his thought is in matters that are immaterial. Therefore, it is better to think about the good that he has now, meaning the fact that now he can think what do for the *Kedusha*. It does not matter what he does, but only that he wants to engage in Torah and *Mitzvot*. Now he already has connection with the Torah and *Mitzvot*, according to the above rule, "Where one thinks, there he is."

Now we should interpret the verse differently: Now he should be "Part from evil," meaning not to think about his bad state, when he was separated, but rather "do good," so everything he wants to do now will concern the good that he should do now.

According to the above, we should ask, How does one go to work in the manner of the left, since then he is in the state of "left," and thinks only about deficiencies, so he is attached to the deficiencies?

The answer is that a person should work on the left line only if first he is in the right line. Only when he is in a state of completeness and feels a good taste in the work, which is called "an ascent," should he dedicate time to the left, as well, to see whether his mind and heart are fine. After this, he will be rewarded with "the Creator gives the soul," called "the soul of life."

What Is the "Right Line," in the Work?

Article No. 38, Tav-Shin-Nun-Aleph, 1990/91

Our sages said (*Avot de Rabbi Natan* 11:2), "Anyone who extols himself with words of Torah is ultimately brought low, and anyone who lowers himself with words of Torah is ultimately raised high."

We should understand why specifically with words of Torah, it is forbidden to take pride. After all, in general, it is forbidden to be proud, as it is written, "Be very, very humble" (*Avot*, Chapter 4:4). Also it was said, "Anyone who is proud, the Creator said, 'I and he cannot dwell in the same abode.'" So, why did they speak specifically about words of Torah?

It is known that we have two discernments in observing Torah and *Mitzvot* [commandments/good deeds]: 1) 613 *Eitin* (counsels [Aramaic]), 2) 613 *Pekudin* [Aramaic: deposits]. These two discernments come to us from two discernments that exist in the world: 1) the purpose of creation, 2) the correction of creation.

In the matter of the purpose of creation, His desire to do good to His creations, for which He created in the creatures a desire and yearning to receive delight and pleasure, this *Kli* [vessel] for receiving pleasure comes from the Creator. Hence, this *Kli* is complete. In other words, a person does not need to work to make for himself a *Kli*, as this comes to him by nature, since wherever one sees that there is something to enjoy, he immediately yearns for it, as it is written, "The eye sees and the heart covets."

However, afterward, a correction was done where in order to prevent the issue of shame when receiving the delight and pleasure a *Tzimtzum* [restriction] and concealment were made, so we cannot see that there is pleasure. Naturally, a person does not see the delight and pleasure so as to yearn for this delight and pleasure that the Creator wants to give to the created beings. But once they have vessels of bestowal, by reception of pleasure in these *Kelim* [plural of *Kli*], the shame while receiving pleasure will be removed from them. At that time, the concealment is lifted and they see the delight and pleasure that the Creator wants to impart upon the creatures.

However, we must know that all of our work is in making the vessels of bestowal, since our *Kli* is against our nature. But how can one go against nature? This is why we begin to observe Torah and *Mitzvot* in order to receive, as *The Zohar* says, that we should observe Torah and *Mitzvot* out of fear.

This fear divides into two manners: 1) observing Torah and *Mitzvot* because of reward and punishment in this world, such as health and provision, and 2) observing Torah and *Mitzvot* because of reward and punishment in the next world, meaning to go to Heaven and not to Hell.

It follows that these two discernments do not contradict the will to receive, which is human nature. Afterward, he enters the work of the "still of *Kedusha* [holiness]," and the "still" is the first quality, where everyone begins. This pertains to the whole collective, meaning that as surrounding, the light shines to all of Israel, meaning to all those with a grip on Torah and *Mitzvot*, the Surrounding Light shines in them, since Surrounding Light means that the light illuminates outside the *Kelim*, since the light needs a *Kli* so as to have equivalence with the light.

In other words, since the light aims to bestow, likewise, the *Kli* should aim to bestow. As long as a person has not qualified his

Kelim to work in order to bestow, the light remains outside the *Kli*. However, from there, it shines to the *Kli*, and by this, the *Kli* gradually acquires a need to equalize with the light, and seeks advice how to equalize with the light, meaning for the *Kli*, called "will to receive," to have the power to work in order to bestow.

The Zohar says that there is a manner of observing Torah and *Mitzvot* out of fear: 3) He observes Torah and *Mitzvot* because "He is great and ruling." This means that the fear that leads him to observe Torah and *Mitzvot* is not because the will to receive will enjoy it, meaning that by observing Torah and *Mitzvot* he will receive some reward that he will enjoy. Rather, the greatness and importance of the King obligate him, since he wants to serve the King, and he does not want any reward for his labor in Torah and *Mitzvot*. Rather, the things he does in order to bestow upon the King are his pleasure.

However, how can one acquire this feeling of the greatness and importance of the King, while there is concealment on the greatness and importance of the King, which was done by the *Tzimtzum* [restriction]? And if so, from where will he take the greatness of the Creator?

Here begins the work in the manner of "faith above reason," where one must believe in the greatness and importance of the King. This work is considered that a person must ask the Creator that "His great name will grow and be sanctified," meaning that the greatness and importance of the Creator will be revealed in the world. As long as one is immersed in the will to receive, we learned that there is a correction called "concealment on Providence," that the Creator leads the world in a manner of good and doing good.

Otherwise, there will be no room for choice, that it will be possible to do something in order to bestow. It is known that smaller pleasures are easier to relinquish and say, "If not in order to bestow, I do not want to use them." But with great pleasures, it is certainly difficult to relinquish them. This is why there had to be concealment on Providence.

However, in order for a person to exist in the world, and without pleasure, there is no existence to the creatures, since the purpose of creation is to do good to His creations, for this reason, the ARI says that through the breaking of the vessels that occurred in the world of *Nekudim*, sparks fell into the *Klipot* [shells/peels] and sustain the *Klipot* so they will not be cancelled. These are called "tiny light," in the words of *The Zohar*, and from this tiny light extend all the corporeal pleasures.

Conversely, the real pleasure is clothed in the Torah. Hence, on corporeal pleasures, where the pleasures are not as great as the spiritual ones, we begin to practice on them how to receive them in order to bestow. To the extent that a person enters the work of bestowal, to that extent the concealment and hiding over the pleasure in Torah and *Mitzvot* depart from him.

However, how does one acquire the strength to work in order to bestow on small pleasures? After all, a person can work only for his own sake. Thus, in what manner can he begin, so he has something over which to relinquish his self-benefit? The answer is that our sages said about this, "The Creator said, 'I have created the evil inclination; I have created the Torah as a spice, since the light in it reforms him.'" In other words, when a person engages in Torah, he must aim that the Torah will give him light, to want to work for the sake of the Creator and not for his own sake. This discernment is called "613 *Eitin* (counsels [Aramaic])." In other words, these are only counsels concerning how to achieve equivalence of form, called "*Dvekut* with the Creator."

Once a person has been rewarded with the *Kli* called "desire to bestow," he is then rewarded with the Torah, which is the names of the Creator. In the words of *The Zohar*, this discernment is called "613 *Pekudin* [Aramaic: deposits]," which means that in each *Mitzva* [singular of *Mitzvot*], a special light that pertains to that *Mitzva* is deposited. This Torah is discerned as "the names of the Creator."

At that time, a person can obtain the delight and pleasure that exist in the thought of creation, called "His desire to do good to His creations," and then he is rewarded with the discernment of "The Torah, and Israel, and the Creator are one." This is the discernment that one should achieve, as it is written in the book *A Sage's Fruit* (Vol. 1, p 118).

However, the heart of man's work begins when a person wants to observe Torah and *Mitzvot* because of the greatness of the Creator, meaning that he wants to achieve a state where all his actions are in order to bestow. At that time, ascents and descents come to a person, since everything is built on faith above reason. Hence, sometimes the faith shines for him, and sometimes it does not shine. At that time, one must believe that "There is none else besides Him," meaning that "There is no other force in the world but the power of the Creator."

Baal HaSulam said that one must believe that the Creator gives the descents, as well, meaning that he should believe above reason that the Creator hears the prayer of every mouth. That is, both that of an important person, and that of an ordinary person. In other words, even if a person feels that he is an ordinary person, that he lacks Torah and is devoid of strength to work, nevertheless, through prayer, the Creator gives him everything, if he prays for the Creator to bring him closer and wants to serve the King without any reward.

However, what can he do if the body disagrees with this? For this reason, he asks the Creator to take him as a servant who will serve the Creator. And although he has no merits over others, he feels an inner drive that awakens him to be a servant of the King. Yet, he has no control over the body, so he asks of the Creator to help him. This is considered that he believes that the Creator hears the prayer of every mouth.

However, when a person feels a lack and feels his own lowliness, and there is a rule that one cannot live from deficiencies, but rather one can live only from fulfillment, for one can live only where one feels the taste of wholeness, therefore, he was given another way to work, called "right line." In this way, one feels wholeness. But here, when one wants to shift from the "left line," it is something that requires correction, which is called "left" in the work, and correction pertains specifically to when there is corruption. Then it is possible to speak of correction.

Therefore, when a person sees in the left line that he has no control over the body, and he does not want to do anything except for his own benefit, how can he then shift to the right line and be happy that he has wholeness and praise and thank the Creator for bringing him closer to His work? After all, they are two writings that deny one another.

The thing is, as Baal HaSulam said, that in the work of the Creator, there are always contradictions, which are called "right" and "left." This is so in the upper worlds, and they are in contradiction to each other until the third line comes and decides between them, as it is written, "Until the third writing comes and decides between them." He said that in the order of the work there are also contradictions, which extend from the upper roots. On one hand, we see that the writing says, "and his heart was high in the ways of the Lord." On the other hand, our sages said, "Be very, very humble." However, they apply to two times, one by one, and only at the end of the work are they applied at one time. In other words, once he comes to the middle line, it is as our sages said, "There are three partners in a person: the Creator, his father, and his mother. His father gives the white; his mother gives the red; and the Creator gives the soul," for only in the middle line are all of them together.

Therefore, when a person walks on the left line, he should be with pride, as our sages said, "and his heart was high in the ways of the Lord." In other words, he should say what our sages said (Sanhedrin 37), "Therefore, each one must say, 'The world was created for me.'" That is, he should try to achieve the purpose of creation, which is His desire to do good to His creations.

Therefore, he should try that the purpose of creation will come true in him, and before he has achieved the goal, he should be deficient and regret that he has not achieved the wholeness that befits the creature that the Creator created. This is called "left," meaning a lack.

However, what should one do before he has achieved wholeness and he is deficient, since a person cannot live on deficiencies and must receive vitality, and we can receive vitality only from wholeness, as from this a person derives delight and pleasure, from this he can exist. But from the left, it is impossible to live.

At that time, a person should shift to the right line, called "wholeness." Yet, how can one receive wholeness when he sees that he is bare and destitute? From what can he receive wholeness? That is, from what can he receive delight and pleasure in this state?

The answer is that at that time, one should say that he does not see that he is more important than other people, who have no privilege to have desire and yearning for Torah and *Mitzvot*. That is, they do not even have a need for *Lo Lishma* [not for Her sake]. Yet, he sees that the Creator has given him a desire and yearning to do something in Torah and work. Although he does not feel any taste in the work, in terms of the work, he does have the privilege of doing something. The only thing is that his intentions are wrong, but he sees that some grip he does have, whereas to others, the Creator did not give the desire and yearning to do something in Torah and work, and he believes that this is a great thing. Although he still does not feel the importance of the matter, he still believes in this above reason.

Moreover, he sees that there are many people who are happy when they engage in Torah and *Mitzvot*. They are glad and regard secular people as mere beasts, but they have no thought at all about the intention. Therefore, why should he not be as happy as they are, who feel wholeness in their work? Why does he deserve greater wholeness? That is, if he sees that he cannot work in order to bestow, he feels deficient. Who says that he deserves a higher degree than theirs?

It follows that a person must lower himself and say that he does not deserve a higher degree than others, and from this a person can receive wholeness, meaning be happy with the little bit of grip on the work of the Creator that he has. From this he should be happy all day long.

According to the above, we should interpret what we asked, "Why is it written, 'Anyone who extols himself with words of Torah is ultimately brought low, and anyone who lowers himself with words of Torah is ultimately raised high'?" We asked, Why is it forbidden specifically concerning words of Torah, since our sages said, "Be very, very humble," and not necessarily concerning words of Torah?

The answer is that this discusses those who want to walk on the path of the Creator on the path of truth, meaning that all their work will be only in order to bestow. They observe what is written, "And his heart was high in the ways of the Lord," and the "pride" is not that he wants something for his own benefit. Rather, he wants to annul before the Creator, and for himself, he wants to put this desire called "will to receive" to death. He wants to observe what our sages said, "The Torah exists only in one who puts himself to death over it."

It follows that his pride is not for someone who is proud, of whom it was said, "Anyone who is proud, the Creator said, 'I and he cannot dwell in the same abode.'" Rather, here his pride is that he wants to put to death his own will to receive and not be like the rest of the people, caring only for their own sake.

And still, they said that there is a time when he should be in lowliness, meaning be content with little. In other words, he does not need to be a servant of the Creator more than others. Rather, as the general public work in action and does not pay attention to the intention, they settle for this and do everything gladly, each according to the degree that he received by upbringing. Hence, at that time he says, "I, too, 'dwell among my own people,' and I do not need greatness."

Indeed, we should understand this, since it is better that he works on the path toward achieving a state of *Lishma*! The answer is that there is a lot of work before we achieve the degree of *Lishma*. In the meantime, during the work, there are ascents and descents because this work is against nature. When a person sees that he is still not advancing in the path toward achieving the desire to bestow, then he is deficient, and a person cannot receive vitality and joy from deficiencies. Therefore, at that time he is without vitality.

This is called "the work of the left." Hence, a person must shift to the work of the right, where "right" means wholeness. When a person feels that he is in a state of wholeness, from this he can derive joy and vitality and enjoy the work he does for the Creator, and praise and thank the Creator for rewarding him with a little bit of grip on the work of the Creator. Otherwise, one is unable to exist and must fall into a state of sadness.

In a state of sadness, a person cannot work. Rather, he can find all his pleasures in sleep, since when a person is asleep, he feels as though he has escaped from his suffering. Because of it, a person must enter the work of the general public. But afterward, a person enters the work of the left once more, but it should be limited and measured. For most of the time, a person should be in the work of the right until the Creator helps him and gives him the middle line, as was said, that there are three partners in a man: the Creator, his father, and his mother.

According to the above, we should interpret what is written (Numbers 24:7), "Water will flow from his buckets." "Water" is called Torah. "His buckets" comes from the word "bucket," meaning the bucket that is used to draw water. *Dli* [bucket] comes from the word *Dal* [poor], which is poverty, and "there is no poverty except in knowledge."

The verse comes to tell us that one who wants to be rewarded with the Torah, meaning that the Creator will open his eyes in the Torah, should go through many, many states until he is rewarded with the opening of the eyes in the Torah. We should know that it is impossible to be rewarded with the Torah before one is rewarded with *Kelim* that are fit for the Torah.

This is why prior to being rewarded with the 613 *Pekudin*, we must first go through observance of 613 *Eitin*, which are counsels how to acquire the means to qualify oneself to achieve the degree of 613 *Pekudin*. At that time, there is the matter of left line and right line. It is known that the beginning should be in one line, after which we shift to the left line, and then the one line becomes the right line. Then, when the one line becomes the right line, it is hard to walk on one line, meaning to be in joy and vitality from engaging only in action and not reflecting on whether it is in order to bestow.

...Now that the time of work on the left has passed, meaning in a state of pride, as in "His heart was high in the ways of the Lord," when he does not want to be like the general public, but wants to work in the manner of individuals, how can he later lower himself and walk on the path that was previously called "one line," which means that he still did not know that there is another line, but now that he sees that there is the matter of left line, how can he lower himself and take back the way that he left and say, "I am returning to the way I said was suitable for ordinary people and not for me"? Thus, it is difficult for him to return to the way that is now called "right line."

He comes to tell us about this, that a person must return to the state of "poor and meager," as though he has no reason in that he is returning to the way of wholeness, which is now called "right." However, each time, he must return to the left. It follows that by his returning to the state of "right" he becomes poor. And from many *Dal* [poor] and meager, a bucket is made, and the bucket becomes buckets, and from them water will flow, and water is called "Torah."

In other words, through these buckets, he will later be rewarded with the Torah. This is the meaning of the words "Anyone who extols himself with words of Torah is ultimately brought low," since he must lower himself and walk on the right, and anyone who lowers himself and walks on the right is raised and he is rewarded with the Torah.

What Does It Mean that the Right Must Be Greater than the Left, in the Work?

Article No. 39, Tav-Shin-Nun-Aleph, 1990/91

The *Zohar* writes (*Nasso*, Item 174), "This *Mitzva* [commandment/ good deed], that the priest should bless the people each day by pointing out the fingers, since the fingers imply the upper one, the five on the right are more important than those on the left, since the right is more important than the left. Therefore, in the blessing that the priest blesses the people, the right should be raised higher than the left."

We should understand what is "right" in the work, what is "left" in the work, and why the right is more important than the left.

It is known that in the order of man's work, when he wants to achieve *Dvekut* [adhesion] with the Creator, which is equivalence of form, meaning to do everything in order to bestow, we should make two discernments: 1) a state of wholeness, where everything he thinks and does has no deficiency, 2) a state of deficiencies, where everything he thinks and does is full of deficiencies.

We need both of those states. The state of wholeness is in order to receive vitality, joy, and pleasure from his states. When a person feels deficiencies in everything he does, he has nothing to live on, since man was created with a nature that he must receive pleasure as long as he is alive. This stems from the purpose of creation, which is because of "His desire to do good to His creations." (In the words of the ARI, this is called "*Zivug* [coupling] to sustain the worlds," since without vitality the world will be cancelled. Hence, this matter is called "perpetual *Zivug*.") This can be only if a person is content with little and is happy with the share that he has, and says that he does not deserve more than the rest of the people.

In the work, this is considered that he says that he is happy with this share, with the fact the Creator gave him a desire and craving to do something in *Kedusha* [holiness]. In other words, he is happy that he can observe Torah and *Mitzvot* [pl. of *Mitzva*] even without any understanding and without any intention. He says that he sees that there are many people who do not even have the little bit of engagement in Torah and work that he has. As in corporeality, a person who wants to be content with little should look at people who live happily although they do not make even half the income that he does. From this, he can be happy with his share in corporeality.

The same is true for spirituality. He is happy with his share when he sees that there are people who have no grip at all on Torah and *Mitzvot*, while he is happy that he has some grip on Torah and *Mitzvot*. From this he derives vitality, meaning he can glorify and praise the Creator for giving him some grip on Torah and *Mitzvot*. We must remember that the gratitude that a person gives to the Creator, at that time he is in a state of closeness to the Creator because the gratitude that one gives is for the present and the past. It follows that he can be in wholeness.

But when a person prays that He will fulfill his heart's wishes, he should strengthen during the prayer with faith that the Creator hears the prayer of every mouth. Otherwise, his prayer cannot be from the bottom of the heart, since he must believe that the Creator hears every mouth. Baal HaSulam said that during the prayer, one should believe what is written, "For You hear the prayer of every mouth," where "every mouth" means even a mouth that is unworthy, meaning full of deficiencies and devoid of merits, still, the Creator helps everyone, only if a person prays from the bottom of the heart, meaning believes above reason in what is written, that the Creator hears every mouth. Only then can one pray with all his heart, meaning without any doubts.

It follows that when one works in the manner of the "left," meaning looks and sees that he is bare and destitute, and wants the Creator to satisfy his wishes, then it is difficult for a person to believe that the Creator will help him, and he needs great strengthening so he can pray with all his heart. For this reason, a person does not receive vitality from the prayer for deficiencies since he is living in doubt. That is, he sees that he prayed several times, and it is as though the Creator does not hear his prayer. Therefore, it is hard for him to derive vitality from prayer.

But in the manner of the right, when he walks on the path of wholeness and is happy with everything he does, from the privilege he has that the Creator lets him do something in Torah and *Mitzvot*, at that time it is forbidden to look at the deficiencies, since one takes vitality only from wholeness. Therefore, a person must make every effort to see that the Creator is complete with all the virtues and depict to himself every depiction in the world about how He leads the world in utter perfection. As Baal HaSulam said, one should believe above reason that the Creator leads the world in complete delight and pleasure, to a point that there is nothing to add to it. And although a person cannot see this before he achieves the desire to bestow, he should still believe that this is so.

It therefore follows that when one walks on the path of wholeness and thanks the Creator, he already knows if he thanks the Creator because he already has faith in the greatness of the Creator to some extent, and this is why he thanks the Creator, for the Creator summoning a lowly person like himself to serve Him, meaning observe His *Mitzvot*. In other words, he is able to observe something in Torah and *Mitzvot* because the Creator has given him a thought and desire to do something in Torah and *Mitzvot*, and this is considered that the Creator has summoned a person and told him, "I am giving you permission to enter the palace of *Kedusha* [holiness] to do some service for Me."

It follows that a person has no doubt about the gratitude that one gives for the past and for the present. Otherwise, if he does not go completely above reason, he is powerless to thank the Creator. Conversely, a prayer is for the future. At that time, he does not know for sure that the Creator will help him, since he cannot say anything about the future.

It follows that although one should work in the manner of the right, as well as in the manner of the left, and we explained that "right" means wholeness, which should be perpetual, since only from wholeness can one derive vitality, but from wholeness, a person cannot engender a higher level because he has no deficiency. Thus, who says that he should go forward, which is considered that he should engender a higher degree (which is called in the words of the ARI, "a *Zivug* for begetting souls," and this *Zivug* is not permanent but only during an ascent).

In other words, wholeness means that he engages in *Hesed* [mercy/grace], although it is an act without an intention, to him it is important and he is happy with his share, since from this a person receives vitality. (As said above, this is called "a *Zivug* to sustain the worlds," which is *Hassadim* [mercies], in the manner of "For He desires mercy." He does not need anything and he is happy with his share, and this is called "a perpetual *Zivug*.")

However, in order to achieve a higher degree, which is called "a *Zivug* to beget souls," since the meaning of engendering souls can come only from deficiencies and not from wholeness, this is as it is written in *The Zohar*, "He who comes to purify." That is, when a person sees that he is impure, meaning he is lying under the governance of the will to receive, which is the *Tuma'a* [impurity] within man's heart, and he does everything and cannot emerge from the control of the will to receive, at that time he prays to the

Creator from the bottom of the heart to help him. Then what our sages said, "He who comes to purify is aided," comes true. And *The Zohar* asks, "With what?" And he replies, "With a holy soul."

We therefore see that specifically from deficiencies we can beget a soul, meaning from a prayer from the bottom of the heart. By this we can interpret the words of the ARI, that the *Zivug* for engendering the souls is not perpetual but is specifically during an ascent. This means that when a person wants to ascend to a higher degree each time and achieve a higher soul, he must search in himself for a lack to fill. This is specifically when he demands help from the Creator, causing him the birth of new souls. In other words, specifically when he does not settle for less and feels his deficiency, it causes him to be given from above more of a soul until he obtains the NRNHY in his soul.

It follows that the way of the right, meaning wholeness, should be perpetual because a person must do everything with vitality, and from deficiencies, a person has no joy so as to derive vitality from being deficient. For this reason, the left, which is a lack, from which one does not derive vitality, since when a person sees that he is deficient, with what can he be happy? Hence, in general, a person should always be on the right line. Only some of the time he is used to dedicating to Torah and work, he should set a special time, when he is not in descent, but specifically when he is in ascent. At that time he will be sure that he will not fall into a state of sadness when he sees his deficiencies.

Rather, then he will be strengthened; he will be able to give a heartfelt prayer, meaning that the confidence that the Creator hears the prayer of every mouth will illuminate for him during the prayer. But during the rest of the hours of the work, he should walk only on the right path, since on the right path, he is always in wholeness with the Creator. Hence, at that time he receives from the Surrounding Light, as the ARI says, that the Surrounding Light shines from afar. That is, Baal HaSulam said that even when a person is still far from equivalence of form, meaning even when a person has still not been rewarded with the desire to bestow, the Surrounding Light still shines for him, and from this a person receives vitality and joy, whereas with the left, it is to the contrary.

According to the above, we should interpret what is written (Numbers 26:53-54), "Among these the land shall be divided for an inheritance. To the large you shall increase their inheritance, and to the small you shall diminish their inheritance." The interpreters of the Torah ask, If it says, "To the large you shall increase their inheritance," it is obvious that "to the small you shall diminish their inheritance," so why the repetition concerning the small? We should interpret this in the work. In the work, it is known that we learn everything in one person. That is, "to the large you shall increase and to the small you shall diminish" applies to the same person.

We should therefore interpret "large" and "small." "Large" means "whole" and "small" means "deficient." As we learn, the right line is called "wholeness," hence the right line is called "large," as one says, "Any grip that I have on the work," he believes that the Creator has given him the thought and desire to observe Torah and *Mitzvot*, and he says that he is not more important than the rest of the people. Rather, as before he began to work on the left line, he had vitality and pleasure in the work that he did, he knew that it was very important and he would certainly receive a great reward for this, so now that he has begun to walk on the left line, he should be in a state of humbleness, as it is written, "Be very, very humble." In other words, even after he has begun to walk on the left line, to see his deficiencies, which the left line shows him, which he received from the state of "His heart was high in the ways of the Lord," but now that he is working in the state of the right, when he should lower himself, this is a lot of work because they are called "two writings that deny one another," and this was not so when he was walking on one line.

Yet, such are the ways of the Creator. A person should believe in the sages that such is the order of the work. It follows that there is a huge difference in the work between his work being in the right or being in one line. But according to what we learn, we need two lines. Both cannot be at the same time in the same subject. Rather, they can be one at a time.

Now the question will be that if we need two lines, and we must dedicate some time to the right, and some time to the left, the question is how much of one's work should he dedicate to walking on the right line, and how much time should he dedicate to walking on the left line.

According to the above said, we should interpret what is written, "To the large you shall increase their inheritance." "Large" means work that is called "wholeness" and "right line," which is called "large," meaning wholeness. "You shall increase their inheritance" means that you will increase the time you dedicate to the right line, giving much of your time of engagement in Torah and *Mitzvot*.

When it says "and to the small, you shall diminish their inheritance," "to diminish" means to lessen, a deficiency called "left line," where one begins to contemplate what he has gained when he left the one line and began the work of bestowal. He sees that not only did he not advance in the work, but he even regressed. That is, now he does not have the vitality and joy he had while walking on one line. Although he prays to the Creator to give him the power of the desire to bestow, he sees that he has prayed many prayers for this but he is not being noticed from above, so many times he wants to escape the campaign. Although the work on the left line is important, for the birth of souls comes specifically from the left line, we must still believe in faith in the sages that we can engage in the left line precisely at a time of ascent, for then a person is strong and can overcome the left through prayer. But only for a little while, as it is written, "To the small you shall diminish their inheritance," where "diminish" means that you will not dedicate to it much of your work time.

It follows that the word "small" has two meanings: 1) "small" as in "deficient," such as when saying, this person has little income, 2) little time.

It follows that when it writes, "to the small you shall diminish," and "diminish" means a lack. Diminishing in the work of bestowal and "diminish" is diminishing in time. Accordingly, we should interpret what it means that the right should be greater than the left in the work, and also what it means that *The Zohar* says that "when the priest blesses the people, he should raise the right higher than the left." We should interpret that "right" indicates wholeness, which is *Hesed*. *Hesed* means that he does not need anything except to give. Therefore, when a person feels his lowliness and says that the Creator is doing *Hesed* with him by giving him some grip on Torah and work, he thanks the Creator for this.

Therefore, when we speak in the work about the priest who blesses the people, since all matters pertain to the same person, the "priest" is a servant of the Creator. He "blesses the people," meaning the person himself, called "the people," in the work. It is as our sages said (Sanhedrin 37), "Therefore, each one must say, 'The world was created for me.'" For this reason, in the work we learn the whole world within one person. "He must raise the right higher than the left," in order to know that the right is more important than the left, although from the left we are rewarded with the birth of new souls.

Yet, when a person engages in deficiencies, he cannot receive from this vitality. For this reason, he must work on the right, as well. *The Zohar* comes to tell us that we should dedicate the majority of our time to the right. This is why he says that "the priest must raise the right above the left," since the right is more important. And in *The Zohar* (*Pekudei*, Item 683), he says, "The most important is that the left will not be greater than the right." This is the meaning of what our sages said (*Yevamot* 63), "One of inferior degree receives a woman" (a person should descend from his degree in order to receive a wife).

There, he speaks in the manner of degrees in the upper worlds. As above, in the upper degrees, so it is below, in man's work, even before one is rewarded with opening the eyes in the Torah. There the meaning of "left" is when the light of *Hochma* shines, which is in vessels of reception. Certainly, this should be in order to bestow, and he still did not receive the right, which is light of *Hassadim*. It is called "left" because everything where there is a deficiency is called "left."

What Does It Mean that the Right Must Be Greater than the Left?

At that time, the path of correction is that the light of Hassadim, called "right," should be greater than the light of *Hochma*. That is, the light of *Hochma* must not take more than half a degree, and the light of *Hassadim*, which is "right" which guards the light of *Hochma* so it stays in order to bestow, should be greater than the light of *Hochma*. At that time, the light of *Hochma* exists in the degree, and this is the meaning of the priest, when he blesses, should raise the right above the left, meaning that the *Hesed* should be more important than the left.

This is the meaning of what is written, "This is the meaning of 'one who is of inferior degree receives a woman.'" It means that when a person comes to receive the light of *Hochma*, which is *Malchut*, where *Malchut* is called "bottom *Hochma*," he should not take her in her state of *Gadlut* [greatness/adulthood]. Rather "inferior degree," meaning when one comes to receive the light of *Hochma*, called "woman," which is *Malchut*, one should try that she will already be in a state of descent, meaning that she has only half of what she had. At that time he can receive *Hassadim*, and the *Hassadim* will be more than the *Hochma*. Then the words *"One of inferior degree receives a woman"* will come true.

According to the above-said, we should interpret what is written (Sanhedrin 44b), "Rabbi Elazar said, 'One should always precede prayer to trouble.'" We should interpret that one does not go into the work of the left before he first worked in the manner of the right, which is regarded as wholeness, meaning that he does not lack anything and he thanks and praises the Creator for giving him some grip on the work of the Creator, and then he begins the work of the left. At that time, he sees that he is in trouble, that he has neither Torah nor work that is suitable for one who is serving the Creator. At that time, he feels how far he is from the work of the Creator, meaning from working for Him, namely working only with the aim to bestow contentment upon his Maker, and not at all for his own benefit. At that time, he sees how the body objects to this, and he does not see that he will ever be able to do anything only in order to bestow.

It follows that when he begins the path of the left, this is called "trouble," and he has no other choice but to pray to the Creator to help him and give him the desire to bestow, called "second nature." At that time, the prayer is from the bottom of the heart, and the Creator hears his prayer.

Accordingly, we should interpret what our sages said, "One should always precede prayer to trouble," since it is possible that when he comes to work in the state of the left and sees the state of lowliness that he is in, he might fall into despair and want to escape the campaign. This is called "trouble," and he must precede with a prayer, meaning first see if he will have the strength to pray when he is in a state of trouble. Otherwise, he must not begin the work of the left line. This is the meaning of what they said, that the "priest who blesses the people should raise the right higher than the left." In other words, the right should be greater than the left. This means that he must wait for the right time to exit from the work of the right to the work of the left.

We must remember that the work of the right, which is called "wholeness," is the work of the general public. It is work in practice, meaning he observes Torah and *Mitzvot* because of the commandment of the Creator and in order to receive reward in this world and in the next world. This is called "work in practice." But the intention to bestow, which is called "the work of the left," this he does not touch. Hence, a person feels wholeness during the work.

This work of wholeness is called "one line." That same work of wholeness of the general public, when he begins to work with the intention, that same one line, meaning the practice of the general public, acquires a different name: Now it is called "right line." Hence, it is now difficult to shift to work on the line of wholeness of the practice when it receives a new name, "right."

What Are Truth and Falsehood in the Work?

Article No. 40, Tav-Shin-Nun-Aleph, 1990/91

We should understand how truth and falsehood pertain to the work of the Creator. This implies that one can be a servant of the Creator even though it is a lie. How can such a thing be said?

It is written in *The Zohar* ("Introduction of The Book of Zohar," Item 175), "The share of the Creator is to delight the poor, for on these days, the holidays, the Creator comes to see His broken *Kelim* [vessels], and sees that they have nothing with which to rejoice. He weeps for them."

He interprets these words in the *Sulam* [Ladder commentary on *The Zohar*] as follows: First we need to understand the interpretation of our sages (*Midrash Rabbah*, Portion 6), that at the time of the creation of the world, when He said to the angels, "Let us make man in our image," *Hesed* [mercy] said, "Let him be created, for he does *Hassadim* [mercies]; Truth said, "Let him not be created, for he is all lies"; *Tzedek* [justice] said, "Let him be created, for he does righteousness"; Peace said, "Let him not be created, for he is all strife." What did the Creator do? He took Truth, and cast it to the earth.

We know the words of our sages, "One should always engage in Torah and *Mitzvot* [commandments/good deeds], even if *Lo Lishma* [not for Her sake], since from *Lo Lishma* he comes to *Lishma* [for Her sake]." Because of his lowliness, a person cannot engage in His *Mitzvot* right away in order to bring contentment to his Maker. By nature, he cannot make a move if not for his own sake. Hence, first he must engage in *Mitzvot Lo Lishma*, meaning out of self-benefit. However, he still draws abundance of *Kedusha* [holiness] while performing the *Mitzvot*, and through the abundance that he draws, he will eventually come to engage in *Mitzvot Lishma*.

Truth complained about the creation of man, saying "He is all lies," etc., how can such a man be created, who from the beginning engages in Torah and *Mitzvot* in complete falsehood, meaning *Lo Lishma*? But *Hesed* said, "Let him be created, for he does mercies," etc., by which he will gradually be corrected until he can engage in all the *Mitzvot* in order to bestow. Likewise, Peace complained that "He is all strife," but *Tzedek* said, "Let him be created" because through the *Mitzva* [singular of *Mitzvot*] of charity to the poor that he does, he will gradually approach the quality of bestowal until he comes to engage *Lishma*. Once all of their arguments were heard, the Creator agreed with the angels *Hesed* and *Tzedakah*, and threw Truth to the ground, meaning permitted engaging in *Mitzvot* initially in *Lo Lishma*, for even though it is a lie, it will eventually become *Lishma*, and then Truth will rise up from the earth.

Maimonides says there (*Hilchot Teshuva*, Chapter 5), "Therefore, when teaching little ones, women, and uneducated people, they are taught to work only out of fear and in order to receive reward. Until they gain much knowledge and acquire much wisdom, they are taught that secret little-by-little."

From the words of Maimonides, we see that we must begin the work of the Creator in *Lo Lishma*, and we must not even reveal that there is such a matter as *Lishma* to them. Rather, they must know that they're observing Torah and *Mitzvot* in order to receive reward is real wholeness, and there is nothing to add to this, other than in quantity, meaning to dedicate more time and effort to observe

Torah and *Mitzvot*. They should be happy that by observing Torah and *Mitzvot* they will have plentiful reward.

It follows that in order for them to be complete servants of the Creator, they must not know that there is the matter of *Lishma*, since they are still not ready to begin to work *Lishma*. Hence, should they be told that the main work is *Lishma*, they will say, "How can we observe Torah and *Mitzvot Lo Lishma* if this is not the real work?" And since they still cannot work *Lishma*, they will remain empty handed both ways.

In other words, *Lo Lishma* will not be important to them, and they will see that they cannot work *Lishma*. For this reason, it is forbidden to reveal to them that there is a matter that we must work in order to bestow. But when they do not know, they think that they are true servants of the Creator and that they are righteous. Hence, from this they will have strength to work, since they are happy that they are servants of the Creator, and they consider other people, who do not observe Torah and *Mitzvot* as they do, as beasts and animals, and that they have no more brains than that of beasts and animals.

Concerning the scrutinies, he wrote in *Tree of Life* (presented in *Beit Shaar HaKavanot*, Item 107): "The Creator gave the Torah and *Mitzvot* to Israel only in order to sort, cleanse, and remove the dross from the silver, which is the dressing for the soul. Through man's intention in Torah and *Mitzvot*, the clothing of the soul is completed. Through the Torah, *Noga* of *Yetzira* is cleansed, a clothing of *Ruach*, and through practical *Mitzvot*, *Noga* of *Assiya* is cleansed, and becomes a clothing of *Nefesh*."

This means that we cannot say that the performance of *Mitzvot* and Torah without an intention are not true. Rather, it is implied from the words of the ARI that through all of man's actions, the scrutinies of *Kedusha* are sorted out of the *Klipot* [shells/peels], to which they descended at the time of the breaking of the vessels. However, we should distinguish between *Mitzvot* without an intention and Torah without an intention, and between Torah and *Mitzvot* with an intention, as was said, "and through the practical *Mitzvot*, *Noga* of *Assiya* is cleansed and becomes a clothing for the *Nefesh*."

Concerning *Lo Lishma*, which is called "a lie," we should interpret that since the purpose of creation is to do good to His creations, and in order for man to obtain this in practice, meaning to see that the delight and pleasure are revealed in the world, the creatures cannot see this before they have the real *Kelim* by which to see the delight and pleasure revealed in the world.

Therefore, to the creatures, it is still not revealed that the purpose of creation is really to do good to His creations, since they see that they are suffering torments in the world, each in his own way. Thus, we can interpret that as long as the creatures observe Torah and *Mitzvot* not with the aim to bestow, they are unable to see the truth that there is in the purpose of creation—to do good.

Therefore, this means that concerning those who observe Torah and *Mitzvot* and have not been rewarded with aiming to bestow, although in truth scrutinies were made for the *Kedusha* by observing Torah and *Mitzvot* even if without the intention, meaning that the *Kedusha* increases through their actions, this is only with respect to the existence of *Kedusha*. Nevertheless, the creatures are still unable to see what happens through their actions, meaning what corrections are done by their work even if *Lo Lishma*.

It follows that when we speak of falsehood, that we say that *Lo Lishma* is called "a lie," it is with respect to the creatures. That is, they are still unable to see the truth about observing Torah and *Mitzvot* without the intention. But in truth, corrections and scrutinies are made in *Kedusha*.

We must believe the words of the ARI that each and every act in Torah and *Mitzvot* makes corrections to such an extent that we should ask, concerning what we see, that the rule is that if a person can make his neighbor not desecrate the Shabbat [Sabbath], if for example, the neighbor needs his help, and because of it the neighbor will observe Shabbat, then a person must act so he will not desecrate the Shabbat.

What Are Truth and Falsehood in the Work?

We should ask, But if there is no intention here to observe the Shabbat, and he observes the commandment that his friend imposes on him, so what good can emerge from such work? However, every single act we do, even without an intention, does its thing. That is, it makes scrutinies for *Kedusha*, except the creatures still cannot see the corrections because they might blemish, since they are still under the governance of the will to receive.

For this reason, before he sees the corrections that are done by him, he still cannot receive from the abundance that is revealed through his actions. Hence, when they do not see the abundance that is revealed, they cannot blemish since they do not see that there is something to receive. However, one must believe that each and every act in Torah and work is important, and so he must believe.

Only after one is rewarded with receiving the second nature, called "desire to bestow," he will be rewarded with seeing the truth, that the purpose of creation is to do good to His creations. It follows that when we say that *Lo Lishma* is called "a lie," it is from man's perspective, for man still does not see that the purpose of creation is to do good to His creations.

Accordingly, we can understand why *Lishma* is called "truth," since by being rewarded with *Lishma*, a person should achieve the degree of "love of the Creator," by His behavior with the person himself. That is, when a person receives abundance from the Creator, he sees the truth, that the purpose of creation is to do good to His creations. Moreover, a person should be rewarded with seeing that Providence behaves with all creations in a manner of good and doing good.

This is a great degree, when a person sees how the Creator behaves with him in person in a manner of good and doing good. However, a person must see that the Creator behaves this way with all creations—in a manner of good and doing good. Because of this, *Lishma* is called "truth," for by work in the state of *Lishma*, a person is rewarded with seeing the truth, that the Creator behaves with all creations in a manner of good and doing good.

This is as it is written in the "Introduction to The Study of the Ten Sefirot" (Item 97): "For this reason, our sages warned us concerning the necessary condition in the practice of Torah, that it will be specifically *Lishma*, in a way that one will be awarded life through it, for it is a Torah of life, and set his mind and heart to find 'the light of the King's face' in it, that is, the attainment of open Providence, called 'light of the face.'"

In other words, as long as one has not been rewarded with *Lishma*, he is in concealment of the face, meaning that he still does not see how the Creator leads the world as The Good Who Does Good. It follows that he is in a state of falsehood. That is, when he says what they said, that the purpose of creation is to do good to His creations, it is a lie, since we see the opposite.

But one who learns Torah *Lishma* is rewarded with seeing the truth because he himself has been rewarded with seeing the delight and pleasure he is receiving from the Creator. Moreover, he must come to a state of wholeness and see how the Creator behaves with the whole world with the purpose of doing good to His creations. It follows that truth and falsehood pertain to the attainment of the person himself. Accordingly, it follows that one who learns Torah *Lo Lishma*, which is considered a lie, is only because he is unfit to see the truth, that the Creator leads the world in a manner of good and doing good.

This is as the ARI says, that all of man's actions in *Kedusha* make corrections, but a person still cannot see what is done with the Torah and *Mitzvot* that the creatures do even without the intention, meaning even in *Lo Lishma*, but for their own sake. For this reason, Maimonides says that we must begin the order of the work with children and women in order to receive reward, since the performance of *Mitzvot* in themselves make corrections.

Baal HaSulam said about what our sages said (*Avot*, Chapter 3:18), "Israel are beloved, for they are called 'The children of the Creator.' They are greatly favored, for they are called 'The children of the Creator,' as was said, 'You are the children of the Lord your God.'

He said that being called 'The children of the Creator' is in general, but being greatly favored is in person. He asks, what is being 'greatly favored'? He replied, 'The great favor is in that it is known to them, meaning that they know and feel that they are called 'The children of the Creator.'"

Here we can interpret similarly. That is, in terms of the action without the intention to bestow, called *Lo Lishma*, the people of Israel are called "children of the Creator," because they engage in Torah and *Mitzvot* in practice, this, too, makes great corrections, as the ARI said. However, it is not known to them. In other words, they cannot see what corrections are done by their work.

Conversely, after they are rewarded with *Lishma*, it becomes known to them what they are doing. This is as it is written, "Rabbi Meir says, 'Anyone who engages in Torah *Lishma* is rewarded with many things. Moreover, the whole world is worthwhile for him, and the secrets of Torah are revealed to him.'"

We should interpret that "the whole world is worthwhile for him" means that he already see the truth about the purpose of creation, that it is to do good to His creations. The evidence of this is that at that time, he sees that "the whole world is worthwhile for him," since he feels the delight and pleasure.

Also, we should interpret the meaning of "the secrets of Torah are revealed to him." This means that he is rewarded with seeing how through his work in Torah and *Mitzvot*, corrections are done above. But before he is rewarded with engaging in Torah and *Mitzvot Lishma*, although corrections are done through his work in Torah and *Mitzvot*, he cannot see it before he is rewarded with vessels of bestowal.

Accordingly, we should interpret what our sages said (*Avot* 1:17), "It is not the learning that is the most important, but the work." Here before us are two things: 1) actions, 2) intentions.

On one hand, we understand that the intention matters most. In other words, when a person does something, good or bad, we should regard the intention, not the act. For example, in a conflict between two people, one took a knife and stabbed the other. Of course, this is a bad deed. The victim sued him and the offender was fined for it.

The offender claimed, "I only stabbed this man in the hand, and I only scratched him, but I have to pay him a fine. And yet, I saw that not long ago, this man went into a hospital and a doctor cut open his stomach and took something out, and he paid the doctor a lot of money. And I, for the tiny cut I caused him, I have to pay him, the opposite of what happened with that doctor?!"

"The answer is simple," said the judge. "We follow the intention. Since you stabbed him because you wanted to enjoy, you have to pay for the pleasure you had. But when the surgeon cut his flesh with a knife, he wanted the patient to enjoy. Therefore, the patient should pay the doctor." We therefore see that what counts is the aim and not the act. Thus, why did our sages say, "It is not the learning that matters most, but the action"?

In spirituality, concerning Torah and *Mitzvot*, the work matters most, as in the words of the ARI, that through performance of *Mitzvot*, scrutinies of holy sparks are sorted out of the *Klipot* [shells/peels]. However, a person cannot see this before he has vessels of bestowal, or he will see what is done with his work and it will go to his vessels of reception, and he will send it all back to the *Klipot*. It follows that the work is what matters most.

But if he can make the intention in order to bestow, as well, then through the intention that lies over the action he ascends to a higher degree, as was said above, "Through man's intention in Torah and *Mitzvot*, the clothing of the soul is completed. Through the Torah, *Noga* of *Yetzira* is cleansed, a clothing of *Ruach*, and through practical *Mitzvot*, *Noga* of *Assiya* is cleansed, and becomes a clothing of *Nefesh*."

For this reason, the act is what matters most, and to the act, we must also add the intention. We must believe that as far as branch and root go, all the corporeal things that happen here derive from upper roots. That is, as corporeal actions correct the body, and without them the body cannot exist, it is likewise in matters of the soul: Without performance of Torah and Mitzvot, there is no nourishment to the soul so it can exist.

This is as presented in the book Beit Shaar HaKavanot (Item 83), "Know that in Adam HaRishon, all the scrutinies of all the worlds and all the souls were sorted, and all the beasts were sorted. But the still and vegetative were not fully sorted; this is why they eat, in order to sort them. When they sinned, the souls and beasts returned to the depth of the Klipot, and only the pure beasts are sorted through our eating, and likewise the still and vegetative."

It therefore follows that specifically through our eating in practice, the still, vegetative, and animate are sorted, and all we need is to add to it the aim. But without the act, the aim does not help. Therefore, we should not say, "Why put Tefillin if the intention is what matters? He can aim the intention of the Tefillin and does not need to observe in practice." However, the act is the main thing, and the aim is the addition.

Therefore, as in corporeality, if a person makes the aim of eating or the aim of drinking, but does not eat or drink in practice, he will die. Likewise, if a person does not observe Torah and Mitzvot in practice, his soul, which receives its nourishment from the work in Torah and Mitzvot, will have nothing on which to live.

This is the meaning of "It is not the learning that matters most, but the action," meaning an actual act, in practice. Afterward, as an addition, we also need an aim over the actions that a person does. This is regarded as "still of Kedusha [holiness]." From the still, we can arrive at the state of vegetative, animate, and speaking.

According to the above, we can understand what is said above concerning the Creator coming to see His broken Kelim, for in the end, he will achieve Lishma and Truth will rise up from the earth. He says there (p 173 [in Hebrew]), "This is the meaning of the breaking of the vessels that occurred prior to the creation of the world. Through the breaking of the vessels of Kedusha and their fall to the separated BYA, sparks of Kedusha fell with them to the Klipot, and from them come the pleasures and all sorts of penchants into the domain of the *Klipot*, which they pass on for man to receive and enjoy, and thereby cause every kind of transgression. However, along with it, He gave us Torah and *Mitzvot*, so that even if one begins to engage in them while still in *Lo Lishma*, meaning for one's own pleasure, to satisfy his lowly lusts, in the end, through them he will achieve *Lishma* and will be rewarded with the purpose of creation, to receive all the pleasantness and good in the thought of creation, in order to bestow contentment upon Him."

We should remember the rule in the order of the work, that one need not examine himself to see if he is fine or not. That is, if a person sees that he is not alright, this is the time when he should pray to the Creator to help him be fine. This is specifically when one feels that he has some closeness to the Creator. At that time, he is permitted to regard his situation with criticism. But when a person feels that he is removed from the work, meaning that he does not have a desire for the work, at that time he must not examine himself and pray. Rather, he must pay attention and say, "Whatever grip I have on the work, I am happy with it, and I thank the Creator for it." But at that time, he should not pray to the Creator to bring him closer. And concerning the prayer that he should pray to the Creator to bring him closer, this should be specifically when he has some ascent in the work.

This is as it is written in *The Zohar* (*VaEra*, Item 102), "Come and see, in the day, he engaged in Torah to complement the judgments, and at night he engaged in singing and praising until the day came because all through the day he engaged in complementing and scrutinizing the judgments, which are 'left.' At night, he engaged in praises, which are *Hassadim*."

Hence, the above explanation is that specifically during the "day," meaning during an ascent, he engaged in the left, to sort the judgments. But at "night," when it does not illuminate, he engages in praises.

What Should One Do If He Was Born With Bad Qualities?

Article No. 41, Tav-Shin-Nun-Aleph, 1990/91

It is written in *The Zohar* (*Nasso* 41), "One's actions reflect the *Partzuf* that is on him, which is why he says that their countenance testified to the form that was on them, or from the *Merkava* [chariot/structure] of the four elements of the world, which are fire, wind, water, and dust (FWWD), in which there are neither the good inclination nor the evil inclination. Rather, they are like the beasts of the world."

This means that the merging of the body engenders in a person the qualities, and this does not pertain to the evil inclination. For example, if one has more of the "water" element, he is lustful. If he has more of the "fire" element, he is petulant. If he has more of the "wind" element, he is arrogant, and if he has more of the "dust" element, he is lazy. But this has nothing to do with the evil inclination. This means that all the qualities that exist in a person that extend from the four qualities FWWD have nothing to do with the evil inclination.

The question is, What is the evil inclination? We should say about this that the evil inclination is what tempts a person to do things against the will of the Creator. A person must first believe in the Creator, and then it is possible to say that he is doing things against the will of the Creator, and then he begins to sin because of the evil inclination and does not want to obey the Creator, who gave Torah to His people, Israel.

Rather, the only reason they are (who do not achieve faith in the Creator) harming others is because of the merging of the four elements, as said in the words of *The Zohar*, which says, "of the four elements, in which there are neither the good inclination nor the evil inclination. Rather, they are like the beasts of the world," in whom there is no connection to faith in the Creator. But for man, where there is the matter of faith, there begins the matter of the evil inclination, when he does not believe in the Creator, and the good inclination is when he does believe in the Creator. That is, one who believes in the Creator, meaning believes in reward and punishment, in him begins the work of the evil inclination and the good inclination. But those who have no interest in faith in the Creator are as beasts.

Yet, we have to say what *The Zohar* says, that they belong to the four elements and have no connection to the evil inclination or the good inclination. This is with respect to the work. But with respect to the revealed, meaning to the rules, they are subject to every punishment and judgment that the courthouses impose upon them, for there one cannot say, "I have no evil inclination and I do not deserve to be punished," and to say that he comes from the four elements.

We must say that *The Zohar* speaks from the perspective of the work and not from the perspective of the revealed Torah, where it speaks in terms of actual practice. Rather, *The Zohar* speaks from the order of the work, where it can be said that a person belongs to the four elements but still has no connection to the evil inclination, since in the work, we begin to speak of the evil inclination from the time when a person begins to believe in the Creator. At that time, we speak of the good inclination or the evil inclination.

What Should One Do If He Was Born With Bad Qualities?

However, concerning faith in reward and punishment, we should also make two discernments: 1) Reward and punishment that are interpreted that if he walks on the straight path, he will receive in return a reward that he will be happy in this world and will also be happy in the next world. And if he does not walk on the straight path, he will be unhappy. 2) Reward and punishment that are interpreted that if he walks on the straight path, as the sages have arranged for us, and will believe in their words, then the reward will be that they draw near to the Creator. Conversely, if they do not believe in the sages, who determined for us how to walk in the ways of the Creator, they will be punished. The punishment is that they will be far from the Creator and will not be given help to draw near the Creator. That is, their reward will be that they will be given from above a desire to bestow, which is a second nature, and their punishment will be that they will remain immersed in self-love and will ache because they are not advancing.

This is considered that they are "placed under the governance of the evil inclination," that they are separated from the Creator and cannot bond with Him, and it hurts them that they are placed under the governance of evil. That is, we cannot say that a person is punished but he does not feel that he is punished, meaning does not suffer from being under the governance of evil.

Rather, "punishment" means that he suffers because he is under the control of the evil inclination, meaning he feels that it is bad through suffering. This is regarded as a person being "placed under the governance of the evil inclination," meaning that it hurts him. Conversely, those who are placed under the governance of the evil inclination but do not suffer, in terms of the work, this is considered that they still do not have the evil inclination, that they still do not feel that they are placed under the governance of the will to receive, called "evil."

However, we must understand, if, according to the merging of the body, a person is incapable of doing good and must exert more than other people to do good, how does it help us that *The Zohar* says that the bad he does is like a beast? What is the advice that he would be able to do good? That is, what would help him to later obtain the good inclination and the evil inclination?

Our sages said (*Rosh Hashanah* [beginning of Jewish new year] 17), "The eyes of the Lord your God are on her, at times for better, at times for worse. At times for better—how? If Israel are complete wicked in the beginning of the year and are allotted few rains, but in the end they repent, it is impossible to add to them because the sentence has been given. Instead, the Creator pours them down in time on a soil that needs them, all according to the soil." (RASHI interprets "the soil that needs them"—the fields and vineyards and gardens.) "At times for worse, how? If Israel are complete righteous in the beginning of the year, they are allotted many rains, but in the end, they move astray. It is impossible to lessen them, since the decree has already been given, but the Creator pours them down not in their time, on soil that does not need them. (RASHI interprets "not in their time"—before sowing, and "on soil that does not need them"—in forests and deserts.)

We should understand what this matter comes to teach us in the work. According to what *The Zohar* says, there are people who were created according to a merging of the four elements and have no connection to the good inclination or the evil inclination, but are like the beasts of the world. This means that good inclination and evil inclination mean that there is the matter of choice, where one can overcome the evil. But in the quality of "beasts," it means that the qualities they have cannot be changed. Thus, what should one do if he were born with bad qualities and his nature cannot be changed? How can he have choice, which is the work of overcoming of the good inclination over the evil inclination?

According to the above, we should interpret that although one is born with bad qualities in which there is little good, when he walks on the straight path, meaning asks the Creator to help him overcome the bad, although the bad within him is bigger than in the rest of the people, and it is impossible to change nature, the Creator gives him the strength to use his qualities, in which there is little good. However, whatever good he does have works within him, meaning that the Creator helps him from above so that whatever powers he does have, he uses them in the right place.

For example, if he has stamina to learn only one hour, he learns specifically in books that bring him the light of Torah, meaning that through them he acquires the importance of the work of the Creator and receives an awakening that it is worthwhile to cling to the Creator. And when there is a little bit of thinking concerning work, he does not think, "What will I get out of this work?" Rather, he thinks, "What can I give to the King so I will connect with Him?" When he prays, since he knows that he is not gifted and cannot think great and profound thoughts, when he prays, he simply imagines to Whom he prays, meaning with Whom he speaks and what he asks of Him to give him. He says, "I know my lowliness, that I am worse than the rest of the people, so the rest of the people can overcome their evil and do not need Your help so much, whereas I have neither power nor brains, so have mercy on me." Because he prays from the bottom of the heart, the Creator hears his prayer. Hence, he uses all of his small powers in the right place and at the right time.

But if a person is sentenced through the four elements to have good qualities and virtues, yet he is not rewarded, meaning he does not walk on the straight path—to ask the Creator to help him walk on the right path, his gifts are used in a place where they are not needed. That is, all the powers and talents go to a place that will not yield anything in spirituality with respect to the work, as it is written, "not in their time, before the sowing." In other words, his work, despite the great effort and depth he puts into it, will not yield anything. This is the meaning of "on a land that does not need them—in forest and deserts." This means that all the powers and gifts and all the good qualities are used in a place that will not grow, meaning that will not lead him to *Dvekut* [adhesion] with the Creator. In other words, he will not trouble himself to find the right guide and will not pay attention to learn specifically in books that lead to nearing to the Creator.

It follows that the fact that man was created from four elements has no connection to the evil inclination or the good inclination.

But afterward, when he begins the work and wants to draw near the Creator, then begins the matter of the evil inclination, when a person begins to see that there is evil in him and it pains him. Then, when he sees that he has no good qualities, he prays to the Creator to help him. At that time, the Creator summons all his powers and the little bit of talent that he has. The Creator assembles everything and concentrates all the powers that he can, so it will all be in order to achieve *Dvekut* with the Creator.

It follows that although it is said that man's character does not change, through the evil inclination, when a person begins to work and sees that he suffers from being removed from the Creator, through prayer, when one prays to the Creator and believes what is written, "for You hear the prayer of every mouth," meaning even a mouth that comes from a person who is not gifted and is powerless to overcome, and also has bad qualities, and he is worse than the rest of the people, and this comes to him because he was created from the four elements (fire, wind, water, and dust), and according to the merger of the four elements in his body, he has bad qualities. It follows that he has nothing to add to this.

Yet, when one begins to work in Torah and *Mitzvot* [commandments/good deeds], it causes him to know that there is the matter of the good inclination and the evil inclination, as he writes in the *Sulam* [Ladder commentary on *The Zohar*] (*Beresheet Bet*, Item 103), "If one engages in Torah and *Mitzvot* even for his own pleasure, through the light in it he will still feel the lowliness and the terrible corruptness in the nature of receiving for oneself. At that time he will resolve to retire from that nature of reception and completely devote himself to working only in order to bestow contentment upon his Maker. Then the Creator will open his eyes to see before him a world filled with utter perfection without any deficiencies whatsoever."

According to the above, we see that although a person is born with the four elements and has no connection neither to the good inclination nor to the evil inclination, and he is like the beasts of the world, and these qualities cannot be changed, still, through engagement in Torah and *Mitzvot*, he comes to know and feel that there is the matter of good inclination and evil inclination, and then he can pray to the Creator to help him emerge from the control of the evil inclination. At that time, one concentrates on using all of one's powers in the right place. That is, whatever forces he has, it is enough for him to use to an extent that will be able to give him the ability to achieve *Dvekut* with the Creator.

This is the meaning of "At times for better—how? If Israel are complete wicked in the beginning of the year and are allotted few rains." We should interpret that when he is born, he has bad qualities in terms of the merger of the body. This is considered that they were "allotted few rains." "Rains" are the power that yields fruits, called "fuel [or motivation]" in the work. It is written, "In the end they repent, it is impossible to add to them because the sentence has been given." This means that they were already born with the merger of the body in the four elements, but "the Creator pours them down in time on a soil that needs them." That is, the rains, which are the fuel, the powers with which we work, are concentrated so as to be used only for what is required.

Let us take "fire," for example. On one hand, man enjoys the fire. When man has fire, he can cook, he can use it to light up the darkness, and it can warm him in the winter. Therefore, essentially, we can say that fire came to the world in order to correct it. On the other hand, if a person is not careful and misuses it, this fire brings destruction and ruin to the world, for through it, man sometimes becomes poor and indigent, even if previously, he was very wealthy. Sometimes, fire brings death to the world.

Likewise, in the work, man's powers can bring correction to the world. If one uses the powers according to the order of correction, the forces bring delight to the world. As said above, if a person walks on the path of correction, the little powers he has are enough for him to achieve his completion. We see that even something that can harm the world, if we use this power, called "fire," for example, in a manner of correction, the whole world benefits from it.

It is likewise in the work: When the Creator gives the required help, the power of the fuel called "rains" is enough for him to bear fruit, as there is a rule in *Kedusha* [holiness], that a person should bear fruit in the work, whereas concerning the *Sitra Achra* [other side], it is called "Another god is sterile and does not bear fruit."

According to the above, we should interpret what our sages said (*Nidah* 16b), "Rabbi Hanina Bar Papa says, 'That angel appointed over pregnancy is called *Laila* [Hebrew: night]. It takes a drop and places it before the Creator and says to Him: 'Master of the world, what shall become of this drop? Will it be a mighty one or a weakling, a wise one or a fool, rich or poor?' But 'wicked or righteous' it did not say. It is as Rabbi Hanina said, 'Everything is in the hands of heaven except for fear of heaven.'"

Baal HaSulam asked about this, If this drop is sentenced to be a fool, how can there also be a choice for the better afterward? After all, there is a rule that one does not sin unless a spirit of folly has entered him. Thus, how can one choose the good, since he is born with a spirit of folly, so how can he keep himself from transgressing when the spirit of folly is within him?

According to what we explained concerning man, when he is born according to the merger of four elements, for which he has bad qualities, but it is not connected to the evil inclination or the good inclination, but he is like the beasts of the world, yet by engaging in Torah and *Mitzvot* even for his own benefit, through the light in it, he will feel the lowliness and terrible corruption that there are in the nature of receiving for oneself. At that time he will resolve to completely devote himself to working only in order to bestow contentment upon his Maker, and then the Creator will open his eyes.

Also, we should interpret here that although the drop is sentenced to be a fool, by engaging in Torah *Lo Lishma* [not for Her sake], the light in it will reform him. That is, the light in Torah *Lo Lishma* can shine for him so he will feel the bad in him. That is, although there is a rule that a fool does not feel, for how can one who was born from a drop that was sentenced to be a fool feel the difference between good or bad, this is so from the perspective of the birth itself, from the angle of the drop, that it was sentenced to be a fool. At that time, he is considered "a fool does not feel." But through the light of the Torah, he receives the feeling of good or bad to such an extent that through the recognition of the bad, which he received through the light of Torah, he is then rewarded with opening the eyes.

However, we should ask, Why does the Creator sentence a drop to be a fool? It seems as though the Creator deliberately causes him not to be able to overcome the qualities with which he were born. We should interpret as Baal HaSulam said, that many times, the Creator does something to a person that seems as though the Creator acts to that person's detriment. But we should ask according to the rule, "The Creator does not complain against His creations," so why does the Creator make it so it seems as though He caused man to be unable to overcome?

The answer is that the Creator wants the creatures to know that He is not limited in His actions. That is, achieving *Dvekut* with the Creator is out of one's hands, but rather comes specifically by help from above, when the Creator gives a person a second nature, called "desire to bestow," and to the Creator, it makes no difference whether he should help him a lot or a little. Also, we should interpret here, as well, that the fact that the Creator sentences the drop to be a fool, it is in order for man to know that to the Creator, there is no difference between having great powers or small ones, whether he is very wise or a fool. Only if one understands that he must ask the Creator to help him, the Creator helps him. That is, after he received the light of Torah, through the Torah in which he engaged for his own pleasure, called "will to receive for his own benefit," if he asks of the Creator, he is rewarded with the Creator opening his eyes and will show him a world full of utter perfection.

According to the above, we can interpret what our sages said (*Taanit* 7), "Anyone who engages in Torah *Lishma* [for Her sake], his Torah becomes to him a potion of life. And anyone who engages in Torah *Lo Lishma*, it becomes to him a potion of death."

This is perplexing: Before a person is rewarded with his actions being for the sake of the Creator, he still cannot learn *Lishma*. So why did they say (*Pesachim* 50), "One should always engage in Torah and *Mitzvot Lo Lishma* since from *Lo Lishma* he comes to *Lishma*." How can it be said that a person should first learn *Lo Lishma*, if he puts into himself a potion of death?

We should interpret according to the above, that man, who comprises four elements, still does not have connection to the evil inclination or to the good inclination. Rather, as said in the *Sulam* [Ladder commentary on *The Zohar*], it says there by learning Torah for one's own pleasure, this is called *Lo Lishma*, meaning for one's own benefit, still, through the light in it, as said in the *Sulam*, "Through the light in it he will feel the lowliness and the terrible corruptness in the nature of receiving for oneself. At that time he will resolve to retire from that nature of reception and completely devote himself to working only in order to bestow contentment upon his Maker. Then the Creator will open his eyes."

Therefore, this means that only through the light of Torah, by learning Torah *Lo Lishma*, the light in the Torah will make him understand and feel that if he learns *Lishma*, meaning in order to bestow, he will be rewarded with the light of life and he will see a world filled with abundance. And if he does not, but rather stays in self-reception, his state will be "the potion of death." That is, he will feel the corruption that there is in self-reception, and he will remain separated from the Life of Lives.

It follows that specifically when he begins to learn *Lo Lishma*, the light in the Torah makes him understand what is "the potion of life" and what is "the potion of death." By this, he will later be rewarded with the opening of the eyes and will see a world filled with abundance.

What Is, "An Ox Knows Its Owner, etc., Israel Does Not Know," in the Work?

Article No. 42, Tav-Shin-Nun-Aleph, 1990/91

It is written, "An ox knows its owner, and a donkey its master's manger; Israel does not know, My people do not understand." We should understand what is the question, for he says that the ox knows, and the donkey knows its master's manger, but Israel do not. That is, man certainly has more brains than a beast, so he asks, Why does Israel not know and "My people does not understand" who is the Provider and Giver of nourishments to the created beings?

We could say that "The ox knows its owner" is not like Israel. The ox and the donkey see who feeds them, unlike Israel, and the people of Israel do not see who is their Provider, and they must only believe that the Creator gives them all they need.

In other words, the people of Israel must believe that the Creator nourishes and provides for the world. So what is the question, Why do the ox and the donkey know who provides for them and Israel do not know? If Israel could see the Creator giving them food, like the ox and the donkey, they would be like the ox and the donkey, with the same knowledge as those of the ox and the donkey. But we must believe what is written, "You open Your hand and satisfy the desire of every living thing," for this can be only by faith and not by knowledge like the ox.

Therefore, we should understand what is the question, "Why does Israel not know?" First, we must understand why He gave faith to man. That is, anyone who has some brains understands that if the Creator wants people to observe the Torah and *Mitzvot* [commandments/good deeds], if man could see His Providence openly, and would not have to believe that the Creator leads the world with a guidance of good and doing good, but rather each one would see His Providence, then the whole world would be servants of the Creator and would observe the Torah and *Mitzvot* with love.

Open Providence is as it is written ("Introduction to The Study of the Ten Sefirot," Item 43), "If, for example, the Creator were to establish open Providence with His creations in that, for instance, anyone who eats a forbidden thing would immediately choke, and anyone who performed a commandment would discover wonderful pleasures in it, similar to the finest delights in this corporeal world. Then, what fool would even think of tasting a forbidden thing, knowing that he would immediately lose his life because of it? Also, what fool would leave any commandment without performing it as quickly as possible?"

So why did the Creator not do this, but did everything in a manner that we must believe, and not by way of knowing? Baal HaSulam said that we must believe that the Creator is almighty. So why did He choose that we would go specifically by the way of faith and not by the way of knowledge? It must be that the Creator understood that the way of faith is better in order to ultimately achieve the purpose of creation, and this is why He gave us the way of faith.

What Is, "An Ox Knows Its Owner, etc., Israel Does Not Know"?

Concerning faith, there are many interpretations. That is, each one has his own meaning. But in truth, any meaning of faith that a person chooses is called "faith." This is as is presented in the "Introduction to The Study of the Ten Sefirot" (Item 14), "'He whose Torah is his trade,' we should interpret that the measure of his faith is apparent in his practice of Torah because the letters of the word *Umanuto* [his trade] are the same [in Hebrew] as the letters of the word *Emunato* [his faith]. It is like a person who trusts his friend and lends him money. He may trust him with a pound, and if he asks for two pounds he will refuse to lend him. He might also trust him with one hundred pounds, but not more. Also, he might trust him with all his properties without a hint of fear. This last faith is considered 'whole faith,' and the previous forms are considered 'incomplete faith,' but rather as 'partial faith.' Similarly, one allots oneself only one hour a day to practice Torah and work out of the measure of his faith in the Creator, and the third does not neglect even a single moment of his free time without engaging in Torah and work."

According to the above, we see that every Jew has the quality of faith. Yet, why did the Creator choose specifically the way of faith? It is because as said above, the way of faith is the most successful for a person to thereby achieve the purpose of creation, meaning to receive the delight and pleasure that He had in the thought of creation, which is "His desire to do good to His creations."

However, we should understand what are the ways that one can follow in order to achieve the completion of the goal. The answer is that man must perform the correction of creation. This means that the vessels of reception that the Creator created in the creatures, this desire is in oppositeness of form from the Creator, whose desire is to bestow. Hence, man should correct himself by obtaining the desire to bestow. This is called the "correction of creation," and this is all of man's work, to achieve *Dvekut* [adhesion] with the Creator, which is the meaning of "equivalence of form."

Hence, if it were revealed that the guidance by which the Creator leads the world is in a manner of good and doing good, it would be utterly impossible for man to choose, meaning to observe Torah and Mitzvot in order to bestow. Rather, another reason would compel him to observe Torah and Mitzvot, which is the punishment, meaning out of self-benefit and not because of the commandment of the Creator, as said in the "Introduction to The Study of the Ten Sefirot."

Hence, His guidance is concealed and man must believe, and then there is room for choice. In other words, there is room to say that he works in order to bestow. That is, a person engages in Torah and Mitzvot although he still does not feel any taste in Torah and Mitzvot, meaning the taste of Torah and the taste of Mitzvot cannot be said to be the reason that obligates him to observe them, since he still does not feel any flavor.

But with corporal pleasures, where the pleasure is known and not believed in, the pleasure that a person sees in something compels him to receive the pleasure. For this reason, if the pleasure in Torah and Mitzvot were revealed—that there is the real pleasure, as the ARI said, that corporeal pleasures have no more than the holy sparks that fell into the Klipot [shells/peels], which is only a "thin light"—if the pleasure in Torah and Mitzvot were revealed, the creatures would certainly be compelled to observe Torah and Mitzvot out of self-benefit.

This is not so when one observes Torah and Mitzvot not because he feels any flavor in it. Rather, sometimes he performs the acts of Torah and Mitzvot by coercion, even though the body objects to this. Yet, we should ask, Why does one force oneself and overcomes the will to receive, which wants rest? The person says that this is the whole difference between man and beast. A beast has no brains; only the pleasure determines what to do or not to do.

But man, who was born with reason, no longer looks at the pleasure as the basis, meaning that this is his guide and where there is more pleasure, this is where he should go. Rather, a person always thinks that he must walk on the path of truth, meaning that the measurement of the work is the truth. He walks on this path and does not look at the sensation of pleasure, that this is his guide. Instead, a person always thinks about the truth, whether what he is about to do now will truly yield a good thing for him.

For this reason, when one takes upon oneself the kingdom of heaven, called "faith," when one wants to engage in Torah and *Mitzvot* for the sake of the Creator, and he wants to bring contentment to his Maker, a person does not regard the thing he is doing, but he regards the truth. In other words, since the Creator gave us Torah and *Mitzvot*, we want to do His will so as to delight Him, by observing His *Mitzvot*.

Therefore, when, for example, a person wears a *Tzitzit* [a mandatory Jewish fringed undergarment], he does not look at whether the body will enjoy his wearing the *Tzitzit*, especially when he is careful to wear a very fine *Tzitzit*, as our sages said (*Shabbat* 133), "This is my God, and I will praise Him. Adorn yourself before Him with *Mitzvot*. Make for Him a handsome *Sukkah* [Tabernacles Feast booth], and a handsome *Lulav* [Tabernacles Feast palm branch], and a handsome *Shofar* [ram's horn to blow in], a handsome *Tzitzit*, a handsome book of Torah."

However, a person always looks at how he can please the Creator. That is, he understands with this mind that the fact that the Creator gave us the commandment to love the Creator is not because the Creator needs our love. Rather, everything that the Creator has commanded us to do and to observe His commandments is only for our sake. In other words, by this, a person will achieve the purpose of creation, which is to do good to His creations.

But a person knows that he has a nature called "will to receive" for his own sake and not for the sake of others. This makes it difficult for him to say, although he understands that man is not like a beast, that we can say that specifically where one feels that he will receive pleasure, there he can exert to obtain the pleasure. However, if one is told that he should love the Creator, a person can understand this only when he sees the greatness and importance of the Creator, then we can speak of love.

But when a person does not see the importance of the Creator and must believe, here begins man's work, meaning work that pertains to the quality of man and not to the quality of beast, for the matter of faith belongs to man's work, and not to the work of a beast.

However, the measure of faith should be the same as the measure of knowledge that the beast has. Otherwise, this is still not regarded as "faith," if there is a difference for him between faith and knowledge.

In other words, man should be like a beast: As the beast knows only what it sees, so man should go with faith, as a beast does with knowing. Otherwise, what is the difference between man and beast? Thus, faith should be as knowledge.

According to the above, we should interpret what we asked about what is written, "An ox knows its owner, and a donkey its master's manger; Israel does not know, My people do not understand." How does he compare Israel to an ox and a donkey? After all, the ox and the donkey see who feeds them, whereas Israel do not see and must believe, so where is the similarity?

The answer is that the main difference between man and beast is that a beast has no knowledge. Therefore, among the beasts, the sensation of pleasure is all that determines whether or not to perform an action. But for man, who has brains and knowledge, he should not consider the pleasure in the matter but rather the truth in the matter.

Therefore, when we are given faith, as it is written, "and they believed in the Lord and in his servant Moses," when He gave us this work, Israel should be in a state of knowing, meaning faith, which Israel must take upon themselves as knowing is for beasts.

There is a question regarding this: Why must faith in Israel be the same as knowing is for beasts, as this is their basis? And also, why does Israel "not understand," meaning that their faith is not like knowledge?

It is written, "My people does not understand." "My people" means "ordinary people," whereas "Israel" is already a higher degree, as it is known that Israel has the letters of *Li-Rosh* [lit. I have a head]. This is why he says, "Israel does not understand." Why? Because "My people does not understand." When they were "My people," to understand the measure of faith that they must obtain, they thought that partial faith was enough for faith. Hence, they settled for little and thought of themselves as "Israel," although they were still not rewarded with "complete faith," so that it is similar to knowing in beasts.

It follows that the order of the work should be that a person should achieve faith that is as knowing. In other words, a person begins to understand that we must do everything in order to bestow contentment upon one's Maker. Therefore, when one walks on this path, when he sees that the body does not enjoy the thing he wants to do, he should say to his body, "I am not going to do something that you will enjoy; I am going to do something that the Creator will enjoy. Therefore, what you are asking of me, to avoid doing this until you agree, you do not count as far as the thing I am doing for the sake of the Creator."

But the body asks, "What will you get out of working for the sake of the Creator?" meaning "What pleasure will you derive from this?" After all, one does not do anything without reward, so "What is the reward that you hope to receive in return for this?"

The answer should be that we were given the *Mitzva* [sing. of *Mitzvot*] of faith, as it is written, "And they believed in the Lord and in His servant Moses," "so I believe that I am serving a great King, although I still have no feeling of the greatness of the Creator. Yet, I believe in His greatness and I enjoy serving a great King, and this is my pleasure. Therefore, all your questions can be only about faith—why I believe. But when I believe in complete faith, my faith is like knowing."

We see that when we know of a person who is superior, such as a king or a high ranking minister, or someone who is famous, a great person, it is inherent in nature that we surrender before that great person. This has nothing to do with religion; it is a law of nature that it is a privilege for the small to serve the great. But in work, where greatness and smallness are not revealed and we must believe, there is work there because by nature, a person cannot do anything unless he sees and understands with his mind.

Hence, when one takes upon himself faith like knowing, he no longer needs to argue with the body, since he tells the body, "I see that you are telling me anything because you are saying only one thing, that you cannot accept the faith that I have taken upon myself. Therefore, with such an argument about faith, I have nothing to argue with you about. Therefore, I am telling you what I am doing now, and you disagree. Yet, I am not waiting for your consent, since to me, faith is like knowledge."

It therefore follows that all of man's work is to obtain the power of faith, since man is unable to defeat the evil in him by arguing, since in the external mind, the body is always right. Only if a person answers to the body with faith above reason can he defeat the body.

Therefore, one should prepare before he does something in *Kedusha* [holiness], that thanks to the act of *Kedusha* that he is going to do now, he will receive faith in return for the work. He should believe that he does not need anything other than faith in the Creator, and he can obtain faith when the Creator gives it to him by his doing things above reason, meaning by coercion. That is, many times, he should force himself and aim that thanks to the coercion he will be rewarded with faith in the greatness and importance of the Creator.

However, one should know that when he works in order to bestow, he has ascents and descents. This is so because through the ascents and descents, a person receives the ability and possibility to tell good from bad, for it is known that one cannot understand anything sufficiently if he does not have the opposite of what he has.

It is written about this, "as the advantage of the light from within the darkness," meaning that we cannot recognize the importance of the light unless from within the darkness. He suffered and was tormented by the darkness, so when the light came, he knew how to appreciate it. Likewise, a person cannot appreciate the importance of the state of ascent unless he has descents opposite it. Only then can he appreciate the importance of the light, meaning the ascent.

Otherwise, it is like giving gems and jewels to an infant, and the infant does not know how to value them, and people come and take from him the good things, since the baby does not know why he needs to keep the jewels. Naturally, anyone who wants, takes from the children the good things.

Likewise, a person who does not know the value of *Kedusha* [holiness], if he is given some *Kedusha* so as to advance in the work, the *Sitra Achra* [other side] comes and takes it from him, since he is unable to understand that the little bit of *Kedusha* he has acquired requires care so that the *Sitra Achra* will not pull the *Kedusha* out of his hand.

Hence, when he has descents, he remains with *Reshimot* [recollections/memories] of what he had, and then he knows how to be careful so that the *Sitra Achra* will not pull it out of his hand. For this reason, a person believes that the Creator does everything, and there is no doubt that the Creator does everything for man's sake, so the descents that he receives, he says that the Creator sent him these states for his own benefit.

This gives a person strength not to escape the campaign although he does not see that the Creator watches over him, meaning feels that the Creator helps him. Rather, not only is he not advancing in the work, but he has even regressed. Yet, if he believes that the Creator helps him by sending him the descents, then he no longer escapes the campaign.

Instead, he says that the Creator does help him, but not in a way that the person understands, meaning in ascents. Rather, the Creator helps him through descents. This is why this faith makes him stronger so he does not escape the campaign. Instead, he waits for the help of the Creator and prays that he will have the strength to continue the work until the Creator opens his eyes and he will be rewarded with *Dvekut* with the Creator.

According to the above, we should interpret what our sages said (*Berachot* 54), "One must bless on the bad as he blesses on the good." This means that if one believes that the Creator leads the world in a manner of good and doing good, why does he feel that there is bad in him? It is as though the Creator is giving him evil. Therefore, our sages said that one should believe that this bad must be for the better.

In the work, we should interpret that we see that when one begins to work in a manner where "all his actions are for the sake of the Creator," meaning that everything he does is because he wants to bestow upon the Creator and not for his own sake, at that time, he comes into states of ascents and descents.

When faith shines for him, he is in a state of ascent. That is, he understands that it is worthwhile to work only for the sake of the Creator. Afterward comes a descent, where thoughts come to him—"What will I get out of working for the sake of the Creator and not for my own sake?" Sometimes, the descent he suffers is so deep that he wants to escape from the campaign.

At that time, the question is, Why is it that before he began the work of bestowal, he was always in high spirits, and now he often feels that he is far from the work altogether and does everything by force? But there is a rule, "a *Mitzva* induces a *Mitzva*," so why did he receive a descent?

The answer is that the fact that a person feels that he is in descent, called "a state of evil," is also for his best, for specifically by both can he be rewarded with help from the Creator. This is the meaning of "One must bless on the bad."

What Is, "You Will See My Back, But My Face Shall Not Be Seen," in the Work?

Article No. 43, Tav-Shin-Nun-Aleph, 1990/91

It is known that the order of the work in order to achieve the purpose of creation, which is to do good to His creations, is in two manners:

1) The manner of the "mind," which is faith above reason, is a manner that is called "against reason." That is, the reason of a person determines whether something is worth doing or not. According to the rule that one cannot go against reason, it follows that a person takes upon himself to serve the Creator even if the mind does not understand that it is worthwhile. And yet, a person takes upon himself faith in the sages, who determined for us how to serve the Creator.

They said that we must follow the rules of the Torah and not according to the intellect, and this is called "mind."

2) The manner of the "heart," meaning the will to receive, and he must work against the desire, meaning work and do things in order to obtain the desire to bestow. This is called "heart."

Since man, by nature, is born with a will to receive for himself, when he wants to work in order to bestow, he is shown so he will know that the will to receive is bad. However, he must not see right away how much the will to receive controls him, meaning to know how bad it is and that it controls us to the point that one is unable to emerge from its control by himself.

If one were to see the power of the evil within him, and how far he is from the Creator because of this evil, he would say, "The control of the evil in me is bigger than in the rest of the people, so how can I defeat it? I am wasting my effort since it will all go to waste, for I see no way out of the control of the will to receive, and the will to receive is all the bad, meaning the only obstructor from achieving *Dvekut* [adhesion] and equivalence of form. Therefore, it is better for me to escape this campaign.

But since the bad is not shown at once, but bit by bit, by giving him an ascent, so he thinks he no longer has any bad, since during the ascent he feels that he is close to the Creator and no longer needs the Creator to help him anymore because he thinks that he will remain in this accent forever, for now he sees that everything is folly and all that matters is nearing the Creator, but since a person should see all the bad within him, so he can pray with all his heart, for only then does he have a complete *Kli* [vessel], meaning a real lack, he therefore receives a descent from above. In other words, he is shown some more of the evil that is found in the will to receive, and which he did not think about. This continues repeatedly and each time, a little more evil is revealed to him. If he does not escape the campaign, when he reaches the bottom of his evil, the Creator gives him the required help, which comes to him in order to save him from the control of the evil within him. At that time, a person is rewarded with the desire to bestow, called "second nature," and then he receives the "opening of the eyes in the Torah."

It therefore follows that it is not as one thinks about how the order of the work should be according to his view. Rather, the Creator has a different order. It should be said about this, "For My thoughts are not your thoughts, nor your ways My ways" (Isaiah 55). In other words, a person understands that the order of the world is that a person learns some science or profession, and each day he advances and understands more and more until he grasps his field of expertise in full. Therefore, once he is accustomed to the work, as he received while learning, meaning that all that we should work on is the practice. In other words, one is taught to take upon himself faith, to believe in the Creator, and believe in the sages who set up for us the way by which to observe Torah and *Mitzvot* [commandments/good deeds], and all that one needs to remember while engaging in Torah and *Mitzvot* is that he is observing the *Mitzvot* of the Creator, who commanded us through Moses and sages that followed him, and by this we will be rewarded in this world and in the next world. This is the manner of the beginning of man's work in Torah and *Mitzvot*.

This is called "work in practice," meaning that one should remember while observing Torah and *Mitzvot*, that he is observing the commandment of the Creator. This is called "work of the general public." This is also called "still of *Kedusha* [holiness]."

Afterward, when he is accustomed to work in practice and gladly observes it, since he was rewarded with observing the *Mitzvot* of the Creator, we can speak of the intention. However, before one observes the Torah and *Mitzvot* like the general public, meaning in practice, we cannot speak to that person about the intention. This is as Maimonides said, that the intention, which is called *Lishma* [for Her sake], is not revealed to any person. Rather, "Until they gain knowledge and acquire much wisdom, they are shown that secret bit by bit."

This means that Israel in general, which are called "still of *Kedusha*," faith shines for them as "Surrounding Light," and from this, a person can observe Torah and *Mitzvot* in practice. However, those who are still not observing Torah and *Mitzvot* even in the manner of the general public, it is certainly impossible to speak with them about the intention.

Conversely, those who are fine in terms of the general public, yet feel an inner drive that there is also the matter of intention, since they heard that there is also the matter of having to do all the deeds for the sake of the Creator, called *Lishma*, a desire awakens in their hearts to be among the people who engage in Torah and *Mitzvot* for the sake of the Creator.

There are several interpretations concerning "for the sake of the Creator." 1) He engages in Torah and *Mitzvot* for the sake of the Creator, meaning he is not observing Torah and *Mitzvot* for respect or for money, but only because the Creator commanded us through Moses, that we must observe His *Mitzvot*. This is why we observe and not for respect or for money. It follows that this is called "for the sake of the Creator," meaning because the Creator commanded us to observe the Torah and *Mitzvot*.

However, in return for this, a person wants the Creator to reward him, as our sages said, "You can trust your landlord to reward you for your work" (*Avot*, Chapter 2:21).

There is a second meaning to the matter of "for the sake of the Creator." Self-benefit is not the reason that obligates him to observe Torah and *Mitzvot*, but the importance and greatness of the Creator obligates him to engage in Torah and *Mitzvot*. In other words, the reason he wants to engage in Torah and *Mitzvot* is to serve the King and observe His commandments.

It follows that the reward is not the reason, as we explained about the first manner of "for the sake of the Creator," where the reason why he observes Torah and *Mitzvot* is his desire that the Creator will reward him, since he does not observe Torah and *Mitzvot* for people, but he works in concealment so that no one knows of his work in Torah and *Mitzvot* but the Creator, so he wants the Creator to reward him. It follows that self-benefit is the reason.

But when he wants to work only because of the greatness of the King, this is called "for the sake of the Creator," meaning that the intention of the reward is that he is serving the Creator. This is as it is written in the *Sulam* [Ladder commentary on *The Zohar*] ("Introduction of The Book of Zohar," Item 191), "that he should fear the Creator (which is why he observes Torah and *Mitzvot*) because He is great and rules over everything."

It therefore follows that precisely when one works not in order to receive reward, but his intention is for the sake of the Creator, namely that the greatness of the Creator obligates him to observe Torah and *Mitzvot*, this is called *Lishma*. That is, it is not the reward but the greatness of the Creator that is the reason why he observes Torah and *Mitzvot*. Therefore, we should ask, What does it mean that they said, "You can trust your landlord to reward you for your work" if the person is not working for a reward?

We should interpret that those who work not in order to receive reward, it means that they want to work in order to bestow. However, the body objects to this and they cannot overcome the will to receive for themselves. Yet, they desire this and pray to the Creator to help them be able to work without any reward. At that time, the Creator hears their prayer and gives them a second nature, called "desire to bestow," and this is their reward, that they are rewarded with working only for the sake of the Creator.

However, we should know that precisely when one begins to work in order to bestow, when he wants to achieve this degree, since it is against nature and one cannot come to this by himself, but the Creator must give him the desire to bestow, since there is a rule that there is no filling without a lack, for it is impossible to fill something where there is no receptacle, called "lack," and since the lack over inability to perform acts of bestowal is also not in one's hands to feel, but this feeling, that a person must work in order to bestow, a person asks, "For what purpose do I want to perform acts of bestowal?" So one must first feel that without the desire to bestow he is deficient, meaning separated from the Creator due to disparity of form. Yet, this, too, one cannot feel, but rather this, too, meaning the feeling of the evil that exists in the will to receive for oneself, that by this he becomes separated from the Creator, this, too, he cannot understand, since he asks, "What will you get out of doing everything in order to bestow?" With these questions, he loses the desire and the need to do everything in order to bestow.

Thus, precisely through the light in the Torah, which shines for a person even when he learns *Lo Lishma* [not for Her sake], this light gives a person the ability to feel the lack and the need to obtain the desire to bestow. However, one is not shown all the bad that is in the will to receive, but is shown a little bit each time. After each descent, when he sees that he is separated and has no desire to work, he is given an ascent. And after each ascent he gets another descent until all the bad is revealed to him. Then, once he has a complete lack, he receives from above the desire to bestow. But in the middle of the work, when a person suffers a descent, he wants to escape from the campaign. This state is called *Achoraim* [posterior/back], meaning that the faith he draws in the work does not illuminate for him, and he understands that the Creator should behave with him as he understands, yet the Creator does what He wants, and not what the person wants—who thinks that the order in the work should be similar to every profession that a person learns, and that each day he advances. Here, however, a person sees that each day he is regressing, meaning each day, he sees that he is in a state of *Achoraim*. But in truth, the Creator behaves with him as He thinks, and not as the person thinks.

Accordingly, we see that the order of the work is opposite from man's view, for man understands that by having an ascent in degree each time, he will achieve the completion of the goal, but the Creator thinks to the contrary—since if a person were to remain in a state of ascent, he would think of himself as complete. That is, he would not see any deficiency in his work, and then he would remain in a state of still. He would not feel that the bad in him due to the will to receive is bad, since he would not see that it obstructs him from engaging in Torah and *Mitzvot*, and he would not know what is *Achoraim*, meaning what it means that the Torah and *Mitzvot* do not shine. Rather, he would always be happy that he is serving the Creator and observing His commandments. There is a rule that from above, no redundancies are given, meaning that when one does not feel that he is missing the essence, it is forbidden to give him extras.

There is a rule that when a person is deficient on life's necessities, meaning when he is deficient of the breath of life, called "*Dvekut* with the Creator," called "whole faith," it cannot be said that he should be given extras, namely things that a person does not feel he needs, and without which he cannot live. In spirituality, this is called "extras." That is, precisely when a person asks the Creator to give him something that he needs so much, to the point that without it, his life is worthless, this is called "necessity," and this is called "a real desire," meaning a lack that is worthy of being satisfied. But if his desire is not as great, it is regarded as "redundancies."

Therefore, when one is satisfied with Torah and *Mitzvot* in practice, it cannot be said that he should be given a greater degree, since he is not so needy of salvation. It follows that one cannot ascend the rungs of holiness unless he feels that he is in utter lowliness. This is called "a state of *Achoraim*." Thus, when he is in a state of *Achoraim*, he can receive a *Kli* [vessel], called "desire to receive help from above." And the help that comes from above is called "a soul," as it is written in *The Zohar*, "He who comes to purify is aided." He asks, "With what?" and the answer is "with a holy soul."

Each time he asks for help, he receives a greater degree until he is rewarded with attaining the *NRNHY* in his soul.

By this we should interpret what we asked, What is, "And you will see My back, but My face shall not be seen"? We should interpret "And you shall see." It means that if a person wants to be rewarded with "seeing," meaning with opening the eyes in the Torah, namely the Torah that is the names of the Creator, a person cannot be rewarded with this during an ascent, when he sees that the Torah and *Mitzvot* shine for him and give him satisfaction, and he wants to have a higher degree each time, as is done in corporeal matters, where each time a person sees that he is adding in obtaining what he wants, both when he learns some profession or some science. It follows that the person is always in ascent, called *Panim* [face/anterior].

In spirituality, it is to the contrary. Specifically from the state of *Achoraim*, from states that do not illuminate, meaning specifically from descents, when more bad appears in him each time, meaning the measure of the bad in the will to receive, how it obstructs one from achieving the goal for which he was created. This is so because a person cannot receive help from the Creator unless in a state where he feels the real deficiency. It follows that a person cannot say that the Creator is not looking at him when he sees that he is regressing. Rather, this *Achoraim* that a person feels comes from above. That is, the Creator has given him help by his seeing the bad that is in the will to receive.

It follows that the person is advancing, but not according to the person's view, but according to the Creator's view, as it is written, "For My thoughts are not your thoughts." This means that the Creator first helps him by making him feel each time more of the measure of evil that is in the will to receive, for as said above, it is impossible to reveal to him all the bad at once, but each time, a small amount is revealed in him, since if a person sees all the bad at once, he will escape the campaign. Therefore, it is revealed to him little by little until he sees its real measure. At that time he has a real need for His help, and then he is rewarded with extending the *NRNHY* in his soul.

This is the meaning of what is written, "And you will see My back." Precisely through the states of *Achoraim* can one be rewarded with the goal.

By this we can interpret what is written (Deuteronomy 7:7), "The Lord did not set His love upon you, nor choose you because you were more in number than any people, for you were the least of all peoples."

What Is, "You Will See My Back, But My Face Shall Not Be Seen"?

We should ask, What does this come to teach us? Does anyone think that the people of Israel are more numerous than all the nations, so the verse comes to tell us so we will not be mistaken that the Creator chose us because the people of Israel are more numerous than all the nations? Rather, we should interpret that when we speak of the work, whether we speak of Israel, or whether we speak of the nations of the world, we are speaking within the same person, as it is written in *The Zohar*, "Every person is a small world in and of itself."

Therefore, we should interpret that sometimes, a person is in a state where the quality of Israel within him is greater than the quality of the nations of the world in him. In other words, he is in a state of ascent. This is so when he feels that he is complete in Torah and *Mitzvot*. Therefore, by this one can be rewarded with the love of the Creator, since it makes sense that when one feels that he is walking in the right path, according to one's view, when he is working in the manner of the general public, and because of this the Creator should love him, to this comes the answer, "The Lord did not set His love upon you, nor choose you because you were more in number than any people."

The question is, Why does the Creator not favor a person when he feels that he is serving the Creator in completeness? The answer is as said above, that the person does not need the Creator's help in order to be rewarded with the Creator's love, since he feels that he is complete in terms of the practice, that he is a "still of *Kedusha*."

But the verse says, I favor you "for you were the least of all peoples." In other words, specifically from the state where you feel that you are the least of all the peoples, that all the desires of the nations of the world govern you, and the Israel in you does not merit a name, and you see the bad within you to its true extent, then you pray that I will help you. And since now you have a real need, since you feel how far you are from doing anything in order to bestow, then comes the right time to help you, since then you are asking for necessity and not for extras.

In a state of ascent, a person does not need the Creator to help him, except for extras, as it is written, "The Lord did not set His love upon you, nor choose you because you were more in number than any people," for then you do not need Me for necessities, since your state is "more in number than any people," and you feel that you are governing the evil in you in the quality of the general public, which is the practice. So why did the Creator want you? It is precisely from the states where you are "the least of all peoples," when the nations of the world govern the quality of Israel in you, and you cry out to Me, "Help!" with all your hearts.

Then I love you, and only then can I keep all that I promised the forefathers concerning the inheritance of the land, for now you have the *Kelim* [vessels] to receive My blessing, meaning vessels of bestowal, for when one has vessels of bestowal, he can receive the blessing from above.

It follows from all the above, that a person does not need to be impressed when during the descent, the bad comes to him to argue with him, and makes him think, "You see that you are not advancing in the work, so I advise you to run from this path, which is work of bestowal, and go work in the manner that the general public work, meaning only in practice." This is the time of choice—to overcome and say, "Now I see the truth, how far I am from the Creator and only He can help," and to believe what is written, "For You hear the prayer of every mouth," meaning even though he is not worthy of being helped, the Creator still helps. Therefore, he says, "I will certainly get help from above, since I feel that the help that the Creator will give me now is truly "reviving the dead." But if a person is not rewarded, he escapes from the campaign and says that this work belongs to those who are gifted, but he is unfit for it. Yet, our sages said about this, "The ways of the Lord are straight; the righteous walk in it, and the wicked fail in it." Therefore, do not run away!

What Is the Reason for which Israel Were Rewarded with Inheritance of the Land, in the Work?

Article No. 44, Tav-Shin-Nun-Aleph, 1990/91

The verse says (Deuteronomy 9:5), "It is not for your righteousness or the integrity of your heart that you are going to inherit their land, but it is because of the wickedness of the nations that the Lord your God is driving them out from before you, and in order to fulfill the oath that the Lord swore to your forefathers."

We should understand this, for it implies that the reason that the Creator gave the inheritance of the land to the people of Israel is as it is written, "because of the wickedness of the nations the Lord your God is driving them out from before you." That is, were it not for "the wickedness of the nations," there would not be any interest in giving the inheritance of the land. We should also understand the second reason. He says that it is because "the Lord swore to your forefathers." Were it not for the oath, would the Creator not need to give the land to the people of Israel?

This is difficult to understand. Our sages said, "The world was created only for Israel." This means that all the good things that exist in the world are for Israel. This implies that it is for different reasons that the people of Israel are given the good, expansive, and coveted land, a land flowing with milk and honey.

The text provides two reasons:
1) the wickedness of the nations,
2) the oath that He swore to your forefathers.

Yet, the writing tells us that we should not be mistaken that the reason He is giving us the inheritance of the land is our righteousness and the integrity of our heart. Rather, it is for the two above-mentioned reasons.

Baal HaSulam said about what is written (Genesis 15:7-14), "And He said to him, 'to give you this land to inherit it.' He said, 'how will I know that I will inherit it?' And He said to Abraham, 'Know for certain that your descendants will be strangers in a land that is not theirs, and they will torment them four hundred years, and afterward they will come out with great possessions.'"

He asked, what is the answer that the Creator replied to what Abraham asked, "How will I know that I will inherit it?" The Creator said, "Know for certain that your descendants will be strangers in a land that is not theirs, and afterward they will come out with great possessions." This means that the answer was to the question, "How will I know?" That is, Abraham says that he wants guarantees about the inheritance, so the Creator answers him so that by this answer he will be certain of the inheritance of the land. Thus, we should understand the answer, for it contains a guarantee of the inheritance.

He said that this means that when the Creator told him "to give you this land to inherit it," Abraham saw the greatness and importance

The Reason for which Israel Were Rewarded with Inheritance of the Land

of this land, since the matter of the inheritance of the land refers to *Malchut*, which receives all the lights from above and bestows upon the souls, since *Malchut* is called "the assembly of Israel."

Abraham saw according to the rule that "There is no light without a *Kli*," meaning that "there is no filling without a lack," that if the Creator were to give to Israel a little bit of illumination and awakening from above, they will settle for little and will have no need for higher degrees. As a result, Abraham saw that there was no way for the people of Israel to receive the inheritance of the land, since they have no need for it.

This was the question, "How will I know?" It is not that he did not believe what the Creator had told him. Rather, his question was that he said that he could not see them having a need for it. It is like giving something precious to a person who has no need for it. He cannot enjoy it. It follows that even if they are given the inheritance of the land, without the need, they will not be able to enjoy it. Although from the perspective of the giver, everything is fine, if the lower one has no need, what can the giver do? This is what Abraham asked.

The answer was "Know for certain that your descendants will be strangers." That is, they will be in exile in Egypt, which is called "a land that is not theirs," meaning that the people of Israel, who want to work for the sake of the Creator, the Egyptians will control them. Each time, the people of Israel will want to come out of exile, as it is written (Exodus 2:23), "And the children of Israel sighed from the work, and their cry went up to God from the work." Generally, the nations of the world are called "will to receive for oneself." However, there are many desires in the will to receive, and each desire is attributed to a specific nation. This is why they are called in general, "the seventy nations of the world," corresponding to the seventy discernments in the desire. This extends in a manner of "one opposite the other," meaning opposite the seven *Sefirot* of *Kedusha* [holiness], which are *HGT NHYM*, each of which consists of ten *Sefirot*, which together make seventy nations.

Also, there is the discernment of "Israel," which are named after *Yashar-El* [straight to the Creator]. These are opposite from the will to receive for oneself, but are rather discerned as the desire to bestow upon the Creator. In other words, he wants to bring contentment to his Maker.

Therefore, since the Egyptians controlled them, they had to do all their work for the Egyptians, and not for the Creator. This is why it says, "And the children of Israel sighed from the work." It means that the children of Israel wanted to work for the sake of the Creator but the Egyptians controlled them; this is why they sighed. That is, they saw that not only were they not progressing, they were retreating. This is why it is written, "And their cry went up to God from the work."

Then, when they saw that they could not emerge from exile by themselves, they asked the Creator, as it is written, "And their cry went up to God." That is, the Creator helped them come out from the exile in Egypt. This is as *The Zohar* says about what was said, "He who comes to purify is aided." It asks, "With what?" And it replies, "With a holy soul."

It follows that specifically when they are under the governance of evil do they see—each time more so—the governance of evil. At that time, a person comes to feel two things: 1) The will to receive, which is the governance of the Egyptians, is so bad that it removes him from the Creator. That is, before he began the work in order to bestow, he did not know how much harm the will to receive causes him. This is so for the known reason that a person is not shown the power of the evil at once. Rather, he is shown bit by bit, for otherwise he will immediately escape from the work and say that this is not for him.

According to the above, we should interpret the words of Maimonides, who says that the matter of *Lishma* [for Her sake] is not revealed to a person at the beginning of the work, but "Until they gain knowledge and acquire much wisdom, they are shown that secret little by little." We should understand what it means that "they are shown that secret little by little." We should understand how there can be such a thing as "little by little." After all, when a person is told that he must do everything *Lishma*, everything is revealed to him. What else is there to reveal?

We should interpret that when he says "they are shown," who is it who shows them this secret of the matter of *Lishma*? We should also understand what he says, "Until they gain knowledge and acquire much wisdom." Who knows that one has been rewarded with "Until they gain knowledge and acquire much wisdom"?

We can understand this as *The Zohar* says about the verse, "Or make it known to him that he has sinned." He asks, "Who made it known to him?" and he replies, "the Creator." We should understand why he says that the Creator makes it known to him that he has sinned. In what way did He inform him? We should interpret this in the manner that is written in the *Sulam* [Ladder commentary on *The Zohar*] (*Beresheet Bet*, Item 103), "If one engages in Torah and *Mitzvot* even for his own pleasure, through the light in it he will still feel the lowliness and the terrible corruptness in the nature of receiving for oneself. At that time he will resolve to retire from this nature of reception and completely devote himself to bestow contentment upon his Maker. Then the Creator will open his eyes to see before him a world filled with utter perfection without any deficiencies whatsoever."

Now we can understand how the Creator informs him "that he has sinned." We should interpret that even when a person learns *Lo Lishma* [not for Her sake], the light in it informs him that the will to receive is the cause of all the evil, the obstructor to man's ability to receive these delight and pleasure that He wishes to give to the created beings. And the light in the Torah is regarded as the Creator notifying to a man that he has sinned.

We should also interpret why Maimonides says that we must begin to accustom a person to work in *Lo Lishma*, and not in *Lishma*. This is so because the matter of *Lishma* is revealed to a person by his receiving the light of the Torah. It follows that if he does not engage in Torah even if *Lo Lishma*, from where will he take the light of the Torah? This is why Maimonides says that we must begin with *Lo Lishma*.

By this we will understand what we asked, "Who knows if they have been rewarded with "much wisdom," so it is permitted to reveal to them the matter of *Lishma*? The answer is that the light in the Torah knows how much they are inspired by the light of Torah, and to that extent it is possible to reveal to them the matter of *Lishma*.

By this we will understand what Maimonides says, that they are shown that secret little by little. It means that the matter of for the sake of the Creator means not for one's own sake. A person must feel what is not for one's own sake, and this reveals to him the light of the Torah. Hence, each time, the light shows him the amount of bad that is in the will to receive, since through the light that a person receives from the Torah, he sees each time a little bit of the bad that there is in the will to receive. This is why he says that he is shown "little by little."

Evil is interpreted in two manners: 1) the quality of the evil, meaning how much one loses by receiving for himself 2) how much the body objects to the work of bestowal.

Those two, a person receives from the light in the Torah little by little. This is the meaning of the words "They are shown that secret little by little." That is, through the light that he receives from the Torah in *Lo Lishma*, he reveals the two above matters. In other words, the measure of the evil found in the will to receive, and the measure of resistance of the body, each time to a greater extent, when one sees that he is able to overcome. This is why it says, "little by little," meaning that each time, the light reveals to him, which is called that it is impossible to reveal to him at once.

Now we can understand what we asked, Why does the writing say that specifically through the wickedness of the nations, they were rewarded with the inheritance of the land? The reason is as the Creator promised Abraham, that in this way, meaning if Israel suffer from the Egyptians in exile, meaning all the nations of the world, with all the bad qualities in them, want to control the people of Israel, and the people of Israel want specifically to do everything for the sake of the Creator and not for the sake of the seventy nations. At that time, they feel the lack and they will see that they are powerless to overcome them.

Then it will be as it is written, "And the children of Israel sighed from the work, and their cry went up to God from the work." At that time, the Creator will give them the required help for this. That is, each time, they will be rewarded with a "holy soul," and this will be the reason that the children of Israel will need to receive the inheritance of the land, since they will receive it out of necessity, to save themselves from the control of the nations of the world.

This is the meaning of the words, "but it is because of the wickedness of these nations that the Lord your God is driving them out from before you." In other words, specifically through the wickedness of the nations, the Creator can give them the inheritance of the land of Israel, since the sensation of bad when they reveal that this evil obstructs from achieving nearness to the Creator, for this is all that we need, since the matter of "near and far" in spirituality is the matter of equivalence of form. When there is equivalence of form between the light and the *Kli* [vessel], the light dresses in the *Kli*.

Hence, the sensation of evil, called "wickedness of the nations," causes the need to be rid of the bad, and then a person begins to purify himself from reception for oneself, and sees that it is out of his hands. At that time, he begins to pray to the Creator to help him, as our sages said, "He who comes to purify is aided." As said in the words of *The Zohar*, he is given a holy soul. In other words, each time, he receives help from above by being given a soul. It follows that the ascents and descents are the reason that cause the need and desire to receive the inheritance of the land.

This is why he says that the reason is that "the Lord swore to your forefathers." That is, it is not that the reason is that He swore to your forefathers, and this is why He is giving them the inheritance of the land. We asked, but our sages said about what is written,

"*Beresheet* [in the beginning], there is no *Resheet* [beginning] but Israel." It follows that it was all for Israel and not because of the oath He swore to the forefathers.

Yet, we should interpret that when the people of Israel are qualified to receive the inheritance of the land, when they have a need for the inheritance of the land because, as he says, "but it is because of the wickedness of these nations that the Lord your God is driving them out from before you," this is the reason that the children of Israel will inherit the land.

It is known that "land" is called *Malchut*, and *Malchut* is called "the assembly of Israel," since she assembles within her everything that there is in ZA, who is called "Israel." This is called "the unification of the Creator and His *Shechina* [Divinity]." Through this unification, abundance pours out to the souls.

All this comes from the beginning of the thought of creation, as our sages said, "There is no beginning but Israel." This means that the purpose of creation, which is His desire to do good to His creations, refers to the children of Israel. But in what way will they receive the delight and pleasure? The text tells us about this, that the main reason by which they are made fit to receive is the "wickedness of the nations," and also "to fulfill the oath that the Lord swore to your forefathers." The inheritance of the land is as He notified Abraham when Abraham asked "How will I know that I will inherit it?" The Creator's answer was that the children of Israel would be in exile, meaning in the "wickedness of the nations."

It therefore follows that a person cannot ascend the rungs of holiness unless he feels a deficiency in the state he is in. That is, the deficiencies and suffering he feels give him a need to find a way by which to satisfy his deficiencies. But if he does not feel any lack within him, although he might know that there he has deficiencies in the work, but this does not pain him, so this lack cannot be satisfied because he does not seek counsels for it, and without an awakening from below, meaning without a person asking the Creator from the bottom of the heart, the prayer cannot be answered because if he is not suffering from the absence, he cannot ask with all his heart.

This is as it is written in the Midrash, "Seeking good" (Psalms 23), "'For the Lord your God blessed you in all the works of your hands, even if you sit idly.' The meaning of 'all the works of your hands' is that if he did, he is blessed, and if not, he is not blessed."

We therefore see that without an awakening from below, meaning if there is no work on the part of the lower one, the blessing cannot come. The question is, Why? The answer is that when a person begins to work, the work gives him the need for it. That is, there is a difference in the need for the matter. This means that we should understand to what extent a person wants to obtain what he wants, since the work and the counsels that a person invests in order to obtain what he wants expand the lack for the matter, so when he obtains it, he will be able to enjoy it.

Therefore, when speaking in the work, although there is a need within man to ascend in the work, that need still does not make within him a necessity for the matter. So naturally, when he is given something from above, and he still does not know how to appreciate what he is given, he will lose it into the *Sitra Achra* [other side], since he will not be wise enough to know how to appreciate something in spirituality.

This is as our sages said (*Hagigah* 4), "Who is a fool? He who loses what he is given." That is, when a person does not know how to appreciate when he is given some nearing from above, it promptly leaves him and he suffers a descent, since he does not know how to keep the nearing.

Normally, if someone is permitted to enter somewhat into the King's courtyard, he is concerned and seeks ways by which to enter the King's house and he does not settle for being in the King's courtyard. Therefore, when a person is brought a little closer, he is happy that he was brought closer and does not worry about finding ways to go forward. Therefore, that person is thrown out. Then, when he suffers a descent, which is called "a road accident," meaning that he had an accident as he was going to approach the King.

That is, another car crashed into his car, meaning that the car of the corporeal world crashed into the car of the desire to bestow, and then all the vitality that he had from the desire to bestow departed from him and he was left unconscious. In other words, now he feels that he no longer has spiritual life. Rather, until he gradually recovers and begins to feel that his entire vitality, on which he now lives, is only from the will to receive for himself, at that time, he begins to seek advice once more how to reenter the work of bestowal.

It follows that in order to have a deficiency, to need to ascend the degrees of the work of bestowal, he is given from above the descent, so he would have a need to advance, since without a real need, a person cannot receive what he should obtain. Hence, if a person wants to keep himself from having a road accident, he should keep himself so he does not crash with the car of the will to receive. By this he will be certain that he will not lose what he is given, meaning the ascent he has received.

According to the above, we should interpret what is written (Deuteronomy 5:15), "Remember that you were a slave in the land of Egypt, and the Lord your God brought you out from there." We should interpret that in the work, a person must remember that he had a descent before he came to an ascent, meaning that the Creator let him feel the bad in him. In other words, a person should believe that this feeling, that he is a slave among the Egyptians, namely that he has no permission to do anything for the sake of the Creator, but all that he does is only for the sake of the Egyptians within man, this comes from the Creator.

Afterward, he must remember that now that he is in a state of ascent and feels that he is somewhat close to *Kedusha* [holiness], he must remember that he should go forward. Therefore, now he must remember that as he was previously a slave, meaning that he was in a state of descent, now he also needs to find within him a lack, so he will need to go forward. Otherwise, he will have to be given a descent from above, since without a need, a person cannot advance and must stay in the state he is in. Therefore, in order not to need to be given a descent, during the ascent he must find within him a place of lack. This is the meaning of what is written, "Remember that you were a slave in the land of Egypt, and the Lord your God brought you out from there."

It therefore follows that a person should begin the work like the general public, meaning in practice, and to aim that it will be for the sake of the Creator. This means that a person observes Torah and *Mitzvot* [commandments/good deeds] because the Creator gave us the Torah of life, where by observing what the Creator commanded us, we will be rewarded, as our sages said, "You can trust your landlord to reward you for your work." By this, we will be happy in this world and happy in the next world.

The fact that we must believe that even if views and thoughts that do not let us believe come to us, we must ask the Creator to give us the power to believe. Afterward, there is a higher degree, which is "not in order to receive reward." Rather, he is rewarded with feeling that observing Torah and *Mitzvot* is regarded for him as though he is serving a great King. From this, we come to inherit the land.

What Does It Mean that a Judge Must Judge Absolutely Truthfully, in the Work?

Article No. 45, Tav-Shin-Nun-Aleph, 1990/91

Our sages said (*Shabbat* 10), "Any judge who judges absolutely truthfully, it is as though he becomes partners with the Creator in the work of creation."

We should understand the following:

1) What is "truthful judgment" and what is "absolutely truthful judgment"? It seems as though there could be a truthful judgment, but the "absolute" will still be missing, although in general, it is truthful. Also, what does "absolutely" mean? That is, what does the "absolutely" add to us?

2) What is the meaning of "it is as though he becomes partners with the Creator in the work of creation"?

3) Why specifically if it is "absolutely truthful" can he become partners with the Creator in the work of creation, whereas if it is merely "truthful," he cannot become partners? We should understand the reason, meaning the connection between being "absolutely truthful" and the work of creation.

It is known that the work of creation, which is the creation of the world and all that is in it, was with the aim to do good to His creations. In that sense, the world emerged with both the lack and the satisfaction of the lack. This is called "the world of *Ein Sof* [infinity/no end]." At that time, the upper light filled the whole of reality of creation.

However, in order to prevent the matter of shame, there was a correction called *Tzimtzum* [restriction], which is a concealment and hiding so the delight and pleasure that the Creator wants to impart upon the creatures will not be apparent in the world before they can aim to bestow contentment upon the Maker.

For this reason, it is upon creation to correct the matter of shame, namely that they must aim in order to bestow. Since the creatures were created with a nature of a desire to receive for oneself, since the Creator wants the creatures to enjoy the abundance that He wishes to give them, He created in them a desire and yearning for the matter. Hence, if the creatures must act to the contrary, to receive with the aim to bestow, this is a lot of work. This is considered that we must make *Kelim* [vessels] that are fit to receive the delight and pleasure, and that there will not be any shame while receiving the pleasures.

It therefore follows that the *Kli* [vessel] that should receive the abundance from the Creator consists of two discernments: 1) a desire to receive pleasure, 2) the intention should be in order to bestow.

It follows that in order for the purpose of creation to be carried out, namely for the creatures to receive delight and pleasure, we should note two partners in the making of the *Kelim*: 1) the Creator, who gave the will to receive, 2) the intention with which the creatures should receive what they receive. This is called "receiving in order to bestow."

The *Kli* that is fit to receive the delight and pleasure is made of those two.

Accordingly, we should interpret what we asked, What does it mean that they said, "It is as though he becomes partners with the Creator in the work of creation"? We should understand what it tells us that they say "as though." The thing is that from the perspective of the light, which is the delight and pleasure, only the Creator gives. In this, we cannot speak of a partnership. But with regard to the *Kli*, there we can speak of a partnership, since the Creator gave the will to receive and the yearning to receive pleasure, and the creatures give the other half of the *Kli*, namely the desire to bestow. In other words, we attribute the part of the *Kli* that is the will to receive to the Creator, and the other part of the *Kli*, the desire to bestow, we attribute to the creatures; this is what the creatures make. Thus, there are two partners in the *Kli*.

This is as it is written in *The Zohar* ("Introduction of The Book of Zohar," Item 67), "'And to say to Zion, 'You are My people.'' Do not pronounce 'You are My people [*Ami*],' but 'You are with Me [*Imi*],' with a *Hirik* in the *Ayin*, which means partnering with Me. As I made heaven and earth with My speech, so you." That is, I started creation by creating the will to receive, and you must finish, meaning place the intention to bestow on the will to receive. This is called "partnership."

It follows that the partnership stems primarily as a result of the *Tzimtzum* and the concealment that were made on the vessels of reception. That is, the light departed because of the correction of the *Tzimtzum*, but through the correction called "in order to bestow," the light can shine once more, to the extent that the *Kli* has a desire to bestow.

Accordingly, we should ask: It is written, "The whole earth is full of His glory," and it is also written in *The Zohar*, "There is no place vacant of Him" (no place is vacant from the Creator). This means that there is no place of concealment or *Tzimtzum* in the world. Yet, we see that when a person comes to a descent, he is under the governance of concealment and *Tzimtzum* and does not feel any spirituality.

The thing is that from the perspective of the Creator there is no *Tzimtzum* and "The whole earth is full of His glory." However, "You are until the world was created, and You are once the world was created." We should interpret that just as before the world was created (*Olam* [world] means *He'elem* [concealment] and hiding), the Creator still filled the whole of reality; likewise, "once the world was created (when the concealment and hiding were created), the Creator also fills the whole of reality, and there was no place vacant of the Creator. However, He is concealed from the creatures; they do not feel Him because of the correction, so there will not be the matter of shame.

It follows that the concealment and hiding that a person feels in the work begins specifically when he wants to be rewarded with *Dvekut* [adhesion] with the Creator, as it is written, "and to cleave unto Him," which is the matter of equivalence of form. This means that as the Creator wants to delight His creations, man should try to make bringing contentment to the Creator his only concern in life.

In order for one not to fool oneself and say that he has no concern for himself, and his intention is only to bestow upon the Creator, when he is given a descent from above, when he does not feel any flavor in Torah and *Mitzvot* [commandments/good deeds], a person can see his true state, whether he has no desire for himself and all his thoughts are for the sake of the Creator, or for his own sake. During the descent, a person should say, "I do not care how I feel when I engage in Torah and *Mitzvot*, since all my thoughts are to benefit the Creator. Therefore, I do my part and I believe that the Creator will enjoy it. Concerning the thought that we should think this way, I receive it from faith in the sages." Conversely, when his aim is his own benefit, he says otherwise.

This is as it is written in the article "The Order of the Work" by Baal HaSulam (Item 4), "When attributing the work to the Creator, he should believe that the Creator accepts our work, regardless of how the work seems." A person should only attribute the work to the Creator; this is enough.

Therefore, during the descent, he can see his true state in the work. But the main point is that at that time, he must strengthen himself with faith that "The whole earth is full of His glory." Thus, even if a person is in a state of lowliness, he must not say that in this place, we cannot say that "The whole earth is full of His glory." Rather, one should believe what is written, "His glory fills the world," and it is only hidden from him, and that it was done so that he would have room for choice, and to work in order to bestow and not for his own sake, for because of his aim for his own benefit, he cannot work gladly, since the will to receive for himself does not feel any flavor.

At that time, a person can be pleased that now he has a place where he can say that he is working only for the sake of the Creator. If he cannot overcome and be happy about this work, he should say, "I am happy that I see the truth, that I am far from the work of truth. Hence, now I have a chance to ask of the Creator from the bottom of the heart to help me. Otherwise, I will be lost because I see that I am powerless to overcome and emerge from the governance of the will to receive for oneself."

We therefore see that the order of the work is that a person should ask for reward for his work in Torah and *Mitzvot*, by which he will achieve working for the sake of the Creator. This is considered that a person must acquire vessels of bestowal by which he will be able to receive the delight and pleasure, as this was the purpose of creation "to do good to His creations."

This is as our sages said, "The Torah and *Mitzvot* were given only so as to cleanse Israel." That is, the reward they ask in return for observing Torah and *Mitzvot* is the cleansing, meaning the intention, that by observing Torah and *Mitzvot* they will be rewarded with the desire to bestow, as our sages said, "The light in it reforms him."

What Does It Mean that a Judge Must Judge Absolutely Truthfully?

Accordingly, we should interpret what we asked, What does it mean that they said, "Any judge who judges absolutely truthfully becomes partners with the Creator in the work of creation"? The question is, What is "truth" and what is "absolute truth"?

The answer is, as I wrote (Article No. 44, *Tav-Shin-Nun-Aleph*), that there are two discernments concerning "for the sake of the Creator": 1) He is not working for people's respect or for money. Rather, he is working humbly with the Lord your God, and all his work is in order to observe Torah and *Mitzvot*, which the Creator commanded us. Therefore, he asks the Creator to give him in this world life, health, provision, and so forth. Also, He should reward him in the next world, as it is written in the Torah, "If you obey, I will give grass in your field." That is, the Creator will reward him. This means that the *Mitzvot* he observes are only for the sake of the Creator.

2) He works for the sake of the Creator, and even his intention is for the sake of the Creator. That is, he does not want any reward, but everything is for the sake of the Creator. This is regarded as the aim also being for the sake of the Creator.

Therefore, we should interpret that mere "truth" means that only his actions are for the sake of the Creator, but he still cannot make the intention for the sake of the Creator. Therefore, when speaking in terms of the work, it means that any person who wants to judge himself and see his situation in the work needs to be a truthful judge.

Although he is a truthful judge, who sees that all his actions are for the sake of the Creator, that judge still cannot be "as though he becomes partners with the Creator in the work of creation." That is, the work of creation is the creation of the world, where the intention was to delight His creations. A correction was made so that in order to avoid the bread of shame, the creatures must make the other half of the *Kli*, which is the aim in order to bestow. And since he judges truthfully, he is still unfit to receive the delight and pleasure because there is still disparity of form between him and the light. Hence, he cannot be a partner.

Conversely, a judge who judges absolutely truthfully, meaning that the aim is also for the sake of the Creator, then there is already a correction of the vessels of reception, so there is equivalence between the *Kli* and the light. At that time, the light can shine in that *Kli* and that judge becomes a partner, since he gave the partnership of the *Kli*, meaning the desire to bestow that is on the *Kli* of the will to receive, called "receiving in order to bestow." This means that only now that he has finished the *Kli* can the purpose of creation, which is the work of creation, be revealed to the lower ones, since the matter of shame has been corrected because they can already receive everything in order to bestow.

However, when a person places a judge to judge his situation, to see whether he prefers the love of the Creator to self-love, and the judge should determine the truth of the matter, this should not be his main work. On the contrary, his main work should be to exert in the "right," meaning to engage in Torah and *Mitzvot* and receive from this wholeness and joy because he was rewarded with engaging in Torah and *Mitzvot*. It does not matter how much love he has at that time for Torah and *Mitzvot*. Rather, the very observance of the *Mitzvot* without any conditions, he believes that this is a great thing when a person attributes the work to the Creator, regardless of the form of his work, for the Creator accepts everything.

This work is called "right" and "wholeness," and from this a person receives vitality, to have the strength to later walk on the "left," as well, meaning to place a judge who will pass a truthful judgment about the real nature of his work. However, this should be only part of the time that he gives to serving the Creator. The majority of the time of work should be on the right. This is regarded as two legs, since it is impossible to walk on one leg and advance in the work.

By this we should interpret what is written, "'Peace, peace, to the far and to the near,' said the Lord, 'and I will heal him.'" We should interpret "far" and "near" in the work. "Far" means left line. That is, when a person places a judge to judge how he behaves in the work, he sees how far he is from the Creator. "To the near" means when a person returns to working on the right line, which is when he sees only wholeness. That is, he values the work and considers even a small grip on Torah and *Mitzvot* as a fortune, since he does not even deserve the little bit of nearness. Hence, in a state of "right," a person is considered "close to the Creator."

But those two lines are disputed with each other, since they contradict one another. At that time comes the middle line and decides and makes peace between them. This is regarded as the Creator making peace between them, as it is known that the Creator is called the "middle line."

It is known that the order of the work is that we begin to work on one line, which is the work of the general public, who regard only the action. There, everyone is more or less content with the work. We should know that on one line, the Surrounding Light shines in general, which is light that shines from afar. That is, a person is still far from equivalence of form, yet receives illumination from this light. At that time, there is no issue of "two writings that deny one another" in him, for he has only one way.

But when a person shifts to the left line, when he wants to repent, this can be only when he places a judge to examine his situation. If the judge is truthful, he sees that he is not all right, meaning that everything he does is for his own benefit. Then he has room to pray that he wants to repent, meaning to return to the Creator, to be adhered to the Creator and not to be separated. Then his one line becomes the right line.

According to the above, we should interpret what our sages said (*Midrash Rabbah* 19), when Reuben started with repentance, as it is written, "The child is gone, and I, where do I go?" We should interpret that this indicates that the order of repentance is when a person says, "The child is gone."

It is known that there are two forces within man: 1) an old and foolish king, 2) a poor child, as it is written (Ecclesiastes 4), "A poor and wise child is better than an old and foolish king." This means that when a person begins to repent, he should know on what to repent. This is implied by what Reuben said, "The child is gone, and I, where do I go?" That is, the child, who is called "good inclination," is gone, and all that one sees is that the body is completely controlled by the old and foolish king, which is the "evil inclination," and it is known that the good inclination is called "desire to bestow," and the evil inclination is called "will to receive."

It follows that before a person sees that the will to receive controls him and that this control harms him, causing him to be far from the Creator, he still has nothing on which to repent. Only when he sees that "the child is gone" does he acquire a place of lack on which to repent, meaning to return to the Creator, which is called "*Dvekut* [adhesion] with the Creator." That is, where he was previously far from the Creator, now he has become near to the Creator, and this is called "repentance."

This is also called "left line," following the rule, "Anything that requires correction is called 'left.'" Since a person must also be in wholeness called "right," it creates "two writings that deny one another, so the third writing will come and decide between them." In other words, at that time the Creator gives him the desire to bestow, and then he obtains true wholeness. That is, then he is rewarded with the Torah, called "The Torah, and Israel, and the Creator are one."

However, he should not forget that although the work should mainly be on the right, called "wholeness," that a person takes fuel from the right, still, progress in the work, meaning achieving the completeness of the goal of receiving the delight and pleasure, depends specifically on the left, since there he sees his lack and has room to correct that lack through prayer that the Creator will satisfy his lack. A person advances only by the help of the Creator, as *The Zohar* writes, that the help that comes from above is called "a holy soul." This is how he advances until he is rewarded with achieving the purpose of creation, which is the delight and pleasure.

Now we can interpret what is written (Psalms 78), "He chose David His servant and took him from the sheepfolds, from the care of the sheep with suckling lambs He brought him up to shepherd Jacob His people, and Israel His inheritance." We should interpret why He chose David His servant; what merits did he have over others? He says about this, "and took him from the sheepfolds." We should interpret "sheepfolds" as food. That is, what was his food? He says, sheep. Sheep, explained Baal HaSulam, means "exits."

That is, when a person feels that he has emerged from the work of the Creator, that he is in descent, he should not be alarmed by this. On the contrary, this gives him room to pray to the Creator to deliver him from the control of the bad and bring him closer to Him. For this reason, each exit that he had gave him fuel and what to pray for. Conversely, when a person is always in ascent, he has no need to advance. This is the meaning of the words "and took him from the sheepfolds."

Also, it is written, "He brought him up." We should interpret that "up" means ascents. "Brought him up" means that after the ascents, which is descents, He brought him "to shepherd Jacob His people." "Jacob" is considered *Yod-Akev* [heel], since heel is called "faith," which is something that a person tramples with his heels. That is, it is something of inferior importance. In other words, specifically from states that are after the ascents, which are descents, specifically from the descents, he would shepherd his faith.

This means that from the descents, he took strength to expand the faith. This is the meaning of the words "Jacob His people," meaning the Creator's people. "And Israel His inheritance" means that after he has been rewarded through the descents into the state of *Yod-Akev*, which is faith, he was rewarded with the "inheritance of the land." This is why it is written, "Israel," for afterward, he achieved the degree *Yashar-El* [Israel, lit: straight to the Creator]. Then he achieved the inheritance of the land, which is the purpose of creation. This is the meaning of the words "Israel His inheritance."

However, we must not forget that the primary attention in the work should be given to the right line. We advance from the state of the left, as well, but we cannot walk without the right, for a person must be in gladness, as it is written, "Serve the Lord with gladness," and we can receive this only from the right line. Although this contradicts the left line, but since a person must be in high spirits, which is obtained only when a person believes in the Creator and has faith in the sages, who told us that a person should try to appreciate all his actions, even if they are still not in the manner that they should be, to the extent that a person thanks the Creator, even for small things that he can do, it connects him to the Creator.

What Is the Son of the Beloved and the Son of the Hated in the Work?

Article No. 46, Tav-Shin-Nun-Aleph, 1990/91

The Midrash says (presented in *Baal HaTurim*) about what is written, "If a man has two wives, the one loved and the other hated." He says, "'If a man has two wives' is the Creator. 'Loved' are the idol-worshippers, to whom He shows His face, and 'hated' are Israel, from whom He hides His face."

We should understand this, since it contradicts all the places that write that the Creator loves His people, Israel, as it is written (Malachi 1:2-3), "'I loved you,' says the Lord. But you say, 'How did You love us?' 'Was not Esau Jacob's brother?' declares the Lord. 'Yet I loved Jacob and I hated Esau.'" Also, we say, "Who chooses Israel, His people, with love."

We should interpret this in the work: It is known that in the work, we speak of everything within one body. For this reason we should interpret saying "two wives" to mean that they are in the same body. This means that there are two forces within man: 1) the desire to receive for one's own benefit, 2) the desire to bestow, to do everything for the sake of the Creator.

Those two are called "two wives." In other words, we should determine within man the quality of the "seventy nations of the world," and the quality of "Israel." We attribute the "nations of the world" to the will to receive for one's own benefit, and we attribute "Israel" to the desire to bestow upon the Creator.

We should know that those two desires come from above, meaning that only the Creator gives them and it is not within man's hands to take them by himself. Rather, the first force, called "will to receive for oneself," comes to a person without any effort. As soon as one is born, he has this force. But the second force, the "desire to bestow," does not come from above without labor. This means that first one must seek ways by which to obtain it, and only then does he receive from above the desire to bestow. However, it is not given without labor.

We should understand the reason that the desire to bestow is not given without labor, and the will to receive is given without labor. This is so because in order to achieve the purpose of creation, which is to do good to His creations, He had to create a creation that contains the will to receive pleasure, since without a desire, it is impossible to enjoy anything. Hence, the Creator placed within creation the desire to receive pleasure.

This means that if man did not have it when he was born, it would be impossible to be called "creature," since this shows us the matter of creation "existence from absence," meaning that a desire and need were created, where he wants to satisfy his need. For this reason, this desire comes immediately, without any effort. In other words, were it not for the will to receive, there would not be any development, so there would be anything in the world, since we learn everything only by the power of the will to receive, which pushes us to go forward. For this reason, this desire comes to us without any effort.

But concerning the desire to bestow, the Creator does not give it to us without any effort. That is, once we have creation and the

Creator should give fulfillment to the creatures, He gives them what they demand and say that they need. At that time the Creator fills their lack. It therefore follows that all the effort that a person makes in Torah and *Mitzvot* is in order to obtain the lack for the desire to bestow. That is, as man understands that without a desire to receive pleasure, a person cannot live in the world, meaning that if a person sees that if he has nothing to give to his will to receive so it can enjoy, the person knows that he will not be able to exist in the world, since without vitality he is in conflict with the purpose of creation, to do good to His creations.

Likewise, a person must come to feel that unless he has the desire to bestow, by which he can achieve *Dvekut* [adhesion] with the Creator, he also has no life or pleasure in this world. In other words, he sees that he has no satisfaction in life. For this reason, he wants to achieve wholeness, for there must be delight and pleasure in creation. However, without the desire to bestow, a person cannot achieve wholeness. This state is called "lack and need," and when a person has such a lack, he receives from above, from the Creator, the second desire called "desire to bestow."

For this reason, one should do all that he can in order to acquire a lack for the desire to bestow. However, one must know that although he wants to do everything in order to bestow, the body does not let him emerge from its governance, and this causes one descents and ascents. That is, once the will to receive prevails over the desire to bestow, meaning that the will to receive brings him desires and thoughts that it is correct, meaning that it gives him a greater taste for self-love, which means that the will to receive, which is the "nations of the world," receives more flavor each time, so when it acquires more strength, it cancels the need for the desire to bestow.

Hence, all the labor that one has given in order to obtain the need for the desire to bestow departs from him, and the person agrees, during the descent, with the will to receive for oneself. However, afterward, the person recovers and begins once more to work and labor in order to obtain the need for the desire to bestow, and then the will to receive prevails once more. It follows that this is the cause of ascents and descents.

This situation continues until a person comes to a resolution that without His help, it is impossible to attain, not necessarily the actual desire to bestow, but even the need for the desire to bestow also ascends and descends to the point that several times he came to a state where he saw that he could not make any more efforts than he already has. Therefore, he wants to escape the work.

However, we should ask, Why did the Creator make it so there are ascents and descents? As said above, it is in order for man to need to move forward and not settle for little. For this reason, he receives a descent from above. In other words, a person is helped to advance by lowering him from his degree. This causes him to reflect and see what is required of him from above, and for which he was lowered from his degree.

This causes a person to pray to the Creator for help. The help that one receives from above is the preparation because of which he will obtain a soul, as it is written in *The Zohar*, that he is helped by "a holy soul." It follows that both the ascents and the descents come from above. That is, the descents, too, help a person, and because of them he achieves the goal he should achieve.

By this we should interpret what *The Zohar* says (*VaYishlach*, Item 4), "If a man comes to be purified, the evil inclination surrenders before him and the right governs the left. And both the good inclination and the evil inclination join to keep man in all the roads he travels, as it is written, 'For He will give His angels charge over you, to keep you in all your ways.'"

We should understand how it can be said that the evil inclination keeps a person walking on the straight path. After all, it advises a person not to walk in the way of Torah, fails him in all his ways, and detains him from working for the sake of the Creator but only for his own sake. Thus, we should know how the evil inclination helps him.

The descents that a person receives, when the evil inclination gives him thoughts that are foreign to the spirit of Torah, cause him descents. According to a person's opinion, it must be that the evil inclination brought him the feeling that love of self is more important than love of the Creator, and that this is the cause of the descents.

But in truth, one should believe that the Creator does everything. In other words, the Creator sends these descents to a person in order for them to give man momentum in the work so he will not be content with little. When a person feels that he does all that he can in Torah and *Mitzvot*, and he cannot discern the matter of the intention for the sake of the Creator, or that he is working for his own benefit, since when one works in the manner of the general public, an illumination shines on a person as Surrounding Light, giving him satisfaction so he will not feel any lack in his work.

Only when one wants to work in the manner of individuals, meaning that the aim will also be for the sake of the Creator, and not specifically the act (as said in Article No. 45, *Tav-Shin-Nun-Aleph*), then he is notified from above that he is not all right, and from this he falls into a descent. At that time, one sees his real situation and begins to seek a way by which to emerge from the control of self-love.

It therefore follows that were it not for the evil inclination, which brings him the state of descents, he would remain in a state of ascent and would not need to achieve the goal of *Dvekut* with the Creator. It follows that the evil inclination is an angel of God, a messenger of the Creator to keep him from staying in a state of "still of *Kedusha* [holiness]," but rather needing to advance. This is why he says, "For He will give His angels charge over you, to keep you in all your ways." Thus, the evil inclination is also a messenger of the Creator to keep the person.

According to the above, we should interpret what we asked concerning the words of the Midrash that says, "'If a man has two wives' is the Creator. 'Loved' are the idol-worshippers." How can it be said that the Creator loves the idol-worshippers? We should interpret that when it says, "If a man has two wives," it means that the Creator gives to a person two wives, meaning two desires, one loved, meaning the will to receive for one's own sake. This is called "idol-worshippers," meaning not for the sake of the Creator but for one's own sake.

That desire is called "loved," meaning that the creatures love this desire because the Creator shows them the face. In other words, the Creator created the world because of His desire to do good to His creations. This is considered that the Creator is showing them the face, meaning to the will to receive, for it is impossible to receive pleasure if there is no yearning for the pleasure. Because of this, the Creator shows the face to the will to receive pleasure. That is, All that one does for oneself, one enjoys, and this is considered that He shows him the face.

Yet, why is this called "idol-worshippers"? The answer is that since there was a correction that in order to avoid the issue of shame, it is forbidden to receive in order to receive. One who does receive in order to receive is called in the work, "idol-worshipper." In other words, he does not work for the sake of the Creator but for his own sake. In the work, this is called "foreign work," "idol-worshipping." Although in terms of the actions, he is considered "Israel" and a "servant of the Creator," in terms of the work, which is to bestow, this is called "idol-worshipping," meaning work that is foreign to us.

Since a person is born with an inherent nature to work only for one's own sake, which a person calls "loved," since the Creator shows them the face, as long as one works for his own sake, he has a desire to work, since by nature, he loves working for the will to receive. But when one wants to work for the sake of the Creator, which is to benefit the Creator and not himself, this desire belongs to the quality of "Israel" in a person, and that desire is called "hated," since the Creator hides the face from them.

In other words, in order for one to be rewarded with "Israel," the Creator hides His face from them, since when a person wants to walk in a manner where all his actions are for the sake of the Creator, in order to be able to receive in order to bestow, there had to be a concealment and *Tzimtzum* [restriction] on the Torah and

Mitzvot [commandments/good deeds], so they would be able to say that they are observing Torah and *Mitzvot* without any reward, but only for the sake of the Creator. Since this is against nature, the body hates this work. And if a person wants to work specifically for the sake of the Creator, he has no other choice but to pray to the Creator to give him the strength to overcome the will to receive and subdue it

A person receives this power from above, as it is written, "He who comes to purify is aided." That is, he is given a soul from above. It follows that specifically by having hatred for the quality of "Israel" in a person, he cannot overcome, since the body hates bestowal. At that time, there is room for one to truly be rewarded with the degree of "Israel" by asking for help from above.

This is the meaning of what was said, that from the two forces that there are in man—the evil inclination and the good inclination—a person can achieve the completion of the goal, for both of them keep him from veering off from the right path, neither to the right nor to the left, but to come to achieve the completeness of the goal, which is to receive the delight and pleasure that the Creator wants to impart upon the creatures.

It therefore follows that the "loved wife" is the idol-worshippers, and the "hated wife" is Israel. To this we should add that those two forces, the will to receive and the desire to bestow, are also called "man" and "beast." That is, the will to receive in man is regarded as a "beast," belonging to the quality of animals, in whom there is only self-benefit, and the "speaking" is the quality of "man," which is the desire to bestow that man should achieve, and which he can achieve only through great efforts for the above reason, that by nature a person cannot understand how to do anything for the sake of the Creator.

That is, a person is concerned with satisfying the demands of his "beast," but what the "man" in him demands, a person cannot satisfy. Rather, this requires asking the Creator to give him the power to overcome his "beast," for without the help of the Creator, governance is given to thoughts and desires that hate the quality of "man" and the quality of "Israel," which is the quality of "man," as our sages said, "You are called 'man,' and the idol-worshippers are not called 'man'" (Yevamot 61). Thus, the "hated woman" is "Israel," from whom the Creator hides His face.

According to the above, we should interpret what our sages said (Avot 1:15), "Welcome every person." We should understand what this tells us in the work. When a person wants to do something for his quality of "man," and since the quality of "man" is hated, since all of man's concerns are only to satisfy the demands that his "beast" demands, and the body loves the quality of the beast, but as for the quality of "man," which is "Israel," the body hates it; therefore, our sages came and warned, "Welcome every person," where "every" means even all that is discerned as "man."

In other words, we should appreciate even a small thing, if it pertains to the quality of "man." Our sages told us that we should try to welcome the quality of "man," and not as it seems to us as hated because the Creator hides His face from them. Rather, we should go above reason and welcome every person above what the mind of our body tells us. That is, we must do things that are suitable for the quality of "man."

Although the "beast" within us screams and says that the work we want to do for the quality of man are unsuitable for sane people, since what we are, a demanding beast, this is acceptable, and the evidence is that the body loves this work. But what he wants, to work for the quality of "man," you see that the body hates this. Clearly, the mind makes sense, since it says that by working for the quality of "beast," this is reasonable and suitable for an intelligent person, while the work that you want to do for the quality of "man," this is an act of a "beast," meaning mindless.

Our sages tell us about this that we should not listen to what the body says, that it is making the argument of a "human," but rather to welcome every "quality of man," and say, "Although according to the mind and reason, the quality of man is hated, I believe in the words of the sages and I welcome them."

By this we should interpret what our sage said, "Man and beast You deliver, O Lord." These are people who are as cunning in their reason as people, and pretend to be as beasts. That is, although rationally, you are correct, and a person should walk on the path that he loves, still, "he pretends to be a beast," mindless, and goes with faith above reason.

However, we should believe that by observing Torah and *Mitzvot* in practice in every detail and precision, thanks to the actions, we are rewarded with the Creator helping us from above so we will have the strength to go forward and be rewarded with obtaining the goal, which is that man will receive the delight and pleasure that there is in the purpose of creation. This is so because when we observe Torah and *Mitzvot* unconditionally, but only because of the commandment of the Creator, this is called an awakening from below. By this, the light and abundance extend from above, and they can emerge from the governance of evil.

This is as our sages said (RASHI in the name of *Machilta*) about what is written (Exodus 13:12), "When I see the blood, I will pass over you, and no plague will befall you to destroy you." (He asks), "'When I see the blood?' But everything is revealed before Him! But the Creator said, 'I look to see that you are engaged in My commandments, and I pass over you.'"

We see that our sages said that so that no plague would befall them, meaning to emerge from the control of the evil, called "death," as our sages said, "The wicked in their lives are called 'dead,'" we were given the work in practice. Thanks to the work we do, the Creator is revealed to us, as it says, "And it shall be as a token for you." What do we learn? "In return for the *Mitzva* that you are performing, I will have mercy on you." Thus, thanks to the practice of *Mitzvot*, a person is saved from the governance of the will to receive, called "evil inclination," and is rewarded with obtaining the desire to bestow.

However, one who walks on one line, who is satisfied with practice, when he works for the sake of the Creator and does not consider the intention, that the intention will also be for the sake of the Creator, he cannot obtain the desire to bestow, called *Dvekut* [adhesion]. This is so because he has no lack. Hence, these people who have already shifted from one line to the right line, when they see their lowliness, that there is not a single organ in that person that wants to do anything for the sake of the Creator, they yearn for the Creator to deliver them from death, meaning from the governance of self-love. At that time, his way to be rewarded with the Creator being revealed to him, meaning to be rewarded with the desire to bestow, which is when one is adhered to the Creator, a person can be rewarded with it only thanks to the practice, when he wants the reward for observing Torah and *Mitzvot* will be *Dvekut* with the Creator. This is the meaning of "In return for the *Mitzva* [sing. of *Mitzvot*] that you are performing, I will have mercy on you." That is, He has mercy on us and saves us from death, which is the governance of the will to receive.

However, we see that man can do anything that is not on the path of correction. We see that this applies both in adults and in little children. And especially, we see this in little children since with grownups, everything already involves several reasons, so we cannot see the truth. But with children, we see this more openly, that children can toil all day, but if we ask them to do something, they say that they have no energy for the work. We should know that this extends from the world of *Nekudim*, where there was the breaking of the vessels. For this reason anything that does not pertain to correction, we have the strength to do. But if it pertains to correction, there is already labor involved due to the resistance of the body.

Hence, when a person walks on one line, he can observe Torah and *Mitzvot* in every way. But when he goes on the right line, when the work is on the path of correction, the person should then make great efforts to walk on the path of the "right." This is why we need strengthening.

What Does It Mean that the Right and the Left Are in Contrast, in the Work?

Article No. 47, Tav-Shin-Nun-Aleph, 1990/91

The verse says (Deuteronomy 29:8), "Keep the words of this covenant and do them so you may be wise in all that you do." We should understand why he says, "Keep and do them so you may be wise in all that you do." This implies that doing is so that by this "you may be wise in all that you do." It follows that doing is like a preparation, where by doing, we will be able to be wise in what we do.

This means that there are two matters to discern here in the work: 1) The act, as it is written, "and do them." 2) The learning in the doing, as it is written, "so you may be wise in all that you do." Ostensibly, this is a contradiction: On one hand, it means that the main thing is the act, as it is written, "and keep and do them." But then, it is written, "so you may be wise in all that you do." This implies that doing is only a means by which to achieve understanding with the intellect and knowledge.

The Zohar says that we should make two discernments in the 613 *Mitzvot* [commandments/good deeds]: 1) It calls the first discernments "613 *Eitin* [Aramaic: counsels]." 2) It calls the second discernments "613 *Pekudin* [Aramaic: deposits]."

The difference between them is that *Eitin* means that that thing is not the goal, but only advice how to achieve the goal. Thus, it is difficult to understand why he says that the 613 *Mitzvot* are only counsels, and then he says that they are called "613 *Pekudin*."

He interprets in the *Sulam* [Ladder commentary on *The Zohar*] ("Introduction of The Book of Zohar," "General Explanation for All Fourteen Commandments and How They Divide into the Seven Days of Creation," Item 1), "When rewarded with hearing 'the voice of His word,' the 613 *Mitzvot* become *Pekudin*, from the word *Pikadon* [Hebrew: deposit], for in each *Mitzva* [singular of *Mitzvot*], the light of a unique degree is deposited, which corresponds to a unique organ in the 613 organs and tendons of the soul and the body. It follows that while performing the *Mitzva*, one extends to its corresponding organ in his soul and body the degree of light that belongs to that organ and tendon."

Therefore, according to what he interprets there in the *Sulam*, we should interpret simply that he says that "In all things there are *Panim* [anterior/face] and *Achor* [posterior/back]. The preparation for something is called *Achor*, and the attainment of the matter is called *Panim*. Similarly, in Torah and *Mitzvot* there are 'We shall do' and 'We shall hear.' When observing Torah and *Mitzvot* as 'doers of His word,' prior to being rewarded with 'hearing the voice of His word,' the *Mitzvot* are called '613 *Eitin*,' and are regarded as *Achor*."

Accordingly, we can understand what we asked, Why does it say, "Keep and do them"? which implies that doing is the most important, and afterward he says, "so you may be wise." That is, when I tell you, "Do them," it is only a preparation to attain the actions. It follows that the main thing is the learning, the intellect, and the mind, and not the action.

The answer is that the main thing is the action, since without the actions we cannot obtain anything. But through the actions we can obtain *Dvekut* [adhesion], called "equivalence of form," since from *Lo Lishma* [not for Her sake] we come to *Lishma* [for Her sake]. Hence, the actions are the most important.

In the actions themselves, we need to make two discernments:

1) The actions themselves, when they are still means. That is, they are only a preparation by which to obtain the vessels of bestowal. After he obtains through the actions the *Kelim* [vessels] called "desire to bestow," he obtains the light that is clothed in the actions.

This means that all the actions that he did prior to being rewarded with vessels of bestowal, although then, too, the light was clothed in Torah and *Mitzvot*, but it was as a deposit that is clothed in Torah and *Mitzvot*. In other words, he was unable to see what was in the Torah and *Mitzvot* because he still did not have the *Kelim* that are suitable to the light. But afterward, when he is rewarded with vessels of bestowal, he receives the light that is clothed in Torah and *Mitzvot*, and then we see that before he was rewarded with seeing, the light was already clothed in the 613 *Mitzvot*, but it was there as a deposit.

Therefore, this is not a contradiction that first it says that the action is the most important, as it is written, "and do them," since we begin with action and end with action, but there is a discernment in between, meaning before he is rewarded with vessels of bestowal or after he is rewarded with vessels of bestowal. This means that through the actions, he is rewarded with *Kelim*, and then, through the actions, he is rewarded with the light. This is called "so you may be wise in all that you do," meaning that afterward he is rewarded with "Learn and know Me."

However, we must remember that before we are rewarded with vessels of bestowal, when we want to be rewarded with working for the sake of the Creator and not for our own sake, there are many ups and downs in this work. It is known that the body objects to work that aims to achieve *Dvekut* with the Creator, and once the good within man prevails, and once the bad within man prevails. This is called "the war of the inclination." In other words, there is work in action, which is the work of the general public, who should aim that the acts they do will not be for the purpose of respect, money, and so forth, but for the sake of the Creator.

Hence, those who want to work for the sake of the Creator do their deeds in concealment. The measure of concealment is as Baal HaSulam said, that a person should behave just like the people in his surroundings. In other words, he should not be conspicuous in his environment. If he shows that he slights customs that are practiced in his surroundings, or that he is stricter in some matters more than is customary in his surroundings, the work of that person is no longer in a state of concealment, since when people are in a certain environment, if one of them does something different from the environment, that person draws attention from the society and everyone looks at him. It follows that his work is not in concealment.

These people feel the taste in the work as Surrounding Light, which shines to the general public of Israel. This is as it is written, "I am the Lord, who dwells with them in the midst of their impurity." This means that although a person has not been purified of self-love, and all his work is in order for the Creator to reward him in this world and in the next world, they are still regarded as working for the sake of the Creator.

In this work, a person can see his progress, since each day he adds Torah and *Mitzvot*. Naturally, he can derive from this vitality and joy and can observe what is written, "Serve the Lord with gladness." It is known that this work is called "one line." In other words, a person does not know that "for the sake of the Creator" is something that requires special attention. Rather, like the rest of the people, they have faith in our sages, who said, "One should always engage in Torah and *Mitzvot*, even if *Lo Lishma* [not for Her sake], since from Lo *Lishma* he comes to *Lishma* [for Her sake]." However, he does not think that these work and intention require time and work. He thinks that it comes naturally, without any special work, as our sages said, "From *Lo Lishma* we come to *Lishma*." For this reason, this work is called "one line."

But if a person comes to understand that for the sake of the Creator is special work, that this work does not pertain to the general public, but only to those who received an awakening from above that the intention should also be to bestow, that it is something special, and begins to examine whether he can work for the sake of the Creator and not for his own sake, to this work the body objects, since it is human nature that he does not understand anything that is not for his own benefit.

Here begin the above-mentioned ascents and descents. It follows that the examination that the person did on his actions, whether they are for the sake of the Creator or for his own sake, when he sees his lowliness and how far he is from this work, a person should pray to the Creator to give him the power to overcome the will to receive for oneself.

At that time, sometimes the body argues, "You saw how many times you prayed to the Creator to help but you did not receive any help. Therefore, it must be that this work is not for you." A person cannot always overcome such complaints. In that state, one remains as though dead, completely lifeless, and naturally, he cannot persist and continue in this work.

This path is called "left line" in the work, since there is a rule that anything that requires correction is called "left."

Therefore, in the work, a person must not engage in this manner, meaning to examine whether his work is in wholeness. Rather, as is said ("Order of the work," Item 9), where he says, "In the work on the left, half an hour a day is enough."

The majority of man's work should be on the right line, called "wholeness." In this work, a person should be without criticism, to see if his work is in wholeness. A person should say, "Even though my actions in Torah and *Mitzvot* are incomplete, I am still grateful to the Creator for giving me the intellect and will to have some grip on *Kedusha* [holiness]. That is, whatever grip I have, I regard as a great fortune, since I see that many people in the world have no connection to Torah and *Mitzvot*, so I am happy with my share, that I was given some contact. And since I believe that this is an important thing, the little bit of contact with spirituality is more important to me than my whole life in this world. I do not deserve to be given more than I have, and the rest of the time I am confused by all kinds of nonsense that I cannot overcome. Therefore, I am happy all day long and this gives me high spirits, since I know my lowliness. Therefore, I am thankful to the Creator for the small part with which I have been privileged."

According to the above, we should interpret what is written (Deuteronomy 26:11), "You shall rejoice in all the good which the Lord your God has given you." We should understand this. Should one be commanded to rejoice if he has abundance? Naturally, when one has abundance, he is happy. If it is otherwise, if he does not have abundance, then it can be said that he should be ordered to be happy. Therefore, what does it imply that it says, "You shall rejoice in all the good which He has given you"?

We should interpret this in the work. There is a matter of work of the right and of the left. "Right" is called "wholeness," when one has already begun to walk on the path toward obtaining vessels of bestowal, when he has already entered the left line, meaning that he wants to see the truth, whether he can work for the sake of the Creator and not for himself. This causes one ascents and descents in the work, and as a result, a person has no fuel to continue the work. Rather, the left line shows him the truth, that he should not fool himself that he has already achieved his wholeness.

However, in order to have motivation to work, a person can receive this only when he feels wholeness in the work. At that time, he has joy from what he is doing. However, since the right and left contradict one another, meaning that either one feels that he has wholeness, or that he is deficient, but how can there be two opposites in one subject?

The answer is that although they are in one subject, they are still in two times. That is, there is a time when a person should be in lowliness, and there is a time when one should be in pride. This is as Baal HaSulam said, that in the work, there are always two opposites: 1) Our sages said, "Be very, very humble." It follows that the essence of man's work is to try to be low in his spirit. 2) It is written, "And his heart was high in the ways of the Lord." This means that a person should be proud, meaning to try to be proud and not look at the general public. Instead, he should try to be higher than the general public. It follows that we should ask about this, too, how can there be two opposites in one subject? Here, too, we must answer that this refers to two times, one after the other, for then both can exist.

However, we should ask why we need these opposites. That is, why do we need this oppositeness, and why is one way—either lowliness or pride—not enough?

The answer is that we must walk on two lines, the right, as well as the left, even though they contradict one another. That is, precisely when they contradict one another, they yield the result that we need in order to obtain the purpose of creation, which is His desire to do good to His creations. That is, it is impossible to receive the delight and pleasure from the Creator before we have corrected ourselves with vessels of bestowal, which is the meaning of equivalence of form.

Therefore, although by nature, man is born with a desire to receive for his own benefit, when a person is told to observe Torah and *Mitzvot*, we must say that by observing Torah and *Mitzvot*, you will be rewarded in this world and in the next world. To the extent of his faith in reward and punishment, he observes Torah and *Mitzvot*. Although he is working for the sake of the Creator, meaning he wants to receive reward from the Creator and not from people, since he does not engage in Torah and *Mitzvot* for people to see how he works, but his work is only for the sake of the Creator, because of the commandment of the Creator, this is still called *Lo Lishma*.

That is, although in practice he engages in Torah and *Mitzvot* only for the sake of the Creator, his intention is his own benefit. Hence, this is called *Lo Lishma*. Yet, our sages said, "One should always engage in Torah and *Mitzvot Lo Lishma*, since from *Lo Lishma* he comes to *Lishma*." A person should say, "I dwell among my own people," meaning that each one should work like the rest of the public. But without special attention, the person will remain in *Lo Lishma* and will never achieve the purpose of creation.

For this reason, at that time a person should say, "And his heart was high in the ways of the Lord," meaning "I do not want to be at the degree of lowliness like the general public. I do need to achieve the purpose of creation." This is considered that he begins work in criticism to see how much he prefers the love of the Creator over his love of self. This criticism makes him deficient, and he begins to seek advice how to emerge from the governance of self-love.

However, here, in this state, when there is a war between the will to receive in a person and the desire that is now within him, which wants to acquire the desire to bestow, sometimes the desire to bestow prevails, and sometimes to the contrary, and the will to receive prevails. This is why at that time there are ascents and descents. A person should know that while he is in a state of deficiency, he has nothing from which to draw vitality, and then he has no fuel to continue the work in Torah and *Mitzvot*. This is why he must shift to the right line.

The right line is actually one line. That is, the same order of work that he had while working only in action, called *Lo Lishma*, should be applied now. That is, he needn't pay attention whether his work is *Lishma*, rather now he should say that he is not more important than other people, and as the rest of the people who work in *Lo Lishma* are satisfied with the work and are high-spirited, likewise, he, who is worse than they are, certainly does not deserve a more important place in the work.

In other words, even compared to the rest of the workers, he is at a lower degree than they are in both quantity and quality, and he must thank the Creator for giving him a thought and desire to do something in spirituality, as this is a gift from the Creator, who has rewarded him with a little bit of work in Torah and Mitzvot, for he does not even deserve this much, as he sees that there are many people who have no connection to Torah and Mitzvot. At that time, when one feels himself in wholeness, that person is called "blessed." Baal HaSulam said about this that when one feels blessed, he can adhere to the Blessed, as it is written, "The blessed clings to the Blessed."

Therefore, precisely from this state, a person receives fuel for the work. When a person works on the left line, he is in a state where he should say, "and his heart was high in the ways of the Lord." That is, he must not regard the general public, but rather be at a higher degree than the general public. This applies only when he works on the left line.

Afterward, he should shift to the right line, of which our sages said, "Be very, very humble." For this reason, he truly is humble. At that time, a person should know that he is not more important than others, and he is happy that he was given from above the desire and yearning to do something in Torah and Mitzvot. This is the meaning of the words "rejoice in all the good," meaning even anything, from this a person should receive joy.

Now we can understand why the right and the left must be in contrast in the work. It is so because a person must work in two manners: 1) in wholeness. At that time he can receive fuel for the work, since it is impossible to live on negation. Hence, the majority of one's time, he should be in the work of the right. But when one feels satisfaction in one's work, who causes him to advance? After all, there is a rule that if a person feels no deficiency, he does not change his way, since he is satisfied.

For this reason, we must shift to the left line, to examine his actions, whether they are done in order to bestow. From this he can see what there is to correct, so he will achieve the purpose of creation, and the deficiency that a person sees in his work makes him advance.

In other words, if he sees that he is not walking on the right path, he will certainly want to correct himself, since during the examination, a person can see the truth, since if he is not walking on the path of truth, a curse befalls him, as it is written (Deuteronomy 28:41), "You shall have sons and daughters but they will not be yours, for they will go into captivity."

We should interpret that in the work, "sons and daughters" are the good deeds of the righteous, as was said about what is written, "These are the generations of Noah; Noah was a righteous man." They asked, "'These are the generations [offspring],' it should have mentioned the names of his sons. Why does it say 'Noah was a righteous man'? Rather, we learn that the primary offspring of the righteous are good deeds."

Accordingly we should interpret "You shall have sons and daughters." This means that you will do good deeds, but when you want to see what good deeds you did, you will have nothing to see. But, you engaged in Torah and *Mitzvot*, and yet you do not feel that you did something in the work. We should ask, "But you engaged in Torah and *Mitzvot*, so where did the good deeds that you did disappear?"

The answer is that they went "into captivity." That is, they were taken captive by the *Klipot* [shells/peels]. This is why they disappeared from the horizon and you cannot see them. This pushes a man to seek advice how to emerge from the governance of the will to receive for himself. Baal HaSulam said that after a person has repented, he brings back out to *Kedusha* all his work that fell into the *Klipot*, as it is written, "He swallowed down riches, and he will vomit it out."

But before one repents, his work makes the sea of the *Sitra Achra* [other side], as it is written, "There is the sea, great and broad, in

What Does It Mean that the Right and the Left Are in Contrast?

which are swarms without number, animals both small and great." He said that they are small animals and big animals that the person had and which were lost from him, fell into that sea. But afterward, he takes it all back.

It therefore follows that both lines are required. Precisely by being in contrast, they yield the required result in order to achieve the purpose of creation, which is "to do good to His creations." We should also know that concerning "right," which is wholeness, a person can use it only when he can lower himself. But as for the left line, he can use it precisely when he is in a state of pride.

www.ingramcontent.com/pod-product-compliance
Lightning Source LLC
Chambersburg PA
CBHW051707160426
43209CB00004B/1049